# BURNING
# ALL
# ILLUSIONS

# BURNING
# ALL
# ILLUSIONS

Writings from
*The Nation*
on Race

1866–2002

EDITED BY PAULA J. GIDDINGS

Thunder's Mouth Press/Nation Books
New York

BURNING ALL ILLUSIONS: *WRITINGS FROM* THE NATION *ON RACE*
*1866-2002*

Compilation © 2002 Avalon Publishing Group Incorporated

Published by
Thunder's Mouth Press/Nation Books
161 William St., 16th Floor
New York, NY 10038

Nation Books is a co-publishing venture of the Nation Institute and
Avalon Publishing Group Incorporated.

Library of Congress Control Number: 2002103622

ISBN 1-56025-384-3

9 8 7 6 5 4 3 2 1

Book design by Michael Walters
Printed in the United States of America
Distributed by Publishers Group West

# Contents

Introduction: Paula J. Giddings                                           1

## PART ONE

## BEHOLDERS                                                               5

The South As It Is, March 15, 1866                                         7

The Washington Riots, August 9, 1919                                      11

Faith Adams: A Question to Democracy, November 10, 1920                   13

William Ellery Leonard: The Lynching Bee, December 29, 1920               22

William Pickens: Jim Crow in Texas, August 15, 1923                       34

Gustavus Adolphus Steward: "White," October 17, 1923                      39

Robert Herrick: The Race Problem in the Caribbean,
        June 18, 1924                                                     44

W. E. Burghardt Du Bois: The Primitive Black Man,
        December 17, 1924                                                 50

Langston Hughes: The Negro Artist and the Racial Mountain,
        June 23, 1926                                                     54

Sherwood Anderson: Look Out, Brown Man!,
        November 26, 1930                                                 60

Claude McKay: Harlem Runs Wild, April 3, 1935                             65

Carleton Beals: The Scottsboro Puppet Show, February 5, 1936             69

Langston Hughes: Laughter in Madrid, January 29, 1938                     75

Roi Ottley: I Met the Grand Dragon, July 2, 1949                          78

Langston Hughes: Brotherly Love, August 18, 1956                          83

W. E. B. Du Bois: I Won't Vote, October 20, 1956                          84

Dora Byron: Courage in Action: On a Florida Newspaper,
        December 1, 1956                                                  88

Wilma Dykeman and James Stokely: Montgomery Morning,
        January 5, 1957                                              93

Barbara Deming: In the Birmingham Jail, May 25, 1963              100

Howard Zinn: Incident in Hattiesburg, May 18, 1964               103

LeRoi Jones: In the Ring, June 29, 1964                          110

Peter de Lissovoy: Moments in a Southern Town,
        December 21, 1964                                         114

Aaron O. Wells: The Doctor, December 28, 1964                    124

Ralph Ellison: "Tell It Like It Is, Baby," September 20, 1965   128

Paul Delaney: Black Cops in the South, July 31, 1976            145

James Baldwin: Open Letter to the Born Again,
        September 29, 1979                                        155

James Baldwin: Notes on the House of Bondage,
        November 1, 1980                                          159

Patricia Vigderman: From Rags to Rage to Art, Review;
        Alice Walker's *In Search of Our Mothers' Gardens*,
        December 17, 1983                                         168

Patricia J. Williams: Among Moses' Bridge-Builders,
        May 23, 1994                                              174

John Edgar Wideman: Doing Time, Marking Race,
        October 30, 1995                                          183

Patricia J. Williams: Different Drummer Please, Marchers!,
        October 30, 1995                                          187

Nell Irvin Painter: A Different Sense of Time, Review;
        *The Future of Race*, H.L. Gates & C. West, May 6, 1996   190

John Leonard: Shooting Women, Review;
        Toni Morrison's *Paradise*, January 26, 1998              196

PART TWO

REPORTERS                                                                 205

News of the Day: The Freedmen, February 14, 1867                          207

Editorial: Land for the Landless, May 16, 1867                            209

Open Letter to Gen. Grant, May 28, 1874                                   213

Letter to the Editor: The Situation in South Carolina,
    April 19, 1894                                     214

Letter to the Editor: The Race Riots in North Carolina,
    November 17, 1898                                  217

Editorial: France and Morocco, August 29, 1907                            219

Book Review: *The Souls of Black Folk* by W .E. B. Du Bois,
    June 11, 1903                                      221

Oswald Garrison Villard: The Higher Education of the Negro,
    February 18, 1915                                  225

Editorial: Injustice Accorded to Black Soldiers, May 18, 1916             227

Letter to the Editor: Lynching Defended, June 22, 1916                    228

Editorial: Mutiny Condemned, August 30, 1917                              231

E. Franklin Frazier: Garvey: A Mass Leader,
    August 18, 1926                                    232

Oswald Garrison Villard: Issues and Men:
    Walking Through Race Prejudice, January 30, 1935    237

Horace R. Cayton: Fighting for White Folks?,
    September 26, 1942                                  240

Carey McWilliams: Racial Dialectic: Missouri Style,
    February 24, 1945                                  246

Mary Mostert: Death for Association, May 5, 1951                          251

F. Franklin Frazier: The New Negro, July 7, 1956                          253

John O'Kearney: Which Way Harlem? Unity on a Key Issue,
    October 27, 1956                                              258
Howard Zinn: Finishing School for Pickets, August 6, 1960          264
Martin Luther King, Jr.: Report on Civil Rights,
    Fumbling on the New Frontier, March 3, 1962                    270
Hoyt W. Fuller: Rise of the Negro Militant,
    September 14, 1963                                             278
Gordon Englehart: Wallace in Indiana, May 4, 1964                  283
Charles R. Eisendrath: The Black Hessians, January 29, 1968       289
Eulogy for Martin Luther King, Jr., April 15, 1968                294
Hans Toch: Cops & Blacks: Warning Minorities, April 21, 1969      295
John U. Monro: Escape from the Dark Cave, October 27, 1969        302
Charles Gillespie: Jim Brown Comes to Mississippi,
    September 21, 1970                                             316
Jerome H. Skolnick and Steven A. Brick: A Fair Trial for
    Angela Davis?, July 19, 1971                                  325
J. K. Obatala: Where Did Their Revolution Go?,
    October 2, 1972                                               335
Steve Murdock: Florence Rice vs. the Utilities,
    December 25, 1972                                             341
Clayborne Carson: Black Power After Ten Years,
    August 14, 1976                                               343
Jeff Gottlieb and Jeff Cohen: Was Fred Hampton Executed?,
    December 25, 1976                                             354
Richard Severo: Blacks Only Need Apply,
    September 20, 1980                                             367
Randall Kennedy: On Cussing Out White Liberals,
    September 4, 1982                                             373

Andrew Kopkind: Flo Don't Know, April 9, 1988 378

Jon Wiener: Racial Hatred on Campus, February 27, 1989 381

Adolph Reed Jr.: The Rise of Louis Farrakhan,
    January 21, 1991, Part 1 389

Adolph Reed Jr.: All for One and None for All,
    January 28, 1991, Part 2 401

Barbara Smith: Where's the Revolution?, July 5, 1993 414

Derrick Bell: The Freedom of Employment Act, May 23, 1994 418

Roger Wilkins: Racism Has Its Privileges, March 27, 1995 427

Gerald Early: Performance and Reality, August 17, 1998 439

Angela Ards: Rhyme and Resist, July 26, 1999 460

Amy Bach: Unforgiven, January 21, 2002 482

Contributors 493

# BURNING ALL ILLUSIONS

# Introduction

*Paula J. Giddings*

At its inception in 1865, *The Nation*, conceived by abolitionists, set out to keep the blight of slavery from ever afflicting the body politic again. Its tradition established, *The Nation* may not have been the only magazine to see race as an integral part of its mission, but with editors that included Henry Wadsworth Longfellow, James Russell Lowell and Anatole France, its vision might have been the most literary. This is no small distinction. Whatever its different manifestations over time, "race" retains its power through how it is imagined; through how it fitfully lies within those deep cultural recesses that artists have access to.

It was this aspect of *The Nation*'s writings on race that I decided to focus on in selecting from the hundreds articles from 1865 to 2002. The category of "artist" is broad here. It includes the obvious such as James Baldwin, Sherwood Anderson, and Ralph Ellison; but it also applies to lesser-knowns and contemporary writers who made race writing into an art. For example, the magazine published correspondents who traveled widely and wrote their first-person experiences with a novelist's sensibility. In this volume you will read, replete with dialogue, the report of a "special" correspondent who encounters two former slave women while walking from Baton Rouge to New Orleans in 1866. He details the women's descriptions, told with "apparent enjoyment," of the fall of New Orleans to the Union. There is also the first-person narrative of an NAACP official riding a Jim Crow car in Texas; a white woman writing about her experience in a Birmingham jail during the sixties; and Patricia J. Williams' wry—and penetrating—take on the Million Man March.

Such first-person perspectives, published in chronological order, make up Part One of this anthology; Part Two is made up of another category of selections which *The Nation* did superbly well. This is third-person reportage firmly rooted within a particular time, place, and historical moment, proving the adage that the universal is found in the particular. For example, the great sea change of desegregation is distilled through the impressions of an elderly Black gentleman who, with a mixture of fear and determination, sits down in a Whites-only diner—two hours after the passage of the civil rights bill. "Fighting for White Folks?" by sociologist Horace Cayton, written on the cusp of World War II, examines the historical isolation of Blacks from a society that expects them to die for it. The transformative moment of commitment to a cause is told through young Black women students at Spelman College who emerge from the chrysalis of lady-like obedience to become picket-line stalwarts. The issue of police violence is refracted through the murder of Black Panther Fred Hampton; the rise and fall of Black Power—and black students on white campuses—is situated in a particular time and space.

Of course, there are inherent limitations to this approach. Chronological gaps exist because some periods, as well as editors, lent themselves more to such writing than others. The manner of selection and word limitation precluded a thematic approach, although issues which thread through the entire hundred-plus years—racial violence, nationalism, race and foreign policy, the evolution of civil rights legislation— would be good subjects for future books. It must also be said that the approach also undermines the tidiness of representation. There are major events and actors missing. The criteria largely precluded *The Nation*'s historical concern for economic issues. Although gender and sexuality burn beneath every race issue, women are historically marginalized in racial discourses. Especially before the 1990s, and the regular column of Patricia Williams, there were regrettably fewer women, particularly Black women writers, to select from. Still, *The Nation* is one of the few mainstream publications to devote an issue to women, entitled "Black Women Speak," in 1989.

Finally, *The Nation*'s propensity, from its beginnings, to cover more than one side of important questions are underrepresented. For example, although the preponderance of its articles adamantly argued against lynching, this volume contains a 1916 letter to the editor, chillingly well thought out, explaining why he changed from an antilynching view to one that supported it.

How did *The Nation* stand historically regarding racial attitudes—

attitudes in which gender plays an integral part? According to *Nation* historian Richard Clark Sterne, it was James Miller McKim—a co-founder with Frederick Law Olmstead (also the architect of Central Park), Eliot Lawrence Godkin, and Charles Eliot Norton—who was particularly attuned to the need for a publication that sustained the abolitionist spirit after the Civil War. McKim co-founded the American Anti-Slavery Society with the famous abolitionist and *Liberator* editor, William Lloyd Garrison. Abolitionists, of course, were not free from bias, stereotype, or, a certain paternalism—the latter of which was evident in the included editorial against giving former slaves their forty acres and a mule. (They had to earn it, was the conclusion.) On the other hand, as seen in this volume, there are enthusiastic editorials supporting federal aid to Black education and the successful achievement of suffrage legislation in the various states. And significantly, *The Nation* did not shy away from the reporting of racial violence, including that which involved the great taboo, miscegenation, as seen in the news item about the murder of a pregnant Black mistress of a white man who did not want his wife to find out that the victim was carrying his child. And although the seering criticism, in 1874, of the Republicans by Hiram Revels—the Black former U.S. Senator from Mississippi—was used opportunistically in *The Nation* after it had lost its enthusiasm for the Radical Republican program, it is significant that the opinion of a Black Reconstruction leader was published at all. Indeed, *The Nation* compared favorably to its contemporaries such as *Harper's* and *The Atlantic Monthly* which, according to historian Rayford Logan, followed the Plantation Tradition, ridiculed Black freedmen and women, rationalized lynching and sounded alarms about giving Blacks the ballot.

The publication also recognized important ideas, even when it may not have agreed with them. In 1903, for example, when the conservative Black leader and educator Booker T. Washington was near the height of his influence, the magazine, edited at the time by a Washington sympathizer, nevertheless published one of the most supportive and insightful reviews of the book, which galvanized the opposition against him: *The Souls of Black Folk* by W.E.B. Du Bois. The unsigned book review had the stylistic "earmarks" of Oswald Garrison Villard, according to Du Bois's biographer, David Levering

Lewis. Fittingly, Richard Clark Sterne observed that when Villard—the grandson of the abolitionist William Lloyd Garrison, and a founder of the NAACP in 1909— took over *The Nation*'s editorship (and ownership) in 1918, it marked the beginning of its modern period.

Indeed, there is an important and often overlooked relationship between modern race theory—which discounted the biological bases of race—and the NAACP, which attracted liberal social scientists to its ranks and provided public forums for their ideas and findings. Among other alleged "racial behaviors," modern views began to liberate Blacks from the burden of hypersexualization. Without such a perspective, the 1919 article written by a white woman who went into Washington, D.C's Black community to interview men there would have hardly been possible. The unsigned article was written in the wake of a riotous attack on Blacks precipitated by charges that Black men were raping white women.

It might have been Villard who established another modern perspective for the magazine: the contested notion that more than one or two African Americans might know as much about race as whites and, moreover, were capable of writing about it. Subsequently, as seen by the publication of Langston Hughes's article on Madrid during the Spanish Civil War, the more frequent appearance of Black authors was augmented by another contested notion : that the Black perspective enriched the writing about subjects not directly connected to the North American race issue.

The thought and passion that suffuse the contemporary pieces is evidence that *The Nation* 's editors continued to encourage writers to engage the eye and the heart as well as the mind. To bring such resources to the subject of race makes the writing distinctive, rich, and enduring. It also tells us that despite the postmodern efforts to think of race as merely an illusion, it is still a primary means of knowing and interpreting the world.

## PART ONE

# BEHOLDERS

*March 15, 1866*

## The South As It Is.
### From Our Special Correspondent.

*Parish of Orleans, La., Feb. 17, 1866.*
I wished after leaving New Orleans to visit Baton Rouge, and, for the sake of seeing the country and the people between these two cities, I decided to make the journey on foot. My valise and overcoat, therefore, were sent forward by express, and I carried with me only a very light equipment of such things as would be indispensably necessary during a week's walk. I reached the little suburb of Carrollton before twelve o'clock, and there enquired for the road to Baton Rouge. "The river," everybody answered with a stare; "a boat; nobody went by land," and at last they told me to take to the levee. Accordingly I climbed the bank and was fairly on my way. At the end of the first five hundred yards a colored soldier ordered me to halt, and referred me to his officer for the reason. The lieutenant said that he had orders to keep all Jews and peddlers out of the camps; the men were being paid off. Satisfying him that I was not a peddler, he suffered me to pass on, and for a little way I walked in company with two negro women who were going into the country to make a Sunday visit to their relatives. They talked about the capture of New Orleans, the cannonade at the forts, the first appearance of the fleet, and the fright among the citizens. That was the day, one said, when them rebels run all about. Yes, said the other, that was the time when the stripes come off'n their pantaloons! They told her the d—n Yankees had come, and the very first thing they'd blow up the city and kill all the people. They wouldn't kill her, she told 'em. She knowed she'd never done nothin' but work hard; not her, not since they done sell her out o' old Virginny. They told her a heap more 'n she believed. Same as they said that Confederate flag never should come down off 'n the Custom House; the man that laid a hand on it should die sure. But she noticed the Yankee flag went up very quick. As for herself, her mind was all made up to run for them same cannon that talk' down the river, if the Yankees didn't come up.

These recollections the women dwelt on with much apparent enjoyment, as is usual with the negroes whenever they talk of Federal successes. By-and-bye we came upon another guard, and I went on alone, leaving the soldiers examining the baskets of the women to see if they contained whiskey, and soon I fell into the company of a young man who, after finding out my business, informed me that he was a teacher employed by the Freedmen's Bureau, and urged me to spend the night with him. He would show me a *usus naturæ*, he said. He would introduce me to Mr. B——, a man born in the South, once the owner of several slaves, afterwards for a long time an overseer, who was not only a Unionist, but actually believed that the negro was the equal, and in many respects the superior, of the white man, and should be allowed to vote. Mr. B—— was manager of the plantation he was living on, which was only twenty-five or thirty acres further up, and I would find him very hospitable.

I consented to go with him, and as we walked along he bade me remark that the surface of the river was eight or ten feet higher than the land, and that the field-ditches all ran not towards it but away from it. The country along the Mississippi for many miles above and below New Orleans and Baton Rouge was a narrow strip of good land, with the river on one side of it and a swamp on the other. Then each plantation was a strip of land, the most of it worthless, extending back, sometimes many miles, into the swamp water; and in esti-mating the size and value of the farm the important element entering into the calculation was always the number of acres fronting on the levee. The country is exclusively agricultural. It is customary, there-fore, in measuring length to use the measure applied to the farms, and to speak of points upon the road as being so many acres or so many arpents distant from each other.

It was not long before we came to the dwelling-place of my new acquaintance. The house was a low building, shaded by magnolia trees, in the middle of a flat yard, which looked like a goose-pasture with its slippery mud, its short green grass, and shallow pools. His school-house was on the next plantation. On first coming into the service of the Bureau he had been compelled for several months to live in a part of one of the negro cabins; but Mr. B—— had taken him

out of those disagreeable quarters, and established him more com-
fortably where he was then. His pay was eighty dollars a month, the
same with that given other teachers of his rank. Those of lower grades
received sixty-five and sixty dollars a month, and no one was
employed without first passing a thorough and severe examination.
In no other State, he thought, had the rate of wages for teachers in
freedmen's schools been so very high, and from all I hear of the examination to which teachers in Louisiana have been subjected, I should
say that the standard of qualification also has been exceedingly high.
General Baird's recent order, directing that the negroes shall hereafter
pay the expenses of their schools, goes into operation in March, and
during February all schools are suspended. Meantime agents go
about explaining its provisions to the people. Its effect, this teacher
thought, would be to diminish considerably the number of persons
under instruction. Anticipating its promulgation, he had offered to
keep his school open during the intermission if each pupil would pay
one dollar. Formerly, he had eighty-three pupils; now he has only
thirty-five. But, if I am not mistaken, a compulsory support of schools
is intended.

At night we walked out half a mile to the negro quarters of a
neighboring plantation, and visited the cabin of one of the laborers.
Several of his friends dropped in, and the schoolmaster directed the
conversation to the subject of education. Two men were spokesmen
for the others, and presented the different aspects of the question.
Here they were, one said, working for only twenty-five dollars a
month. Out of that amount they had to buy food and clothes and
everything else they wanted, and were also taxed half a dollar a
month to pay for the regular visits of the doctor. If he ordered medicine, that had to be paid for. Mr. M——, their employer, didn't want
women in the field—not now, at any rate—and the man's wages were
all that was coming in. It was pretty tight living, and come to put on
a school tax on top, nobody could stand it. The wages all went for
victuals. How could they save a dollar a month for schools?

The other man, a carpenter and engineer, said that the school tax
wouldn't be a dollar; it would be only seventy-five cents a month. Mr.
M—— had explained that all out to them; and by-and-bye the women

would have work as well as the men, and would be getting half a dollar and a dime a day for it. Education was the greatest of all things. What made the difference between a white man and a black man? Knowledge and wisdom. Look at this: Mr. M—— hired him and paid him thirty dollars a month, and he had to find himself out of it; but he hired Baptiste and paid him a hundred dollars a month and found him everything he wanted. Now he could do the work Baptiste did, just as well, and perhaps a little better; but when it came to taking a pencil and paper and calculating and figuring, he couldn't do it. Baptiste could tell the feet in a load of boards; he couldn't. Education was the thing. "For we old gineration," he thought, it was too late to go to school; but the children ought to be educated. Leaving learning to your children was better than leaving them a fortune; because if you left them even five hundred dollars, some man with more education than they had would come along and cheat them out of it all; but learning they could keep. He ended by begging the teacher if his boys would learn their lessons in no other way to whip them night and morning. The little girl was more easily managed; she sometimes sat up half the night over her geography book. The other men fully agreed with him as to the importance of education; it was the tax that frightened them, and they so poor; but of course they meant to keep their children in school as long as they could.

Going back in the dark, we could hear the steamboats panting down the distant river, but could only see them as moving clusters of lights, floating as it seemed in the air, the river was so high above us. Mr. B—— had returned in our absence, but had immediately gone away again, for a squad of soldiers, searching for a stolen mule, had forcibly taken away one of his, and he had ridden to the camp to recover his property. He had not come back when I rose in the morning, and I lost the opportunity of talking with him.

*August 9, 1919*

## The Washington Riots

To the Editor of *The Nation*:

Sir: On Tuesday night, when so many in Ledroit Park feared a mob and a general massacre, and when most white men believed that a white woman who ventured into that section would be literally devoured, I took it into my head to go there, and go I did. I went for several reasons. One was to prove that a white woman could do it; another, because I knew what had been done by the authorities and thought that a little reassurance from a lone and harmless woman might go a good way, for I guessed the probable psychological state in that section. Besides, I wanted to know at first hand what the Negroes were doing and thinking. I found out. If I talked to one colored man, I talked to a hundred and fifty. Occasionally I would stop to speak to one I knew; oftener I would accost a group of unknown men and ask them for their views. Always and everywhere I met with courtesy and attention. As we talked, men would appear from the shadows—seemingly from the night itself—until there were perhaps twenty of us. Only once did I see a policeman, who glanced at us curiously, but said nothing and passed slowly on. And when we had finished our talk, the group would melt into nothingness and I would proceed on my quest.

I saw no women at all. And the men—why, those men were not out to "start something." They were armed, most of them, and were quite frank about it, but they did not want a fight. They said they were out to see if a mob were coming, and, if there were, they were going home to barricade themselves; then, if the mob tried to get in, there was trouble ahead. As one put it: "A man would be less than a man if he didn't fight for his family and his home." Their state of mind was not primarily fight. It was fear, a perfect hysteria of dread lest, as more than one expressed it, "a new East St. Louis" was at hand. And, as with all hysteria, a small occurrence would have set them off in a frenzy. Dynamite! They were TNT. Again and again I was asked: "Is a mob gathering on

Pennsylvania Avenue? Will they come up and burn us out? Is the Park cordoned? For they did not dare go downtown far enough to see if the troops were really there. Over and over, I heard the pathetic question: "Do the white folks care? Does anyone care? Are they really doing anything?" I told them that the best of the whites did care, but that we were helpless. I told them also that measures had really been taken that afternoon and what they were—that there really was military, as well as police, protection. One queer old man remarked: "Well, I reckon somebuddy do care, or a white lady wouldn't come out to tell us about it." A one-handed soldier said: "I enlisted; I gave the country my hand, and I was ready to give more. When I was in France, I was a man and a soldier, but when I get back here, I'm not a citizen; I'm not a man, even—just a big, black brute." It was not said bitterly; it went deeper than bitterness. He spoke like a man with a broken heart. Another said: "They say this is to protect the white women. My father was in charge of a whole plantation and a family of white women during the Civil War. They weren't afraid to leave the white women with us then, and Negroes are no different now."

Many of them expressed a liking for, and confidence in, the captain of the precinct, and, when a man of one race speaks well of a man of another, during a race riot, that means something. But they spoke of the lack of colored police, and of the fact that Negroes were being dropped from the force and that none had been appointed since 1910. "You know," they said, "that we could talk better to colored police. They would reason with the people and not just knock them 'round. They know who the people are and what is going on, and they could stop a lot of trouble without arrests. But they don't *want* to give us a chance."

I saw but one noisy Negro, a half-witted and dishevelled-looking fellow, talking loudly and belligerently. Him two colored men seized and thoroughly shook, telling him that if he did not "shut up and get home," he would certainly find things happening to him. Once an excited Negro boy came flying on a bicycle with the news that a white mob had formed inside the cordon and was on its way. "Let's go meet them," said one young hothead. This was at once negatived. "We'll watch and see if they are coming, and if they are, we will go home and lock the doors. That's what Captain Doyle said, and he knows what's what." So, for a few tense moments, we stood peering into the drizzly gloom, not knowing what might after all be about to come. But all was quiet, and we silently drifted on our ways.

And thus it went for two hours. I met them—not savages, not red-handed murderers, but citizens, hunted and terrified, looking more or less hopelessly to their Government for aid; human beings craving the hand of brotherhood, and cut to the very heart. I thought of Belgium. I remembered that my country stands abroad for liberty, justice, and the rights of men, though she has them not at home. How blind we are, we Anglo-Saxons, who talk of Freedom and have not yet freed our souls. But still I hope and dimly see a dawn—red, it is true, but still a far-off dawn.

A white man once said to me: "You talk like a Negro. You seem at times to identify yourself with them. Have you lost your race consciousness?" I replied: "I hope I think enough like them to show you how they feel. I hope I always lose race consciousness when it stands in the way of my consciousness of common humanity." Then he said a queer thing: "I do not know whether you are mad or inspired." I had been thinking of going to Serbia, but I believe my duty is here. I believe that our country needs all of us who are standing along the color line. I am ready to do anything possible, to whatever limit. If you, to whom I look as a leader in this situation, should ever need my services, you have but to speak. My soul is aflame, not with the glare of the destroying torch, but with the steady, incandescent glow which cannot be extinguished.

*November 10, 1920*

## A Question to Democracy

*Faith Adams*

The Gold Star has disappeared from my neighbor's window, for two years have elapsed since the Armistice. The boy who went out from the house next door was the eldest of the family. I know that he died for Democracy. Yet I never saw the gold emblem that marked his sacrifice without being conscious of a vague uneasiness because I know that my neighbor's son died for something he had never known and would not have known had he lived.

When the L——s first moved into our street in B—— they caused no small commotion. They were the only middle class colored people in our small suburban community. There are, of course, plenty of colored people beyond the railroad in Shantytown, plenty, that is to supply our needs in regard to laundresses, scrubwomen, and children's nurses, but the idea of a colored physician and his family moving into one of the best houses on Elm Street was preposterous. As the nearest prospective neighbors of the invaders, we were objects of sympathy. Our friends expected us to become the leaders of an opposition and I do not know exactly why we failed to live up to their expectations. In some ways it would have been easier, but something in me—perhaps a strain of Abolition ancestry—asserted itself in a sudden burning shame at the thought. We declined to lead a movement to make it impossible for the L——s to enter the home they had bought. But in spite of our defection they did not succeed in entering their house until a lawsuit bitterly contested at every point had been won by them in several courts. In coming, they brought with them a problem which has never been solved and which has maintained its rigid outline, through all the patriotic enthusiasm that swept away a dozen hyphens and consolidated every other element in our community during the war, a problem which persisted in spite of the Gold Star that used to hang in my neighbor's window.

The trouble encountered by the L——s was not an isolated phenomenon. It was a characteristic and attendant circumstance of every act of their lives. I wonder if any reader, whatever his or her views on the Race question, has ever paused to consider, not so much its profound and significant aspects but the comparatively simple one which finds its origin in the mere inconvenience of being a Negro in a hostile white community, especially the daily and hourly inconvenience of being that complex, highly sensitized creature, an intellectual Negro in a hostile white community. "But why do they come here?"

lamented my white neighbors. "Why don't they stay with their own people?" ask those who feel that the troubles are of their own making. I believe that the answer is simple. They want the same advantages for their children that we want for ours. They moved to Elm Street to obtain those advantages in the face of our antagonism, rather than live in Shantytown, or in the South from which they came, or in the crowded insanitary districts which are usually the only ones accessible to urban negroes. So far as possible in our Christian Democratic community, we have made it impossible for them to achieve this. Of course we have not been entirely successful. We are a Northern community and there are still traces of respect for the individual's civil rights written into our laws and upheld by our courts. We have so far succeeded, however, that I, who gave no sons to my country, cannot remember the Gold Star that used to hang in my neighbor's window without a feeling of humiliation.

Primarily, the problem of my neighbors concerns their children. If America means anything to us, it means the future of our children, a future presumably freer, happier, surer than that of any children in the world. It does not mean this to the L——s. They have three children since their elder boy was killed, two daughters of sixteen and ten, respectively, and a boy of eight. The second daughter, Katherine, is the one I know best. She and my ten-year-old daughter are classmates. They walk to and from school together and are friends after a fashion, and yet I know that there is not an aspect of their environment that is the same to both. The very feeling of the sun and wind on her face is a different thing to my colored neighbor's little daughter than it is to mine because she is colored. My ten-year-old is a tomboy. In her short vigorous life she has never stopped to think whether she was "nice" or as good as anyone else. Her speech and manners are free, emphatic, and quite devoid of grace. She tears her clothes, falls into the pond, climbs trees, walls, roofs, and anything else which can be climbed, hitches her sled on to passing teams despite emphatic warnings and stands cheerfully somewhere between the foot and the middle of her class. She goes forth unconcernedly on errands, or pursues adventurous ends of her own. She is a perfectly ordinary, very healthy and really nice child, far less talented than sensitive little

Katherine, but she has never in her life been afraid or unwelcome or very unhappy. Her world has boundless horizons and endless possibilities of adventure. It may seem a small thing to you but, remembering my own childhood, there is nothing for which I am more thankful than that my children can have adventures. Our town and the world are decently safe for Elizabeth or relatively so. She may break an arm or a leg one of these days, but I know that her heart and her spirit will not be broken. I realize that Katherine's mother does not share this security, that there is no aspect of life in our charming village that is not haunted for her by shapes of shame and terror. Each day she wakes to a dread of things unbelievably ugly from which she cannot shield her child. I know that she awaits Katherine's return from school each day in fear of seeing in the child's face that some irreparably cruel thing has happened to her.

Meanwhile Katherine's clothes are always immaculate, her ways are gentle, her speech is soft and punctiliously correct. She stands well in school and is particularly gifted in music and drawing. If the color line does not hem them in too closely, by the time she graduates my neighbors hope to send her to an art school for a year and then, perhaps, to Europe. It will take money, of course, and their means are slender, but where else, they ask passionately, can she possibly fulfill the promise that is in her.

Barbara, the older daughter, will enter college this fall. She was to have had the R—— College scholarship, awarded every year to a member of the graduating class of the High School, but as the L——s say quietly, "something happened." Something usually does happen in such cases it seems, so they were not much surprised. Whether or not they are right, I cannot say, but they and hundreds of colored people like them, people of sober judgment and integrity believe that in such contests they are habitually cheated by white people. Barbara was admittedly the best student in her class. If the scholarship had been awarded according to precedent it would have gone to her as the holder of the highest general average for the entire four years, but this year the Faculty Committee departed from precedent and awarded it to Ruth H——, our minister's daughter and holder of the second highest average. Ruth's work, they said, showed more originality. Is this happy result merely a departure from hide-bound academicism and as such to be applauded or just what the L——s think it, the cheating of a sixteen-year-old child out of the fruits of four years' work? In any case, everyone was glad for Ruth, a general favorite, and her father has allowed her to accept. Barbara will enter college, of course, but she will have to work a little harder to make both ends meet. Already she is a little older, a little quieter.

And so it goes! The only one of my neighbor's children who still seems quite merry is Archie, the youngest. He is delicate and does not go to school, but studies at home with his mother. I like to see him laughing and tumbling about the lawn like any other boy of eight, but I know that if he were to venture outside the gate and a block or so down the street, he would find the hereditary enemy lying in wait for him. He did venture once, and his mother had to explain to him when he came back bruised and troubled why the white boys called him names and threw things at him. They weren't "tough" boys either, nor members of the white gangs that the L——s moved from the city to avoid, but the nice little sons of some of our leading citizens. When they discussed the invasion of the L——s at home and abroad in loud and angry tones, those same citizens did not intend to suggest to their sons that it was a good game to hunt down Archie, but somehow the boys have learned that he is an intruder and so in the good old tribal fashion transmitted by their parents, they threw stones and shouted "nigger." Archie never goes out alone now and Katherine usually goes to school with Elizabeth. "It's a little safer for a girl!" Mrs. L——s says wistfully. Just how safe it is, I know from what Elizabeth has told me of the jeers that Katherine daily endures. It is Elizabeth, and not Katherine, who resents those jeers and who, on occasions, puts Katherine's tormentors to flight, while Katherine walks on quietly, "just as if she didn't care!"

You see, Katherine is not only a little ten-year-old girl; she is a representative of her race, and so are all the L——s. The freedom and unconsciousness of normal, happy childhood are not for her, as they were not for Barbara and as they will not long be for Archie. Compared with her, how robust and spontaneous my Elizabeth seems. Elizabeth can forget herself. This is just what Katherine can not do.

Her shrinking self-consciousness is a distressing thing. But even if she could lose herself in work or play, how quickly she would be forced to remember. Alone, Katherine might perhaps forget for a moment that she is colored, but the world about her never forgets. To that world she is colored first, and a child with a child's needs afterwards.

As it is with the children, it is with their elders in a far greater degree. They, too, are the representatives of their race first, human beings only secondarily. Just what this means in actual nervous strain, if in no other way, is a difficult thing for any of those who belong to the dominant race to estimate. It means eternal vigilance and eternal self-consciousness. It means doubt, hesitation and never-ending complications in the most commonplace incidents of daily living. It means, even under such favorable conditions as obtain in B——, a constant uncertainty of life, health and happiness. How great a gift my own careless certainty of a very few elementary things now seems to me! In particular the certainty I have of meeting in the ordinary walks of life with ordinary courtesy, decency and fair play; of always meeting in an emergency with deep kindliness, dormant before perhaps, but called into being by nothing more than my need of it; my certainty of fellowship, of equality, of respect if it is due me; my certainty of getting pretty generally anything which I honestly work or pay for and sometimes more than this, and of foretelling the morrow with some accuracy and laying my plans accordingly for myself and my children. Can you imagine being able to take none of these things for granted? If you can, your imagination serves you better than most in trying to realize what daily life means to the L——s.

In one of our "high-brow" monthlies, an American woman wrote recently of her readiness to kill in defense of what "middle class America" meant to her. It meant just such a safe, sure, happy freedom from dependence on the irrational and violent in human nature as it does to me. It does not mean this to the L——s, and yet they, too, are of "middle class America." They give it their passionate loyalty and hold it to be good, except in so far as it excludes them or others because of race, creed or color—a loyalty which is constantly and tragically betrayed by the reality, while the weakness of my own *weaker* faith in its institutions is constantly being justified. Do you think I am exaggerating? Then consider for a moment these parallels in the lives of two middle-class Americans, Mrs. L. and myself.

If I want to go away for the hot weather, all I have to do is to look up some jolly mountain or seashore spot within my means, pack my bags and go. Mrs. L. cannot do this. Of all the wealth and loveliness of our natural resources, the greater part is closed to her. Hotels, boarding houses, and camps are almost entirely in the hands of white people who exclude colored ones. There are a few, a very few, resorts for colored people but they are generally crowded and not always desirable. To rent or buy a summer cottage, however simple, is difficult and expensive. Too many white people refuse to have colored neighbors! Long trips are not to be thought of because it is necessary to depend on hotel and sleeping-car accommodations. Just once, in the flush of youth, Dr. and Mrs. L. did attempt a trip. They took their oldest children to see Niagara and the Great Lakes. The experience was one they have never cared to repeat. So the L——s spend the summer in sunbaked B. There are worse hardships, of course, and yet why should the desirable thing which for me is so simple, that is, to give Elizabeth the wild freedom of the woods or an outing at the beach for two months each year, be impossible for them? They do spend a few days sometimes in a small colored hotel at a glittering resort on the Jersey coast, but they do not call it "taking their children to the country," and neither, I think, would you.

Again, let us say that a member of my family is stricken suddenly with a serious illness, or requires an immediate operation. It is a hard time and an anxious one, but how comparatively smooth and simple my course will be. I speak as a representative of middle-class America who can pay more or less for what she needs, and leave aside for the moment all question of economic injustice. My family physician will make all arrangements. I have my choice of the best doctors, the best private accommodation, the best nurses I can afford, and I will be pretty sure of sympathetic interest and helpfulness from all with whom I come in contact. When Barbara L——s was suddenly stricken with appendicitis, there was not a hospital, public or private in B——, or in the nearest big town, where she could get a room. They finally rushed her to the nearest big hospital and took their chances in the ward, already overcrowded, knowing that for the urgent care she needed, they had to depend upon overworked, indifferent nurses, and doctors in an institution which excluded colored people as doctors, nurses, or private patients. "It's when you're in a hurry that being colored really matters" was Mrs. L's comment on this occasion. These serious discriminations have their more trivial counterparts in almost every incident in our daily lives. If I wish to go down town to shop or for any other purpose, it is a simple matter. I can be served with reasonable promptness and civility in any store I see fit to enter, while Mrs. L. may be obliged to wait indefinitely or be ignored altogether by saleswomen who do not like her complexion. If I cannot get home to luncheon I eat downtown at the first tea-room or dairy lunch that comes to hand. Once when Mrs. L. was delayed beyond the noon hour, she tried to get food in three or four such places and, failing to obtain service in any of them, finally lunched on a bar of chocolate in the public square. It is possible that she would eventually have been served had she persisted. There is a law on the statute books covering such cases, but she preferred an unsatisfactory luncheon and her subsequent headache to further rebuffs. Again, if a good concert or a good play comes to town, I take Elizabeth as a matter of course. She has not so far evidenced any great enthusiasm for the concerts. Mrs. L. does not take Katherine, who is really musical and would love to go, because she can never be sure that the tickets she buys, or perhaps reserves by telephone, will really be honored. If they are for the gallery, the chances are that they will be, but even this is not a certainty. Besides she does not always want to sit in the gallery. You and I could do this with no feeling of discomfort. It is a part of our white freedom that we can, but then we have never been segregated into galleries or winced under the phrase "nigger heaven."

For our freedom is far more than the freedom from unpleasant occurrences. It is freedom from the expectation of such occurrences; from the constant apprehension of unfairness and of hostility or condescension in those we meet. It is freedom from the constant necessity of being on the defensive, of living forever isolated in a lonely little hell of self-consciousness. It is the priceless freedom of the mind and it contains the possibility of a fellowship as wide as the world. I cannot believe that even the close bond of suffering which unites those we exclude from it compensates them for its loss. That there are some compensations cannot be denied. Their lives gain in intensity. They know race loyalty and kinship and pride such as few of us even dream, and also sometimes practice detachment and irony to a degree few of us suspect, but surely these are shadowy substitutes for the whole of life. To live warped and ingrowing, however intensely, however sustained by pride, or irony, or the sense of having a cause, is not a substitute, it seems to me, for living fully and freely and to the limit of our powers.

The war which cut so sharply across our lives, obliterating race and class lines, once seemed about to wipe out even the barriers which separated the L——s from the rest of us. We were all Americans with a common cause—Democracy. In the name of Democracy we drafted black and white Americans impartially and sent them out to die. We taught them both to make sacrifices, to work and fight and save. We sold them both Liberty Bonds and Thrift Stamps and urged on both alike the need of war time effort and economy. But there Democracy ended. It drafted Robert L——s. It has since taken his life. But it excluded his mother from the workrooms of the Red Cross organization in B—— just as it has excluded and separated colored people the country over in every kind of war and war relief work. Democracy does not mean social equality, I may be told at this point, and there are many whose chosen work it seems to be to popularize this misconception. But if it does not mean equality, it means nothing. We did not knowingly go out to fight for "Democracy-within-caste-limits." It is not an inspiring slogan. Certainly it was not for such a qualified Democracy that Robert L——s and other young colored Americans died. What they really died for, I do not know. Neither do I know what of faith or despair or necessity drove them to their death in the American Forces. But I do see in the memory of my colored neighbor's Gold Star the most insistent question that has yet been put to our Democracy.

*December 29, 1920*

## The Lynching Bee

*William Ellery Leonard*

Here at the crossroads is the night so black
It swallows tree and thicket, barn and stack,
Even though the sickle of the new moon hang,
Keen as a knife, bent like a boomerang,
A witch's bangle in the Zodiac.
Black on the crossroads . . . but in skies off yonder
There broods a fiery gloom, a hectic glow,
Like the last twilight just before the thunder,
Or omens of doomed soothsayers, long ago . . .
Today the veriest dog or mule would know
It only means a lighted town thereunder.

Honk, Honk!
On to the fork! Honk! Honk!
You hear?
From hand-squeezed bulb and belching conch!
Honk! Honk!
Down in the hollow now, but near.
How many there?—
Honk! Honk!
Topping the hill off there—
Behind the foremost cone of glare—
That, like the swift typhoon,
Sweeps on along each length of rut
And makes their ridges as clear cut
As in Uganda at high noon
Stand out the Mountains of the Moon.

Honk—for the brasses and cat-gut!
Honk, Honk—for cymbals and bassoon!
New times, new music, and new fun!
Though Bottom's gone and Oberon,
With Satyr, Dwarf, and pet Baboon,
Midsummer nights have still their rites.
Honk, Honk: "We've caught the coon!"
("Honk" means they've caught the coon.)

They stop—they jerk—they chug—they back.
And in a monstrous ring, they park,
With ghostly cones converging from the dark
Upon a central tree all split and black,
Whose limbs and leaves are caverned out of sight
In the eternity of night.
It's like a magic circle where
Snake-dancers, striped, brown, and bare,
With pouch in waving hand and horns on hair,
In old times swayed and swung
And called on Tunga-Tung,
With nasal *ang* and guttural *unk*
Around a lightning-blasted trunk,
Or hissed in chorus with a serpent-stare.
Yet nothing like this there—
It's only the sign-board of the town's,
And crossroads cottonwood by Farmer Brown's.

It's only twelve true men in pants and coats
(The sort who pay their bills, and cast their votes,
Or file to jury boxes on hot afternoons) . . .
Each with a finger on a trigger,
Dragging by ropes, around his gullet tied,
With hobbled legs and arms well lashed to side,
The best of all buffoons—
A banjo-boy and jigger,
A hovel-doorway bawler of coarse tunes.

Like Caliban he shuffles, only bigger;
Or Ourang-outang, only larger-eyed—
A bandy-leggèd nigger,
Quite jerky, but all silent down inside.

They take the rope off at the tree—perhaps
Won't hang him after all?—These humorous chaps!
Just make him dance amid the glare
For women-folk and boys and girls back there,
Still in their seats?
Make him show off his feats?—
Stand on his head-piece while he eats
Hoe-cakes or possum sweets?
Or turn him up, and have him wag his ears;
Or wriggle and wrinkle scalp and brow,
Like a fly-bitten back of Holstein cow,
And throw from pate a bowl or plate,
While underneath he grins and leers?—
He'll butt his thick skull 'gainst the trunk, I think,
And then draw back, guffaw, and wink.

Not so. They pay a chain out link by link.
Hear it rattle, hear it clink!
A good stout chain so much can do!—
As dancing bear and old-time showman knew,
Or bloodhound leashed at kennel door in straw.
And down along the Nile,
With Pharaoh's Sphinx in view,
The Coptic coolies, with a chain or two
Around his belly, tail, and jaw,
Aboard the freighter hoist the crocodile
For Circus or for Zoo—
A stout chain holds,
Come fear or fire, whatever's in its folds.

They strip him, overalls and shirt,

They set his back against the tree,
They wind the links so tight about,
In girdles two and three. . . .
And yet it hardly seems to hurt—
For not a word says he.
Honk! Honk!

He stands five fathoms deep in glare agrin.
Honk, Honk! Honk, Honk!
His skin-bark on the tree bark-skin,
Trunk grafted on to trunk.
Honk! Honk! . . .
The graft should take, for they are close of kin—
Both sprung of one old soil of earth,
Both fed on rain and air and dirt from birth,
Both tough and stark and thin . . .

One steps with jack-knife up. And he
Will cut the bark of which dark tree?
Nigger or cottonwood?—With that
He gelds him like a colt or cat!
But the coon's caterwauls and wails
(Honk, Honk! Honk, Honk!)
Fall thin and blurred and flat—
While every conch-horn at him rails:
"No more he'll spawn in bush or bed,
With cocaine crazed, with whiskey drunk,
A charcoal woolly head,
Or yellow half-breed brat!"
Honk, Honk!

Another comes with brush and pot,
And smears him over, as with ointment hot.
Honk! Honk!
Good fellow, at your trellised house in town,
You boil the tar to indigo and brown,

Shimmering in sunshine, bubbling to the brim—
Why waste it at the crossroads here on him?
Tar on your driveway, rolled in grit,
Makes you a roadbed firm and fit;
Tar on your upturned row-boat sinks
In all the nail-holes, joints, and chinks;
Tar on your gadding daughter's white kid shoe
Was black, and tickled you all through;
But, brother, with the brush and pot,
Tar does no good on hide of Hottentot—
Or have you feathers in a bag or two?—
If so, by now, he'd just as lief as not.
Honk! Honk!

With rags, and straw, and sticks, and other toys,
In run the women-folk and girls and boys.
They'll prod his ribs? tickle his arm-pits? sop
His sweating cheeks, as with a pantry mop?
Such crossroads pranks are not just right
For decent town-folk, it would seem . . .
(Or is this only a midsummer dream
In innocent midnight?) . . .
Besides they haven't the heart. They drop
Their knickknacks at black ankles and bare feet,
And cool him from the spouts of cans
(Fetched from below-stairs, under washing pans
Porcelain-lined and scoured so white).
And then they all, excepting one, retreat,
Back through the length of light.

This one is honored over every other—
She is the dead child's Mother.
And the two glare and glare
At one another
In two eternities of hate and pain,
Yet with such monstrous union in despair,

Such hideous sameness in their haggard shapes,
The one, the other,
That you would say the twain
Seemed like a savage sister and twin-brother
Dying of hunger out among the apes.

Her hand is clutching her unsuckled breast—
You know the rest:
The bloody curls, the dainty skirt a shred,
The sprawling hand-prints on the legs and head,
Her body's little body in a shed. . . .
Then down she kneels;
You see her hunched back and her upturned heels. . . .
But not the scratch and scratch,
Not the small flame that tips the second match. . . .
And not her hands, her face, her hank of hair—
As when a Java woman kneels in prayer,
Under a temple-hut of thatch,
Before some devil-idol standing lone—
Not far from jungles and the tiger's lair—
Carved from the teak-wood to a jet-black face,
With Pagan wrinkles, curving pair by pair,
With set grimace,
And two great eyeballs, staring white in stone. . . .
Whilst smoke curls roofward from its hidden base. . . .
The Mother rises . . . will depart. . . .
Her duty done . . . and her desire. . . .
And as she turns, you see a strange
And quiet rapture of most uncouth change.
For from her burning marrow, her crazed heart,
She has transferred the fire
Of horror and despair
To the dumb savage there. . . .
She has transferred, she thinks, the fire to him.
Honk, Honk! let lights be dim!
(And now the lights are dim.) . . .

And for a moment is the night so black
It swallows tree and coon and all the pack,
And lets the sickle of the new moon hang,
Keen as a knife, bent like a boomerang,
A witch's bangle in the Zodiac.
Gone is the light that played upon the tree,
But at the cottonwood's own base
Another light now takes its place—
And there is still so much for us to see.
Honk! Honk!
There have been many bonfires on the earth,
Born out of many moods and needs of men:
As when the maskers, in their twilight mirth
On Wessex heaths, would burn Guy Fawkes again;
As when the bustling country-side in dread
Against the Armada's coming set the beacons,
In the heroic English days, on Beachy Head,
When the midsummer sea-winds blew;
As when the village dames and Yankee deacons
Out on the common had a barbecue;
As when the boys in South and North
Still make the boxes blaze and crackle on the Fourth.
The ghouls and witches too
In olden times and regions far away
Danced at their wonted rendezvous
Upon the Brocken on the first of May,
Screaming round the bonfire's light
All through Walpurgis Night.—
Honk! Honk!
There is much fascination in a flame—
Not least, whenever it has sprung
In intertwining tongue and tongue,
And left the one small spot from whence it came—
Faster, faster, higher, higher,
Shapes of wing, and wave, and lyre,
Shapes of demon-heads and peaked caps

And flying smocks, and shreds and scraps
Of all fantastic things without a name.
Tongue after tongue in middle air—
Snatched from existence, how and where?—
There is much fascination in a flame—
Not least, when it is yellow, blue, and red,
With blackness for a background and a frame,
Still fuel-fed
With straw and wood and tar and kerosene,
And some organic matter still alive.—
Its witcheries of color, how they strive!—
Even though some smudge and smoke may get between.

Yet two vast bloodshot eyeballs by their might
Out-top the flame, though from the flame their light—
Two eyeballs wrought (like eyeballs of the steer's
Or dog's, or cat's, or woodchuck's, or a deer's)
By one blind Nature in a mammal's womb—
By one Herself with neither eyes nor ears,
Nor birth, nor breath, nor doom.
The two vast eyeballs grow and grow,
Till, to the masters of the revels,
They seem the eyeballs of the devil's
Ascending from hell-fire down below.
The masters will not have it so:
A pole, all glowing charcoal at the tip—
Zip, Zip! Zip, Zip!
Honk, Honk! Honk, Honk!
And the blind savage at the flaming tree
No more will glare so monstrously.

But on the crossroads our midsummer dream
Converts each flame into a scream, a scream—
A shriek, a shriek!
The horns honk at them as a hose at fire;
But still with every honk they come,

Shriek after shriek,
But fiercer, faster, higher!
(And all the while before, he was as dumb
As Roman martyr, schooled to turn the cheek.)
Honk, honk, away to left and right!—
Between the honking and the shrieking black
The odds (awhile) are ten to one tonight
In favor of the blazing maniac!
All ancient Africa is in his yells:
The wounded zebra's neighing, the gazelle's
Fierce whinny at the salt-lick, and the goat's;
The roars of lions, with distended throats,
Over the moonlit rocks for hollow hunger;
The bellowing elephants, with jaws agape,
And lifted trunks that thrash across their backs
Like writhing pythons or the great sea-conger,
Their monstrous hindlegs bogged beyond escape
In fire-swept jungles off their beaten tracks.
All Africa is in the Negro's shrieks:
The forests with their thousand parrot-beaks,
From Nile and Congo to the Cape;
But the Gorilla, the man-ape,
With his broad, hairy, upright chest,
Seems to out-scream the rest.
All Africa is in his agony:
The human ladings at the western coast,
The slave-ship, and the storm at sea,
The naked bodies (never very old)—
Dragged, sick and crippled, from the fetid hold
And over the pitching gunwales tossed,
Both male and female, overboard,
While sharks, careening on their backs,
In the green swells with scudding foam astreak,
Ate up the blacks,
And crew and captain prayed the Lord,
Or crammed fresh oakum in the leak.

All Africa is on his lips:
The million sweats, the million bloody whips,
The million ankles festering in a cord—
The unborn baby still between the hips,
The bent gray head along the rice-swamp humming,
"O Massa Gawd, I'se coming."

His voice has come from other times and places. . . .
And hence away it carries far and far. . . .
For in mid-darkness, level with a limb,
Above the flames and smoking tar,
Ride feather-crested heads that bob at him,
With peering faces,
There—and—there—and there!
Faces, Faces,
Sudden and weird as those that loom and peep
Upon us nightly just before we sleep.
No hands, nor arms, nor tomahawks you see,
No thighs in buck-skins dyed and slashed,
No moccasin, no foot, no knee,
Not even a copper torso brave and bare
From many a war-path scarred and gashed—
But only faces, faces, faces,
Riding in the air—
Faces, faces, faces, faces,
Feather-crested with long braided hair,
Peering with an old desire
From the gloom upon the fire,
Summoned back from Otherwhere. . . .
Summoned back from What-has-been:
"Is that a Jesuit father at the stake
Burning for his Jesus' sake?—
He hung us crosses round our necks to save—
But when the Mohawks to our village came
They killed both squaw and brave;
We Hurons put the Mumble-Jumble to the flame.

The cross it was no good to make us win—
It was bad medicine!"
And Seminole, Pawnee, and Sioux,
Apache, Blackfoot, Chippewa, and Crow,
Each gloats as if he saw anew
His own best captive of the long ago. . . .

The faces fade away. . . .
The Negro's cries
Have joined the uncouth sounds of Yesterday—
The incantations to the blood-red moon,
The ululations in the eclipse at noon,
The old palm-island lullabies
That ring-nosed crones were used to croon,
Squatting circle-wise. . . .
And the twelve Shadows to the fire fling
Great logs with fungus, spines, and rotted pith,
And great dead boughs with thin and sprawling arms
(Fetched from about a long abandoned spring,
And toad-stool woodlots of surrounding farms)
As if to cage in wickerwork therewith
(Like the wild people of a South-sea myth)
The Demon-in-fire from everything it harms. . . .
The Negro's corpse will take strange shapes,
As the flames gnaw it, flesh and bone;
But neither men shall see, nor apes,
For it shall burn from now alone.
Alone . . . and up and up . . . and down and down. . . .
While honkers honk it back to town.

At last the stench, or glow of embers, brings
The wolves, or wolf-like things. . . .
Such as on earthquake midnights prowl around
Smoulder of fallen beams and littered ground,
And tear from dead hands golden finger-rings,
But though they crouch in slow two-legged stealth,

Their hunt is not for wealth.
They paw into the cinders, as with hooks. . . .
Snatch something out,
With gloating, starveling looks . . .
A bit of rib . . . or skull . . . or crup . . .
Hot ash and finger knuckle . . .
They wrap them up,
And putter round about . . .
And chuckle . . .
And foot it off and down the road,
Past the weasel, skunk, and toad,
The barnyard rat,
The hooting owl and the whirring bat.

But over the spot of glowing embers, listen,
The poplar's leaves are rustling like the rain
That patters on my garden-shrubs by night. . . .
The dew may glisten,
The south-wind come this way again,
And wander thither,
But the charred cottonwood has caught the blight. . . .
Its leaves shall wither.
Here on the fork, except that spot of red
(Still fierce as some primordial desire),
All lust is dead:
The lust to breed, the lust to burn;
The rut of flesh, the glut of fire. . . .
Lift up the head,
If still you can, and turn
To the great spaces of the skies.
Black . . . black . . . all black . . .
The moon has set—perhaps elsewhere to hang,
Keen as a knife, bent like a boomerang,
A witch's bangle in the Zodiac . . .
Black . . . black . . . all black . . .
Though dawn be pregnant with her enterprise,

And stars perhaps will keep . . .
Black . . . black . . . and over yonder,
The glow is gone from all the town thereunder . . .
And all the people sleep . . . and sleep . . . and sleep*
   *(You cringe and shrink?—
   It makes your own eyes in their sockets ache?
   O squeamish listener, but think
   It's all a midnight dream, and no one is awake;
   And in the morning, with the bobolink,
   We'll see together, you and I,
   The flowers, the fields, the sun, the sky.
   And the magnolia blossoms, white and pink.)

*August 15, 1923*

## Jim Crow in Texas

*William Pickens*

The classics tell about the tortures invented by the Sicilian tyrants, but the Sicilian genius for cruelty was far inferior to that of the fellow who contrived the Jim Crow car system to harass the colored population of the South. There are tens of thousands of white people in this country who would be uncompromisingly opposed to this exquisite torture if they only understood it. But *they* are not "jim crowed," they have not the experience, and they do not and almost *cannot* understand what the colored brother finds to complain of. Have you noticed how difficult it is to explain a sensation or a pain to some one who never experienced it?

Fourteen States have Jim Crow car laws. Not one of them maintains "equal accommodations" for colored people, although the law generally calls for accommodations "equal in all points of service and convenience," so as to square with the Fifteenth Amendment.

Nobody expects the railroads to go to the expense of duplicating their accommodations for the colored, non-voting, minority population. The result is that the colored traffic is usually attached to the general service with the least possible expense: a small waiting-room in one corner of the station, generally unswept and otherwise uncared-for; a compartment in one end of the white men's smoker for all the colored people—men, women, and children—to ride in; generally no wash basin and only one toilet for both sexes; with no privilege of taking meals in the diner or buying a berth in a sleeper. Colored passengers taking a journey of several days must either carry cold food enough to last or else buy the high-priced trash of the newsboy. A colored woman traveling three nights from El Paso, Texas, to Charleston, S. C., with a baby and small children, is compelled to carry cold food and to sit up on straight-backed seats for the whole trip. A colored woman of Portland, Oregon, editor of a paper there, bright, intelligent, and attractive, respected by the best-known white and colored people of the State, was visiting her parents in Texas, carrying her infant and a small child of three years. On their third night's ride, in Texas, she was compelled to get up, dress herself and babies, and vacate her berth because some short-distance white passengers objected to her presence in the car. A colored person who was hurrying from Florida to undergo an operation by an expert in Chicago had to risk death by a twenty-four-hour ride in a Jim Crow day coach. Sick colored people sometimes have to be carried on stretchers in the baggage car.

Let us look at an actual case of Jim Crow, which is typical of practically the whole South. This system is not designed to rid white people of the mere physical presence of the Negro, for a white man who objects to a colored person who rides in the other end of the car may have a colored servant with his family in his end of the car, and this colored servant may sleep in his house and be a wet-nurse for his baby. I shall use the first person singular and attempt to tell of Jim Crow experiences, without exaggeration and without abatement. I sit in a Jim Crow as I write, between El Paso and San Antonio, Texas. The Jim Crow car is not an institution merely to "separate the races"; it is a contrivance to humiliate and harass the colored people and to torture them with a finesse unequaled by the cruelest genius of the heathen world. The cruder genius broke the bodies of individuals occasionally, but Jim Crow tortures the bodies and souls of tens of thousands hourly.

In the last two months I have ridden many thousands of miles in comfortable Pullman reservations out from New York to the great Northwest, with many stops and side trips; then down from Tacoma and past the Golden Gate to the City of the Angels, from the red apples of Spokane to the golden apples of the southwestern Hesperides; and then on by the petrified forest, the great canyon, and through the ancient cliff-dwellings of man to Albuquerque, New Mexico. In Albuquerque I had bought my reservation to El Paso, Texas. El Paso is where the train would enter Texas, and both my tickets terminated there. But so thoroughly is it understood that Jim Crowism is not designed merely to "separate," but also to humiliate, colored passengers that the thing is always in the consciousness of the railway employees, even those who operate in and out of Jim Crow territory, and they begin to "work on you" as soon as you buy a ticket that leads even to the limbo of this hell.

"Well, you can't ride in this car after you get into Texas. You'll have to get out of this car in Texas, and I suppose you know that?" This from the Pullman conductor, in a very gruff and loud voice, so that the whole car might hear him, while he and others stare and glare upon me. His speech is absolutely unnecessary since my tickets call only for El Paso, but the object is to "rub it in." I answered with not a word nor a look, save such mild and indifferent observation as I might bestow upon idiots who should spit at me or lick out their tongues as I passed by their cells of confinement.

In El Paso, because of the miscarriage of a telegram, my friends did not meet the train and I had to call them up and wait till they came down. I was meanwhile shown to the "Negro" waiting-room, a space of about twenty by twenty, away off in one corner of the station structure like a place of quarantine or a veritable hole in the wall. I had to traverse the entire length of the great main waiting-room in order to reach this hole. This main waiting-room has all the conveniences, 'phone booths, ticket offices, and what not. And whom do you suppose I saw in this main waiting-room as I passed through? Not only the "white people," but all the non-American "colored peoples," yellow Chinese, brown Japanese, and the many-colored Mexicans, some dirty with red handkerchiefs around their necks and carrying baskets and bundles with fruits, vegetables, and live chickens. These Mexicans are the people whom the colored soldiers of the Twenty-fourth Infantry held off those white people some years ago. And if we should go to war with Japan the colored American will again be expected to rush forth from that hole in the wall to the defense of his white compatriot. I say all this without the slightest feeling of animosity toward any race, and absolutely without scorn of any human misfortune. I am only stating the case plainly. And when I reached the little humiliating hole assigned to "Negroes," I found there only four or five colored people, all intelligent, not one of them conspicuously unkempt like some of the Mexicans in the main waiting-room. Those Mexicans were being treated as human beings, as they should be treated. These colored people knew that this arrangement was not so much for their separation as for their humiliation and attempted degradation, and it formed the burden of their conversation.

I stayed in El Paso two nights and three days. Its colored people are alert to the situation. By means of their automobiles they protected me against the "rear-seat" treatment of the electric street cars. They took me across the shallow Rio Grande into Mexico, just a few hundred yards from Jim Crowism. And over there, bless you, white and black people come out of Texas and gamble at the same table, drink at the same bar, and eat in the same restaurant, while the dark and almost black Mexican stands around as the policeman and the law.

Then I went to buy a ticket for San Antonio. I did not expect to buy a Pullman ticket, but I did expect to buy a day coach ticket on any train. But I found that colored passengers are allowed to go to San Antonio on but one train a day, the one that leaves at night. The morning train carried only Pullmans, and colored folk are made to wait twelve hours longer for the train that carries a Jim Crow compartment. A colored man's mother may be dying in San Antonio, but he must wait. Any Mexican, however, whom the colored infantry fought on the border and did not happen to kill, can ride on any train. Any foreigner, or any foreign spy who happens to be loose in the land, can travel freely, but not the mothers or wives or sisters of the black Americans who fought, bled, and died in France. All the rest of the world, be he an unlettered Mexican peon, an untrammeled Indian, or a representative of the uncivilized "white trash" of the South, can get either train; but the Negro, be he graduate of Harvard or bishop of the church, can go only once daily. Now if the Negro can be limited to once a day while others ride on any train, the Negro can be limited to one day a week while others ride seven, or even to one day a month while others ride thirty.

I took the train that leaves at night. It is a ride of about twenty-four hours. Through friends it had been arranged that I be given a berth, late at night, after all the white people had gone to sleep and could not see me, and perhaps be called early before any of the whites were up. The money was accepted from my friends, even tips, but only the porter was sent to bring me a pillow into the Jim Crow car, and they still have the money. In the morning I went back to see if I could get some breakfast in the dining car, before 7 o'clock, before the whites got hungry. And what did I find as I passed through the whole string of Pullman cars in the rear? All the races of the world, as usual, save only the most loyal of all Americans.

In the Jim Crow car there was but one toilet and washroom, for use of colored women and men. And the Jim Crow car is not a car, mind you, but only the end of a car, part of the white men's smoker, separated from the white smokers only by a partition that rises part of the way from the floor toward the ceiling, so that all the sickening smoke can drift over all night and all day. And yet what do you suppose the colored porter said as he swept out the Jim Crow end this morning? Nobody asked him, he volunteered as he swept: "Well, this is the cleanest floor I have to sweep every morning. Them white folks and Mexicans and things back yonder sho' do mess up the floors!"

When I reached the dining-car there was not another person there. I was asked did I "want anything." I replied briefly, breakfast. Then there was confusion and much conferring between the steward and several colored waiters at the other end of the car. The steward kept glancing at me meanwhile, as if endeavoring to "size me." Finally I was given a seat at the end of the car where the porters eat. Oatmeal, eggs, and postum were brought, and then a green curtain was drawn between me and the rest of the vacant dining-car! Remember, this did not all happen in some insane asylum, but in Texas. The check on which I was to order my food was a green check, a "porter's check," so that I should not need to be treated to such little formalities as an extra plate or a finger bowl. I deliberately wrote my name down in the blank for "porter," but I was charged a passenger's fare. It all meant that I would not eat any more that day, although I was not to reach San Antonio till eight or nine at night.

One must be an idiot not to comprehend the meaning and the aim of these arrangements. There is no such thing as a fair and just Jim Crow system with "equal accommodations," and in very human nature there will never be. The inspiration of Jim Crow is a feeling of caste and a desire to "keep in its place," that is, to degrade, the weaker group. For there is no more reason for a Jim Crow car in public travel than there would be for a Jim Crow path in the public streets. Those honest-souled, innocent-minded people who do not know, but who think that the Jim Crow system of the South is a bona-fide effort to preserve mere racial integrity on a plane of justice are grievously misled. Any man should be permitted to shut out whom he desires from his private preserves, but justice and Jim Crowism in public places and institutions are as far apart and as impossible of union as God and Mammon.

*October 17, 1923*

## "White"

*Gustavus Adolphus Steward*

I

When Everett took a job as truck driver for a large Philadelphia concern he did not say that he was "colored." Tall, white, with brown hair and brown eyes, and with Caucasian—or should I write Nordic?—

features, nothing in his physical appearance betrayed his "race." Week in and week out he worked steadily, apparently giving entire satisfaction, earning the praise of his boss. Suddenly he was "let go." A *real white man*, a friend from his Jersey home, happening to secure work for the same firm, had given the information that Everett's mother and father, sisters and brothers, all of whom he personally knew, were "colored."

"But I'm the same man I was yesterday, ain't I?" protested Everett to the boss.

"Why yes, but you're colored. It would hurt the business—the other men won't work with a——."

All right, then, he'd *be* "colored," he determined, as he stamped out, flaming.

In New York he applied to the Pullman Company for a job as a sleeping-car porter. The man at the desk looked up at him in amazement and replied: "We can't use white men as porters."

"But I'm not white, I'm colored," Everett fiercely declared. No use. The other, unconvinced, waved him politely out. Everett was never sure whether the man believed him simply a plain liar or a new brand of interesting lunatic.

## II

The widow Moore is the daughter of her former Virginia master by one of his slaves. She is stately, gray-haired, with bluish-gray eyes, and far from unfashionable in dress. She listed with the Barton Rental Agency a piece of property she owns, and did not state that she was "colored." In due time Barton's "For Rent" sign appeared in the front window of her vacant house. Some time later she called at the agency. Mr. Barton told her that her house seemed a bit hard to rent, that is, to desirable tenants. She should be patient, however. The house would certainly be rented, and to first-class people, too. They did not rent to any other class.

"Of course," he continued, "we could easily rent to colored, for example, but—"

"Well, why not? Colored people are good people, aren't they?"

"I'm not saying they aren't, but when they get into a property it depreciates. If you should want to sell later, you would lose money. Moreover, any agency which places colored among white people thereby earns an undesirable and unprofitable reputation. We therefore make it a business point not to—"

"Have you had any applications from colored people?"

"Oh, several."

"Then rent it to them. Why keep the house idle if they are good people and can pay?"

"Sorry, madam, but we shall have to decline—"

As the widow Moore was leaving Barton's office, she had a consuming desire to fling back at him the scorching words: "I'm colored." She thought how much she would enjoy seeing him writhe as they annihilated him. Instead she went out and rented her house—to "colored."

## III

The brown letter carrier bought a house in the very middle of a block occupied entirely by whites. When the day to move came, he went to his work as usual, while his blonde, pink-cheeked, blue-eyed wife superintended the transfer of their household goods. She wore no tag stating that she was "colored."

Her new neighbors watched the emptying vans from behind front-room curtains and upstairs windows. Late in the afternoon, when the greater part of the preliminary "settling" was over, the lady next door ventured over.

"You must be tired, working here all day by yourself. I just thought I'd run in and ask you if you would not like to come over and have a cup of hot tea or something with me." The blonde wife went.

The brown letter carrier finished his day's work, hurried to the new home, slipped into rough clothes, and began to busy himself about the yard. The lady next door and his wife were in the midst of a pleasant neighborly chat, finishing their luncheon. The former was saying: "I'm so glad I had a little something in the house. It's such an awful job to move. Now, anything I can do until you get straight, let me know. Just come right over any time and use our stove and things until yours is connected." The postman's wife thanked her.

"Your yard man has come, I think," the neighbor continued, as she saw the brown man in overalls in the yard.

"Oh, that's my husband," said the carrier's wife, and without waiting to see what visible effect this pronouncement had—an omission she now decidedly regrets—she ran out to him. But the lady next door "does not speak" now, and the neighborhood bristles with antipathy against the interlopers.

## IV

None of his friends seems to have known what blood mixture filled Norton's veins. He himself was able to account for three strains— American Indian, American white, and Mexican. He had the complexion of an Italian, his head was covered with a mass of deepest black hair, and he wore the long curling mustache of the vogue which preceded the present truncated, stubbly fashion. At any rate he certainly did not state that he was "colored."

When I first met him he was a night clerk in the Brookline, Massachusetts, post office, dreaming of the day when, with a friend who was both violinist and composer, he would entrance a waiting world with the beauties of an exceedingly graceful light opera to the preparation of which they both devoted all their spare moments. Suddenly he became violently religious, and vehemently damned the very art to which hitherto he had been ardently attached. He joined a church in the shadow of Faneuil Hall. He and his wife became prominent in its activities, and with the inspiration and approval of its pastor, he prepared himself for missionary work in India. The missionary board approved his application. He went to the New York offices to complete preliminaries. Somehow information seems to have reached the board that he was "colored." Perhaps some member of the church had drawn that conclusion from the fact that his wife was indubitably "colored," and this startlingly subversive intelligence had been communicated to the board. At any rate, upon seeing him the good gentlemen of the missionary board were sure that some unaccountable mistake had been made.

They were profuse in their apologies. In spite of their written approval of his application for service in India which he held, it seemed that they had intended to state "service in Africa." It is reported that they oiled their explanation of this unusual blunder with the same old quasi-pious stuff which white Christians too frequently employ when confronted with a Negro demanding mere human consideration. "Colored people are so much happier among their own, you know." "Africa should make a particularly compelling appeal to every consecrated colored man," and so on.

But Norton was interested in souls, he said, and not in the color of human skins. He left the board's rooms convinced that there was a mistake and that he had made it. He had seriously misjudged the board. Bitterly he reflected afterwards that he had thought that they were Christians!

His missionary zeal did not at once abate, and so he started with his wife on a tour through the South, with the avowed purpose of converting the Negroes there. He had desperately determined to *be* "colored." They got as far as Petersburg, Virginia, became upset and frightened at the hostility they engendered among the Negroes by their frank, somewhat superior-minded assumption that they needed conversion, and returned, cured, to the North, where Norton accepted the pastorate of a church in a New England town. But his disillusionment must have been both thorough and permanent, for not long afterward he had given up religious work for good and was driving a huge auto truck for some New York business house.

One winter morning he was found frozen to death in the city's streets. It is said that his mind had become deranged from brooding over his abortive missionary efforts. His widow now does uplift work in a Jim Crow Y. M. C. A. in a Southern city. And the soft-voiced, elderly gentlemen of the missionary board, one supposes, still approve "colored" missionary applicants for service—in Africa only.

*June 18, 1924*

## The Race Problem in the Caribbean
*Robert Herrick*

II. The French Way
*(In a previous article, printed in* The Nation *of June 11, Mr. Herrick described the situation existing in the British islands.)*

It is only sixty miles from the English island of St. Lucia to Martinique, less than forty miles from Martinique to the English island of Dominica. Both these British islands retain positive indications of French influence, distinguishing them from Barbados or Antigua, which are purely English. The colored population of St. Lucia and Domenica understand and largely use among themselves a French patois and their folk literature betrays the contacts they have had with their immediate neighbors. Moreover, there are subtler marks of French blood and French influence among many of the natives who have been under English rule exclusively for more than a century, testifying to the potent quality of the French culture. Yet when one passes in the night from one of these English islands to Martinique he wakes up to a new world, still predominantly colored, but with a vivid contrast in appearance and spirit that seems more marvelous the longer he remains in the French colonies. From the same materials, practically, physiographically, and racially, the French have made an utterly different compound culturally, which promises if permitted to endure to differentiate itself more and more from the English product.

I felt it that first Sunday morning of my visit to Martinique while taking my early coffee on the terrace of the hotel and watching the stream of colored folk on their way to mass in the cathedral. Color was the first note of contrast with the English settlements—color in the houses, in the costumes of the women, in the vivid madras, the picturesque foulards—I had never seen such amazing contrasts of color in dress. Purples and greens and yellows, all violently yet agreeably thrown together. And color in the people themselves. Here was not a people of whites and blacks (or even mulattoes). These women and children—for there were few men in the church-going crowd—were of every possible shade of brown, ivory, reddish bronze, yellow. Few were either dull or vivid black, as in Barbados and Trinidad. At this first glance it was evident the mixing of races had gone on in Martinique for a much longer time and more commonly than in any English island. Further acquaintance with conditions in the French islands confirmed this impression: of the one hundred and seventy-five thousand inhabitants of Martinique not more than two thousand are pure white, and an astonishingly small percentage of the majority are pure black, or *nègres*, as they are called. The great majority of the one hundred and seventy-five thousand have some white (a few, Indian) blood. Here, then, on a small scale, one might observe the results of an almost free miscegenation between whites and blacks and, if true, witness the dire degeneration that such a miscegenation is supposed to produce!

It is a commonplace that the French (and Southern Europeans generally) evince no such instinctive repugnance to the black race as the Anglo-Saxon; they intermarry with colored peoples and admit them quite freely to civil equality, even to a sort of social equality. The French colonials, during the days of slavery, endeavored unsuccessfully to keep the white stock pure by making stringent laws against the freeing of black women for the purpose of marriage, but to how little avail the sight of the present highly varied colored population is evidence. The fact was that the French colonial in those illicit relations with dark women which all colonial societies have suffered was much kinder, more humane, more open, and less ashamed of his irregular establishments than his English neighbors. For example, in the old days it was customary for the white man to give land or houses to his colored mistress, to admit the relationship. As a consequence one finds that today the colored offspring of miscegenation will speak with pride of his white father or grandfather. Instead of becoming neither a good white nor a good black, as the American has it, the French mixed blood is conscious of a superiority, and whether due to a real improvement of stock or to the benefit of a better upbringing, the lightly colored folk are the ones to be found in responsible positions, in trade and in the civil service. In fact if there is ever a race conflict in the French islands it will come about because of competition for control between the pure blacks, the plantation hands, who are less advanced, and the mixed breed who are socially conscious and ambitious—not between the white and the black. For here, as in the English Antilles, the white has already practically given over the hopeless struggle for racial dominance. Their numbers are falling every decade, and their wealth.

But it is not only by a franker mixing with the "inferior race" that the French colonial has brought about this situation, so different from that of the English colonies. Something besides the touch of white blood has gone to creating the allure, the grace, the subtle sense of independence, of quick-witted equality, all of which and more make the French colored man, woman, or child a different creature from the English colored. That superb carriage of the body, which Lafcadio Hearn was never weary of remarking thirty-five years ago, and which, especially among the colored women of Martinique, is as true today as then, that readiness of tongue and readiness of wit come from something other than mingling of blood. Across the tiny place from my hotel in the Fort de France was the *Palais de Justice*, with the usual flamboyant Gallic proclamation of *Liberté, Egalité et Fraternité*. These noble human ideals are probably no better observed in these distant dependencies of France than in Algiers or Tonquin—or Paris, for that matter. But that extravagant motto, for all its absurdity, splashed as it is across the façades of all French buildings, has put something into the French democracy which every other democracy in the world lacks. Just as the French conscript army seemed to me the most democratic army in the world, the most citizen army (probably far more so than the communist army) so the French colored folk carry themselves as do no other Negro people I have ever seen. There is no servility (and little insolence) in their attitude, but a consciousness of freedom and equality. This, with their vivid sense of color, with their charm, and their very great personal beauty makes them the most attractive colored people I have known in the world. Here for the first time I at least came to realize that it was stupid to speak of black or colored, indiscriminately en masse; that there was as great physical and personal individuality, as many shades of complexion and casts of features and degrees of beauty or charm among dark-skinned people as among Nordics! It is only the stupid—and brutal—egotism of a dominant race that lumps under one undiscriminated heading all the qualities of another race. Individuality and variety are not merely potentially but actually existent in black as in white. These the French culture has evoked.

Two obvious agencies have assisted in creating the French colored civilization—the Catholic church and the public schools. The French colonies are saturated with Catholicism. Not even in Brittany is the wayside shrine, the wayside cross, the *calvaire* as common as in Martinique. And whatever else one may find to say about Catholicism it inculcates in its lowliest representatives a spirit of Christian equality. The old white priest standing beneath the stone cross on the green hillside of Morne Rouge, surrounded by his black congregation who had made with him, singing, the stations of the cross that Lenten Sunday of March called them "mes frères" in his simple address, in no Pickwickian sense. So, too, the schools are crowded, where the youth are taught by white and colored men and women; taught at least to read and write French, so that practically every person in the colony can speak intelligible French, aside from the patois, which is unfortunately destined to die out. Possibly the Great War has had its part in this making of a French colored civilization. For somewhere in every hamlet there is a tablet bearing the names of many colored citizens who died in France fighting side by side with white Frenchmen. An extraordinary number of these colored men went overseas to fight. In the little hamlet of Lorain I counted over a hundred names on the memorial tablet of those who had died in the war. (Such strange names, too, suggesting Carib descent, African, East Indian coolie, Spanish and Portuguese, beside "Creole," that is white colonial.)

Another important question, of course, is the land question. Wherever in these tropical islands the "inferior race" has been able to get hold of land in sufficient amount to live off it, the social product differs from that in places where, as in Barbados, the land is still held in the form of large plantations to be exploited by dependent blacks at a low wage. In the French islands the land is in small patches, no doubt largely because of the tumbled, broken, volcanic nature of the country. There are comparatively few large holdings. The characteristic thing in Martinique is the small cabin with a field of two, worked—and really worked—by the owner and his family. Of course this development is deplored by the white colonial who finds that it restricts his supply of labor, and who grumbles inevitably at the "lazy nigger." And paradoxically in these densely populated islands there is an almost universal "labor problem." But looking at the matter solely from the aspect of the colored colonial the small-holding type of development makes for independence, and charm, also cheapness of living. The by-ways of Martinique, the little valleys, the mountain slopes, are garden patches, supporting an animated, fairly industrious, vivid, and articulate colored race.

The first question the American traveler is asked in Martinique by both white and colored, asked with curiosity and agitation, is: "What is your country going to do with us? Will the United States take the French Antilles in payment of war debts?" This trade which so far as I know has never been seriously considered in the United States (outside such circles of blatant imperialism as the Chicago *Tribune*, and among the boosters for a bigger navy) is passionately discussed and patriotically dreaded down there in the French Antilles. The local newspapers, inflamed by suggestions from the French press, print furious denunciations of the scheme, and the white colonials express more or less politely their natural disgust of the idea. Recalling the type of rowdy, booze-hunting American citizen whom the great excursion steamers periodically set loose in their ports, one should not be surprised or offended at this repugnance to becoming more closely associated with the richest and most powerful nation in the world.

But considering the matter more seriously I asked myself why should the handing over of these lovely, fertile islands to the United States be the unmitigated disaster that it unquestionably would be to their present inhabitants? The answer to this question reveals the secret of our failure in handling our own race problem and the success of the

French way with the same problem. Ignoring the economic working of the Eighteenth Amendment in a rum-making territory (which has largely devastated the Virgin Islands we bought from the Danes and which would simply prostrate Martinique and Guadeloupe) the graver reason is that our prejudices unfit us to govern or assimilate a colored people. We should inevitably create another and worse Porto Rican sore, and ruin something fine of great promise if permitted to work itself out, and that is the creation of a French colored civilization. The root of that civilization is the frank acceptance of what we hypocritically shudder at and surreptitiously practice, miscegenation. We have a huge literature, probably largely unscientific, on race hybridization, and the popular mind in America is so clouded on this subject, so closed, and so inflamed that we should consider and treat the populations of these islands merely as "niggers," offending their pride, ignoring their just claims to individuality, probably trying to suppress their language, as we are engaged in suppressing Spanish in Porto Rico. We are the most intolerant people in the world, as we have recently demonstrated to the Japanese, and the most ignorantly prejudiced, as we are engaged in demonstrating in Haiti. In Martinique and Guadeloupe we should have a more advanced people to deal with than in either Haiti or Porto Rico, and one that the usual American administrator would not have the imagination to understand.

No, the hope for these French foster children, as in a somewhat different way it is for the English colored populations, is to be allowed to extend self-rule, to develop themselves in a climate to which they are admirably adapted—even at the expense of less sugar, cocoa, limes. The world needs the harmonious development of the culture of these mixed white and black people far more than it needs more sugar and other tropical riches. It needs the gaiety, the beauty, the vivid color sense of the French mulatto—another demonstration of the age-old fact that white and black have mingled without terrible consequences, as among the Mediterranean peoples. And America needs the object lesson which the French are giving of a possible humane solution of the race problem.

*December 17, 1924*

## The Primitive Black Man

*W. E. Burghardt Du Bois*

I began to notice it as I entered southern France. I formulated it in Portugal. I knew it as a great truth one Sunday in Liberia. And the Great Truth was this: efficiency and happiness do not go together in modern culture. Going south from London, as the world darkens it gets happier. Portugal is deliciously dark. Many leading citizens would have difficulty keeping off a Georgia "Jim Crow" car. But, oh, how lovely a land and how happy a people! And so leisurely. Little use of trying to shop seriously in Lisbon before 11. It isn't done. Nor at noon; the world is lunching or lolling in the sun. Even after 4 p.m. one takes chances, for the world is in the Rocio. And the banks are so careless and the hotels so leisurely. How delightfully angry Englishmen get at the "damned, lazy" Portuguese!

But if this of Portugal, what of Africa? Here darkness descends and rests on lovely skins until brown seems so luscious and natural. There is sunlight in great gold globules and soft, heavy-scented heat that wraps you like a garment. And laziness; divine, eternal languor is right and good and true.

I remember the morning. It was Sunday, and the night before we heard the leopards crying down there. Today beneath the streaming sun we went down into the gold-green forest. It was silence—silence the more mysterious because life abundant and palpitating pulsed all about us and held us drowsy captives to the day. Ahead the gaunt missionary strode, alert, afire, with his gun. He apologized for the gun, but he did not need to apologize to me, for I saw the print of a leopard's hind foot. A monkey sentinel piped, and I heard the whir of the horde as they ran.

Then we came to the village. How can I describe it? Neither London nor Paris nor New York has anything of its delicate, precious beauty. It was a town of the Veys and done in cream and pale purple—still, clean, restrained, tiny, complete. It was so simple and quiet there in the great wide world. Its arms were wide—it was no selfish place, but the central abode of fire and hospitality, was clean-swept for wayfarers, and the best seats were bare. They quite expected visitors, morning, noon, and night; and they gave our hands a quick, soft grasp and talked easily. Their manners were better than those of Park Lane or Park Avenue, Rittenhouse Square or the North Shore. Oh, much better and more natural! They showed breeding.

The chief's son—tall and slight and speaking good English—had served the late Colonel Young. He made a little speech of welcome. Long is the history of the Veys and comes down from the Eastern Roman Empire, the great struggle of Islam and the black empires of the Sudan.

We went on to other villages—dun colored, not so beautiful, but neat and hospitable. In one sat a visiting chief of perhaps fifty years in a derby hat and a robe, and beside him stood a shy young wife done in ebony and soft brown, whose liquid eyes could not meet ours. The chief was taciturn until we spoke of schools. Then he woke sud-denly—he had children to "give" to a school. There was a pile of brown coffee heaped in the center of the village. I see the last village fading away: they are plastering the wall of a home, leisurely and carefully. They smiled a goodby—not effusively, with no eagerness, with simple friendship, as we glided under the cocoa trees and into the silent forest, the gold and silent forest.

And there and elsewhere in two long months I began to learn: Primitive men are not following us afar, frantically waving and seeking our goals; primitive men are not behind us in some swift foot-race. Primitive men have arrived. They are abreast, and in places ahead of us; in others behind. But all their curving advance line is con-temporary, not prehistoric. They have used other paths and these paths have led them by scenes sometimes fairer, sometimes uglier than ours, but always toward the Pools of Happiness. Or, to put it otherwise, these folks have the leisure of true aristocracy—leisure for thought and courtesy, leisure for sleep and laughter. They have time for their children—such well-trained, beautiful children with perfect, unhidden bodies. Have you ever met a crowd of children in the east of London or New York, or even on the Avenue at Forty-second or 142nd Street, and fled to avoid their impudence and utter ignorance of courtesy? Come to Africa and see well bred and courteous children, playing happily and never sniffing and whining.

I have read everywhere that Africa means sexual license. Perhaps it does. Most folk who talk sex frantically have all too seldom revealed their source material. I was in West Africa only two months, but with both eyes wide. I saw children quite naked and women usually naked to the waist—with bare bosom and limbs. And in those sixty days I saw less of sex dalliance and appeal than I see daily on Fifth Avenue. This does not mean much, but it is an interesting fact.

The primitive black man is courteous and dignified. If the platforms of Western cities had swarmed with humanity as I have seen the platforms swarm in Senegal, the police would have a busy time. I did not see one respectable quarrel.

Wherefore shall we all take to the Big Bush? No. I prefer New York. But my point is that New York and London and Paris must learn of West Africa and may learn. The one great lack in Africa is communication—communication as represented by human contact, movement of goods, dissemination of knowledge. All these things we have—we have in such crushing abundance that they have mastered us and defeated their real good. We meet human beings in such throngs that we cannot know or even understand them—they become to us inhuman, mechanical, hateful. We are choked and suffocated, tempted and killed by goods accumulated from the ends of the earth; our newspapers and magazines so overwhelm us with knowledge—knowledge of all sorts and kinds from particulars as to our neighbors' underwear to Einstein's mathematics that one of the great and glorious joys of the African bush is to escape from "news."

On the other hand, African life with its isolation has deeper knowledge of human souls. The village life, the forest ways, the teeming markets bring an intimate human knowledge that the West misses, sinking the individual in the social. Africans know infinitely fewer folk, but know them infinitely better. Their intertwined communal souls therefore brook no poverty or prostitution—these things are to them ununderstandable. On the other hand, they are vastly ignorant of what the world is doing and thinking and of what is known of its physical forces. They suffer terribly from preventable disease, from unnecessary hunger, from the freaks of the weather.

Here, then, is something for Africa and Europe both to learn; and Africa is eager, breathless, to learn—while Europe? Europe laughs with loud guffaws. Learn of Africa? Nonsense. Poverty cannot be abolished. Democracy and firm government are incompatible. Prostitution is world old and inevitable.

Whereupon Europe proceeds to one of two programs:

1. To force Africa into modern work-slavery by whip and gun.
2. To tempt Africa into work profitable to Europe by catering to her present wants.

And then across these programs with absolutely no reference to them logically or physically run the amazing missionary efforts.

The net result is disintegration. Disintegration toward death as in the Belgian Congo. Disintegration toward European life as in French Senegal. Disintegration toward modern machine methods as in Sierra Leone. Disintegration by absorption into another group as in Liberia, where the new Liberian is more and more of native blood and American training.

Most people would disagree with the attempt to force Africa into work slavery and assume that this program is obsolete in Africa. It is not. It is, on the whole, the main and predominant program. On the other hand, the second program of catering to the wants of Africa may be good and may be bad, and is usually bad. Everything depends upon which wants are catered to, and how they are catered to, and with what objects and ideals. One may cater to the wish for alcoholic stimulants by synthetic gin, or one may cater to the need of knowledge by establishing schools; and between these two runs the gamut of the universe. As a matter of fact, what one does cater to is to those wants the satisfaction of which makes the largest profit for the importer. And one does this without any reference to the ultimate effect upon the people. One copies the beautiful cloth patterns of the West African artisan and his dyes, and floods West Africa with machine-made garments, beautiful and striking in many ways, but far less beautiful, of course, than the native garment, and at the same time driving the native artisan out of the market.

What shall one do? Here again one must do the thing most profitable to the importer. Bring down palm oil and ivory and wild rubber. All this beginning of trade and intercourse with the modern world is a matter which ought to call for the wisest thought and most farseeing philanthropy. It is left today in the hands of the most selfish and ignorant white traders. One could envisage in West Africa a missionary effort that would uplift the world: trained physicians and nurses, masters of industrial processes guided by ideals which make industry cater to human development and uplift; wise men trained in anthropology and history to observe and copy the ancient and in many respects magnificent native organizations; and teachers who know how to teach.

*June 23, 1926*

## The Negro Artist and the Racial Mountain

*Langston Hughes*

One of the most promising of the young Negro poets said to me once, "I want to be a poet—not a Negro poet," meaning, I believe, "I want to write like a white poet"; meaning subconsciously, "I would like to be a white poet"; meaning behind that, "I would like to be white." And I was sorry the young man said that, for no great poet has ever been afraid of being himself. And I doubted then that, with his desire to run away spiritually from his race, this boy would ever be a great poet. But this is the mountain standing in the way of any true Negro art in America—this urge within the race toward whiteness, the desire to pour racial individuality into the mold of American standardization, and to be as little Negro and as much American as possible.

But let us look at the immediate background of this young poet.

His family is of what I suppose one would call the Negro middle class: people who are by no means rich yet never uncomfortable nor hungry—smug, contented, respectable folk, members of the Baptist church. The father goes to work every morning. He is a chief steward at a large white club. The mother sometimes does fancy sewing or supervises parties for the rich families of the town. The children go to a mixed school. In the home they read white papers and magazines. And the mother often says "Don't be like niggers" when the children are bad. A frequent phrase from the father is, "Look how well a white man does things." And so the word white comes to be unconsciously a symbol of all the virtues. It holds for the children beauty, morality, and money. The whisper of "I want to be white" runs silently through their minds. This young poet's home is, I believe, a fairly typical home of the colored middle class. One sees immediately how difficult it would be for an artist born in such a home to interest himself in interpreting the beauty of his own people. He is never taught to see that beauty. He is taught rather not to see it, or if he does, to be ashamed of it when it is not according to Caucasian patterns.

For racial culture the home of a self-styled "high-class" Negro has nothing better to offer. Instead there will perhaps be more aping of things white than in a less cultured or less wealthy home. The father is perhaps a doctor, lawyer, landowner, or politician. The mother may be a social worker, or a teacher, or she may do nothing and have a maid. Father is often dark but he has usually married the lightest woman he could find. The family attend a fashionable church where few really colored faces are to be found. And they themselves draw a color line. In the North they go to white theaters and white movies. And in the South they have at least two cars and a house "like white folks." Nordic manners, Nordic faces, Nordic hair, Nordic art (if any), and an Episcopal heaven. A very high mountain indeed for the would-be racial artist to climb in order to discover himself and his people.

But then there are the low-down folks, the so-called common element, and they are the majority—may the Lord be praised! The people who have their nip of gin on Saturday nights and are not too important to themselves or the community, or too well fed, or too learned to watch the lazy world go round. They live on Seventh Street in Washington or State Street in Chicago and they do not particularly care whether they are like white folks or anybody else. Their joy runs, bang! into ecstasy. Their religion soars to a shout. Work maybe a little today, rest a little tomorrow. Play awhile. Sing awhile. O, let's dance! These common people are not afraid of spirituals, as for a long time their more intellectual brethren were, and jazz is their child. They furnish a wealth of colorful, distinctive material for any artist because they still hold their own individuality in the face of American standardizations. And perhaps these common people will give to the world its truly great Negro artist, the one who is not afraid to be himself. Whereas the better-class Negro would tell the artist what to do, the people at least let him alone when he does appear. And they are not ashamed of him—if they know he exists at all. And they accept what beauty is their own without question.

Certainly there is, for the American Negro artist who can escape the restrictions the more advanced among his own group would put upon him, a great field of unused material ready for his art. Without going outside his race, and even among the better classes with their "white" culture and conscious American manners, but still Negro enough to be different, there is sufficient matter to furnish a black artist with a lifetime of creative work. And when he chooses to touch on the relations between Negroes and whites in this country with their innumerable overtones and undertones, surely, and especially for literature and the drama, there is an inexaustible supply of themes at hand. To these the Negro artist can give his racial individuality, his heritage of rhythm and warmth, and his incongruous humor that so often, as in the Blues, becomes ironic laughter mixed with tears. But let us look again at the mountain.

A prominent Negro clubwoman in Philadelphia paid eleven dollars to hear Raquel Meller sing Andalusian popular songs. But she told me a few weeks before she would not think of going to hear "that woman," Clara Smith, a great black artist, sing Negro folksongs. And many an upper-class Negro church, even now, would not dream of employing a spiritual in its services. The drab melodies in white folks' hymnbooks are much to be preferred. "We want to worship the Lord correctly and quietly. We don't believe in 'shouting.' Let's be dull like the Nordics," they say, in effect.

The road for the serious black artist, then, who would produce a racial art is most certainly rocky and the mountain is high. Until recently he received almost no encouragement for his work from either white or colored people. The fine novels of Chesnutt go out of print with neither race noticing their passing. The quaint charm and humor of Dunbar's dialect verse brought to him, in his day, largely the same kind of encouragement one would give a sideshow freak (A colored man writing poetry! How odd!) or a clown (How amusing!).

The present vogue in things Negro, although it may do as much harm as good for the budding colored artist, has at least done this: it has brought him forcibly to the attention of his own people among whom for so long, unless the other race had noticed him beforehand, he was a prophet with little honor. I understand that Charles Gilpin acted for years in Negro theaters without any special acclaim from his own, but when Broadway gave him eight curtain calls, Negroes, too, began to beat a tin pan in his honor. I know a young colored writer, a manual worker by day, who had been writing well for the colored magazines for some years, but it was not until he recently broke into the white publications and his first book was accepted by a prominent New York publisher that the "best" Negroes in his city took the trouble to discover that he lived there. Then almost immediately they decided to give a grand dinner for him. But the society ladies were careful to whisper to his mother that perhaps she'd better not come. They were not sure she would have an evening gown.

The Negro artist works against an undertow of sharp criticism and misunderstanding from his own group and unintentional bribes from the whites. "O, be respectable, write about nice people, show how good we are," say the Negroes. "Be stereotyped, don't go too far, don't shatter our illusions about you, don't amuse us too seriously. We will pay you," say the whites. Both would have told Jean Toomer not to write "Cane." The colored people did not praise it. The white people did not buy it. Most of the colored people who did read "Cane" hate it. They are afraid of it. Although the critics gave it good reviews the public remained indifferent. Yet (excepting the work of

Du Bois) "Cane" contains the finest prose written by a Negro in America. And like the singing of Robeson, it is truly racial.

But in spite of the Nordicized Negro intelligentsia and the desires of some white editors we have an honest American Negro literature already with us. Now I await the rise of the Negro theater. Our folk music, having achieved world-wide fame, offers itself to the genius of the great individual American Negro composer who is to come. And within the next decade I expect to see the work of a growing school of colored artists who paint and model the beauty of dark faces and create with new technique the expressions of their own soul-world. And the Negro dancers who will dance like flame and the singers who will continue to carry our songs to all who listen—they will be with us in even greater numbers tomorrow.

Most of my own poems are racial in theme and treatment, derived from the life I know. In many of them I try to grasp and hold some of the meanings and rhythms of jazz. I am sincere as I know how to be in these poems and yet after every reading I answer questions like these from my own people: Do you think Negroes should always write about Negroes? I wish you wouldn't read some of your poems to white folks. How do you find anything interesting in a place like a cabaret? Why do you write about black people? You aren't black. What makes you do so many jazz poems?

But jazz to me is one of the inherent expressions of Negro life in America: the eternal tom-tom beating in the Negro soul—the tom-tom of revolt against weariness in a white world, a world of subway trains, and work, work, work; the tom-tom of joy and laughter, and pain swallowed in a smile. Yet the Philadelphia clubwoman is ashamed to say that her race created it and she does not like me to write about it. The old subconscious "white is best" runs through her mind. Years of study under white teachers, a lifetime of white books, pictures, and papers, and white manners, morals, and Puritan standards made her dislike the spirituals. And now she turns up her nose at jazz and all its manifestations—likewise almost everything else distinctly racial. She doesn't care for the Winold Reiss portraits of Negroes because they are "too Negro." She does not want a true picture of herself from anybody. She wants the artist to flatter her, to make the white world believe that all Negroes are as smug and as near white in soul as she wants to be. But, to my mind, it is the duty of the younger Negro artist, if he accepts any duties at all from outsiders, to change through the force of his art that old whispering "I want to be white," hidden in the aspirations of his people, to "Why should I want to be white? I am a Negro—and beautiful!"

So I am ashamed for the black poet who says, "I want to be a poet, not a Negro poet," as though his own racial world were not as interesting as any other world. I am ashamed, too, for the colored artist who runs from the painting of Negro faces to the painting of sunsets after the manner of the academicians because he fears the strange unwhiteness of his own features. An artist must be free to choose what he does, certainly, but he must also never be afraid to do what he might choose.

Let the blare of Negro jazz bands and the bellowing voice of Bessie Smith singing Blues penetrate the closed ears of the colored near-intellectuals until they listen and perhaps understand. Let Paul Robeson singing Water Boy, and Rudolph Fisher writing about the streets of Harlem, and Jean Toomer holding the heart of Georgia in his hands, and Aaron Douglas drawing strange black fantasies cause the smug Negro middle class to turn from their white, respectable, ordinary books and papers to catch a glimmer of their own beauty. We younger Negro artists who create now intend to express our individual dark-skinned selves without fear or shame. If white people are pleased we are glad. If they are not, it doesn't matter. We know we are beautiful. And ugly too. The tom-tom cries and the tom-tom laughs. If colored people are pleased we are glad. If they are not, their displeasure doesn't matter either. We build our temples for tomorrow, strong as we know how, and we stand on top of the mountain, free within ourselves.

*November 26, 1930*

## Look Out, Brown Man!

*Sherwood Anderson*

In Georgia, Alabama, Louisiana, Arkansas, Texas, Mississippi, and even in Indiana and Ohio, the big shuffle-footed Negroes' Negro man, the so-called "bad one," goes about on the alert now. He has to be careful. These aren't good times for a Negro man to be too proud, step too high. There are a lot of white men hard up. There are a lot of white men out of work. They won't be wanting to see a big proud black man getting along. There'll be lynchings now.

Such a Negroes' Negro man doesn't always remember to be polite and courteous to whites. He isn't slick and fawning. He's not a white man's Negro. There are wenches like that, too—thick blood in them, heads held high. You'll see one of that kind occasionally on a country road in Georgia, a fine proud one. Such a carriage she's got, such a swing to her hips.

Look out, brown man!

You'd think, if you listened to Northern people talk, or to professional Southerners in the North, that all Negroes were alike. I've heard them say, "Why, I can't tell one Negro from another." Might as well say, "I can't tell one field from another, one mountain from another, one river from another." Some can't.

They say, "It's different down South. The Negro knows his place down there." They mean to say he always goes fawning, taking off his hat to any kind of low-grade white, getting off the sidewalks. Why, you'd think, to hear them talk, that Southern Negroes, particularly in the far South, were just dogs. Not very high-class dogs at that. There is a kind of dog that always goes about like that, his tail always between his legs.

As though any decent Northern or Southern white man, or woman, would want a Negro man, or woman, to be like that.

There are whites that do want it. Second-, third-, and fourth-rate whites they are. They are in the ascendancy in a lot of places in the

South now, have been in the ascendancy ever since the Civil War. Before that they were there of course, but they were kept under. Why, you can find as many loose-lipped, boastful, slack-eyed, second-rate whites in the American South as in any place on earth. Who do you suppose does the lynching down there, in the dreadful ugly little towns?

The cheap ones got into power in a lot of places in the South after the Civil War because the whites with class to them got killed in the war. Or they lost all they had. The first-rate families in the far South are surprisingly feminine now. I mean there aren't any men left in some of the families, just a few high-class women hanging on. They don't do any loud talking about killing Negroes—the Southern people with class to them, men or women. I think the real Southern people, of the old South, always did understand the position of the Negro pretty well. There was a situation. The South had something on its hands—"our peculiar institution," the statesmen from down there called it. It was peculiar, all right.

You had to assume that all Negroes were natural servants, that they liked being in a subordinate position in life. They gave love and devotion to the whites, expecting nothing.

I can't see why a Negro should be any different than any other man about all that. A man does what he has to do. How many whites are there in subordinate positions in life, doing what they don't like to do, being pretty polite about it, too?

I can't see this sharp difference between the impulses and desires of Negroes and myself. I think decent Negro men and women have the same feelings I have. They have, under the same circumstances, the same thoughts, the same impulses. I've been about Negroes a lot. I've watched them—that's my specialty, watching people—I've talked to them.

"But you can't understand the thoughts and feelings of a Negro," men say. I've asked a good many Negroes about that. "If you can get on to yourself a little I guess you can get on to me," the Negro says.

"Why," someone says, "you've got something primitive here." Sure you have. You've got the difference of a few thousand years out of the caves and forests. How old is the human race anyway? How much difference do a few thousand years make? And anyway we haven't any pure-blooded Africans here—not any more.

I know this—that the people with some class to them, both men and women of the South, never have talked so big about the difference. These people always did recognize a certain position they were in and that the brown men and women about them were in. It was a difficult position. Slavery never was any good. It wasn't any good for the whites or the blacks either. Most of those who talked so big about the glories of slavery never did have any slaves. The intelligent, human white man of the old South did the best he could with life there, as he found it, and the intelligent brown man did the same.

They got to a kind of friendship, too. Don't think they didn't. Once I was walking with such a white man in a city of the far South when a loose-tipped, cunning-eyed brown man came shuffling up to him and asked for money.

"I'se in trouble, Mr. White," he said.

"You are, eh?"

"Yessah, Mr. White."

"Well then, where is your white-man friend? Why don't you go to him?"

"Because, sah, I ain't got no white-man friend."

"You ain't, eh? Well then, I'll tell you something—the Southern white man who hasn't a Negro-man friend and the Southern Negro man who hasn't a white-man friend isn't any good. . . . You get out of here. You make yourself scarce."

That is about the attitude of the intelligent white or brown man or woman in both the old and the new South, as far as I have been able to get at it. The trouble is there are not enough intelligent whites and browns. Which race has the best of it in that, I don't know. That's one of the things you can't find out. There are all kinds of shades to intelligence. You don't find it all in books, I know that.

You have to think about the Negro with a little intelligence, a little sympathy. You have to consider his position in our civilization. You have to remember that not so many white men and women are anything so very special. Hardly any of us are anything so very special really.

You have to think of what the Negro has done in his position, how well he has handled it, both in the North and in the South.

Then you have to remember also that there are Negroes who are not white men's Negroes. I dare say there were proud men, fierce men, fighters and strutters among the tribes in the forests over there in Africa, too. The blood these men must have come down, some of it, into some of our blacks, some of our browns.

I, for one, can imagine how such a man feels sometimes, when he has to knuckle under. I'm a white man and I've had to knuckle under to second-rate white men myself. I've had to laugh when such a one laughed, listen to his dull yarns, pretend to be impressed when he talked like a fool. I've done it. I've sat in advertising conferences, out in Chicago, for hours at a time, listening to some big windy man talking nonsense. I've sat there smiling, being polite, nodding my head, looking impressed.

I remember one such advertising conference when I sat like that for four hours. I was fingering a heavy inkwell that happened to be on the table before me. I wanted particularly, I remember, to bounce it off the head of a certain vulgar fat man who kept several of us there the four hours that day while he talked about himself. He was telling us what a big man he was, but he wasn't big. It turned out just as I thought it would. What he wanted us to do for him, and what we did, over our protest, broke him. I'm glad it did.

The whites in America have got the Negro into a certain position in our civilization. We present-day whites didn't put him there. We are in rather tight times. The Negro, because of his long subjugation, because he has known, has been taught by the circumstance of his position, a lot about sliding through such times, will get through the present situation better than a lot of whites. He will know how, will have been taught by life how to do it.

That will make a lot of second-, third-, and fourth-rate whites jealous and sore. There'll be lynchings now. You watch. There'll be women insulted.

You'll be surprised, if you watch it, how few first-class white women will be insulted. Most of the women insulted will be the slack wives or daughters of slack second-rate whites, and in this situation the fawning, polite white man's Negro will get through all right.

The fellow who has to look out now is the Negroes' Negro.

Don't strut much these days, big boy.

Walk carefully now.

Some of us understand how you like to strut, how it is in your blood. A good many of us don't mind an occasional strut ourselves. Why, most of the strutting songs, to which we strut, when we do strut, we got from you.

We'll be your friend, if we can, big boy, but it's going to be rough going. There'll be lynchings now. It is a time to walk softly. If you have any intelligence, brown boy, Negroes' Negro, remember that it has been by remaining friends with the intelligent people among the whites, by having an understanding with them, that the browns have got along with the whites as well as they have.

Why, I am talking to Negroes now.

Bear this in mind, Negroes' Negro. There are a good many of us whites who are, more than we like to admit, in the same position as you. If your people have been slaves, so have ours; if you have been in a subordinate position in life, so have we.

There are a good many kinds of slavery in this life.

More brains, white man and brown man, for God's sake, more brains!

Look out, big brown boy, the lynchers are loose.

*April 3, 1935*

## Harlem Runs Wild

*Claude McKay*

*New York, March 25*

Docile Harlem went on a rampage last week, smashing stores and looting them and piling up destruction of thousands of dollars worth of goods.

But the mass riot in Harlem was not a race riot. A few whites were jostled by colored people in the melee, but there was no manifest hostility between colored and white as such. All night until dawn on the Tuesday of the outbreak white persons, singly and in groups, walked the streets of Harlem without being molested. The action of the police was commendable in the highest degree. The looting was brazen and daring, but the police were restrained. In extreme cases, when they fired, it was into the air. Their restraint saved Harlem from becoming a shambles.

The outbreak was spontaneous. It was directed against the stores exclusively. One-Hundred-and-Twenty-fifth Street is Harlem's main street and the theatrical and shopping center of the colored thousands. Anything that starts there will flash through Harlem as quick as lightning. The alleged beating of a kid caught stealing a trifle in one of the stores merely served to explode the smoldering discontent of the colored people against the Harlem merchants.

It would be too sweeping to assert that radicals incited the Harlem mass to riot and pillage. The Young Liberators seized an opportune moment, but the explosion on Tuesday was not the result of Communist propaganda. There were, indeed, months of propaganda in it. But the propagandists are eager to dissociate themselves from Communists. Proudly they declare that they have agitated only in the American constitutional way for fair play for colored Harlem.

Colored people all over the world are notoriously the most exploitable material, and colored Harlem is no exception. The population is gullible to an extreme. And apparently the people are exploited so flagrantly because they invite and take it. It is their gullibility that gives to Harlem so much of its charm, its air of insouciance and gaiety. But the façade of the Harlem masses' happy-go-lucky and hand-to-mouth existence has been badly broken by the depression. A considerable part of the population can no longer cling even to the hand-to-mouth margin.

Wherever an ethnologically related group of people is exploited by others, the exploiters often operate on the principle of granting certain concessions as sops. In Harlem the exploiting group is overwhelmingly white. And it gives no sops. And so for the past two years colored agitators have exhorted the colored consumers to organize and demand of the white merchants a new deal: that they should employ Negroes as clerks in the colored community. These agitators are crude men, theoretically. They have little understanding of and little interest in the American labor movement, even from the most conservative trade-union angle. They address their audience mainly on the streets. Their following is not so big as that of the cultists and occultists. But it is far larger than that of the Communists.

One of the agitators is outstanding and picturesque. He dresses in turban and gorgeous robe. He has a bigger following than his rivals. He calls himself Sufi Abdul Hamid. His organization is the Negro Industrial and Clerical Alliance. It was the first to start picketing the stores of Harlem demanding clerical employment for colored persons. Sufi Hamid achieved a little success. A few of the smaller Harlem stores engaged colored decks. But on 125th Street the merchants steadfastly refused to employ colored clerical help. The time came when the Negro Industrial and Clerical Alliance felt strong enough to picket the big stores on 125th Street. At first the movement got scant sympathy from influential Negroes and the Harlem intelligentsia as a whole. Physically and mentally, Sufi Hamid is a different type. He does not belong. And moreover he used to excoriate the colored newspapers, pointing out that they would not support his demands on the bigger Harlem stores because they were carrying the stores' little ads.

Harlem was excited by the continued picketing and the resultant "incidents." Sufi Hamid won his first big support last spring when one of the most popular young men in Harlem, the Reverend Adam

Clayton Powell, Jr., assistant pastor of the Abyssinian Church—the largest in Harlem—went on the picket line on 125th Street. This gesture set all Harlem talking and thinking and made the headlines of the local newspapers. It prompted the formation of a Citizens' League for Fair Play. The league was indorsed and supported by sixty-two organizations, among which were eighteen of the leading churches of Harlem. And at last the local press conceded some support.

One of the big stores capitulated and took on a number of colored clerks. The picketing of other stores was continued. And soon business was not so good as it used to be on 125th Street.

In the midst of the campaign Sufi Hamid was arrested. Some time before his arrest a committee of Jewish Minute Men had visited the Mayor and complained about an anti-Semitic movement among the colored people and the activities of a black Hitler in Harlem. The *Day* and the *Bulletin*, Jewish newspapers, devoted columns to the Harlem Hitler and anti-Semitism among Negroes. The articles were translated and printed in the Harlem newspapers under big headlines denouncing the black Hitler and his work.

On October 13 of last year Sufi Hamid was brought before the courts charged with disorderly conduct and using invective against the Jews. The witnesses against him were the chairman of the Minute Men and other persons more or less connected with the merchants. After hearing the evidence and the defense, the judge decided that the evidence was biased and discharged Sufi Hamid. Meanwhile Sufi Hamid had withdrawn from the Citizens' League for Fair Play. He had to move from his headquarters and his immediate following was greatly diminished. An all-white Harlem Merchants' Association came into existence. Dissension divided the Citizens' League; the prominent members denounced Sufi Hamid and his organization.

In an interview last October Sufi Hamid told me that he had never styled himself the black Hitler. He said that once when he visited a store to ask for the employment of colored clerks, the proprietor remarked, "We are fighting Hitler in Germany." Sufi said that he replied, "There is no Hitler in Harlem." He went on to say that although he was a Moslem he had never entertained any prejudices against Jews as Jews. He was an Egyptian and in Egypt the relations between Moslem and Jew were happier than in any other country. He was opposed to Hitlerism, for he had read Hitler's book, "Mein Kampf," and knew Hitler's attitude and ideas about all colored peoples. Sufi Hamid said that the merchants of Harlem spread the rumor of anti-Semitism among the colored people because they did not want to face the issue of giving them a square deal.

The Citizens' League continued picketing, and some stores capitulated. But the Leaguers began quarreling among themselves as to whether the clerks employed should be light-skinned or dark-skinned. Meanwhile the united white Harlem Merchants' Association was fighting back. In November the picketing committee was enjoined from picketing by Supreme Court Justice Samuel Rosenman. The court ruled that the Citizens' League was not a labor organization. It was the first time that such a case had come before the courts of New York. The chairman of the picketing committee remarked that "the decision would make trouble in Harlem."

One by one the colored clerks who had been employed in 125th Street stores lost their places. When inquiries were made as to the cause, the managements gave the excuse of slack business. The clerks had no organization behind them. Of the grapevine intrigue and treachery that contributed to the debacle of the movement, who can give the facts? They are as obscure and inscrutable as the composite mind of the Negro race itself. So the masses of Harlem remain disunited and helpless, while their would-be leaders wrangle and scheme and denounce one another to the whites. Each one is ambitious to wear the piebald mantle of Marcus Garvey.

On Tuesday the crowds went crazy like the remnants of a defeated, abandoned, and hungry army. Their rioting was the gesture of despair of a bewildered, baffled, and disillusioned people.

*February 5, 1936*

## The Scottsboro Puppet Show

*Carleton Beals*

*Decatur, Alabama, January 27*

The Scottsboro trial is a puppet show. The principals are jerked through their ordained parts with such fidelity to class and racial and regional traditions, their motives and emotions so faithfully obeying established patterns, that it is difficult, even on the scene, face to face with reality, to realize that these are human beings, or that nine Negro boys, after five years of incarceration, are still fighting for their lives. The vulgar tragi-comedy of the plot being enacted here in the little cotton and mill town of Decatur in the northern red-hill district of Alabama, the pettiness of the judge, the trickery and the demagogic ambitions of the prosecution, and the hatred of the poor-white-trash spectators, relieved only by the gleam of starved lust when they listen to salacious testimony or their amens of approval when the judge squashes the argument of the defense, make it difficult to appreciate that here is being decided a case which may well mark the beginning of a new chapter in the history of the South and of the nation.

It would be easy, too, to forget these things for the quaintness of the scene and the types. An unshaved jury commissioner in a frayed collar and greasy suit that hangs in folds tells you at length in an almost unintelligible dialect how he has been reducing. A ruddy deputy sheriff with a big paunch and gold lodge pin tells you of the cars he saw piled up in the blizzard while he was bringing the nine Negro prisoners from Birmingham to the courtroom. "The damn' niggers," he tells you with comfortable joviality, "ain't wo'th all this heah trouble." A court clerk spends all his recess periods examining the chaw twists of tobacco of the courtroom folk—scarcely a man is unable to produce one, and the court proceedings are punctuated constantly by the spurt of tobacco juice on the floor and wall. The whole courthouse from basement to attic, despite the most amazing collection of spittoons I have ever seen under one roof, is stained with brown juice.

An old man with a mop of uncut and never-combed white hair hanging about a gossipy, womanish face hops in on a home-made crutch, with one shriveled foot wrapped in dirty cloths sticking out sideways. He leans over the rail and wisecracks at the defense attorneys, then hops from person to person in the courtroom urging vengeance.

Prosecutor Thomas E. Knight, Jr., who has played sharp politics with this case and has ridden on the backs of these Negro boys into the lieutenant governorship and expects soon to ride into the governorship, peers from unexpected places in the courtroom with glazed blue eyes. His smile of victory and smug contempt draws back frog-like across his narrow face like a stretched rubber band. During a recess he foregathers with some of the correspondents. With two armed deputies on either side, the Negro defendant Haywood Patterson sits over against the wall.

Knight has been very successful with this case. He knows the temper of local juries and how to appeal to them. He never misses an opportunity to show contempt for that foreign country "New Yawk" and by implication to cast contempt on the defense attorney, Samuel S. Leibowitz, who after Clarence Darrow is probably the most brilliant criminal lawyer in the country. Furthermore Knight's own father sits on the Supreme Court bench of the state of Alabama and helps write the confirmations of the verdicts rendered by the local farmer juries. But during this last trial Knight has been rather subdued. The defense opened with a plea that he retire from the case because the Alabama constitution prohibits a public official from holding two public posts, and because if Ku Klux Klan Governor Bibb Graves should die or leave the state, Knight, as acting governor, would have to pass on any plea for clemency from the boys he helped to condemn. Throughout the trial the defense ironically referred to him only as "Governor."

A jury venireman approached me in the corridor during recess to tell me he did not believe anything he read in the newspapers. A lean, red-headed fellow with steel "specs," he moved his quid of tobacco to one side of his mouth to tell me of the origin of the "nigger" race—he had just solemnly sworn to the court he had no racial prejudices. Cain, it seemed, after killing Abel, went off to the land of Nod where he "knew a woman." "Now mos' folk don't go on and think things out. The Bible never says sexual intercourse, it jus' says a man knows a woman. But the Bible tells that there couldn't be no human folk at that time in the land of Nod. Now jus' put two and two together. Cain had offspring in the land of Nod, so he had him a female baboon or chimpanzee or somethin' like that. An' that's how the nigger race started."

After the geniality of the first day the courtroom setting became grim and harsh as it filled up with a rougher, though orderly crowd. Judge William Washington Callahan drove through the proceedings with relentless speed, making no concessions for delay of witnesses or anything else. Judge Callahan is a man over seventy whose son was recently acquitted of murder through a temporary-insanity plea. The Judge has a lashing tongue and indulges in salty dialect witticisms that usually fall viciously at the wrong moment. With his wispy white hair, his choleric rumblings, his easy mouthing of legal and constitutional formulas, he is, as one writer said, a Hollywood version of a Southern judge.

A climax in the trial was reached on the second day, after seven wearying hours in the foul-aired courtroom, when the two defense attorneys called for a mistrial, accusing the judge of impatience, irascibility, continued ridiculing of the physical and other evidence of the defense, and repeated remarks made to prejudice the jury. Judge Callahan declared that if he had made any improper remarks he was willing to apologize, and in a tone of cold fury denied the motion. He then charged the jury not to heed the remarks of the defense, nor were the jurors to be prejudiced against the defense because of their motion. Subsequently the defense made five other mistrial motions which were denied.

At the outset Judge Callahan ruled out as evidence the defense model of the fatal freight train that ran between Stevenson and Paint Rock five years ago with its human cargo of young derelicts and two mill trollops, Victoria Price and Ruby Bates. "That train is a useless waste of time," snapped the Judge. "It would take half a day longer and is no help to anybody." Actually, without the model train no proper reconstruction of the details is possible. When the defense insisted, the Judge roared out, "I cain't waste time this way. How will you get it set up as it was?"

The model was identical with that admitted by Judge Callahan at the previous trial, but he now demanded that the defense produce evidence. As the defense was not expecting to be asked for witnesses until late afternoon, the train conductor was not available, and most of the witnesses were required to go through long-winded unintelligible explanations which could have been settled at once by the model. In a previous trial Judge Callahan sarcastically remarked about the train, "Go ahead and set it up before Santa Claus gets it."

Late in the afternoon, after two-thirds of the evidence was in, the defense was able to call Conductor R. S. Turner to identify the model train again. Callahan again objected, "All I see it does, it takes up a lot of time"; and throughout the trial he seemed to take the attitude that the loss of five minutes was more important than the lives of the nine Negro boys. As the conductor started to testify, the Judge bellowed at him to ask him the total number of box cars on the train, and before the conductor could make his calculations rushed to another question in such a way as to imply lack of credibility in the witness. Frequently throughout the trial, whenever any witness seemed likely to make a statement that threw light on the facts, the Judge would roar over the bench at him, interrupting and confusing the evidence.

As in all previous trials the star witness of the state, since Ruby Bates recanted her testimony, was Victoria Price. She entered the courtroom well dressed in blue wool and brown velvet coat, and was not, as before, chewing snuff. In an earlier trial she had testified that one of the Negro boys had held her mouth so she couldn't take a spit. On this occasion she altered her testimony in a few key matters, declaring, for instance, that the gravel car was filled up only to two and a half feet from the top as compared to a foot and a half in her previous statements. But when the defense attempted to bring out the contradictions of Victoria Price's testimony with her statements in previous trials the Judge promptly sustained the objections made by the prosecution. The court ruled out all evidence bearing upon the past conduct of Victoria Price—her jail convictions, her various marriages, her actual relations with Jack Tiller, a married man, her profligacy with two different men on the two nights preceding the supposed rape. But in his charge to the jury Judge Callahan declared that the credibility of Victoria Price was not in question, because the defense had not produced evidence showing bad character or untruthfulness.

She sat with her back half turned to the defense except during cross-examination. She spit out her words venomously at the defense with a hard crease in her thin mouth, and this time in her evidence increased the number of scratches on her body, but denied the disfigurations on her face to which she had previously testified and which had been denied by half a dozen witnesses. In this trial she put the supposed blow on her scalp instead of on her forehead over one eye. When no signal for a given reply was forthcoming from the prosecution, toward which she constantly glanced, she would answer sullenly, "I cain't remember." Several times during interruptions she sat smiling at Prosecutor Knight from behind a blue handkerchief.

The local prosecuting attorney and Sunday School teacher, Malvin Hutson, opened the jury pleading. Spitting his cud of tobacco into a spittoon and dropping his legs over the table, he combed his hair, smoothed his tiny black bow tie, and talked for a few seconds to the jury in an intimate low tone. His plump boyish face gradually flushed, and suddenly he sobbed out in a tone that shook the windows, "Save the pure womanhood of Alabama!" From then on he alternately roared and sobbed about the courtroom in a voice that would have filled the Metropolitan Opera House, giving a cross between a sermon and a stump speech and devoting only a few brief moments to actual summing up of the evidence. "Women, red, white, black, or green, depend upon this jury for protection," he insisted. He pictured the long fight of the pitiful Victoria Price for vindication, without which the jurors would have to "hang their heads." Whether "in overalls or in furs" a woman was protected by the law of Alabama against the vilest crime of the human species, that of rape, a crime which put any man lower "than the birds of the air, the fish of the sea, or the beasts of the fields." Even dogs choose their mates. The law reached "from the mountain tops to the swamps and caves" to protect "the sacred secret parts of the female," and now almost in tears, he assured the jurors that "Victoria Price is a human of the female species." Unless the jury upheld the law, women "might have to buckle six-shooters about their middles." The penalty for rape in Alabama is death, a penalty prescribed in accordance "with the wisdom of the ages."

One prospective juror remarked that Hutson was a "very good" Sunday School teacher. He is such a good Sunday School teacher that Haywood Patterson is to spend seventy-five years in prison.

The knife and gun fracas between a deputy sheriff and Ozie Powell, one of the Scottsboro defendants, which took place on the top of Lacon Mountain on the road from Decatur to Birmingham, helps to obscure the complicated case. The original trial in Scottsboro, with a hurried conviction without proper defense and with a mill band playing "There'll Be a Hot Time in the Old Town Tonight" under the courthouse windows, was a form of legal violence that barely stopped short of a major tragedy. The fact is that since then, during the five years of the case, seven of the defendants have never even been brought to trial. It would be strange indeed if stronger minds than those of these black derelicts were not preyed upon by fear, despair, and hate; and for five years the boys, who have grown into young manhood, have known only the companionship of criminals and riff-raff. Ozie Powell, who by his desperate act further endangered himself and his companions, has been brooding about these things. Jail madness seems the most likely explanation. Unfortunately more than ever the case is restored to the basis of passion, and the racial, social, and legal principles are further obscured. The boys will lose sympathy here and elsewhere, but, just as much as ever, justice as well as the boys will remain on trial.

*January 29, 1938*

## Laughter in Madrid

*Langston Hughes*

*Madrid, December 15*

The thing about living in Madrid these days is that you never know when a shell is going to fall. Or where. Any time is firing time for Franco. Imagine yourself sitting calmly in the front room of your third-floor apartment carefully polishing your eyeglasses when all of a sudden, without the least warning, a shell decides to come through the wall—paying no attention to the open window—and explodes like a thunderclap beneath the sofa. If you are sitting on the sofa, you are out of luck. If you are at the other side of the room and good at dodging shrapnel you may not be killed. Maybe nobody will even be injured in your apartment. Perhaps the shell will simply go on through the floor and kill somebody else in apartment 27, downstairs. (People across the hall have been killed.)

Who next? Where? When? Today all the shells may fall in the Puerta del Sol. Tomorrow Franco's big guns on the hills outside Madrid may decide to change their range-finders and bombard the city fan-wise, sending *quince-y-medios* from one side of the town to the other. No matter in what section of the city you live, a shell may land in the kitchen of the sixth-floor apartment (whose inhabitants you've often passed on the stairs), penetrate several floors, and make its way to the street via your front room on the third floor.

That explains why practically nobody in Madrid bothers to move when the big guns are heard. If you move, you may as likely as not move into the wrong place. A few days ago four shells went through the walls of the Hotel Florida, making twenty that have fallen there. The entrance to the hotel is well protected with sandbags, but they couldn't sandbag nine stories. All this the desk clerk carefully explains to guests who wish to register. But most of the other hotels have been severely bombed, too. And one has to stay somewhere.

The Hotel Alfonso a few blocks away has several large holes through each of its four walls but is still receiving guests. One of the

halls on an upper floor leads straight out into space—door and balcony have been shot away. In one of the unused bedrooms you can
look slantingly down three floors into the street through the holes
made by a shell that struck the roof and plowed its way down, then
out by a side wall into the road. Walking up to your room, you pass a
point where the marble stairs are splintered and the wall pitted by
scraps of iron; here two people were killed. Yet the Hotel Alfonso
maintains its staff, and those of its rooms that still have walls and windows are occupied by paying guests.

The now world-famous Telefonica, Madrid's riddled skyscraper in
the center of the city, is still standing, proud but ragged, its telephone
girls at work inside. The Madrid Post Office has no window-panes left
whatsoever, but the mail still goes out. Around the Cibeles Fountain in
front of the Post Office the street cars still pass, although the fountain
itself with its lovely goddess is now concealed by a specially built
housing of bricks and sandbags, so that the good-natured Madrileños
have nicknamed it "Beauty Under Covers," laughing at their own wit.

Yes, people still laugh in Madrid. In this astonishing city of
bravery and death, where the houses run right up to the trenches and
some of the street-car lines stop only at the barricades, people still
laugh, children play in the streets, and men buy comic papers as well
as war news. The shell holes of the night before are often filled in by
dawn, so efficient is the wrecking service and so valiantly do the
Madrileños struggle to patch up their city.

A million people living on the front lines of a nation at war! The
citizens of Madrid—what are they like? Not long ago a small shell fell
in the study of a bearded professor of ancient languages. Frantically
his wife and daughter came running to see if anything had happened
to him. They found him standing in the center of the floor, holding the
shell and shaking his head quizzically. "This little thing," he said,
"this inanimate object, can't do us much damage. It's the philosophy
that lies behind it, wife, the philosophy that lies behind it."

In the Arguelles quarter to the north, nearest to the rebel lines—the
neighborhood that has suffered most from bombardments and air
raids—many of the taller apartment houses, conspicuous targets that
they are, have been abandoned. But in the smaller houses of one and

two stories people still live and go about their tasks. The Cuban poet, Alejo Carpentier, told me that one morning after a heavy shelling he passed a house of which part of the front wall was lying in the yard. A shell had passed through the roof, torn away part of the wall, carried with it the top of the family piano, and buried itself in the garden. Nevertheless, there at the piano sat the young daughter of the house, very clean and starched, her hair brushed and braided, her face shining. Diligently she was beating out a little waltz from a music book in front of her. The fact that the top of the piano had been shot away in the night did not seem to affect the chords. When passers-by asked about it, calling through the shell hole, the child said, "Yes, an *obús* came right through here last night. I'm going to help clean up the yard after a while, but I have to practice my lessons now. My music teacher'll be here at eleven."

The will to live and laugh in Madrid is the thing that constantly amazes a stranger. At the house where I am staying, sometimes a meal consists largely of bread and of soup made with bread. Everybody tightens his belt and grins, and somebody is sure to repeat good-naturedly an old Spanish saying, "Bread with bread—food for fools!" Then we all laugh.

One of Franco's ways of getting back at Madrid is to broadcast daily from his radio stations at Burgos and Seville the luncheon and dinner menus of the big hotels, the fine food that the Fascists are eating and the excellent wines they drink. (Rioja and the best of wine areas are in Fascist hands.) But Madrid has ways of getting even with the Fascists, too. Mola, a lover of cafes, said at the very beginning of the war that he would soon be drinking coffee in Madrid. He was mistaken. Then he said he would enter Madrid by the first of November. He didn't. Then he swore he would enter the city on the eighth of December. He didn't. But on the evening of the eighth some wag remembered, and the crowds passing that night in Madrid's darkened Puerta del Sol saw by moonlight in the very center of the square a coffee table, carefully set, the coffee poured, and neatly pinned to the white cloth a large sign reading "For Mola."

Bread and coffee are scarce in Madrid, and so are cigarettes. The only cigarettes offered for sale more or less regularly are small, hard, and very bad. They are so bad that though they cost thirty centimos before the war they bring only twenty now despite their comparative scarcity. The soldiers call them "recruit-killers," jocularly asserting that they are as dangerous to the new men in the army as are bombs and bullets.

Bad cigarettes, poor wine, little bread, no soap, no sugar! Madrid, dressed in bravery and laughter; knowing death and the sound of guns by day and night, but resolved to live, not die!

The moving-picture theaters are crowded. Opening late in the afternoon and compelled to close at nine, they give only one or two showings a day. One evening an audience was following with great interest an American film. Suddenly an *obús* fell in the street outside. There was a tremendous detonation, but nobody moved from his seat. The film went on. Soon another fell, nearer and louder than before, shaking the whole building. The manager went out into the lobby and looked up and down the Gran Via. Overhead he heard the whine of shells. He went inside and mounted the stage to say that, in view of the shelling, he thought it best to stop the picture. Before he had got the words out of his mouth he was greeted with such a hissing and booing and stamping of feet and calls for the show to go on that he shrugged his shoulders in resignation and signaled the operator to continue. The house was darkened. The magic of Hollywood resumed its spell. While Franco's shells whistled dangerously over the theater, the film went its make-believe way to a thrilling denouement. The picture was called "Terror in Chicago."

*July 2, 1949*

## I Met the Grand Dragon

*Roi Ottley*

*Atlanta, June 21*
"There ain't a nigger that's the equal of a white man," declared Dr. Samuel J. Green, Grand Dragon of the Ku Klux Klan. He repeated his

statement as a question. His manner was belligerent as he gave me a cold, blue, brittle stare. He clearly indicated what he expected of the Negro before him. He watched my lips carefully.

"I most emphatically do believe a Negro is the equal of a white man," I replied.

The Klan chieftain was visibly shaken. He was not accustomed to having his view of the Negro's status challenged, much less opposed, by a Negro. This exchange began my interview with the most notorious enemy of the Negro, and indeed of progress, in the United States. The interview went on for two and a half hours. What should have been a conversation turned into an argument, because Dr. Green insisted on noisily defending "white supremacy."

I had walked into Green's office in the business section of Atlanta by appointment. I hoped to discover what sort of charlatan was operating this race-ridden organization which hoodwinked poor whites and terrorized Negroes. As I entered, I was surprised by his striking resemblance to Adolf Hitler. Besides sharing the Nazi leader's racial philosophy, the Grand Dragon had the name absurd brush-like mustache, watery blue eyes, slight frame, high-pitched voice, and dictatorial manner.

Eleven men wearing police uniforms were paying their Klan dues when I opened the door. They eyed me suspiciously until Green ordered me to be seated in a rickety chair next to a water-cooler which bore a big sign reading, "For Whites Only." When he had finished collecting the Klansmen's money, a process he seemed to drag out in order to make me wait, he invited me into his private office—a dentist's operating room adjoining a lobby. Away from the critical eyes of his "hooded hoodlums" his manner changed perceptibly and he became more civil. I almost expected him to bring out the mint juleps. But throughout our talk he referred to Negroes as "niggers" or "darkies." He did not address me as "Mister." Actually he talked at me—as white people do with Negroes when they want to avoid using ordinary titles of respect. He frankly refused to have his picture taken with me, explaining almost apologetically that "white people might misunderstand." What he meant was that his fellow-Klansmen might frown upon such social truck with a Negro.

I soon learned that "Doc" Green is a primitive fanatic, without the slightest knowledge of affairs beyond his neighborhood, though he had a professional education. He sounded as ignorant as the lowliest redneck. Perhaps he conveniently refuses to acknowledge anything that happens beyond the borders of Georgia. In any case he knew nothing about Dr. Ralph Bunche, who has won an international reputation for his brilliant work as United Nations mediator in the Arab-Jewish conflict. When I asked him if Dr. Bunche wasn't proof enough of the Negro's equality when given an opportunity to develop his talents and show his competence, the leader of the Klan answered, "I ain't never met that nigger."

I told the Grand Dragon that his theory of Negro inferiority was old hat. I said that scientific thought had long ago exploded his racial theories, that today the whole weight of world opinion was opposed to his ideas. "I'm still livin' in Georgia, no matter what the world and science thinks," he said.

Dr. Green was unmoved when I said that the Ku Klux Klan had given the United States much bad publicity abroad, and had even made people in other countries question the sincerity of America's support of democracy. He didn't seem to care that the Klan is considered America's chief fascist organization. "You'll never get me to recognize a Chinaman, a Jap, or a nigger as my equal," he declared somewhat heatedly. "It's all right to give money to those fleabitten countries to get them on their feet, but we don't want none of their ideas."

At one stage he proudly claimed Scotch-Irish descent and I used this to drive in a point. He had insisted the white man was superior because he had a longer heritage of culture than the Negro. I told him that in London I had heard an Englishman call an Irishman inferior on the same grounds. "Doc" Green quickly amended his parentage. He explained that he was not "quite exactly" Irish in descent, but really Scotch.

Under a deluge of facts he fell back on the Bible as the source of his racial theories. He declared the Klan was a Christian movement which did not preach hate but based its program on the eleventh chapter of Genesis, which, according to his interpretation, reveals that

God segregated the races. "If God wanted us all to be equal," he said firmly, "He would have made all people white men."

Now Klansman Green got down to curbstone conversation. He was immensely tickled by a story he told about an "ole darky" who got stranded in Chicago. The Negro accosted him in the Loop, addressing him as "yo' all good white folks," and complained that he hadn't eaten for days, " 'cause white folks in Chicago will let you come in the front door, but won't feed you in either the back or front." Southerner Green rose to the emergency, especially when he discovered that the Negro was "one of ole Bradley's niggers." He collected twenty-odd dollars from friends, then he took the Negro by the hand, fed him "at one of them places where white folks and niggers kin eat," escorted him to the railway station, bought him a ticket, and gave the conductor strict instructions "not to let this nigger off the train till he reaches Augusta, Georgia."

Green made a point of imitating the Negro's dialect in telling the story, explaining that "the ole darky talked real nigger talk." But I must confess I could detect little difference between the dialect of the Negro and his own broad Southern drawl. It would perhaps shock him to be told that he talks exactly like a blackface comedian.

Expansively Green offered his opinions about the crucial issues facing the South today. He declared he believed in equal education, equal housing, and equal recreational facilities for the Negro, within the Negro community, but that as a humanitarian he couldn't advocate these things openly, since for him to do so, in view of the "prejudice against the Klan," would be to give them the kiss of death. He conceded that the Negro had a right to vote in general elections but not in "white primaries." He offered a unique solution for the mounting problems connected with Negroes moving into so-called white neighborhoods, a trend which is the chief source of racial tensions in Atlanta today. He said white families should be systematically moved from the areas surrounding Negro slums and Negroes moved into the houses abandoned by the whites. But he was unable to say where the boundary between whites and Negroes should begin or end. He speculated on the possibility of corralling all Negroes into one big section.

The Grand Dragon of the Ku Klux Klan is worried about the increasing number of marriages between whites and Negroes in the North. While he was in Chicago he saw a white girl with a brownskin child—a dreadful memory, to judge by his expression when he related the incident. He was very firm that "it ain't gonna happen in Georgia." He felt, too, that stricter laws should be enacted to define a Negro: too many Negroes are passing as white persons. He also wants something done about white women passing as Negroes. Recently he stopped by to inquire about the sick child of a Negro handyman, and a blond woman opened the door, with two blond children about her feet. He wasn't sure if she was white or Negro—and something has to be done about such situations.

Green wants Negroes to believe that he is just a kindly old gentleman who desires nothing more than to see his Negroes happy. He told me how he had given an old Negro Mammy a chicken for Christmas. He was hurt by the behavior of Dr. Benjamin Mays, president of Morehouse College in Atlanta. A few months ago Morehouse College launched a fund-raising drive. To show his good-will Green sent Dr. Mays his personal check for $10. The Negro president promptly returned the check with the brief explanation that the Grand Dragon's money was "unacceptable to Morehouse College." For fear I might think him a liar Green produced the check and note. "Doesn't that prove niggers are prejudiced?" he asked plaintively.

"Doc" Green is a musuem piece. He still regards Georgia as his personal plantation, but he unwittingly offered evidence that the Ku Klux Klan is out of step with many people in the South today. I asked him, "Why do members of the Klan wear disguises?" He replied with remarkable candor, "So many people are prejudiced against the Klan these days that members are afraid they'll lose their jobs, their influence in public affairs, or otherwise be penalized if they are recognized."

*August 18, 1956*

## Brotherly Love
### A Little Letter to the White Citizens Councils of the South

In line of what my folks say in Montgomery,
In line of what they're teaching about love,
When I reach out my hand, will *you* take it
Or cut it off and leave a nub above?

If I found it in my heart to love you,
And if I thought I really could,
If I said, "Brother, I forgive you,"
I wonder, would it do *you* any good?

So long, *so long* a time you've been calling
Me *all* kinds of names, pushing me down—
I been swimming with my head deep under water,
And you wished I would stay under till I drown.

But I didn't! I'm still swimming! Now you're mad
Because I won't ride in the back end of your bus.
When I answer, "Anyhow, I'm gonna love you,"
Still and yet *you* want to make a fuss.

Now listen, white folks!
In line with Reverend King down in Montgomery—
Also because the Bible says I must—
I'm gonna love you—*yes, I will! Or BUST!*

—LANGSTON HUGHES

*October 20, 1956*

## 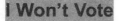 I Won't Vote

*W.E.B. Du Bois*

Since I was twenty-one in 1889, I have in theory followed the voting plan strongly advocated by Sidney Lens in *The Nation* of August 4, i.e., voting for a third party even when its chances were hopeless, if the main parties were unsatisfactory; or, in absence of a third choice, voting for the lesser of two evils. My action, however, had to be limited by the candidates' attitude toward Negroes. Of my adult life, I have spent twenty-three years living and teaching in the South, where my voting choice was not asked. I was disfranchised by law or administration. In the North I lived in all thirty-two years, covering eight Presidential elections. In 1912 I wanted to support Theodore Roosevelt, but his Bull Moose convention dodged the Negro problem and I tried to help elect Wilson as a liberal Southerner. Under Wilson came the worst attempt at Jim Crow legislation and discrimination in civil service that we had experienced since the Civil War. In 1916 I took Hughes as the lesser of two evils. He promised Negroes nothing and kept his word. In 1920, I supported Harding because of his promise to liberate Haiti. In 1924, I voted for La Follette, although I knew he could not be elected. In 1928, Negroes faced absolute dilemma. Neither Hoover nor Smith wanted the Negro vote and both publicly insulted us. I voted for Norman Thomas and the Socialists, although the Socialists had attempted to Jim Crow Negro members in the South. In 1932 I voted for Franklin Roosevelt, since Hoover was unthinkable and Roosevelt's attitude toward workers most realistic. I was again in the South from 1934 until 1944. Here again I did not vote. Technically I could vote, but the election in which I could vote was a farce. The real election was the White Primary.

Retired "for age" in 1944, I returned to the North and found a party to my liking. In 1948, I voted the Progressive ticket for Henry Wallace and in 1952 for Vincent Hallinan.

In 1956, I shall not go to the polls. I have not registered. I believe that democracy has so far disappeared in the United States that no "two evils" exist. There is but one evil party with two names, and it will be elected despite all I can do or say. There is no third party. On the Presidential ballot in a few states (seventeen in 1952), a "Socialist" Party will appear. Few will hear its appeal because it will have almost no opportunity to take part in the campaign and explain its platform. If a voter organizes or advocates a real third-party movement, he may be accused of seeking to overthrow this government by "force and violence." Anything he advocates by way of significant reform will be called "Communist" and will of necessity be Communist in the sense that it must advocate such things as government ownership of the means of production; government in business; the limitation of private profit; social medicine, government housing and federal aid to education; the total abolition of race bias; and the welfare state. These things are on every Communist program; these things are the aim of socialism. Any American who advocates them today, no matter how sincerely, stands in danger of losing his job, surrendering his social status and perhaps landing in jail. The witnesses against him may be liars or insane or criminals. These witnesses need give no proof for their charges and may not even be known or appear in person. They may be in the pay of the United States Government. A.D.A.'s and "Liberals" are not third parties; they seek to act as tails to kites. But since the kites are self-propelled and radar-controlled, tails are quite superfluous and rather silly.

The present Administration is carrying on the greatest preparation for war in the history of mankind. Stevenson promises to maintain or increase this effort. The weight of our taxation is unbearable and rests mainly and deliberately on the poor. This Administration is dominated and directed by wealth and for the accumulation of wealth. It runs smoothly like a well-organized industry and *should* do so because industry runs it for the benefit of industry. Corporate wealth profits as never before in history. We turn over the national resources to private profit and have few funds left for education, health or housing. Our crime, especially juvenile crime, is increasing. Its increase is perfectly logical; for a generation we have been teaching our youth to kill, destroy, steal and rape in war; what can we expect in peace? We let men take wealth which is not theirs; if the seizure is "legal" we call it high profits and the profiteers help decide what is legal. If the theft is "illegal" the thief can fight it out in court, with excellent chances to win if he receives the accolade of the right newspapers. Gambling in home, church and on the stock market is increasing and all prices are rising. It costs three times his salary to elect a Senator and many millions to elect a President. This money comes from the very corporations which today are the government. This in a real democracy would be enough to turn the party responsible out of power. Yet this we cannot do.

The "other" party has surrendered all party differences in foreign affairs, and foreign affairs are our most important affairs today and take most of our taxes. Even in domestic affairs how does Stevenson differ from Eisenhower? He uses better English than Dulles, thank God! He has a sly humor, where Eisenhower has none. Beyond this Stevenson stands on the race question in the South not far from where his grandfather Adlai stood sixty-three years ago, which reconciles him to the South. He has no clear policy on war or preparation for war; on water and flood control; on reduction of taxation; on the welfare state. He wavers on civil rights and his party blocked civil rights in the Senate until Douglas of Illinois admitted that the Democratic Senate would and could stop even the right of Senators to vote. Douglas had a right to complain. Three million voters sent him to the Senate to speak for them. His voice was drowned and his vote nullified by Eastland, the chairman of the Senate Judiciary Committee, who was elected by 151,000 voters. This is the democracy in the United States which we peddle abroad.

Negroes hope to muster 400,000 votes in 1956. Where will they cast them? What have the Republicans done to enforce the education decision of the Supreme Court? What they advertised as fair employment was exactly nothing, and Nixon was just the man to explain it. What has the Administration done to rescue Negro workers, the most impoverished group in the nation, half of whom receive less than half the median wage of the nation, while the nation sends billions abroad to protect oil investments and help employ slave labor in the Union of

South Africa and the Rhodesias? Very well, and will the party of Talmadge, Eastland and Ellender do better than the Republicans if the Negroes return them to office?

I have no advice for others in this election. Are you voting Democratic? Well and good; all I ask is why? Are you voting for Eisenhower and his smooth team of bright ghost writers? Again, why? Will your helpless vote either way support or restore democracy to America?

Is the refusal to vote in this phony election a counsel of despair? No, it is dogged hope. It is hope that if twenty-five million voters refrain from voting in 1956 of their own accord and not because of a sly wink from Khrushchev, this might make the American people ask how much longer this dumb farce can proceed without even a whimper of protest. Yet if we protest, off the nation goes to Russia and China. Fifty-five American ministers and philanthropists are asking the Soviet Union "to face manfully the doubts and promptings of their conscience." Can not these do-gooders face their own consciences? Can they not see that American culture is rotting away: our honesty; our human sympathy; our literature, save what we import from abroad? Our only "review" of literature has wisely dropped "literature" from its name. Our manners are gone and the one thing we want is to be rich—to show off. Success is measured by income. University education is for income, not culture, and is partially supported by private industry. We are not training poets or musicians, but atomic engineers. Business is built on successful lying called advertising. We want money in vast amount, no matter how we get it. So we have it, and what then?

Is the answer the election of 1956? We can make a sick man President and set him to a job which would strain a man in robust health. So he dies, and what do we get to lead us? With Stevenson and Nixon, with Eisenhower and Eastland, we remain in the same mess. I will be no party to it and that will make little difference. You will take large part and bravely march to the polls, and that also will make no difference. Stop running Russia and giving Chinese advice when we cannot rule ourselves decently. Stop yelling about a democracy we do not have. Democracy is dead in the United States. Yet there is still nothing to replace real democracy. Drop the chains, then, that bind our brains.

Drive the money-changers from the seats of the Cabinet and the halls of Congress. Call back some faint spirit of Jefferson and Lincoln, and when again we can hold a fair election on real issues, let's vote, and not till then. Is this impossible? Then democracy in America is impossible.

*December 1, 1956*

## Courage in Action: On a Florida Newspaper

*Dora Byron*

*Atlanta, Ga.*
I crossed the bridge over the still, brown water of the Suwannee river and drove fifteen miles through the pine woods and corn fields to Madison, Florida. There was the town, as I remembered it from twenty years before . . . the courthouse square and the pleasant homes along the oak-shaded streets.

I thought of the year I taught in Madison county, and of the stile over which I climbed into the schoolyard, and of the soup that bubbled on the wood-burning stove in the schoolroom. I thought of Saturday nights when I watched the crowds milling about the stores on the square. I remembered that goods from the stores were piled on sidewalk tables, and I remembered the festive mood of the farmers—white and black—who came to town of a Saturday night. It was innocent and gay and folksy and a glimpse of the genuine rural South, I had thought romantically.

Now the square was the same, except for a bit more neon, a bit more fresh paint. Madison looked prosperous and neat, and parking meters marched in a silver line along the main street. Across from the yellow brick courthouse I saw the new monument, a memorial to local World War II hero Colin Kelly. Four winged marble figures representing the Four Freedoms leaned over the inscription.

The "hearing" for Dr. Deborah Coggins was held in that courthouse, practically in the shadow of the monument, I realized. Young Dr. Coggins, mother of three children and wife of a Madison physician, had been health officer for three North Florida counties, including Madison. She was ousted by the three boards of county commissioners in late September.

I stopped at a restaurant on the corner.

"Is this where that county health officer ate with the Negro nurse?" I asked a waitress.

"No'm. That was next door. We don't serve niggers here." The woman looked at me uncertainly. Which side was I on?

"I'm from Atlanta," I explained. "I read about it in the paper."

"Oh." Relief spread over her face. She brought my order of fried chicken and hot biscuits. "That thing sure is getting us in the newspapers," the waitress offered. "Dr. Coggins is a fine doctor, but she didn't need to eat with a nigger that way. She could have talked to her at the office. We had another public-health doctor here who once worked in Africa. He said there wasn't any difference in white and black folks except that one was black and one was white. He soon went back to Africa where he belonged."

"Was that all Dr. Coggins did? Just eat lunch?"

"She never did anything else as I heard about. But I guess you don't eat with niggers up in Atlanta, do you?"

"There are some places in Atlanta where Negroes and whites may eat together, if you know the places," I said. "How's the editor, Mr. Merchant—is that his name? I read that he defended her in his weekly paper, and appeared at the hearing before the Madison county commissioners. Is he losing business?"

"There's plenty that thinks he won't be able to stay here now," she shrugged.

The waitress joined another behind the counter. "That lady's from Atlanta," I heard her whisper. "She said there are places in Atlanta where white and colored folks can eat together."

"No kidding?" The other woman's tone was incredulous.

At the office of the Madison *Enterprise-Recorder* I found T. C. Merchant, Jr., and his father, publishers and editors of the sixteen-page weekly. Job printing and an office-supply business had pushed the editorial work into a dusty corner of the small shop. No one ever looked less like a crusader than the affable, heavy-set younger Merchant. He pumped my hand and introduced me to the elder Merchant, whose sage manner and intelligent face reminded me of the late Irvin S. Cobb.

Father and son insisted they were not losing business because of the paper's stand. "We lost four subscriptions, but gained several more; and none of the big advertisers' have canceled. However, you know a paper like ours really depends on about fifteen people in a town."

I rode through Madison with the younger Merchant. The car radio was playing hill-billy music from a local station. A Western movie was showing at the local theatre. I thumbed the latest issue of the *Enterprise-Recorder*. I read that Hunter Kelly had been fined for possession of one gallon of moonshine whiskey. The Assembly of God was planning Sunday School "expansion month." Henry Dickinson was injured in a tractor accident. Merchant pointed out the school, the churches and the pretty new restaurant where the fateful luncheon had taken place the month before. "Dr. Coggins had cleared the plan with the owner, the manager and the waitresses," he said. "She and the Negro nurse came in the back door. They ate alone in a private dining room. They wanted to discuss the problem of securing midwives for Negro patients in the area, and Dr. Coggins had such a busy schedule that it seemed the best time to talk. That was all. The complaints and gossip began. A petition was circulated, asking Dr. Coggins to resign. She apologized, promised that it would not happen again, but that wasn't enough." He pulled some letters from his pocket. "These came today. Since the newspaper stories I have been getting lots of mail . . . and some crank phone calls, too. No one has burned a cross on my lawn yet," he smiled.

One letter was from a friend who had been in service with the forty-year-old Merchant. It commended him for his courage. One was unsigned, and began: "You nigger-loving slob." One was from a minister in Philadelphia, asking: "I would like to know what help the churches gave you on the issue?"

"The church members and the ministers have been quiet," said Merchant. "Everyone is quiet. I have lived in this town all my life, except for the years in Harvard Business School and in service. I thought I knew this town and the people. I don't. The town is like some place I have never seen, and the people I grew up with are strangers. They are scared to death. What are they afraid of? I don't know, and I can't make them tell me. Madison is a nice town. I can earn a good living here. Even if many of our best young people do leave for the cities, and even if the population is still 4,000—the same as it was in 1890—it's still a nice town. I love Madison. It is the only home I ever had. But I wonder if I belong any more?"

We drove down the street toward his home, a modern brick-and-glass building in a row of fine frame houses, some over 100 years old. Across the way was the modern home of Dr. Coggins and her doctor husband. The two homes looked too new, as though they belonged to another time that was pushing into the town.

"Her husband is a native of Madison," said Merchant. "Deborah is an independent, outspoken girl, and the best health officer we ever had. She's from Duke University and the University of Washington, but she has tried to adapt herself to our social mores. She does not belong to the NAACP, or advocate integration in the hospital or the school." The controversial Dr. Coggins is taking a refresher course in obstetrics and plans to go into private practice with her husband, the editor told me. "They intend to fight it out right here, and I know they will both have all the patients they can handle." Then he said:

"When I made my speech to the commissioners October 3 the five men sat there with their hands over their faces. They wouldn't look me in the eye. Then I went home, and the first thing I saw was our Negro maid feeding our four-month-old girl. It went all over me! That was all right! No one would object to that. But I knew at that minute Deborah was being fired because she ate a business luncheon with a Negro. I've never thought much about such things. If I thought at all, it was the way Madison thinks, I guess. Until this came along. Now I remember the town ran a Negro barber out in the thirties because he was making too much money, and I remember there was a lynching in nearby Greenville only ten years ago. Who are these people I live with? I have to argue with my neighbors and my relatives. The society editor of my paper is against me. Of course, I know small towns. They forget quickly. Perhaps this will all blow over, but it has done something to me. . . ."

"You are needed here. Please don't leave," I begged as we said goodbye.

I drove away, out onto U.S. 90, where the world whirls through Madison en route from Jacksonville to Tallahassee. I passed the Colin Kelly monument with its winged figures of the Four Freedoms, and passed the two restaurants, one of which once served a Negro woman and a white woman together. I remembered the futile appeal young Merchant had made to the Madison county commissioners: "A physician greater than Deborah Coggins was once criticized for eating with tax collectors and sinners. I am not attempting to make any irreverent comparison, but I sincerely believe that if you fire this girl today you will be doing an evil and unjust act. It is not too late to call a halt to mob pressure and treat this girl with the consideration and respect with which you would want your own wife treated. The eyes of the world are on Madison today. It is up to you, and you alone, to show the world what Southern white men are like."

The five Southern white men voted to fire Dr. Coggins, but another man was seen by the world that day. He was a country editor, T. C. Merchant, Jr. Southern white men can be like that, too, I told myself as Madison, Florida, became a speck in my rear-view mirror.

*January 5, 1957*

## Montgomery Morning

*Wilma Dykeman and James Stokely*

*Montgomery, Ala.*

In the still hours just before daylight on the morning of December 21, fog hung heavy over the dome of Alabama's gleaming white state capitol building. The shrouded streets which stretched away from it through the city of Montgomery were silent. It was easy, in those small hours, to unloose the imagination and wonder if some of the ghosts of 1861 might not be lurking in the "Cradle of the Confederacy" on this morning which was to make Southern history. For if it is true that the hand that rocks the cradle is the hand that rules the world, with a slightly different meaning of words this cradle was presently to be rocked to its foundations.

As daylight came, warm and springlike, Court Square—at the opposite end of the wide main street leading up to the capitol—began to waken. Around the dry fountain, with its tiers of figurines, plump pigeons strutted on the wet pavement. Traffic began to pick up. The giant wreaths of Christmas lights strung across the street became more visible. And the city buses began to roll in and out of the square, loading and unloading passengers. In the doorways of the dress shops, the men's ready-to-wear and hardware stores, the newsstands and the offices and drugstores, people stood watching the buses. This was the morning when a year-old boycott and a generations-old tradition were to end.

Negroes and whites sat or stood at the central segregated bus stop— watching; people drove by slowly, peering from their cars to see what was happening on the buses; and men leaning against the parking meters and standing on the street corners in their shirt sleeves, watched. This was the morning that segregation on the city buses of Montgomery gasped its last and integration breathed its first, and there was tension implied in both the birth and the death.

The morning went quietly. A couple of cars filled with watchful white men in leather jackets parked on two sides of Court Square for the first hour, then slowly moved away. Groups of well-dressed Negro leaders stood at the central bus stop and rode several of the runs. The Rev. Martin Luther King, Jr., who has become the public symbol of the Negro cause, entered a bus and took a seat near the front. The day's pattern developed—most of the buses were only partially filled, but the Negroes rode, for the most part, in the middle seats, a few at the very front, a few at the rear; and the whites rode almost together far to the front. A few whites who were eager for the day to have full meaning rode on the back seat; at least one or two sat by Negroes. By late afternoon the word had gone out over town that "Everything's O.K.; nothing happening."

It was the very calmness of the day that was the great news here. People who said nothing had happened meant nothing violent, to make headlines. Actually a great deal had happened which might make news for years to come. Before a new year can begin, an old year must end. Before a new era of human dignity can be born, old indignities must die. On December 21, an era as well as a year came to an end in Montgomery. It was important that Alabamans and Americans alike should realize that what was disappearing was as meaningful as what was developing.

For one thing, the familiar cardboard signs spelling out segregation were gone from the buses. Gone too was the custom that had compelled Negroes to pay their fares at the front door and then often get off the bus and climb back on at the rear door. And the abusive language of some of the drivers calling their passengers "black apes" and "damned niggers" was stilled. Most apparent of all, perhaps, the stream of walking women had almost disappeared.

"The real power of the boycott was the Negro women," a housewife in one of the white residential areas told us. "Every morning they came by our door here. It was like watching a brook to look out and see them going by steadily for an hour or so every morning and an hour or so every afternoon. And this morning they weren't there. The brook had dried up."

Other things, less tangible but not a whit less real, have gone from Montgomery too. Their essence might be summed up in the words of one Negro: "Now there isn't any more hang-dog looking at a white man. We face him. We got a proud look."

On a street in one of the newer residential areas, as we walked along in the pleasant morning between the rows of green lawns and lush pyracantha bushes heavy with clusters of flaming berries, we saw a carload of young schoolboys slow down just past us and shout something before they roared away. We turned and asked a Negro woman walking behind us what they had hollered. Small and lively as a sparrow in her brown coat and brown head-scarf and brown skin, she smiled at us. "They was just meddlin' me. They have to act theyself up. I don't pay them no mind, when they get through actin' theyself up, everything be all right." She had no resentment against the cruel boys in the present or the bus drivers in the past. "They wasn't all bad. Jus' a few real low mean. My bus driver I hadn' seen in a year welcome me back this mornin'. Like my family I work for: they told me to stay off the buses, they didn' blame us for what we's doin'."

We talked with a Negro man who summed up the remarkable self-control his people had shown in this great victory of their boycott. "We don't use the word 'victory,' " he assured us firmly. 'We don't want to even have the attitude of the word. Like Reverend King told us at one of our meetings, the attitude of 'victory' wouldn't be worthy of us, and it would be a barrier to the growth we hope for in others."

The conduct and accomplishments of the Negroes during the past year have obviously shaken some of the firmest convictions held by the whites. In the beginning of the boycott it was often said that Negroes "can't organize anything but a crap game," and if they did, they "can't hold out." But they did organize, 50,000 strong, and they didn't develop into an army and they didn't degenerate into a mob. They remained individuals united by a vision. In a region where patience on the long haul is considered a somewhat less colorful personal asset than pride in the instant's dramatic gesture, one of the most astonishing features of this boycott, to white residents, was the daily plodding persistence with which the Negroes moved toward their goal.

Then, of course, the white people began to admit the Negroes were organized, but "outsiders" had done it: Communists, "NAACPs," "some of Brownell's gang," "troublemakers" in general. And, of course, the Negroes would submit to the old pressures anyway: a few arrests, some bullying, a few bed-sheets.

"For a while there, the police would stop your car, maybe two or three times a day," one Negro leader said. " 'Get out, nigger.' You'd show your driving license and they'd ask you all the questions already filled out on it. Or they'd book you for going twenty-five miles an hour in a twenty-mile speed zone."

But the spirit didn't break and the Negroes were never provoked into retaliation.

"Then white boys would throw water on us, or a Coca-Cola bottle from a car. Or once in a while they'd spit on us. Even in the last few weeks over twenty cars have had acid thrown on them."

Mass arrest of the famous ninety was the whites' real panzer effort at group intimidation that failed and backfired. "For the first time," a professor at a local Negro college told us, "it became honorable to go to jail. Everybody whose name wasn't on that list felt sort of slighted, like he hadn't done his share." Those who had always been so scared of the police and jail now were clamoring to take the part of the punished.

The final test came when the Ku Klux Klan announced, on the night the Supreme Court handed down its last decision, that it would stage a demonstration in the Negro part of town. Before such a threat the Negro would once have cowered behind closed doors and darkened windows. But this time the Negro community greeted them almost as it would any other parade. As the estimated forty carloads of Ku Kluxers drove by, lights stayed on, doors were ajar, men, women and children watched openly, in silence. It took enormous courage to face this robed and ancient enemy with such nonchalance. In the end it was the Klan that weakened first. Their parade turned into a side street and disappeared. The Kluxers themselves had set the final seal of solidarity and emancipation on the Negro citizens.

Physical intimidation failed—and so did economic threats. For if one fact has emerged clearly to both white and Negro community in this crisis it is the intertwining of their economy. As one person put it: "Our schools may not be integrated, but our dollars sure are." Early in the boycott when the Mayor asked the women of Montgomery not to go after their maids and, if the maid wouldn't walk to work, to fire her, one housewife said, "The Mayor can do his own cooking if he wants to. I'm going after my cook." The Negro women knew their employers well enough, too, to be aware of their general distaste for mops and ironing boards. They knew instinctively that these people might tolerate injustice but never inconvenience.

"They talked about firing all the Negroes in the boycott from their jobs," a Negro man told us. "But then I guess they got to thinking about all those white folk's houses we rent. No payroll, no rent. What would those poor white widows living on their husbands' estates do? And what about all those refrigerators and cars and furniture we owed payments on? The storekeepers didn't want that stuff back. They wanted the money. No, after a little thinking there was very few of us fired from work."

Perhaps the most insidious enemy the Negro of Montgomery faced was his attitude toward himself. Indoctrinated for generations by assurances of his inferiority, in many cases he was uncertain as to his own power to sustain this movement. One will tell you now: "I wasn't sure how well we'd stick together or how long we'd last. But the people were way out ahead of the leaders at first. Then we all went together and there wasn't any doubt we'd go on as long as necessary."

Under these pressures and doubts, the Negroes have discovered the power of their dollars, the strength of their religion and the hidden resources within themselves. And one of the sorest problems facing Negroes everywhere was met and solved: the bridging of that great gap between the really learned and the desperately illiterate. A white woman in Montgomery who had taken part in interracial group meetings said, "You met time and again with the Negro leaders but somehow you felt that you weren't ever touching the real core—couldn't reach that vast group of Negroes to even know what they were thinking. Even their leaders were isolated from them." But those the Rev. King calls "the Ph. D.'s and the D.s" were brought together by the boycott.

This was true because from first to last the movement worked through the churches. "The only way you can reach the great mass of Southern Negroes today is through their churches," one club woman said, "and the churches were the great power behind the success of this Montgomery boycott. It had religious meaning from the beginning."

If there have been improvements in the Negro community of a Sunday, perhaps even more important is the change in the Saturday night world. That cuttings, stabbings and drunkenness have decreased is attested by all the Negroes and admitted by most of the whites. As the pressures of despair and frustration have been partially supplanted by the pressures of self-respect and hopefulness, some of the destructiveness has been supplanted by better citizenship.

As the first days of bus integration passed without notable incident (a Negro woman reported she was slapped and shoved by a white man as she left the bus, and a white woman on another bus reported that a Negro man winked at her), some of the white community still were far from reconciled. We saw two young men sitting at the bus stop— wild, blue-eyed boys with sun-hardened skins. "Well, Buck, what we gonna do with these damned niggers?" And one of the leaders of the White Citizens' Council assured us, "The bus situation here is far, far from settled. It can erupt any time. We're doing our best to keep down any violence, but this is a highly charged situation. Some of these boys mean business."

A bulky taxi driver analyzed developments: "It's all looked all right so far. And it may go on quiet enough, if don't nobody get radical. But this thing's touchy. Could be set off any minute. Then who knows what'll happen?"

Another said simply, "The South will always remain the South."

When a shotgun blast was fired at the Rev. King's home on December 23, the pastor did not notify the police. But he mentioned the incident quietly to his congregation during church services. "Even if my attackers 'get' me," he said, "they will still have to 'get' 50,000 other Negroes in Montgomery." He reminded his motionless visitors that "some of us may have to die," but urged his congregation never to falter in the belief that whatever else changed, God's love for all men would continue. "The glory to God that puts man in his place will make brothers of us all," he said. Such calm in the presence of violence must give the whole city pause.

A tentative proposal has been made to start a white bus boycott and organize a white car pool. The illogic of this, in view of the fact that the Negro car pool was ruled illegal a few weeks ago, seems not to have occurred to the proposers. With characteristic Southern humor someone suggested that the Negroes should run an ad in the local paper; "FOR SALE—Slightly used old station wagons for new car pools."!

No matter what may happen tomorrow in Montgomery, the fact remains that the Negro here will never be the same again. What one of the leaders, a tall, dark, articulate man, told us is obviously true: "On December 5 last year, the Negro in Montgomery grew from a boy to a man. He'll never be the same again. A white man had always said before, 'Boy, go do this,' 'Boy, do that,' and the Negro jumped and did it. Now he says, 'I don't believe I will,' or he does it, but up straight, looking at the white man. Not a boy any more. He grew up."

The image of the frontiersman has always been vivid in the American mind and memory. One of our frequent laments today is for the disappearing frontier which has been so much a part of American history. To a visitor in Montgomery there is the suggestion of a new frontiersman. His weapons are those of Thoreau and Gandhi rather than Crockett and Boone, but the wilderness he faces is no less terrifying. Working on the frontiers of a faith and freedom whose meanings and dynamics have been too little explored before this, these new frontiersmen, black and white, may lead us—and some of the colored and white millions of the world—into a new experience of democracy.

*May 25, 1963*

## In the Birmingham Jail

*Barbara Deming*

*Birmingham, Ala.*

The day I went to jail in Birmingham for joining a group of Negro demonstrators—children, most of them—who were petitioning, "without a license," for the right to be treated like human beings ("that's what it boils down to, that's all we ask"), I experienced more sharply than I ever had before the tragic nature of segregation, that breakdown of communication between human and human which segregation means and is.

The steps which took me from the Negro church in which I spent the early part of that day, May 6, sitting among the children as they were carefully briefed and finally, in small groups, one after another, marched, holding hands and singing, into the streets—"marching toward freedom land"—the steps which placed me swiftly then in the white women's ward of the city jail provided a jolt for the mind that can still, recalling it, astonish me.

The comedian Dick Gregory describes his experience of a similar shock the day he arrived here to join the struggle—describes alighting from the plane and buying a newspaper. Not a word on the front page of the events that were shaking all of Birmingham. He had been afraid for a moment that the plane had put him down in the wrong city. Locked in my jail cell, surrounded by new companions now, I too could ask myself: am I in the right city? The events of the day were acknowledged as news here; the presence of hundreds of children crowding the cells below us was the chief topic of the white women; but the break with reality was quite as abrupt as though no word about them had been spoken.

The children were no longer children now, the frail boys and girls I had seen singing and clapping their hands and sometimes dancing for a moment in the aisles of the church to find their courage—the amazing courage to walk out and face fire hoses, police dogs, jail sentences; these were now "juveniles"—a word spoken in horror, as though their youth made them particularly dangerous and untrust-worthy. These were "niggers" now. "Shit, goddam, they must be fighting among themselves already!" "That's right!" "Goddam, you know it!" "Niggers are wild animals! You know it!" "Yes! That's right!" "Better keep the door here locked tight." The voices would rise in a frenzied chorus—statement and refrain; then hush in awe; then, a little later, break out again. One prisoner would hurry in from her post at a particular window in an adjoining cell, from which a bit of the front yard could be glimpsed, and report that she had seen police dogs out there. Perhaps they would all be safe, then, against these devils in the same building. "All you have to say to one of them dogs is 'Git'm!' Just: 'Git'm!' " But perhaps even the dogs were not protec-tion enough. "They ought to throw a bomb in there and blow them all up," one woman cried in torment.

Now and then, when the wind was right, I could hear the chil-dren's voices from their cells, high and clear—"Ain't gonna let nobody turn me round, turn me round, turn me round. . . . Woke up this morning with my mind set on freedom!"—the singing bold and joyful still; and with that sound I was blessedly in their real pres-ence again. I strained to hear it, to bolster my own courage. For now I was a devil too, of course—I was a "nigger lover." The warden had introduced me to my cell mates, in shrill outrage, and encour-aged them to "cut me down" as they chose. They soon informed me that one of the guards had recommended that they beat me up. No one had moved to do it yet, but the glances of some of them were fierce enough to promise it. "What have you got against Southern people?"

I was not an enemy of the Southern people, I answered as calmly as I could. I happened to believe that we really were intended to try to love every person we met as we love ourselves. That would obvi-ously include any Southern white person I met. For me it simply also obviously included any Negro. They stared at me, bewildered, and I didn't try to say any more. I lay down on my bunk and tried to remove myself from their attention and to control my fears of them.

The unreal drama continued throughout the six days I remained in jail. Three times a day we left our cell block to go downstairs for meals, shepherded by the warden. Occasionally, on these trips, a group of the Negro children would have to pass us in the halls. "Huddle back there in the corner!" the warden would cry out to us sharply—"up against the wall!" The women would cower back like schoolgirls, while the terrifying people God had cursed—as the warden regularly informed us—filed past, harmless, and some of them even still joyful.

As the days passed, I stopped fearing my cell mates and made friends with them. After a little while this wasn't hard to do. Every woman in there was sick and in trouble. I had only to express the simplest human sympathy, which it would have been difficult not to feel, to establish the beginning of a friendly bond. Most of the women had been jailed for drunkenness, disorderly conduct or prostitution. That is to say, they had been jailed because they were poor and had been drunk or disorderly or had prostituted themselves.

Needless to say, I met no well-to-do people there, guilty of these universal misdemeanors. A few of the women had been jailed not because they really had been "guilty" once again this particular time, but because they were by now familiar figures to the cops; one beer, the smell of it on her breath, would suffice for an arrest if a cop caught sight of one of them. The briefest conversations with these women revealed the misfortunes that had driven them to drink: family problems, the sudden death of a husband, grave illness. All conspicuously needed help, not punishment—needed, first and foremost, medical help. The majority of them needed very special medical attention, and many while in jail were deprived of some medicine on which they depended. One woman was a "bleeder" and was supposed to receive a blood transfusion once a month, but it was many days overdue. Each one of them would leave sicker, more desperate than she had entered; poorer, unless she had chosen to work out her fine. One woman told me that the city had collected $300 in fines from her since January. From those who have not shall be taken.

One day, in jest, one of the women cried to the rest of us when the jail authorities had kept her waiting endlessly before allowing her the phone call that was her due: "I ought to march with the Freedom

Riders!" I thought to myself: you are grasping at the truth in this jest. Toward the end of my stay I began to be able to speak such thoughts aloud to a few of them—to tell them that they did, in truth, belong out in the streets with the Negroes, petitioning those in power for the right to be treated like human beings. I began to be able to question their wild fears and to report to them the words I had heard spoken by the Negro leaders as they carefully prepared their followers for the demonstrations—words counseling over and over not the vengeance they imagined so feverishly ("They all have knives and guns! You know it!") but forbearance and common sense; not violence but non-violence; I stressed for them the words of the integration movement's hymn: "Deep in my heart I do believe we shall live in peace some day—black and white together." One after another would listen to me in a strange, hushed astonishment, staring at me, half beginning to believe. By the time I was bailed out with the other demonstrators, on May 11, there was a dream in my head: if the words the Negroes in the nonviolent movement are speaking and are enacting ever begin to reach these others who have yet to know real freedom, what might that movement not become? But I was by then perhaps a little stir crazy.

*May 18, 1964*

## Incident in Hattiesburg

*Howard Zinn*

There was one moment of sick humor when the four of us in the FBI office in Hattiesburg, Miss., met the interrogating agent who had come in to get the facts from Oscar Chase about his beating the night before in the Hattiesburg city jail. John Pratt, attorney with the National Council of Churches, tall, blond, slender, was impeccably dressed in a dark suit with faint stripes. Robert Lunney, of the

Lawyer's Committee on Civil Rights, dark-haired and clean-cut, was attired as befits an attorney with a leading Wall Street firm. I did not quite match their standards because I had left without my coat and tie after hearing of Chase's desperate phone call to SNCC headquarters to get him out of jail, and my pants had lost their press from standing in the rain in front of the county courthouse all the day before; but I was clean-shaven and tidy. Chase, a Yale Law School graduate working with SNCC in Mississippi, sat in a corner, looking exactly as he had a few hours before when I saw him come down the corridor from his cell: his boots were muddy, his corduroy pants badly worn, his blue work shirt splattered with blood, and under it his T-shirt, very bloody. The right side of his face was swollen, and his nose looked as if it were broken. Blood was caked over his eye.

The FBI agent closed the door from his inner office behind him, surveyed the four of us with a quick professional eye, and then said soberly: "Who was it got the beating?"

I mention this not to poke fun at the FBI, which deserves to be treated with the utmost seriousness. After all, the FBI is not responsible—except in the sense that the entire national government is responsible, by default—for prison brutality and police sadism. It is just one of the coldly turning wheels of a federal mechanism into which is geared the frightening power of local policemen over any person in their hands.

Chase had been jailed the day before—Freedom Day in Hattiesburg—when a vote drive by SNCC had brought more than 100 Negroes to the county courthouse to register. On Freedom Day, also, fifty ministers came down from the North to walk the picket line in front of the county courthouse, prepared to be arrested.

It was a day of surprises, because picketing went on all day in the rain with no mass arrests, though the picketers were guarded the whole time by a hostile line of quickly assembled police, deputies and local firemen. These arrived on the scene in military formation, accompanied by loud-speakers droning orders for everyone to clear out of the area or be arrested. Perhaps there were no mass arrests because SNCC had been tirelessly putting people into the streets, until police and politicians got weary of trundling them off to jail; perhaps newly elected Mississippi Governor Paul Johnson wanted to play the race issue cautiously (as his inaugural speech suggested); or perhaps the presence of ministers, TV cameras and newspaper men inhibited the local law men.

At any rate, only two persons were arrested on Freedom Day. One was Robert Moses, SNCC's director of operations in Mississippi, who has, in his two years or so in the state, been beaten, shot at, attacked by police dogs and repeatedly jailed—a far cry from his days in Harvard graduate school, though not perhaps, fundamentally, from his childhood in Harlem. Moses was arrested for failing to move on at a policeman's order, across the street from the courthouse.

The other person arrested that day was Oscar Chase, on the charge of "leaving the scene of an accident." Earlier in the day, while driving one of the ministers' cars to bring Negro registrants to the courthouse, he had bumped a truck slightly, doing no damage. But two policemen took note, and in the afternoon of Freedom Day a police car came by and took Chase off to jail. So Freedom Day passed as a kind of quiet victory, and everyone was commenting on how well things had gone—no one being aware, of course, that about 8 that evening, in his cell downtown, Oscar Chase was being beaten bloody and unconscious by a fellow prisoner while the police looked on.

No one knew until early the next morning, when Chase phoned SNCC headquarters. I was talking with a young Negro SNCC worker from Greenwood, Miss., in a Negro cafe down the street, when the call came in. We joined the two ministers, one white and one Negro, who were going down with the bond money. The police dogs in their kennels were growling and barking as we entered the jail house.

Bond money was turned over, and in a few minutes Chase came down the corridor, unescorted, not a soul around. A few moments before, the corridor had been full of policemen; it seemed now as if no one wanted to be around to look at him. After Chase said he didn't need immediate medical attention, we called for the police chief. "We want you to look at this man, as he comes out of your jail, chief." The chief looked surprised, even concerned. He turned to Chase: "Tell them, tell them, didn't I take that fellow out of your cell when he was threatening you?" Chase nodded.

The chief had removed one of the three prisoners in the cell early in the evening, when Oscar complained that he was being threatened. But shortly afterward the guards put in another prisoner, of even uglier disposition. He was not as drunk as the man who'd been taken out, but he was in a state of great excitement. He offered first to lick any man in the cell. Chase said later: "He was very upset about the demonstration—wanted to know why the jail wasn't 'full of niggers.'" He had been a paratrooper in World War II, and told Chase he "would rather kill a nigger-lover than a Nazi or a Jap."

The third man in the cell proceeded to tell the former paratrooper that Chase was an integrationist. Now he began a series of threatening moves. He pushed a cigarette near Chase's face and said he would burn his eyes out. Chase called for the jailer, and asked to be removed from the cell. The jailer made no move to do so. The ex-paratrooper asked the jailer if Chase was "one of them nigger-lovers." The jailer nodded.

What Oscar Chase remembers after that is that the prisoner said something like, "Now I know why I'm in this jail." Then:

*The next thing I can remember was lying on the floor, looking up. I could see the jailer and some other policemen looking at me and grinning. I could also see the other prisoner standing over me, kicking me. I began to get up, was knocked down again, and then heard the door of the cell open. The cops pulled me out and brought me into another cell, where I remained by myself for the rest of the night. . . . I was still bleeding, a couple of hours after the incident. . . . Watching from the door of my new cell, I saw the trusty put a pack of cigarettes and some matches under the door of my attacker's cell. Later I heard police came in and let him out. I could hear them laughing. . . .*

The FBI dutifully took photographs of Oscar Chase and long, detailed statements. Those experienced in the civil rights activities of the past few years will be astonished if anything comes of that.

The beating of Oscar Chase was not extraordinary. In fact, it was a rather mild example of what has been happening for so long in and out of police stations. White field secretaries for SNCC have been beaten again and again in the Deep South: William Hansen had his jaw broken in a jail cell in Albany, Ga.; Richard Frey was attacked on the street in Greenwood, Miss; Ralph Allen was beaten repeatedly in Terrell County, Ga., and John Chatfield was shot in the same county; Robert Zellner has been beaten too many times to record.

Negroes have been beaten more mercilessly, more often, and with less attention: legs have been broken by policemen, faces mashed to a pulp, clubs used again and again on the heads and bodies of black men, women, children. In towns in Georgia, James Williams had his leg broken by police (Americus); Rev. Samuel Wells was kicked and beaten by police (Albany); Mrs. Slater King, five months pregnant, was punched and kicked by a deputy sheriff (Camilla), and later lost her baby. In Winona, Miss., Mrs. Fannie Lou Hamer and Annelle Ponder were beaten by police. Men, women and children were clubbed in Danville, Va., by police. In a Clarksdale, Miss., police station, a 19-year-old Negro girl was forced to pull off her clothes and was then whipped. The list is endless. The FBI has faithfully recorded it all.

Probably the nation doesn't know. It is very much like the Germans and the death camps. There they are, all around us, but we honestly don't see them. Those Americans who do know don't seem to care. Some express concern, but also a sophisticated resignation. Fresh indignation by the naive is met with a knowing smile. "Man, where have you *been*?" After all, long before and far outside the civil rights movement people have been beaten by police, in and out of jail houses, in every state of the Union. We do have what is called "due process" in the United States, but in that long gap between the moment when a friendless individual encounters an armed policeman to the moment when the normal processes of judicial procedure begin to work, the Constitution too often does not exist.

Something needs to be done, at last, about police and jail-house brutality in this country. Perhaps, to start in a moderate and respectable way, some foundation should subsidize a national investigation, supervised by a panel of distinguished jurists, political scientists and churchmen. But even before that, the President and the Attorney General should be pressed to think and to act on the problem.

We need to stop citing the delicate balance between state and nation in our federal system as an excuse for police tyranny; particularly we need to do so in the South. The truth is that we have not been observing the constitutional requirements of that balance. When the Fourteenth Amendment was passed, a hundred years ago, it made explicit what was implied by the loss of half a million lives in the Civil War—that thenceforth state and local governments could not deal with their inhabitants unrestrained by national power. For a hundred years, it has been national law that state and local officials must not discriminate on the ground of color; forty years ago, the Supreme Court began (in the Gitlow case of 1925) to rule that, beyond race, the same restrictions on the states derive from the other guarantees of the Bill of Rights. And statutes going back to 1866 prohibit willful deprivation of a person's constitutional rights by local officials.

In other words, the legislative basis for national protection of citizens against local tyranny has existed for a century. The judicial sanction for federal intervention has been in effect for decades, and the Supreme Court has several times made very clear that the President can take any action he deems necessary to enforce the laws of the land. What has been missing—*and it is a void no civil rights legislation can fill*—is the blunt assertion of Executive power, by an interposition of national force between local police and individual citizens. Ever since the North-South deal of 1877 which put an end to any meaningful reconstruction, political interest, caution and the absence of any compelling necessity have combined to leave the Fourteenth Amendment unenforced by the Executive.

What is required now is the establishment of a nation-wide system of federal defenders, specially trained, dedicated to civil rights, and armed. These special agents would have at their call civil rights attorneys, prepared to use the federal courts and the injunctive process in much bolder ways than the Justice Department has been willing to adopt thus far. They would be stationed in offices all over the South, but also in the North. With the full power of the national government behind them, they would, in many cases, be able to *persuade* local officials to behave. But they would have the authority—already granted to the FBI, but, curiously, never used in civil rights cases—to make immediate arrests when faced with violation of federal law.

Policemen, deputy sheriffs and other local officials must know that they will *immediately* be locked up in a federal penitentiary if they act against citizens in violation of federal law. *Habeas corpus* and due process will be accorded them, but they will face what thousands of innocent people have endured up to now: the burden of raising bail money, of physically getting out of jail, of waiting for slow judicial processes to take effect. The choice is bitterly clear: Either we put up with the jailing and beating of thousands of Negroes and whites who have done nothing but ask for rights asserted in our Constitution, or we put into jail—*without* brutality—enough local policemen and state officials to make clear what the federal system really is. It is not a matter for discussion in Congress, it is a matter for action by the President of the United States.

Federal interposition is needed at three points in the citizen-policeman confrontation: by its mere presence, to act as a preventive; on the spot at the moment of confrontation (up to now, the federal government, given advance notice of danger, has repeatedly refused to send aid); and in the first moments after confrontation, when quick restitution might still be made of an individual's rights. That one phone call which arrested people are often permitted might be made on a "hot line" connecting every local police station with the regional federal defenders' office.

There is genuine misgiving in liberal circles about the creation of such a federal power. But that fear is a throwback to the pre–New Deal failure to recognize that the absence of central power may simply make the citizen a victim of greater local or private tyranny. The storm of economic crisis in the 1930s blew out of sight our Jeffersonian caution in regard to federal power in economic activity. The nation learned that stronger central authority does not *necessarily* diminish individual freedom; it is required only that such authority be specifically confined to designated fields of action.

Our next big psychological and political hurdle is the idea that it is possible—in fact, necessary—to assert national strength on the local level for the protection of the constitutional liberties of citizens. How much more sacrifice will we require from Negroes and whites, bloodying themselves against the wall of police statism, before the nation is moved to act?

*June 29, 1964*

## In the Ring

*LeRoi Jones*

Sonny Liston was the big black Negro in every white man's hallway, waiting to do him in, deal him under, for all the hurts white men have been able to inflict on his world. Sonny Liston was "the huge Negro," the "bad nigger," a heavy-faced replica of every whipped-up woogie in the world. He was the underdeveloped have-not (politically naive) backward country, the subject people, finally here to collect his pound of flesh.

The mock contest between Liston and [Floyd] Patterson was a "brushfire" limited war, Neo-Colonial policy to confuse the issue. Patterson was to represent the fruit of the missionary ethic; he had found God, reversed his underprivileged (uncontrolled) violence, and turned it to work for the democratic liberal imperialist state. The hardy black Horatio Alger offering the glad hand of integration to welcome 20 million into the lunatic asylum of white America.

In this context, Liston the unreformed, Liston the vulgar, Liston the violent, comes on as the straightup Heavy (who still had to make some gesture at the Christian ethic, like the quick trip to the Denver priest before the match, to see if somehow the chief whitie could turn him into a regular fella). "They" painted Liston Black. They painted Patterson White. And that was the simple conflict. Which way would the black man go? This question traveled on all levels through the society, if anyone remembers. Pollsters wanted the colored man in the street's opinion. "Sir, who do you *hope* comes out on top in this fight?"

A lot of Negroes said Liston. A lot of Negroes said Patterson. That old hope come back on you, that somehow this is my country, and ought'n I be allowed to live in it, I mean, to make it. From the bottom to the top? Only the poorest black men have never fallen at least temporarily for the success story. And the poor whites still fall hard.

A white cab driver was turning to see me in his rear-view mirror; he said, "You know that Liston has got the biggest hands of any boxer to come in the ring. You know his arms are 6 feet long. I mean 6 feet long each. He's like an animal. Jesus! He shouldn't even be allowed to fight normal guys." That was the word from that vector of polite society.

The match meant most to the Liberal Missionaries. It was a chance to test their handiwork against this frightening brute. So a thin-willed lower-middle-class American was led to beatings just short of actual slaughter. Twice. And each time Patterson fell, a vision came to me of the whole colonial West crumbling in some sinister silence, like the across-the-tracks House of Usher.

But, dig it, there is no white man in the world who wanted to fight Sonny Liston himself. So the Orwell Synapse takes over. What we cannot gain by experience, we will gain by *inperience*, the positing of a fantasy "event" for what is actually the case. History is changed to correspond with what we all know reality *should* be, a maneuver common to every totalitarian order. The December, 1963 issue of *Esquire* fantasizes with an essay entitled "The Greatest Fights of the Century." Liston beats Marciano, "the most brutal first round ever seen," and he also beats Louis . . . "Louis flew back five feet, fell, and rolled on his face." Having set this up, Dempsey comes marching in like drunk Ward Bond whistling a cavalry tune, to straighten everything out. It is a little hectic (like in *The Spoilers* or when John Wayne is facing a really brave Indian) but the end is never in doubt. As the barbarian climbs through that chink in the wall, IBM! ". . . Liston turned and fell heavily to the floor, his right glove under his face." In the posture of sleep, like a gypsy in the desert, a *fellaheen*. "At six, he rolled over and, back now in his corner, Dempsey smiled." The muscular Neyland-Smith.

See the white man dream? Which is where the whole race has gone: to the slowest. But the mass media make the dream a communal fulfillment, so that now each man who had and has the dream in solitary can share and grow bigger at its concrete illustration. It's like the European painters when they began to paint Arab/Moorish/Semitic experience in medieval middle-European contexts. Christ is then a blond all dressed up in desert clothes but still looking like Jeffrey Hunter. Another smart Germanic type made good. (Practically speaking, for instance, if God were not white, how could He get permission from the white man to make him? If, say, God were black, there would have to be some white man somewhere to tell him what to do, right?)

So now, forget that all this is dream and wish fulfillment, and think of it as a blatant social gesture. This is how the synapse works. We erase the mad-bad big black bad guy by going back in time to get him in a dream; the drop to the canvas takes nearly the whale of the dream, it is so slow and gravityless; you can replay it over and over again—". . . heavily to the floor, his right glove under his face." "Liston vs. Dempsey. . . . Dempsey, K.O., 1:44 of the ninth."

The champ is the big strong likable immigrant who has always done America's chores. He's glad to oblige. We always get to the bad niggers . . . either kill 'em or drive 'em out of the country. Jack Johnson, Henry Highland Garnet, Du Bois, Paul Robeson, Robert Williams, Richard Wright, Sidney Bechet, Josephine Baker, Beauford Deloney, Chester Himes, so many others. The black neurotic beauties trailing dumbly through the "equal" streets of hopeless European cities. All the unclaimed fugitive corpses.

That leaves us with Cassius X. Back in the days when he was still Clay it was easy to see him as a boy manufactured by the Special Products Division of Madison Avenue. Now I think of him as merely a terribly stretched out young man with problems one hoped would have waited at least for him to reach full manhood. Clay is not a fake, and even his blustering and playground poetry are valid; they demonstrate that a new and more complicated generation has moved onto the scene. And in this last sense Clay is definitely my man. However, his choice of Elijah Muhammad over Malcolm X (if indeed such is the case) means that he is still a "homeboy," embracing the folksy vector straight out of the hard spiritualism of poor Negro aspiration. Cassius is right now just angry rather than intellectually (socio-politically) motivated.

The Liston-Clay fight seemed to be on the up and up to me. Liston was way out of shape, expecting young X to be just another weak-faced American. But Cassius can box, and even Liston in shape might have trouble spearing the very quick X. Sonny's risking jail now, where most of the white world would have him (shades of Jack Johnson!) and the possibility of a return match between Clay and Liston grows each day more remote.

But whoever has the heavyweight championship now, or in the future, it is an even remoter possibility that it will be Jack Dempsey, or for that matter any of his Irish progeny. The Dempseys in America, having graduated from the immigrant-newcomer class, don't have to knock heads for a living except as honest patrolmen; their new roles as just Anybody make them as weak and unfit for the task of defeating any of the black heavyweights as any other white Americans, even the honorary kind like Floyd Patterson.

So what kind of men are these who practice such deception on themselves? Oh, they are simply Americans, and some years from now, perhaps there will be this short addition: "you remember them, don't you?"

*December 21, 1964*

## Moments in a Southern Town
**'This Little Light . . .'**

*Peter de Lissovoy*

Two hours after the President put his name to the civil rights bill last July, Nathaniel "Spray-man" Beech pulled open the wood-and-glass front door of the Holiday Inn restaurant in Albany, Ga., and dashed, like musical chairs, to the very first table he saw. In a near corner, a plump, brown-suited woman popped a white hand to her full mouth, but let escape: "Oh my soul and body!" To the right, a child pointed, and its mother slapped the tiny hand and whispered urgently. Spray-man tucked a shirt wrinkle into his black, high-pegged trousers, removed his shades, studied a water glass.

In the split moment that the door stood open, Phyllis Martin, a SNCC field worker from New York, had slipped in before him. Her skin is soft mahogany, her hair natural, a silver-black bowl about her head. She stood, dark-eyed, staring around the dining room, and I came up, after Spray-man, and stood next to her. When the wax-smiling head waitress approached, Phyllis raised her eyes a little and pointed sternly, and the waitress obediently led the way to a central table. After a moment Spray-man summoned up his long limbs, rose, breathing deep and joined us, and by the time we had ordered he was holding down a nervous grin.

But when his steak arrived, Spray-man could hardly eat it. "Jus' ain' hungry," he apologized, more to the meat than anything else. He mopped his forehead with a handkerchief, and leaned over to explain. "What it is, I was expectin' everything but this. I was expectin' this waitress to say, 'Would y'all min' fallin' back out that door you jus' come in at?' The niceness got my appetite, I guess."

At this time, Spray-man was operating a shoeshine stand— among other things, for to "spray" is to hustle—in the entrance way of the Beehive Bar in Albany's Harlem. In his few years, he has seen a great deal of this country and taken his meals from many tables, yet here was one at which he had never expected to sit—nor ever wanted to. The white man could walk as he pleased on his side of town, but let him watch his step in Harlem, that was the geography of Spray-man's pride. And yet, improvised from a harsh reality though his was, pride hates all boundaries, and I was hardly surprised when he told me he wanted to come along when we tried out the new law. If he was supposed to have a right, he would enjoy it—once anyway. In the car, he was full of cracks; and then, in front of the restaurant, I felt him grow tense. A sense of Southern realities deeper than his pride told him he would have to fight, go to jail perhaps, and he was ready.

But the waitress was icily gracious all during the meal. Such was the strength of the President's signature. Nobody sat at the tables directly adjacent to ours, but nobody got up and left. Everybody stared or took pains to avoid staring. Nearest to us, a family of five giggled and glanced as if galloping through some marvelous adventure.

"Reminds me of up North," said Phyllis.

"What—the stares?" I suggested.

"Yeah . . . and the music." From some hidden orifice, the tension-less, sexless music that you hear in airplanes before take-off was falling like gray rain. We decided that the next thing would be to integrate the sounds of places.

Spray-man gave up on his steak about halfway through. When Phyllis finished, the waitress descended upon her plates like a cheery vulture, hurrying us. Abruptly, we were weary. "You 'bout ready?" Phyllis asked. I scraped up a little more and we rose. Spray-man left the waitress an exorbitant tip.

All heads turned to watch us leave. Several white men followed us from the foyer into the parking lot. I started the motor and we rolled out into the street. Spray-man looked out the window. "Well . . ." he started; and then again, "Well . . ." Phyllis turned to him. "What's the matter? Doesn't progress make you happy?"

At about 2 in the morning, Sunday, July 12, Bo Riggins, manager and part-owner of the Cabin in the Pines, tapped me on the shoulder and nodded toward the door. The "Pines" is a bar and dance hall, a key club, a motel, and a restaurant all strung out beneath some scraggly Georgia pine on a lonely road just south of the Albany city limits. With some white money behind it and Bo Riggins fully at the mercy of the Dougherty County police, who are a good deal more rabid than the very rabid city cops, the nightspot had formerly been "black only." When the civil rights bill became law, I took a certain pleasure in seeing it integrated.

But, following me outside this night, Riggins was a frightened man. Sure, he conceded to me, though I had said nothing, there was the new law; but since when had *law* meant anything around here? Somebody might not know who I was. I might get cut, or shot, and where would he be then? He didn't have anything against me personally—nor my color—but he had to think of his business. Couldn't I understand? He paused; but before I could respond, he blurted, "Ah! Here the police now."

Sure enough, a county patrol car had rolled up, and two uniformed men were sauntering over.

"This boy causin' any disturbance?"

"No suh, but I'm scared they be some trouble. It's late. . . ."

"You want him off yo premises?"

"He ain' did nothin', but ita be bes' I think. I don' want him aroun'. . . ."

My mouth full of the irony of it all, I was packed off quickly to the county jail, charged with trespassing and drunk-and-disorderly—the latter a simple frame and the former a matter of law. The chief deputy told me that he didn't know what the country was coming to, and he grew red in the face. He introduced me at the "tank" door ("Comin' up, anothuh nigguh-lovuh . . ."), and I was pitched, biting my lips, into the company of a check-artist, an escapee, a dognapper, two mattress thieves, a wife-beater, a safe-cracker and assorted winos—all very white and proud of it.

The next day, in Harlem, a collection was started for my bond money; but that was going to take time. A friend of mine, a Baptist deacon and old schoolmate of Bo Riggins, paid the man a call to bawl him out and ask him to drop charges. "Now the whites startin' to do right, we can't one of us keep the wrong alive." This was simplifying matters somewhat, because it was white pressure of course that made Riggins do what he had done, but he was the visible opposition. And he was obstinate. Indignation spread in the black community, and was frustrated.

But the reaction among Negroes might have been anticipated. The sentiments of the white men with whom I had to live for a week in jail were a bit more complicated. Had I been arrested while participating in the standard sort of demonstration or sit-in, their response would have been straightforward: open hostility and perhaps the convening of a kangaroo court, with a beating or jail fine as sentence. But as it was, the two initial reactions were a sneering, almost moral disapproval, as if I had been arrested for public indecency, and a simple, stark astonishment that I could have been so stupid, so lacking in imagination, as to think that I could get away with "mixin' " in south Georgia.

Jail is a place for talking, like a barbershop. In a south Georgia jail, all are friends, if not kin, and the jailbirds pass their time reminiscing, berating mutual acquaintances, and reassuring one another of their deeper innocence. There were three real talkers in the cell with me: the escapee, who had sawed through the bars with a file smuggled to him in a bag of crushed ice, only to trip over a sleeping dog a few feet from the jail; one of the mattress thieves, who claimed to have stolen all manner of valuables in his career, only to suffer the irony of being framed as a $5 mattress-pincher; and the fat, hairy safe-cracker, who spent the time he wasn't talking trying to seduce the dognapper, a rosy-cheeked 18-year-old, who threw shoes and tobacco cans at him. Inevitably, my presence injected "race" into every day's bull session. I remember one fragment. The safe-cracker was off chasing his indignant prey; the unsuccessful escapee, the mattress thief and I were leaning on an improvised sofa at one end of the cell:

UE: *The new law . . .*
MT: *What new law?*
UE: *The* nigguh *law. Jesus! The civil rights law. It's gonna change some things, but mos' alla life down heah gonna go on jes' the same. . . .*

*MT: It ain' gonna change me. It ain' nothin' but anothuh civil wah gonna change me an' then they hafta shoot me 'fo I sit down t' table with one a them.*

*UE:* [turning to me] *You see how it is down heah?* [He reached over and pinched the thief's cheek] *This heah a Southern white man. But overlook it. S'posin' it works an' we all mixed up in the hotels an' restaurants. So what? After a while, somebody gonna get tired a the bad feelin'—nigguhs or the white folk one—an' they'll stop comin'. This law ain't gonna mean shit along the whole run a life.*

I had to agree; after all, I was in jail because of my little bit of confidence in the new law. I didn't tell him that I wished the act had some teeth in it; I didn't tell him that I wanted federal armies to make it work, that I wanted stronger, wider legislation in the future. As a matter of fact, there were a whole lot of banners I wasn't waving. I was doing what in a black man would be called "Tomming"—and I was glad I knew how. I wasn't going to get my head broken trying to reform men that nobody—from Jesus to Johnson—could have swayed.

Later in the week, a tall, solid fellow with snakes inked up and down his arms was led in to "sober up." He never got the chance—or perhaps it was a ruse from the start. One of the deputies took a good look at his face and build and promised him a pint of whiskey if he would knock me down a few times. But the others were not much for it, they had gotten used to me and, if they weren't about to lay hands on him in my defense, they weren't going to encourage him either. Most of the fun for him would have been in the applause, so I got off with *buying* him a pint. Liquor can always be had for a price on the Dougherty County Jail black market, though you can't be too sure of your brand. It came in a large, waxed dixie cup. He got properly loaded then, and it was necessary to lose heavily at blackjack to keep him peaceful.

In the end, most of the jailbirds came to pity me. "Boy, that ol' judge gonna hang yo' ass. This south *Georgia*, boy, you can't get away with things like maybe in New York . . ." And when it came to the pinch, it was the law that was the enemy. They kidded me almost warmly when I was called out for the commitment hearing that Attorney C. B. King had arranged. " 'Lessen that nigguh lawyer a yours do some mighty fine talkin', we gonna see you back 'fo long. Save you a place in the game."

The judge dismissed both charges. Bo Riggins couldn't remember anyone who had seen me "drunk and disorderly" and I had several witnesses to swear that I was neither. The judge did not seem to have heard of the civil rights law—or at least considered it irrelevant and inapplicable to the trespassing charge; but he had to dismiss it when Riggins admitted that he never actually asked me to leave, but rather just complied with the apparent wishes of the police in the matter.

It seemed to have gone amazingly smoothly. Outside, Attorney King explained why: An election was imminent. My case was virtually unknown in the white community, the newspapers had made nothing out of it. So the judge could gain nothing by sending me back to jail, and he just might catch a few black votes if he did the "nigguh lawyer" a favor. I wondered if the jailbirds would figure it out. A little later I sent them some ice cream. I was going back to the "Pines" and I didn't know but that I would be seeing them again.

Early on a Saturday afternoon some days later, a dark, gawky boy in jeans and sport shirt was rigging a microphone and amplifier in the barren front yard of an unpainted clapboard house in Harlem. He placed two boxes before the mike, sat upon one, lowered the silver head of the device to the level of his mouth, and then produced a guitar which he picked idly until a great, black woman in pink flowing robes and blue-cloth crown poured suddenly from the house porch and heaved down beside him. She took the guitar and commenced tuning it, hummed and tuned, hummed and tuned, until a crowd had started. And then she sang.

Her voice was weary but warm, thick but expressive, a blues voice. She sang religious songs and old ballads and songs made popular by the Movement. Her favorite, the one she repeated most often during the day and evening, was a talking blues that roved around the chorus: "Oh, there was a death in Dallas that day. . . ." It was not so much ominous or foreboding as just terribly regretful, a sighing, head-shaking exclamation of loss. Like each of her songs, the Kennedy-blues worked into a sermon, the substance of which was invariably, "trust in the Lord, who giveth and taketh away, for they ain't nothin' else trustworthy" (with a few minor forays into such areas as the evil inherent in woman). Then she passed the hat.

The crowd of listeners was always large. I was in Harlem that day and stayed until nearly midnight, listening to her. At about 8 in the evening, the size of her audience reached its peak, spilling over a curbstone in one direction, backing into a gas station in another. There were sharecroppers, factory workers, housewives, dancing, scurrying children, the celebrated and gently lunatic old woman who checks the doors and windows of all the business establishments in Harlem shortly after midnight every night and reports to the cop on the beat any unusual discoveries, happy tonight, shouting, grinning; and the occasional hipster, sheepish at being in this crowd, at wanting to be there, an eye cocked for the running mate who would most surely call sarcastically, "Hey baby, got 'ligion? Go on now—get happy!" About 8.30, a late-model Chevrolet rolled to a halt at the edge of the gathering, and three young white men got out, slamming doors, and moved into the singing crowd.

One of them immediately engaged a Negro youth in nervous, eyes-flicking conversation. The second, a tall and rake-thin fellow, with long, narrow sideburns, began, modestly, to enjoy himself, clapping and singing in perfect rhythm, his face glowing slightly. The third was drunk. For minutes, he seemed uncertain about what was happening or where he was; then, when things began to clear, he started singing and clapping too—or rather shouting hoarsely and beating his hands together at arbitrary and irregular intervals. At this display, his tall friend was shocked to the point of fright. He tried to get the drunk to the car, gave it up when he grew red and loud and stiffly resistant, and then simply moved away, attempting to dissociate himself.

For a long time, the drunken white boy was merely a tiny shallows in a great, fast river, really offensive only to the thinning few around him. Then, suddenly, as if responding to some vision or

internal force, he strode violently forward and demanded the microphone from the ironically—and tolerantly—smiling lady preacher, to
ask: "What y'all starin' at us fo'? We white—sho. But that ain' no
reason to stare. The bill a rights done been pass'! We got a right. We
gonna stay, an I'm gonna as' this kin' lady to sing *Thus lil' light a mine*
fo' the white people a Albany, G-A, who need it, God knows. . . ."

The drunk's two friends were visibly mortified. Not at what he
had said, but at his having said anything at all—at his having drawn
unnecessary and additional attention to their presence. The first
intensified his dialogue with the Negro youth as if to shut out the
awful reality of what had just happened. In a moment, the taller, side-
burned white man had seized his swaying buddy around the shoulders and bundled him, yelling and protesting, off to their car. The
talker trotted to catch up. The car roared and the tall white waved an
apologetic and helpless goodbye from the driver's wheel. The drunk
was slumped in the seat, whooping: "Hooray fo' the nigguhs! Hoo-
hoo-hooray fo' the nigguhs!"

But already the singer had taken up where she had left off.
Nobody much bothered to hear the drunk's rantings; it was a matter
of discipline, a very old discipline.

I was shooting nine-ball in a Harlem poolroom. It was dinner time,
family time, on a Friday night in America, and the room was filled
with people who had no better place to go. I powdered my hands and
sank the winning ball in a combination with the two—and looked up
to see five white hustlers appear in the doorway like apparitions out
of the foggy night, combing their hair, wiping the water from their
foreheads.

"Who wants to shoot?" drawled the skinniest. His voice cracked
at the end, and so he repeated the question with force. It sounded belligerent, so he smiled, stupidly.

Eyes blinked. Bodies stirred. Butterball, who had been napping in
the corner, rose up and stretched his bulk. He settled his red baseball
cap over his eyes. "You got any money, Whitey?" When the white boy
flashed a roll, I stepped back from my table. Butter' picked up a stick
and called for the houseman to rack.

"What's your name, Whitey?"

For a moment, the white fellow wondered how to answer this question most forcefully, and then he simply let it out, a short nasal squeak. Butter' looked down the row of tables: "Hey, Rut! You hear that? Go on look up his daddy in the phone book, fin' out how much coin he got. I'm gonna take all Whitey's money tonight!" He leaned back on the heels of his tennis shoes and laughed with all his weight.

"No you ain't!" Rut, just as heavy as Butter' and infinitely meaner in the eyes, was heaving down the aisle. "Whitey got way more mon-ey'n you can have by y'self, big as you *is*." He stood before the rest of the white team. "Which one a you boys gonna put a ten down on this first game?"

On a Friday night, the poolroom is always crowded by 8. Tonight, when word got around what was happening, old men and young poured in, until the house had to close its doors, so that the players might have space to shoot. It looked like the Olympic games; and, in a sense, it was.

Butter' and Whitey were a good match. They played past mid-night, and, as it turned out, Butter' lost a little. On other tables, "Schoolboy" Terry and Peter "Rabbit" Harris skinned a blond-headed boy whose nickname really was "Whitey," and a laconic, bespecta-cled, middle-aged hustler with a beautiful if inaccurate stroke. Side bets went round and round. On the whole, the whites lost money, but not nearly as much as would be claimed the next day. When it was all over, Butter', gentleman that he is, took the crew around the corner for drinks. "How 'bout it Whitey?" he asked. "We gonna shoot a little over your side tomorrow?"

"Sure."

"Won't be no shit?"

"Not if you bring your money."

For weeks, the game ran on—the white hustlers appearing in Harlem, black hustlers visiting the white poolrooms. "It's the new law," said Butter.' "Integration always starts over sport."

But not every small-town hustler can shoot nine-ball for $5 and $10 a game. Most make their little money disillusioning country boys, in from the dim lights and hacked tables of south Georgia's tinier hamlets, or the Albany workingmen, tanked up and sure that they are the greatest. "Integrated pool" was only for the best, who could win, or lose big money at big matches. The best soon knew one another and were wary; the novelty wore off and the poolrooms, white and black, returned to their normal, and tedious, business.

It is November. The man who signed a bill and integrated the poolrooms is retained in power. I wonder if Butter' voted. Or Spray-man, taking time off from shining shoes.

That first night, after the Holiday Inn, he had been confused; the experience had not had any immediate meanings. But a few hours later, outside a Negro bar in south Albany, called the Playhouse, he had nodded at the crowded doorway: "Lookit all them Negroes, don't know nothin' bout what's happened yet."

A few minutes and a few beers later, he was checking the hand of a girl who was about to drop a dime in the jukebox. He carried a chair to the center of the floor, climbed atop it, shouted the crowd silent and the dancing to a halt, and related, in a loud, laughing voice, the events over on the white side. A few applauded. Most listened politely for a minute or two, but soon conversation started again, and Spray-man was struggling against an indifferent current. He looked over at me, apologetically I felt. I waved with great emotion for him to forget it, but he had his hackles up and went on.

A young man with ironic eyes nudged me. "It's fine," he said. "Fine, if you got plenty money to eat at the Holiday Inn. Me, all I got's this one little quarter, an' I ain't expectin' nothin' soon. Tell y' frien' I'm sorry, but I gotta put it in the piccolo. I'm gonna have me 25¢ worth a soun', an' no history. . . ."

When the music started, Spray-man glanced around angrily. But, when it was clear he was overcome; drowned in sound, he grinned reluctantly, then wide. He shrugged, stepped across the floor to replace the chair and, in a moment was dancing.

*December 28, 1964*

## The Doctor

*Aaron O. Wells*

One evening early last June, I received an urgent call from a colleague and lifelong friend to attend a meeting, mostly of physicians, that had been called to answer a request for emergency medical aid for civil rights workers in Mississippi. The original appeal had come from persons working in the voter-registration summer project. I was unable to attend that first session, but assured my friend that I would be available for the next one.

The first meeting I attended made a tremendous impression on me. I listened to determined and enthusiastic discussion from twenty to thirty persons who sought a program to meet the needs of volunteer workers. (Once in the field, it expanded to consider the health, not only of the freedom workers, but of those whom the workers had gone South to help.) A number of the participants were personally involved, in that they had sons and daughters active in the summer project. We were concerned that here again, in a situation primarily involving Negroes, Negroes were a minority of those seeking solutions to the problems. In less than a week we had decided that the request could be met, and I volunteered to serve with the group, which at that time was so new it had no name. Four physicians were selected as an advance committee to confer in Mississippi with leaders of the Council of Federated Organizations, the National Council of Churches and other leaders in the state. Their task was to determine how our medical presence in Mississippi could be made most effective. They returned with an enthusiastic report, and we assigned medical teams to initiate the program. Before the first team entered Mississippi, this nucleus of dedicated persons found a name—the Medical Committee on Human Rights.

Looking back, I realize that I was slow to decide how I could best serve these obviously dedicated people. A woman colleague whose opinion I have always held invaluable was one of the original members, and her enthusiasm and interest influenced me. Then, too, I had asked my wife, who is a registered nurse, to represent me at an early meeting. Her immediate reaction was to enlist in the project, and soon thereafter she was in Mississippi as the nurse with a medical team.

The response of these two women forced me to consider very seriously my own level of participation. I asked myself whether financial contributions to the various civil rights organizations was sufficient. Would attendance at conferences and occasional health lectures in the context of civil rights fulfill my moral obligation to my people? I decided that these responses were not enough, that I must go to Mississippi.

In the first days there were numerous consultations in New York to secure the approval of the civil rights leadership. At the same time, we were working out a tentative health program which would be applicable to the overall situation, yet flexible enough to meet the needs of each community to be visited. Long hours were spent on the telephone, settling such matters as recruitment and legal advice, but this administrative detail seemed only to heighten our enthusiasm for the main job ahead.

Finally, on August 7, I boarded the plane for Jackson, Miss., assigned to the post of field coordinator for a period of two weeks. During the flight I met Dr. David Spain, the noted New York pathologist, who was going South to observe the autopsied bodies of the three civil rights workers, Schwerner, Chaney and Goodman.

Even while deep in conversation with this fascinating man, I began to grow fearful. I visualized a hostile reception at the airport, for I am a Negro and Dr. Spain is white. My anxiety increased when the stewardess announced that, due to mechanical difficulties, we would be detained in Birmingham, Ala. We were now scheduled to land in Jackson at 10:30 p.m., and it is particularly hazardous for an integrated group to travel after dark.

Dr. Spain and I registered at a newly integrated motel. Our arrival was observed with hostile glances, and we heard angry epithets. We had been prepared for this reception, and it did not change our respective plans; but neither did it do much to ease my mind.

Until early morning, we conferred with Dr. Charles Goodrich, a friend and colleague from New York, on the problems he was having to secure permission to see the bodies of the three murdered young men. Later that day, as the vocal attack increased, I decided that the situation was becoming dangerous and I moved the Negro members of the medical teams from the motel to homes in the community.

This was my first trip to the Magnolia State. I was struck by the physical beauty of the rolling, green countryside, the vast cotton plantations, varied by rotating crops of soybeans, and the ever blue sky. This physical loveliness makes more incredible the brutality which the state imposes on the mass of its impoverished people.

I was fortunate to be given lodgings by one of the Negro ministers of the community. He and his family were warmly hospitable, and it was obvious that they, like others in the area, were determined to assist the movement wherever and whenever they could. Much honor should be paid to the families who temporarily housed us. Without their courageous assistance we would have been unable to organize and develop our program as rapidly as we did. Many of our hosts have since been subjected to harassment and intimidation, but they continue to assist whenever needed.

After much conferring with local and state authorities, we were granted permission to view the bodies of Schwerner, Chaney and Goodman. Our integrated team drove to the University of Mississippi, dreading the mission, and worried as to how we would be received. This was one of many times when I suspected that we were being followed, and wondered what our fate would be if the authorities decided to prevent us from reaching our destination.

I cannot speak in detail of the actual examination, which was conducted by Dr. Spain, for the sight of those dreadfully mutilated young bodies put me in a state of emotional shock. It was at this moment, though, that I resolved finally to dedicate myself to active participation in the Medical Committee for Human Rights.

The following morning, which was Sunday, I completed the orientation program for the medical teams at MCHR's office in Jackson. They were all eager to reach their posts and begin work. Each team was made up of a doctor, a nurse and a driver.

Sunday evening I was asked to discuss MCHR's origin and program at Tougaloo College with newly arrived voter registration volunteers. Most of these people had been unaware of our existence, and they were extremely interested to know how we would participate in the health programs that they hoped to set up in the various communities. They asked about immunization, nutrition, eyesight and dental problems, prenatal and postpartum care, communicable diseases and child care. No one doubted the need for health education in the state.

The following week, I had many such conferences with groups of volunteers, and learned from them more details of the health needs in the areas where they were setting up programs. I also made daily visits to the COFO office, to be sure that the volunteers knew of our medical presence and to answer questions about their own health needs. For those in need of specific medical attention, I enlisted physicians from within the community to participate in MCHR's program, since we are not licensed to practice medicine in Mississippi.

I was able to establish good relations with the doctors in Jackson, both white and Negro. Most of them were glad to have our objectives clarified; they agreed that the group was necessary and offered to cooperate. The assistance of the National Council of Churches was also invaluable. This group had wide experience of social conditions in Mississippi, and it gave expert advice as we began to put individual health programs into operation.

We decided that a scheme of health insurance should be worked out for the civil rights workers. Most of the summer volunteers lived on extremely small budgets, and so that no one would hesitate to seek care when he needed it, we sometimes assumed payment of medical bills incurred in Mississippi. It was also obvious that most of the volunteers had been under great emotional tension and needed rest from active duty with a change of environment. We therefore took immediate steps to get a recreation program under way.

There is great need for health education in Mississippi, with emphasis on prenatal care, for the infant-mortality rate is very high. Most Negro infants are still delivered by midwives, and in many instances the mother has no one in attendance.

Since a socio-economic change is inevitable, I believe that a sound health program should be instituted for all of the impoverished citizens of the state of Mississippi. But until the obstacles are abolished that would prevent Negroes from participation in such a program, MCHR has a big role to play in the so-called Black Belt.

*September 20, 1965*

## "Tell It Like It Is, Baby"

*Ralph Ellison*

> *Dear Uncle Raf*
> ... What are you doing over there in Rome with all those Italians? What do you think about over there? Are you keeping up with what's happening here at home? Have you read about those cracker senators cussing out the Supreme Court and all that mess? Let me hear what a home-boy done gone intellectual thinks when he's away from the Apple and all the righteous studs ... How's the writing going? Do you find it makes a difference being over there? Tell a man how it is. ...

Virgil B., who wrote the above excerpt in 1956 after the Southern Congressmen had drawn up their manifesto against the Supreme Court, is a childhood friend who is now a cook and baker on merchant ships. Inevitably his letters contain a trace of mockery, directed at my odd metamorphosis into a writer, which is meant to remind me whence I come. Nor is he merely amused, he seriously expects insight and eloquence and a certain quality of attention to the reality experienced by our group—demands which since that experience is often bafflingly complex, I am not always able to meet. After answering his letter, however, I was led to make an attempt at an essay which, perhaps because too many things were happening to me at the time, I was unable to complete. My wife and I were living the dormitory life of the American Academy in Rome and I was much preoccupied: with writing a novel, with literary concepts, with reviewing my own life's resources for literary creation, with the experience of discovering a foreign culture in which the old structures and guides that sustained my thoughts, emotions and conduct at home were so relaxed, whether awake or sleeping, that it was as though I was living in a barely controlled chaos.

So the essay failed. I simply could not organize the various elements—literary, political, psychological, personal—into the complex, meaningful whole which my sense of reality and my concern with fiction demanded. But I could not forget the essay, or at least not the dream which was its core: for in its way it seemed to symbolize my state of diffusion, my concerns, conscious and unconscious. Therefore the following attempt at salvage (made at the suggestion of the late David Boroff) represents, if nothing more, a further episode in my discovery that for me it was by no means a simple task to "tell it like it is"—even when the subject was desegregation and the Southern Congressmen's defiance of the Supreme Court. I was outraged and angered by the event, but the anger was not isolated or shallowly focused, rather it suffused my most non-political preoccupations. More unsettling, I discovered that there lay deeply within me a great deal of the horror generated by the Civil War and the tragic incident which marked the reversal of the North's "victory," and which foreshadowed the tenor of the ninety years to follow.

Since I attempted the essay, some nine years ago now, the power of the Southern Congressmen has been broken and the reconstruction of the South is once more under way. Nevertheless, the hooded horrors parading, murdering and shouting defiance in the South today suggest that the psychic forces with which I tried to deal (in both dream and essay) are still there to be dispersed or humanized; the individual white Southerner's task of reconciling himself to the new political reality remains. In retrospect, then, it was perhaps not too naïve after all to have tried to approach the problem consciously through the insights made available by the wisdom of tragedy. One thing is certain, the mind in sleep will have its way, and I *had* fallen asleep while reading Gilbert Murray's

*The Classical Tradition in Poetry*, puzzling over how its insights might possibly be useful to a writer who is American, a Negro, and most eager to discover a more artful, more broadly significant approach to those centers of stress within our national life wherein he finds his task and being.

—*New York, June 1965*

Let me begin a personal dream—for with what are we concerned, the moment we try to think about the problem of desegregation, but the clash between the American dream and everyday American reality; between the ideal of equality and the actuality of our society in which social, educational, and economic inequalities are enforced explicitly on the irremediable ground of race? And even in so practical and (until recently) so far removed an area as that of foreign policy, does not this clash, especially when we regard Asia and Africa, make for an atmosphere of dream-like irrationality?

Perhaps more to the point, when a Negro American novelist tries to write about desegregation he must regard, in all its tortuous ambiguity, the South. And here immediately he confronts three clusters of conflicting images: the myth-image propagated by orthodox White Southern spokesmen, by costume movies and popular novels of the Civil War; the image, almost completely negative, held by self-righteous white Northerners—and not a few Negroes—who have never known the South; and the more heavily qualified image (far more than a simple synthesis of the others) held by his black Southern relatives and their fellow Negroes. Among these images (none absolutely true or false) there is a great clashing, with the exponents of each set making scapegoats of the others: Northerners for Southerners, the South for the North, the black for the white and the white for the black, and when we try to find stable points of reality in this whirling nightmare of terms and attitudes, they change constantly into their opposites.

If we honestly say "Southerner," then we must, since most Negroes are *also* Southerners, immediately add *white* Southerner. If we say "white South" our recognition that the "white South" is far from solid compels us to specify *which* white South we mean. And so on for the North and for the Negro until even the word "democracy"—the ground-term of our concept of justice, the basis of our scheme of social rationality, the rock upon which our society was built—changes into its opposite, depending upon who is using it, upon his color, racial identity, or in what section of the country he happened to have been born, or where and with whom he happens to be at the moment of utterance. These circumstances have, for me at least, all of the elements of a social nightmare, a state of *civil* war, an impersonal and dreamlike chaos. To what then, and in his own terms, does a Negro writer turn when confronting such chaos—to politics, history, sociology, anthropology, art? War, it has been said, is a hellish state; and so, too, is equivocation, that state (born of the Hayes-Tilden Compromise of 1877 and faintly illumined by the candle of liberty) in which we live. It is the candle alone which guides us through our chaos and when the candle flickers we're in the dark. And so in the Roman dark I dreamed.

It was a bright spring morning and I was walking along Classen Boulevard in Oklahoma City. Birds sang high in the trees that lined the walk and I could see the flash of wings and the quick, downward swoop ending in a nervous run along the walk, where, with alerted heads and flipping tails, they busily harvested a horde of catalpa worms. The worms were everywhere, the walk smeared green and white with their pulp and skin. But they were relentless. They kept dropping from the trees to the walk and moving over the curb and into the street in a steady wave, providing an ambulatory feast for the birds. Trying to avoid both worms and smears, I moved past the well-trimmed walks that led through handsome lawns to the distant houses, showing bright and gay with awnings. There were flowers too, and a clarinet running arpeggios in middle register, and the call of a huckster sounding hoarse-voiced in the limpid distance. I was filled with the expectation of some pleasantness, some long looked-for reward. Then it came over me that I was going to see my father.

I hurried now and almost immediately I saw in the distance under the high archway of worm-damaged leaves a tall, familiar man coming toward me. We were approaching an intersection, which he reached ahead of me, and stood looking steadily toward me and I felt a certain joy.

But then, as I drew closer, he was no longer familiar, but a stranger wearing a dull black and gray diamond-checked suit, his face narrow as he watched me out of small, staring eyes. I didn't know him at all, was even uncertain of his race. Standing quite still now, feeling a cold sensation along the ridge of my spine, I looked across the empty street, trying to interpret his accusatory look. We stared for a breathless time, then he turned away, retreating quickly beyond a privet hedge and out of sight, just as a mirror or window pane nearby sent the sun glaring into my eyes. It was odd.

I moved again, feeling now as though I had lost something precious. Who was this man, and what was the meaning of his staring accusation? What had I done—what had I failed to do? Had I been mistaken for someone else? But who?

The weather had changed and the city become strange. I was walking through an arcade lined with shops and on into an old streetcar terminal covered with dirty glass through which the light filtered gloomily down. Passengers stood about in little groups, silently waiting for the long, yellow cars that came and went with a groaning and grinding, the motormen retracting, and shifting the trolley poles with a great showering of sparks. An old man in a white apron and yellow paper cap was selling popcorn and peanuts from a stand topped by a whistle which sent forth a thin plume of steam each time a little mechanical clown, wearing a white, polka-dotted suit and peaked hat with a red pompon, turned the crank of a glass drum containing unshelled peanuts. The man smiled, holding out a paper cone of popcorn, gleaming with butter, as I moved past and out into a great public square, in the center of which I saw a tall, equestrian statue standing level with the second story of the surrounding buildings. The rider, poised in full gallop, stood high in the stirrups flourishing a broad military hat with plume. An expression of victory showed on his bronze face, despite the fact that his saber had lost three-fourths of its blade. Gazing upward past his head, I saw on the balcony of a building across the square the man who had stared; now, accompanied by a mysterious woman, he was looking toward me. They leaned forward, gripping the rail, staring at me intensely. Then a clock struck three with a mournful sound, followed by the creaking of cogs and pendulum—an ancient, dirty, cobwebbed sound. Then a flock of pigeons flew up, casting a shadow between us as they rustled the light with their wings and a voice spoke from a hidden loudspeaker.

"Is he the one?" it said.

"He's the one," a woman's voice answered, "truly."

"Is he the one? I say is he the *one!*"

"He's young, too young; he's not the one. It's been too long."

"Then he's the one," the male voice said. "Strength is not a requirement."

Then I became aware of a crowd standing behind me, before a building decorated with flags and bunting. It was quite hostile and I had the hot feeling that it was capable of almost anything. I moved away, aware that the crowd was following and feeling that somehow I had fallen from a high place, from a cliff or high protecting wall; and now I was running down a hill on which the tracks of a trolley line gleamed, and the air, suddenly breathless, was portentous.

I ran desperately, until, somehow, I was in a dark, colonial alley in Washington. And as I emerged into a crowded thoroughfare it was as though a book of 19th-century photographs had erupted into vivid life. The street was full of rubber-tired carriages—broughams, phaetons, landaus—and I could hear the creak-snap-jangle and thud of wall-eyed pacing horses. Gas lamps flickered the shadows with a chill white light, revealing a relentless crowd moving with sweating excitement, and as I moved out into the crush I became aware of the strangely sinister, high-frequency swishing of women's skirts. All around me people were rushing swiftly past to gather before a building from which, looking past their bobbing heads, I could see a sheet-covered form being removed on a litter.

It was a man, I could see now, his body having lost its covering as his litter-bearers jolted him roughly about. It was a tall man who seemed familiar: there was something about the way the disarranged sheet draped the toes of his shoes. Then it was now and yet another time, and I moved forward with a feeling of dread, thinking, "It's happening again."

*We had said good-by and he had made me a present of the tiny pink and yellow wild flowers that had stood in the vase on the window sill, had put a blue cornflower in my lapel. Then a nurse and two attendants had wheeled in the table and put him on it. He was quite tall and I could see the pain in his face as they moved him. But when they got him covered his feet made little tents of the sheet and he made me a joke about it, just as he had many times before. He smiled then and said good-by once more, and I had watched, holding on to the cold white metal of the hospital bed as they wheeled him away. The white door closed quietly and I just stood there, looking at nothing at all. Near by I could hear my mother talking quietly with the physician. He was explaining and she was asking questions. They didn't talk long, and when they finished we went out of the room for the last time. Holding on to my wrist as I clutched my flowers in my fist, my mother led me down the silent corridor heavy with the fumes of chloroform. She hurried me along. Ahead of us I saw a door swing ajar and watched it, but no one came out, then as we passed I looked inside to see him, lying in a great tub-like basin, waiting to be prepared for his last surgery. I could see his long legs, his knees propped up and his toes flexing as he rested there with his arms folded over his chest, looking at me quite calmly, like a kindly king in his bath. I had only a glimpse, then we were past. We had taken the elevator then and the nurse had allowed me to hold the control and she had laughed and talked with me as we went down to the street. Outside, as we moved along the winding drive into the blazing sun, I had told my mother but she wouldn't believe that I had seen him. I had though, and he had looked at me and smiled. It was the last time I saw my father alive. Years later, while telling me who he was and what he had been and what it meant to be his fatherless child, my mother had said that difficulties with money and the weather caused his body to be withheld from burial until it stank in the dark back room of the funeral parlor. Such was her respect for the naked reality of the human condition. . . . But what quality of love sustains us in our orphan's loneliness; and how much is thus required of fatherly love to give us strength for all our life thereafter? And what statistics, what lines on whose graphs can ever convince me that by his death I was fatally flawed and doomed—afraid of women, derelict of duty, sad in the sack, cold in the crotch, a rolling stone in social space, a spiritual delin-*

*quent, a hater of self—me in whose face his image shows? My mother loved him through all the years, cherished his memory until she died, apotheosized his vital years. For in effect he only perished, he did not pass away. His strength became my mother's strength and my brother and I the confused, sometimes bitter, but most often proud, recipients of their values and their love. . . .*

But as I moved closer now it was Washington again and I could see the man's head snap suddenly back to reveal a short, carefully trimmed beard and I was confused, thinking: *But he didn't wear a beard.* As I pressed forward to get a better look, the crowd came between and I thought: *He's either drunk or sick—but why aren't they more careful?* Some were even laughing.

"What are they laughing at?" I asked a man going past.

"At our American cousin, fool."

"What? Whose—"

Then there came over me an inexpressible anguish, like a great weight suspended on a blunt hook driven through that part of my throat, the region of the thyroid gland, where grief and anguish collect, bearing down like doom.

For now, looking at the balustraded steps I recognized the building, and recognizing the building I knew the man; and knowing the man I wanted to cry, but could not cry. I wanted to scream, but could not scream. And suddenly the air resounded with the obscene melodramatics of the assassin's *"Sic semper tyrannis!"* and the night was filled with a great weeping and a great laughter.

And yet I was still unsure.

"What are they laughing at?" I said.

"Are you kidding, boy?" came the reply. "Face the facts!"

I knew now, even in the dream, that I had fallen out of time into chaos, and although the sight of the body filled me with horror, there was still room for personal embarrassment. And an embarrassment over the embarrassment—a chattering, degenerating echo of vanity before sad public events. For suddenly I discovered that I, whose grandparents were quite young at the time of Emancipation, had become a child again and was dressed in the one-piece garment of a young slave. I had no pants, nor shoes nor underwear; and when I tried in my dual shame to leave the street I was swept forward by the crowd, forced to follow after the litter which was now being moved along the street in what had suddenly become a funeral cortege. And now, though barefoot and quite young, I discovered that nevertheless I was literate, a slave who could read.

For as I was swept along, history-book descriptions of the event flickered through my mind in visual counterpoint and I kept trying to anticipate the route which the crowd would take through the dim and shadowed streets. But nothing was going as it was written. Instead of an escort of grieving high dignitaries, military men and weeping gentlewomen following a flag-draped camion, and with a crowd of weeping, recently freed slaves forming an anguished second line (perhaps the archetype of all such lines, joyful or sad, associated today with their descendants), the slain man, lanky and not yet cold, the complexion darker than I'd ever imagined, and with an ironic yet benign expression on the transcendent features, was being conveyed by a mob.

In a flash it became a carnival, an *Oktoberfest*, a Mardi Gras, with the corpse become the butt of obscene jokes. In the light of the hissing street lamps I saw a burly, bald-headed man waving his arms about, announcing in stentorian tones, "We've caught the old coon at last! Haven't we now!" Then as he broke into a fit of wheezing laughter the others responded, "COON! COON! COON! Hep-hep- Hep-john-step COON-COON!" And it quickly became a wild marching chant that filled me with a special terror. For hearing this epithet applied to the slain leader warned me that something terrible was about to occur, that some further support was to be torn from the foundation of that which I had thought was reality, from that which I held most sacred.

*And how can I be me, if Old Abe be a "coon,"* I thought. *Yes, and how can I be a slave or even human?* And I looked down at my hands, fully prepared to see them turn into hairy paws.

Just then I saw a squat man with a toothbrush mustache shoot out of the crowd flashing a knife in the lamplight, yelling, "Make way! Make way!"

*Please, not that, please not that!* I thought, striking out about me as he bent low over the litter, the knife poised. Then I was spun around and when I looked again, he held a black piece of cloth, a wedge-shaped lapel, its lining gutted, yelling, "Hey! For my grandbaby boy, a souvenir for little Joey!" And this triggered the mob to a frenzy.

They rushed in to rip at the black coat with their fingers, they hacked it with pieces of broken bottle. One elegant man produced a straight-edged razor from the folds of his rich purple cravat and went to work distributing delicate bits of cloth among those unable to share directly in the dismemberment. Bits of cloth flittered down like blackened snow. And the coat swiftly disappearing, they went to work on his trousers.

Someone tugged off a homely gaiter. I saw several men and women, squawking like carrion crows, close in, fighting to take it away. A bent little old woman wearing a poke bonnet like that of the "Old Dutch Cleanser" woman grabbed the gaiter's mate and disappeared. Two small boys snatched off the socks, slashing them to shreds between them with nails astonishingly sharp.

They were insatiable. They ripped up the slain Lincoln's tie. His collar was seized, his white shirt ripped away, his vest torn to surreal tatters.

"Peace, Peace," a thin voice cried. "Remember the old buzzard's advice to its young: Hit a dead head-horse in the eye and move straight up through his vastness. I say: Remember, Find the place, Strike!"

This enthusiastic *elegante* in Edwardian suit and with suave Eliotonian stoop was knocked aside by a rough-looking man who produced the President's stovepipe hat, and I saw him sail it curving through the air and into a second-story window—in which a wrathful woman promptly appeared and sailed it down again, dusting her hands indignantly as the high hat hovered above us like a battered Saturn with its radiant rings turned gray. A man grabbed it as it fell and, turning on his toes like a ballet dancer, jammed it on the head of a floozy, cotton-topped blonde, who wiggling wobbly a few steps, shook her head of cotton-candy hair to the crowd's applause. She wore a feather boa and a skin-tight satin dress, and flouncing about on unsteady legs she showed off a pair of monstrous, heavily-powdered breasts which, as she stumbled and lurched on shoes with vicious heels, kept flipping out of her low-cut bodice and tossing about like two bloated, moon-mad, oxygen-starved flounders. For a fitful moment she caught the crowd's attention by cutting a clumsy cakewalk as she waved the hat and weaved, singing in a tinny little-lost-girl voice,

Come on boys
And name your play
We put the last clean shirt
On Abe today . . .,

punctuated with a suggestion of bump and grind.

We moved again, the crowd growing with every step, the heat oppressive, the noise expanding in hysterical volume. Suddenly I noticed that the body was now being carried by four ragged Negro men who, kicked and pummeled as they stumbled along, held grimly to their burden, their stolid black faces disapproving.

"Get on. Get on!" the crowd cried. But hardly had they gone a dozen feet than they were beaten to a halt and rested the litter high on their shoulders while the crowd jeered at the slain President. He lay now in his underwear, his bony railsplitter's wrists hanging awkward and bare, his thin ankles sticking from the bottom of his under-drawers much as the rapidly growing Uncle Sam of the 19th-century cartoons had stuck from his outgrown heel-strapped britches.

"Stars, stripes and nigger minstrels!" someone called. "Now he's Happy Hooligan!" At which, to the crowd's wild delight, a short, fat man wearing a long, gray coat, and who resembled Edmund Wilson, turned from drinking beer from a tin bucket and shook his head as with sudden revelation. Taking a final sip, he dashed the remains into the street and with an inspired, slow-mushrooming belch, jammed the "growler" on the Great Emancipator's head, clamping the wire handle beneath the bearded chin.

"Beautiful" someone said, "Beautiful!"

The applause was like the shattering of great sheets of glass. Whereupon the inspired fat man completed the Happy Hooligan transformation by pushing the stem of a corncob pipe between the once so eloquent lips, twisting the bowl so that its contents spilled upon the shrunken chest. Then a group of men labored up with a railway baggage wagon and the Negroes were forced to put the body upon it and then made to pull it through the cursing, flailing crowd.

"Push dat barge, boys!" a joker commanded in a thick foreign accent. "Push dat dar ole cotton-picking barge!"

I wanted to kill him along with all the callous crowd, but was too powerless and too fascinated, too held by horror and the anguished need to see it ended.

We were rushing through wide streets now, with broad lawns and stately buildings on either side. The ragged Negroes strained away, conveying now, beside the President, a number of women in tacky Sunday dresses, whose high-laced shoes dangled contentedly as they fluttered beside the body, joking and laughing and plying their little lace, mother-of-pearl-embellished fans. Then straight ahead I saw the Washington Monument, seeming to break through the floor of a barren plain like a periscope from the sea, rushing to meet us. Then we were there, at the base of the austere shaft, where the four Negroes were again beaten to a halt and made to lay their burden on the grass, then sent fleeing into the darkness. I tried to follow them, but was quickly restrained.

*But why not me,* I thought. *Why not me as well?* For I wished to join them in their forced detachment, I envied them their anonymity, their freedom to not participate. But my brown skin and slave's garment notwithstanding, I was held and forced to the front of the crowd.

I found myself standing near a tall, thin grandame who was laughing hysterically, screaming like a great tropical bird. Then she stopped and sniffed solemnly at a bottle of smelling salts, an expression of utmost complacency settling over her thin, aristocratic face, while the others joked, cursed, and made obscene remarks about the President until abruptly the composure of her face broke apart like the shattering of rock, and she laughed to put my teeth on edge. She bent double, then back, her stiff black garments snapping visibly with the motion and enveloping me in the rank fumes of female senility laced with threat and mystery.

Squeezing around her, and against an invisible hand that now seemed to hold me, I looked down at the lanky figure sprawled at the base of the marble shaft, thinking, *Now it's all over, they'll leave him alone, it's over.*

But not yet. I looked up to see a man wearing a voluminous opera cape, and who looked oddly like Mr. Justice Holmes, skipping slowly forward, decorous and tall, and with the toe of his elegant high-button shoe, flipping the corpse into a grotesque attitude. Then, throwing open his cape, he shouted, "Look at these! I say, *look at these!*" sticking a long finger through a series of bullet holes.

"Poor noble man!" they cried. "Poor betrayed innocent!"

"That dirty coon!"

"He did him wrong, the clod! He swindled him!"

"He wasted his land! He spoiled the cream! Get him!" This initiated a contest. Now they pushed one another about as they tried to see who could kick the corpse into the most fantastic positions, standing it on its head, doubling it over, twisting it in the cordwood postures of Dachau, shouting and cursing all the while.

"He's all to blame!"

"Give it to him good. There, there, how about that!"

"Yeah, but now you just watch this."

"That was a good one!"

"Look at ole Abe, he's dead but he won't lie down!"

"Watch it there, McDuffy, turn him over easy—but turn him!" I wanted to cry, my throat feeling as though it would burst apart, but no tears would flow to bring relief.

I closed my eyes as they knocked me about. And I now realized an odd thing. Up to this point, such is the contradiction of the dream, that I had not felt the President was actually dead. He isn't dead: I wouldn't have it so. It was a pitiful denial born of horror, a wish born of an anguished need to deny the hegemony of terrible fact an attitude with which I had been familiar since childhood, when I had been bemused by a recurring fantasy in which, on my way to school of a late winter day I would emerge from a cold side street into the warm spring sun and there see my father, dead since I was three, rushing toward me with a smile of recognition and outstretched arms. And I would run proudly to greet him, his son grown tall. And then I could awake at last from the tortuous and extended dream that was my childhood with my father gone. So urgent had been my need for a sense of familial completeness, to have our family whole and happy as it had been until shortly before I saw him placed at last into the earth, that this thin fantasy had been made to serve for the man of flesh and blood, the man of the tales, the ghost stories, the gifts and strength and love. From the age of three to thirteen, the processes of time and the cold facts of death alike were—in this special area of my mind, for I *understood* death and was eager for change and for my own manhood's attainment—held off by this recurring day-dream.

So I could not believe Mr. Lincoln dead. Thus, so, in the dislocated, is-and-isn't world of dream, I felt that the President bore his indignities out of a temporary weakness incurred by his wound or out of war weariness—even out of a saint-like patience, out of a hero's grace before the mob's wild human need. It was as though the noisy desecration of his body was being accepted as he had accepted the tragic duty of keeping the country unified even through an act of fratricidal war. Or as later it had been his task to seek reconciliation of the sundered parts. Yes, it was no less an act of duty than that of receiving the assassin's bullet in his brain. He is not dead, I told myself in the dream; he is not tolerating the mob's outrages out of the insensitivity of death, but submitting willingly to them out of the most sublime and tragic awareness of the requirements of his fated role. For we must take our heroes where we find them, and in all their wisdom and their guile, and in all their frustrating enigmas as in their bright lucidities.

For in him at least, there was a man who, having taken the oath, would do, and did, all that it was necessary for him to do, even before his own foreboding dream of obliteration.

But now in the suddenly accelerated tempo of the dream the corpse rebelled. I saw it grow rigid, then swell, transformed before my eyes into an advanced state of putrefaction. So inflated was the corpse becoming that soon the underwear resembled the series of inner tubes that form the body of the figure in the Michelin trademark. Death undeniable looked out at me, the sublime mocking its earthly shell.

"Now it is over," I thought. "At last they can see what they've done and I'll awaken."

But not even the ultimate protest of decomposing flesh could halt them. A man reached down and grasped the inflated underwear, trying to tear it away—and it was then that a sound like a fusillade of shots ripped the air and a dense cloud of gray, slime-drenched birds burst up from the earth on swift metallic wings and attacked the onlookers with feet of fire.

Screaming with pain, they burst apart like an exploding grenade, turning to claw at one another as they milled wildly about. And in the confusion I was pinned against the monument, burned by the flying slime. The four Negroes had returned now, and they stood silently, looking first at me and then down at Mr. Lincoln. They grasped with one hand the handles of a black box; in their free hands they carried gleaming spades. There was some cryptic exchange among them, then they looked at me, and now I was no longer a child. The scene became a scene on a movie screen, which I was watching from a distance and with a feeling of utmost clarity, as though I grasped the mystery of all experience. Then, just as suddenly, I was in the scene again, only now the mysterious Negroes were resting on their spades around a great hole. They motioned for me to look over the edge. Approaching fearfully, I looked down, seeing the crowd, transported there, a multitude, some black faces among them, sitting at table making a ghoulish meal of some frightful thing that a white sheet hid from view. Then as I saw something stirring and expanding beneath the sheet, the earth seemed to crumble, plunging me screaming into a terrible wakefulness. . . .

I lay there in the hushed Roman night, aware of a nightingale singing somewhere beyond the venetian blinds, the lonely play of the fountain in the gravel-strewn *cortile* below. The air was breathlessly hot, yet I lay in a cold sweat, trying now, by way of exorcizing the dream, to recall some of Mr. Lincoln's eloquent words—grasping desperately for the Gettysburg Address. I had known it most of my life, had been moved by it even before its implications had become meaningful; had memorized its stately lines as a class assignment back in an old high school named Frederick Douglass; had studied it on my own in Sherwin Cody's little booklet on composition and rhetoric, where it was grouped with passages from *Ecclesiastes* and Benjamin Franklin; had pondered its themes of sectional reconciliation and national rebirth many times long since, as the awareness grew that there was little about it that was simple and that it was profoundly implicated both in my life and in the failure of my promised freedom.

But now, although I could feel the mood of its noble rhythms as physically as the pounding of my heart, the words had hidden themselves, become mute before the vivid mist of nightmare. I sat up abruptly, seeing the dim bars of moonlight seeping through the blinds as the rhythms called forth a swirl of imagery. Then scenes of Charles Laughton performing the title role of the movie *Ruggles of Red Gap* suddenly reeled through my mind. Once more he was the much put-upon immigrant English butler, enduring the jibes and abuses of his *nouveau riche* American employers, whose vulgar "Gilded Age" materialism mocked all that is ideal in the American tradition. And once more, at the high point, he drew himself up proudly to recite the compassionate words uttered by Lincoln at Gettysburg, becoming in their measured flow transformed into a most resonant image of the American's post–Civil War imperative of conscience and consciousness achieved.

So here at last, in remembered art, the words of hope and reconciliation born of war and bloodshed rejoined the hallowed rhythms to dispel the nightmare images of the great man defiled. I was, though badly shaken, at last awakened.

Thank god it was only a dream! But as I became more fully awake it struck me that more dismaying than having such events erupt in one's dream life was that no living hero or surrogate had appeared to play Antony to Lincoln's Caesar. Even the villains were less than individualized, the figure who looked like Mr. Justice Holmes only resembling him and the man in the long, gray coat only looking like Mr. Edmund Wilson (but with no aura of scholarly eminence). And so the women. None struck me as mother-figures, neither the rump-sprung blonde, the poke-bonneted granny, nor the tall boom-and-bust figure in the stiff black dress—though I'm sure that some critic expert in the interior life of writers could write a fascinating essay on these ladies as three phases of the same personage—say: "The Woman as Earth-Mother, as Matron, and as Scold." Seriously, I could not ignore the fact that no one tried to stop the mob, nor that I myself was but a trapped and impotent observer—in fact, most infantile, my mind become an incongruous scene for historical horrors horribly personalized.

But enough, let me not pretend objectivity; my dream, being a dream, was absurd. For how else describe its mixture of obscene, historical and mythical elements? During the bright Roman day I had read my friend's questioning letter, and at night had fallen asleep reading Gilbert Murray's chapter "Hamlet and Orestes," which here would seem to shed no light at all. Yet this immediately suggests, whatever its Freudian implications, a possible relationship between my dream and a pattern of classical tragedy: the hero-father murdered (for Lincoln is a kind of father of 20th-century America), his life evilly sacrificed and the fruits of his neglected labors withering some ninety years in the fields; the state fallen into corruption, and the citizens into moral anarchy, and with no hero come to set things right. Perhaps this is too far-fetched, but when living abroad one is compelled to look homeward through one's own inner eyes and through the objectives that lie at hand. Perhaps, therefore—any lens being better than no lens at all—the present optics provided by Murray's essay on tragedy will serve without too much distortion when we consider the possibility that the last true note of tragedy was sounded (and quickly muffled) in our land when the North buried Lincoln and the South buried Lee, and between them cast the better part, both of our tragic sense—except perhaps the Negroes'—and our capacity for tragic heroism into the grave. On the national scale, at least, this seems true. The sheet-covered figure in my dream might well have been General Robert E. Lee.

So I confess defeat, it is too complex for me to "tell it like it is." I can only suggest that here at least is how the Southern Congressmen's defiance of the Supreme Court joined with matters which bemused my writer's waking mind in Rome; this is how the incident "dreamed." For a writer who depends upon the imagination for his insights and his judgments, perhaps this is usually the way. Current events and events from the past, both personal and historical, ever collide within his interior life—either to be jumbled in the chaos of dream, or brought to ordered significance through the forms and techniques of his art. Following my defeat with the essay, I returned to my novel—which, by the way, has as its central incident the assassination of a Senator.

*Rome 1956*
*New York 1965.*

*July 31, 1976*

## Black Cops in the South

*Paul Delaney*

I first became aware of the police when I was a boy of 7 or 8 in Montgomery, Ala. Their faces were always white; their reputation, bad. It was meant to be that way. In those days that kind of knowledge just sort of came to you. From somewhere, I learned that two Montgomery plainclothes men were known to slap blacks around for no apparent reason other than to put the fear of God in all of us. And if a few slaps didn't do the job, those two men were ready to kill blacks. That pair, and all policemen, were to be avoided at any cost. I can't remember having a single encounter with a policeman when I was a youngster, not even to ask directions.

One incident sticks in my mind: I was bicycling with a friend on a dry, intensely hot Montgomery day, when his uncle drove past, blew his horn and waved to us. Suddenly a police car appeared, pulled his uncle's car over and asked to see his driver's license.

The uncle was a quiet, handsome insurance salesman whom I admired because he always wore a shirt and tie. When he asked why he had been stopped, the officer reached through the window and slapped him, yelling, "Shut up, nigger." My friend and I turned and rode away. We never said a word about the incident to each other or his uncle.

Nevertheless, my contact with Southern white officers was mild, compared to the direct abuse suffered by other blacks. That kind of experience was what accounted for the deep distrust that many blacks harbored against the police, a distrust that continues to this day in some black communities.

When the civil rights movement began in 1960, there were few blacks on Southern police forces and those few were essentially powerless. Departments that did employ any blacks kept them from patrolling in white neighborhoods or in downtown areas and denied them the authority to arrest whites. Being a policeman under those conditions was a frustrating and at times humiliating job.

Today almost every Southern city with a sizable black population has black officers on its police force. They work at downtown intersections, ride side by side with white officers, and arrest any lawbreaker, anywhere. The image of black Southern cops has changed radically from that of a tightly constrained force whose sole duty was to keep the black ghetto in its place to that of dignified, disciplined officers expected and able to serve the entire community. The change—in image and reality—has been a major factor in the South's emergence into a new era of race relations.

A decade or so ago, black policemen were in effect amateur social workers. They cooled tempers in honky-tonks and bars, patched up family quarrels, tried their best to avoid making an arrest. When they did arrest someone, they usually could not transport their prisoner to jail; that job was for a white officer. And when black cops went to court to testify in a case, they were often treated disrespectfully by the judges and other court officials who theoretically were part of the same structure of law enforcement and justice.

As Southern blacks achieved the vote and political power, especially in the rural areas, the first offices they sought were the law-enforcement positions. In predominantly black Lowndes County, Ala., blacks seemed satisfied with taking over the post of sheriff, leaving the white minority to run the rest of the county, as it always had. Sheriff John Hulett says the county had a notorious history of brutality and lynchings; therefore, controlling the sheriff's office "was a high priority and very important for us to get whites off our backs so blacks could walk down the road without fear."

The change has produced a different breed of black cop. Wearing his Afro hairdo as a symbol, he fully expects to participate in all operations of the department and to take advantage of every opportunity, from choice assignments to promotions all the way up the command ladder. "We took more crap than the younger blacks will take today," admits J.D. Hudson, former policeman and now director of the Atlanta Bureau of Correctional Services. To press his expectations and demands, the young black cop of today is organized into black patrolmen's groups in many cities, and he has taken legal steps and other action, such as through the United States Equal Employment Opportunity Commission, to place more blacks on the force and promote those already there.

Ironically, the advances they have made in the station house have created problems for these cops in the black community, where a decade ago they were respected, sympathized with, and welcomed as a happy change from their racist counterparts. During the early 1970s, and to a lesser degree today, the positive image of the black policeman has been tarnished by the suspicions of his friends and neighbors. Activists often accuse black cops of selling out to the white man and joining in the suppression of black rights and aspirations. For veterans of the upward struggle within the police ranks, this has been a bitter pill.

The Joint Center for Political Studies, a Washington-based research organization, reports that in 1975 only Florida, North Carolina and South Carolina, of the traditional eleven Southern states, were without a single black elected law-enforcement official (if the Border States were included to make up the seventeen states of the Old Confederacy, Oklahoma would be added to the list of those without such officials). Atlanta stands alone among major cities, North or South, in having a black police chief, black public safety director and blacks in control of police decision making.

In a way, Atlanta almost single-handedly set the tone for change in the South. The city served as headquarters of the early civil rights movement when both the Southern Christian Leadership Conference of Dr. Martin Luther King Jr., and the youngsters of the Student Non-Violent Coordinating Committee chose it as the base for their operations. By the early 1960s, Atlanta's black leadership had already achieved a status and sense of political power that their opposite numbers in some cities are still struggling for today.

Herbert T. Jenkins was police chief of Atlanta when the change began. Now retired, he recalled recently that blacks were pressing the administration of Mayor William B. Hartsfield, just as they did his predecessor, to break the tradition of black tokenism on the police force in return for the support the blacks had provided, and in recognition of their growing political power.

"Finally, an ordinance was introduced to the Board of Aldermen to hire eight Negro officers, but the board refused to vote on it until the chief made a recommendation," Jenkins said. "It was a major controversy. The Ku Klux Klan filed a suit to try to prevent it, but the Georgia Supreme Court wisely ruled that it was an administrative matter for the Atlanta Police Department.

"Even some blacks didn't want black officers. These were just backward-thinking people who had been adversely affected by the system of segregation. The pressure on me was tremendous; I got all kinds of threatening calls. . . . One caller said he was going to shoot me on sight. I told him, 'if you shoot at me, you'd better hit me first, you S.O.B., because if you don't I'll kill you.'

"We made it very clear that the Mayor, the aldermen and the city were behind the decision. I made the recommendation, but I softened it by saying it was only on a temporary basis and the eight men would patrol only in the black community."

J.D. Hudson was one of the eight. So was Howard Baugh, now a major on the force. Hudson, a thin, wiry and ambitious college student, did not want to be a cop but urged his fellow students to take the examinations for the force. They insisted that he practice what he preached. He came out with top scores, and accepted the job at the urging of black leaders in the community. Baugh, on the other hand, was cut out to be a cop. He had been a Marine sergeant in World War II, and had the demeanor and temperament of a drill instructor. He was a man used to taking and giving orders, an opinionated person. He was also able to listen and he was patient—traits that have served him well as a policeman.

The eight blacks on the force became immediate celebrities in the black community, but were looked upon with scorn by many whites, including some of their fellow officers. Hudson says bluntly: "The department was racist. Most of the white officers had a KKK mentality. They didn't speak to us or recognize us as policemen. They were hostile. They encouraged blacks to attack us and to file complaints against us. A white officer once arrested a black officer.

"White officers provided us with no help at all, except for the white sergeant who was put in command of us. In court, which was segregated, we sometimes found that, in our cases, white policemen showed up as defense witnesses. We couldn't wear uniforms off duty, and we were not allowed in the police station."

The contingent of eight assembled and held roll call in the basement of the Butler Street YMCA, four blocks from Police Headquarters.

"We had a prescribed route from the Y to the black community and we couldn't deviate from it," Hudson continued. "We couldn't respond to calls downtown or 'officer in trouble' calls. We were not given squad cars until the mid-1950s, and then they gave us the old cars when white officers got new ones. As a matter of fact, the department changed colors from black to white cruisers and we got the old black ones that were not repainted.

"In the mid-fifties, we moved from the basement of the Y to the old horse barn after the new station was built. They cut out a special door for us to keep us from coming in contact with whites. By then, we were allowed to bring our own prisoners to jail.

"White patrolmen called us 'boy' and expected us to say 'sir' to them. They felt they could give us orders. When four of us made detective, we were assigned seats in the detective assembly, but we were not allowed to participate in the discussions. We had to do our own typing cause we couldn't use the white female clerks and typists. That was no problem—we could type better anyway."

The commander of the black squad was the late Earl Brooks, a sergeant at the time. Chief Jenkins hand-picked Sergeant Brooks as one of the few whites on the force who he felt could be fair and win the respect and confidence of the black policemen and community. Q.V. Williamson, a black real estate executive and now City Councilman, says Brooks was "different" from others on the force, in that "he had a sensitivity to the black community."

As a result, Brooks was ostracized by the rest of the white department. "He was the buffer between them and us, and he took a lot of abuse," Hudson remarks. "He was not highly educated, but he was human and humane. He was completely on our side, and I'm still not certain if he was driven to that position by the reaction of white officers or whether he felt it deep down."

But it was in the black community that the officers received their greatest consolation. Says Howard Baugh, now soon to retire from a police career he describes as "the most rewarding any person could have": "We were celebrities. We were recognized in the community everywhere we went. Police officer was considered a good job, so we enjoyed status. We had the support of leaders and the people, and this made policing the community easier for us."

Baugh says that, as detectives, he and his partner, C.J. Perry, one of the original eight and now a captain, solved "every single case we worked on, and we had a lot of help and cooperation from the community. The people wanted to help us to succeed. There wasn't the animosity against us that there was against white officers."

Both the black community and black cops got a major psychological lift is 1961, when Jenkins issued an order permitting black cops to arrest whites. He had been in the middle of a raging controversy over the issue, with the black community on one side and small but vociferous white groups on the other.

"It was nearly as controversial as the original hiring of Negro policemen," Jenkins recalls. "There had been a lot of borderline cases, but the black officers were arresting whites. I got a call one night from a couple of them who had found a black prostitute and white man in bed and the officers wanted to know how to handle it. Also, a Klansman called me and asked me how I would like it if my wife was arrested by a black officer. I told him, 'Hell, I wouldn't want her arrested by a white officer either.' " The black cops made the arrest.

With that victory and with the civil rights movement in full swing, law enforcement in the South moved almost overnight into a new era, with Atlanta setting an example for the rest of the region.

Greenville, Miss., is a quiet, clean delta town on the Mississippi River. Although it was caught up in the tide of "the Movement," with numerous civil rights demonstrations, the town never suffered the notoriety of Jackson, or Selma, or Albany. Police Chief Frank C. Skinner says the town has had blacks on the force since the 1940s. He says there were eight on a force of fifty-five in 1966. At present nineteen of the seventy-one officers are black.

C.G. Ward, a black Greenville attorney, says the racial climate in the delta "always was much better than the rest of Mississippi and some other places is the South." He gives much of the credit to the local newspaper, the *Delta Democrat-Times*, and to Bill Burnlee, the current Mayor who was then police chief. Burnlee kept the police from making mass arrests and from creating major confrontations. He kept the lines of communication open between blacks and whites. "He knew that local business couldn't stand a boycott and didn't want any problems. When he ran for mayor, he got 80 per cent of the black vote."

Chief Skinner, 37, a cop since 1962, says he has witnessed a significant change in the make-up of county and town law-enforcement units in that section of the delta. "I can't think of an agency in this area that doesn't have at least one black"—in contrast to a decade or so ago when most had none. The highest ranking black officer on the Greenville force today is a lieutenant. However, the acceptance of Greenville blacks in law enforcement contrasts with their acceptance in other areas. Education, for example. As blacks in the town of 45,000 put "support public schools" bumper stickers on their cars, whites continue to flock to such private, segregated schools as the Central Delta Academy and the Leland Academy.

• • •

Greenville's experience with racism in law enforcement is mild compared to that of Jackson, the state capital. Ed Wansley, 32, a plain-clothes man with the youth division of the Jackson Police Department, remembers when blacks would cross to the other side of the street rather than pass a white policeman walking down Lynch Street. Wansley himself once took part in demonstrations, and was arrested during protests. He never thought he would wind up on the force he once considered ultra-repressive.

"But in 1971 I was living in Philadelphia, and the company I was working for folded," Wansley says. "I called my brother in Jackson and was told that things had changed 180 degrees. I came back, filled out as application for police work, and to my surprise found the department pursuing me rather than the other way around. I was apprehensive because of the whole history of police-black relations. But I am now glad I did. The department is good, although there is still a lot to be done."

Wansley points out that "the younger officers, black and white, but especially white, are nothing like what they were in the old days. Then the average white officer was a big redneck bully who could use only his brawn, because he had no brains. Today, the majority of officers have a better education, many with some college and some with degrees in criminal justice. I have thirty hours to do for a degree. Blacks no longer scratch their heads and say 'yes sir, boss.' They demand respect and they get it." There is a 100 per cent change on the Jackson force.

The ranking black on Jackson's force is Sgt. Robert J. White, superintendent of the youth division. A slow-talking, soft-spoken, affable man whose stomach pokes from under the sweater he wears, he has been on the force for nine years. He saw the changes that Wansley refers to as they came. And when they did not come fast enough, he did something about it. Two years ago, Sergeant White filed a complaint about promotions with the civil rights division of the U.S. Department of Justice. And the department filed an overall suit against discrimination by the city government. The city consented to a decree providing, among other things, that for every white promotion there should be a black promotion. Promotions have been frozen recently, but Chief Lavell Tullos says he soon will announce the promotion of seven white and seven black sergeants to lieutenant. Sergeant White hopes to be among them.

During the civil rights movement, two cops in particular personified the struggle. One was black, Howard Baugh of Atlanta; the other was white, Eugene "Bull" Connor, police commissioner of Birmingham.

Night after night, national TV audiences watched those two men handle demonstrators and demonstrations. Connor, confronting mass marches in the spring of 1963, used water hoses and police dogs on groups that included elderly people and elementary-school children. It was a no-win tactic that added fuel to the demonstrations and earned Birmingham a reputation it is only now overcoming. Other police officials put their towns on the map in a similar way; Jim Clark of Selma was a notorious example.

Howard Baugh's methods were different. He developed them during intense protests against segregation at Leb's restaurant in downtown Atlanta in 1964. Baugh perhaps was representative of the positive physical presence and mental attitude of black cops during the movement. He considered his task distasteful, but did it. Better him than a white cop, he reasoned.

Seven years earlier, Baugh had performed another task that tore him up inside. He had to order the arrest of twenty-five black ministers who had violated a city ordinance by taking seats designated for whites only on city buses.

"Chief Jenkins said he wanted me to make the arrests, and I protested that I would not do it," Baugh recalls. "He then said if I didn't do it, he'd send the biggest, burliest redneck cop to do it. He knew I wouldn't allow that. I caught hell from many people in the black community, and I felt like hell over it. But the irony of the whole thing was that it was all staged, I learned later. It was a setup between city and black leaders to get a test case to take to court. Jenkins knew that, but he didn't tell me."

Jenkins later chose Baugh to take command of the units at Leb's, the biggest assignment a black officer had yet been given. "We didn't run in with night sticks and pistols drawn," Baugh says. "We allowed those demonstrators who did not want to go to jail to leave. We didn't drag them by the hair to paddy wagons, and we kept away Klan demonstrators.

"But I still felt like hell. I had a sense of guilt in one respect and a sense of dedication in another. I felt bad about arresting black folks who were demonstrating at a restaurant that was conducting business unconstitutionally."

Another assignment Baugh had was guarding Dr. King when the rights leader was in Atlanta. Baugh disagreed with demonstrations, but felt their goals were honorable. He also disagreed with Dr. King, especially when the leader came out against the war. When the Marine veteran could no longer restrain himself, he went to Dr. King. "I told him I was disenchanted with him for coming out against the war. I thought we had a right to be in Vietnam. I asked him how the hell could he advocate people not to fight for their freedom. . . .

"He said that if he were going to be an advocate of nonviolence, he had to go all the way; therefore he could not advocate nonviolence in this country and fighting in Vietnam.

"When I left him, something came over me. I was a completely changed man, even my views on policing. For example, when I was arresting a person I felt I had to be absolutely right in taking away this person's freedom."

As the civil rights movement turned more militant in the middle and late 1960s, black cops found themselves in a predicament they had not faced seriously before: to black militants, the blue uniform became an ugly symbol, and black faces in blue were as much "pigs" as their white counterparts. "It really got nasty for us," Baugh recalled. "It took getting used to, being spat on and called a pig. I didn't mind whites doing it, but it really hurt when blacks said it."

At the same time that they were haranguing black cops, however, militants were also demanding community control of police and calling for more black policemen. The pressure paid off. Almost every department stepped up its recruitment of blacks. Some of the additions to the force inevitably came from the ranks of those making the demands, thus bringing to the force a different breed of officer, and a different attitude toward race. Recently, a major issue in Jackson was the complaint by black cops about discrimination in assignment of interracial details: white superior officers did not hesitate to team up black females and white male officers, but would not assign a black male and white female together. Chief Tullos says he solved the matter by issuing an order barring discrimination in any assignment.

Older black officers feel they laid the groundwork that made it easier and smoother for the younger generation. And some of the old-timers feel they paid their dues in both the white and black communities. Says Baugh: "My family caught hell. It was most difficult for my son to decide which side he wanted to be on. He tried the Black Panther side, and then he tried the police side. He's been a cop now for seven years.

"Our social life was cut down 99 per cent, but my wife never whimpered. She stayed with it, and still does. It was a loneliness very few men have to live with. But it was something that had to be done."

*September 29, 1979*

## Open Letter to the Born Again

*James Baldwin*

I met Martin Luther King Jr. before I met Andrew Young. I know that Andy and I met only because of Martin. Andy was, in my mind, and not because he ever so described himself, Martin's "right-hand man." He was present—absolutely present. He saw what was happening. He took upon himself his responsibility for knowing what he knew, and for seeing what he saw. I have heard Andy attempt to describe himself only once: when he was trying to clarify something about me, to someone else. So, I learned, one particular evening, what his Christian ministry meant to him. Let me spell that out a little.

The text comes from the New Testament, Matthew 25:40: *Inasmuch as ye have done it unto one of the least of these my brethren, ye have done it unto me.*

I am in the strenuous and far from dull position of having news to deliver to the Western world—for example: *black* is not a synonym for *slave*. Do not, I counsel you, attempt to defend yourselves against this stunning, unwieldy and undesired message. You will hear it again: indeed, this is the only message the Western world is likely to be hearing from here on out.

I put it in this somewhat astringent fashion because it is necessary, and because I speak, now, as the grandson of a slave, a direct descendant of a born-again Christian. *My conversion*, as Countee Cullen puts it, *came high priced/I belong to Jesus Christ.* I am also speaking as an ex-minister of the Gospel, and, therefore, as one of the born again. I was instructed to feed the hungry, clothe the naked and visit those in prison. I am far indeed from my youth, and from my father's house, but I have not forgotten these instructions, and I pray upon my soul that I never will. The people who call themselves "born again" today have simply become members of the richest, most exclusive private club in the world, a club that the man from Galilee could not possibly hope—or wish—to enter.

*Inasmuch as ye have done it unto the least of these my brethren, ye have done it unto me.* That is a hard saying. It is hard to live with that. It is a merciless description of our responsibility for one another. It is that hard light under which one makes the moral choice. That the Western world has forgotten that such a thing as the moral choice exists, my history, my flesh, and my soul bear witness. So, if I may say so, does the predicament into which the world's most celebrated born-again Christian has managed to hurl Mr. Andrew Young.

Let us not belabor the obvious truth that what the Western world calls an "energy" crisis ineptly disguises what happens when you can no longer control markets, are chained to your colonies (instead of vice versa), are running out of slaves (and can't trust those you think you still have), can't, upon rigorously sober reflection, really send the Marines, or the Royal Navy, anywhere, or risk a global war, have no allies—only business partners, or "satellites"—and have broken every promise you ever made, anywhere, to anyone. I know what I am talking about: my grandfather never got the promised "forty acres, and a mule," the Indians who survived *that* holocaust are either on reservations or dying in the streets, and not a single treaty between the United States and the Indian was ever honored. That is quite a record.

Jews and Palestinians know of broken promises. From the time of the Balfour Declaration (during World War I) Palestine was under five British mandates, and England promised the land back and forth to the Arabs or the Jews, depending on which horse seemed to be in the lead. The Zionists—as distinguished from the people known as Jews—using, as someone put it, the "available political machinery," i.e., colonialism, e.g., the British Empire—promised the British that, if the territory were given to them, the British Empire would be safe forever.

But absolutely no one cared about the Jews, and it is worth observing that non-Jewish Zionists are very frequently anti-Semitic. The white Americans responsible for sending black slaves to Liberia (where they are still slaving for the Firestone Rubber Plantation) did not do this to set them free. They despised them, and they wanted to get rid of them. Lincoln's intention was not to "free" the slaves but to "destabilize" the Confederate Government by giving their slaves reason to "defect." The Emancipation Proclamation freed, precisely, those slaves who were not under the authority of the President of what could not yet be insured as a Union.

It has always astounded me that no one appears to be able to make the connection between Franco's Spain, for example, and the Spanish Inquisition; the role of the Christian church or—to be brutally precise, the Catholic Church—in the history of Europe, and the fate of the Jews; and the role of the Jews in Christendom and the discovery of America. For the discovery of America coincided with the Inquisition, and the expulsion of the Jews from Spain. Does no one see the connection between *The Merchant of Venice* and *The Pawnbroker*? In both of these works, as though no time had passed, the Jew is portrayed as doing the Christian's usurious dirty work. The first white man I ever saw was the Jewish manager who arrived to collect the rent, and he collected the rent because he did not own the building. I never, in fact, saw any of the people who owned any of the buildings in which we scrubbed and suffered for so long, until I was a grown man and famous. None of them were Jews.

And I was not stupid: the grocer and the druggist were Jews, for example, and they were very very nice to me, and to us. They were never really white, for me. The cops were white. The city was white. The threat was white, and God was white. Not for even a single split second in my life did the despicable, utterly cowardly accusation that "the Jews killed Christ" reverberate. I knew a murderer when I saw one, and the people who were trying to kill me were not Jews.

But the state of Israel was not created for the salvation of the Jews; it was created for the salvation of the Western interests. This is what is becoming clear (I must say that it was always clear to me). The Palestinians have been paying for the British colonial policy of "divide and rule" and for Europe's guilty Christian conscience for more than thirty years.

Finally: there is absolutely—repeat: *absolutely*—no hope of establishing peace in what Europe so arrogantly calls the Middle East (how in the world would Europe know? having so dismally failed to find a passage to India) without dealing with the Palestinians. The collapse of the Shah of Iran not only revealed the depth of the pious Carter's concern for "human rights," it also revealed who supplied oil to Israel, and to whom Israel supplied arms. It happened to be, to spell it out, white South Africa.

Well. The Jew, in America, is a white man. He has to be, since I am a black man, and, as he supposes, his only protection against the fate which drove him to America. But he is still doing the Christian's dirty work, and black men know it.

My friend, Mr. Andrew Young, out of tremendous love and courage, and with a silent, irreproachable, indescribable nobility, has attempted to ward off a holocaust, and I proclaim him a hero, betrayed by cowards.

*November 1, 1980*

## Notes on the House of Bondage

*James Baldwin*

Gabriel's trumpet is a complex metaphor. Poor Gabriel is not only responsible for *when we dead awaken*—heavy enough—but he must also blow that trumpet *to wake the children sleeping.*

The children are always ours, every single one of them, all over the globe; and I am beginning to suspect that whoever is incapable of recognizing this may be incapable of morality. Or, I am saying, in other words, that we, the elders, are the only models children have. What we see in the children is what they have seen in us—or, more accurately perhaps, what they *see* in us.

I, too, find that a rather chilling formulation, but I can find no way around it. How am I, for example, to explain to any of my tribe of nieces and nephews and great-nieces and great-nephews how it happens that in a nation so boastfully autonomous as the United States we are reduced to the present Presidential candidates? I certainly do not want them to believe that Carter or Reagan—*or* Anderson—are the best people this country can produce. That despair would force me onto the road taken by the late, Guyana-based Jim Jones. But there they are, the pea-nut farmer and the third-rate, failed, ex–Warner Brothers contract player, both as sturdy and winning as Wheaties, and as well equipped to run the world as I am to run a post office.

There they are. And there is, also, the question, *Who you going to vote for, Uncle Jimmy?*

It can be said, of course—and let me say it before you do—that I am speaking as a black American. My testimony can, therefore, be dismissed out of hand by reason of my understandable (thank you) but quite unreasonable bitterness.

Well, I have had my bitter moments, certainly, days and ways, but I do not think that I can usefully be described as a bitter man. I would not be trying to write this if I were, for the bitter do not, mainly, speak: they, suddenly and quite unpredictably, act. The bitter can be masters, too, at telling you what you want to hear because they know what you want to hear. And how do they know that?

Well, some of them know it because they must raise their children and bring them to a place, somehow, where the American guile and cowardice cannot destroy them. No black citizen (!) of what is left of Harlem supposes that either Carter, or Reagan, or Anderson has any concern for them at all, except as voters—that is, to put it brutally, except as instruments, or dupes—and, while one hates to say that the black citizens are right, one certainly cannot say that they are wrong.

One has merely to look up and down the streets of Harlem; walk through the streets and into what is left of the houses; consider the meaning of this willed, inhuman and criminal devastation, and look into the faces of the children. *Who you going to vote for, Uncle Jimmy?*

*John Brown*, I have sometimes been known to say, but that flippant rage is, of course, no answer.

But, if we're to change our children's lives and help them to liberate themselves from the jails and hovels—the mortal danger—in which our countrymen have placed us, the vote does not appear to be the answer, either. It has certainly not been the answer until now.

Here one finds oneself on treacherous ground indeed. I am, legally anyway, an adult, a somewhat battered survivor of this hard place, and have never expected my power to vote to have any effect whatever on my life, and it hasn't. On the other hand, I have been active in voter registration drives in the South because the acquisition of the vote, there and then, and even if only for local aims, was too crucial and profound a necessity even to be argued. Nor can it be denied that the sheer tenacity of the black people in the South, their grace under pressure (to put it far too mildly) and the simple fact of their presence in the voting booth profoundly challenged, if it did not expose, the obscene Southern mythology.

Thus, though there is certainly no New South yet, the old one has no future, and neither does the "old" North. The situation of the black American is a direct (and deliberate) result of the collusion between the North and South and the Federal Government. A black man in this country does not live under a two-party system but a four-party system. There is the Republican Party in the South, and there is the Republican

Party in the North; there is the Democratic Party in the North and the Democratic Party in the South. These entities are Tweedledum and Tweedledee as concerns the ways they have been able, historically, to manipulate the black presence, the black need. At the same time, both parties were (are) protected from the deepest urgencies of black need by the stance of the Federal Government, which could (can) always justify both parties, and itself, by use of the doctrine of "States' rights."

In the South, then, the Republican Party was the *nigra's* friend, and, in the North, it was the Democrats who lovingly dried our tears. But, however liberal Northern Democrats might seem to be, nothing was allowed to menace the party unity—certainly not niggers—with the result that the presumed or potential power of the black vote in the North was canceled out by the smirk on the faces of the candidates in the South. The party had won—was in—and we were out. What it came to was that, as long as blacks in the South could not vote, blacks in the North could have nothing to vote for. A very clever trap, which only now, and largely because of the black vote in the South, may be beginning to be sprung.

The American institutions are all bankrupt in that they are unable to deal with the present—resembling nothing so much as Lot's wife. When Americans look out on the world, they see nothing but dark and menacing strangers who appear to have no sense of rhythm at all, nor any respect or affection for white people; and white Americans really do not know what to make of all this, except to increase the defense budget.

This panic-stricken saber rattling is also for the benefit of the domestic darker brother. The real impulse of the bulk of the American people toward their former slave is lethal: if he cannot be used, he should be made to disappear. When the American people, Nixon's no-longer-silent majority, revile the Haitian, Cuban, Turk, Palestinian, Iranian, they are really cursing the nigger, and the nigger had better know it.

The vote does not work for a black American the way it works for a white one, for the despairingly obvious reason that whites, in general, are welcomed to America, and blacks, in general, are not. Yet, risking a seeming contradiction, one may go further and point out that America's egalitarian image is very important to American self-esteem. Therefore, blacks from the West Indies, say, or Africa, who arrive with no social or political quarrels with the United States, who have already been formed by the island, or village community, and who bring their mercantile skills with them, are likely to fare much better here than Sambo does—for a brief and melancholy season. Since the entire country is bizarre beyond belief, the black immigrant does not quarrel with its customs, considering that these customs have nothing to do with him. He sticks to his kith and kin, and saves his pennies, and is the apple of the white American eye, for he proves that the Yankee-Puritan virtues are all that one needs to prosper in this brave new world.

This euphoria lasts, at most, a generation. In my youth, the West Indians, who assured American blacks that *they*, the West Indians, had never been slaves, ran their stores, saved their pennies, went bankrupt and, as a community, disappeared—or, rather, became a part of the larger black community. Later on, the Puerto Ricans were hurled into this fire and, after the brief, melancholy and somewhat violent season, we began to compare notes, and share languages, and now here come, among others, the Haitians, and the beginning of the end of the doctrine of divide-and-rule, at least as concerns the dark people of the West.

The white person of the West is quite another matter. His presence in America, in spite of vile attacks on "the foreign-born," poses no real problem. Within a generation, at most two, he is at home in his new country and climbing that ladder. If there is trouble in the Irish, Italian or Polish ward, say, the trouble can be contained and eliminated because the demands of these white people do not threaten the fabric of American society. This proved to be true during even the bloodiest of the worker-industrial clashes: white workers opted for being white first and workers second—and, in the land of the free and the home of the brave, who said that they had to remain workers? It was easy enough to turn the white worker against the black worker by threatening to put the black man in the white man's job, at a lower salary. Once the white worker had fallen into this trap, the rest was child's play: the black was locked out of the unions, the unions and big business got in bed together and, whenever there was trouble in the ghetto, white America, as one man, cried, *What does the Negro want?* Billy clubs, tear gas, guns and cold-blooded murder imposed a sullen order, and a grateful Republic went back to sleep.

This has been the American pattern for all of the years that I have been on earth, and, of course, for generations before that, and I have absolutely no reason to believe that this leopard has changed his spots. Nixon was elected, after all, received his "mandate," by means of the Omnibus Crime Bill and the "Safe Streets Act" ("safe streets" meaning *keep the nigger in his place*) and his crony, the late and much lamented Gov. Nelson Rockefeller, who was responsible for the Attica slaughter, passed the Hitlerian "No-Knock Stop and Frisk Law," which brought every black person in New York a little closer to the madhouse and the grave. The Nixon career was stopped by Watergate, God be praised, and by the intervention of a black man, thank our ancestors; but Attorney General John Mitchell had already corralled several thousands of us, black and white, in a ballpark.

The United States is full of ballparks. My black vote, which has not yet purchased my autonomy, may yet, if I choose to use it, keep me out of the ballpark long enough to figure out some other move. Or for the children to make a move. Or for aid to come from somewhere. My vote will probably not get me a job or a home or help me through school or prevent another Vietnam or a third World War, but it may keep me here long enough for me to see, and use, the turning of the tide—for the tide has got to turn. And, since I am not the only black man to think this way, if Carter is re-elected, it will be by means of the black vote, and it will not be a vote for Carter. It will be a coldly calculated risk, a means of buying time. Perhaps only black people realize this, but we are dying, here, out of all proportion to our numbers, and with no respect to age, dying in the streets, in the madhouse, in the tenement, on the roof, in jail and in the Army. This is not by chance, and it is not an act of God. It is a result of the action of the American institutions, all of which are racist: it is revelatory of the real and helpless impulse of most white Americans toward black people.

Therefore, in a couple of days, blacks may be using the vote to outwit the Final Solution. Yes. The Final Solution. No black person can afford to forget that the history of this country is genocidal, from where the buffalo once roamed to where our ancestors were slaughtered (from New Orleans to New York, from Birmingham to Boston) and to the Caribbean to Hiroshima and Nagasaki to Saigon. Oh, yes, let freedom ring.

*Why are you voting for Carter, Uncle Jimmy?* Well, don't, first of all, take this as an endorsement. It's meant to be a hard look at the options, which, however, may no longer exist by the time you read this, may no longer exist as I write.

I lived in California when Ronald Reagan was Governor, and that was a very ugly time—the time of the Black Panther harassment, the beginning (and the end) of the Soledad Brothers, the persecution, and trial, of Angela Davis. That, all that, and much more, but what I really found unspeakable about the man was his contempt, his brutal contempt, for the poor.

Perhaps because he is a Southerner, there lives in Carter still—I think—an ability to be tormented. This does not necessarily mean much, so many people preferring torment to action, or responsibility, and it is, furthermore, a very real question (for some; some would say that it's not a question at all) as to how much of Carter belongs to Carter. But if he can still be tormented, he can be made to pause—the machinery can be made to pause—and we will have to find a way to use that pause.

It is terror that informs the American political and social scene— the terror of leaving the house of bondage. It isn't a terror of seeing *black* people leave the house of bondage, for white people think that they *know* that this cannot *really* happen, not even to Leontyne Price, or Mohammad Ali, who are, after all, "exceptions," with white blood, and mortal. No, white people had a much better time in the house of bondage than we did, and God bless their souls, they're going to miss it—all that adulation, adoration, ease, with nothing to do but fornicate, kill Indians, breed slaves and make money. Oh, there were rough times, too, as *Shane, True Grit* and *Rocky* inform us, but the rules of the game were clear, and the rewards demanded nothing more complex than stamina. God was a businessman, like all "real" Americans, and understood that "business was business." The American innocence was unassailable, fixed forever, for it was not a crime to kill a black or a red or a yellow man. On the contrary, it might be, and was most often so considered, a duty. It was not a crime to rape a black or red or yellow woman—it was sport; besides, *niggers ought to be glad we pump some white blood into their kids every once in a while.* The lowest white man was more exalted than the most articulate or eminent black: an exceedingly useful article of faith both for the owners of the Southern fields and the bosses in the Northern sweatshops, who worked this exalted creature past senility to death.

Thus, what the house of bondage accomplished for what we will call the classic white American was the destruction of his moral sense, except in relation to whites. But it also destroyed his sense of reality and, therefore, his sense of white people had to be as compulsively one-dimensional as his vision of blacks. The result is that white Americans have been one another's jailers for generations, and the attempt at individual maturity is the loneliest and rarest of the American endeavors. (This may also be why a "boyish" look is a very decided advantage in the American political and social arena.)

Well, the planet is destroying the American fantasies; which does not give the Americans the right to destroy the planet. I don't know if it is possible to speak coherently concerning what my disturbed countrymen want, but I hazard that, although the Americans are certainly capable of precipitating Armageddon, their most desperate desire is to make time stand still. If time stands still, it can neither judge nor accuse nor exact payment; and, indeed, this is precisely the bargain the black presence was expected to strike in the white Republic. It is why the black face had always to be a happy face.

Recently, the only two black shows on Broadway were minstrel shows. There was a marvelous current between the blacks on the stage and the blacks in the audience. Both knew why the white audience was there, and to watch white audiences being reassured by a minstrel show can be grotesque and sorrowful beyond belief. But the minstrel show is really no different from the TV screen which celebrates, night after night and year after year and decade after decade, the slaughter of the Native American and pretends (in spite of *Roots*, which demands a separate assessment) that the black enslavement never occurred.

Well. It did occur, and *is* occurring all up and down America, as I write, and is crossing borders and being exported to various "under-developed" portions of the globe. But this endeavor cannot succeed, with force or without it, because the center of the earth has shifted. The British Prime Minister, for example, is a grotesque anachronism, and the world is not holding its breath waiting to see what will happen in England; England's future will be determined by what is happening in the world.

I am speaking of the breakup—the end—of the so-overextended Western empire. I am thinking of the black and nonwhite peoples who are shattering, redefining and recreating history—making all things new—simply by declaring their presence, by delivering their testimony. The empire never intended that this testimony should be heard, but, *if I hold my peace, the very stones will cry out.*

One can speak, then, of the fall of an empire at that moment when, though all of the paraphernalia of power remain intact and visible and seem to function, neither the citizen-subject within the gates nor the indescribable hordes outside it believe in the morality or the reality of the kingdom anymore—when no one, any longer, anywhere, aspires to the empire's standards.

This is the charged, the dangerous, moment, when everything must be re-examined, must be made new; when nothing at all can be taken for granted. One looks again at the word "famine." At this hour of the world's history, famine must be considered a man-made phenomenon and one looks at who is starving. There is nothing even faintly ridiculous, or unfair, in these apprehensions, which are produced by nothing less than Western history. Our former guides and masters are among the most ruthless creatures in mankind's history, slaughtering and starving one another to death long before they discovered the blacks. If the British were willing to starve Ireland to death—which they did, in order to protect the profits of British merchants—why would the West be reluctant to starve Africa out of existence? Especially since the generation facing famine now is precisely that generation that will begin the real and final liberation of Africa from Europe. It is, in any case, perfectly clear that the earth's populations can be fed if—or, rather, when—we alter our priorities. We can irrigate deserts and feed the entire earth for the price we are paying to build bombs that we will be able to use, in any event, only once; after which whoever is left will have to begin doing what I am suggesting now. It would be nice if we could, for once, make it easy on ourselves.

The elders, especially at this moment of our black-white history, are indispensable to the young, and vice versa. It is of the utmost importance, for example, that I, the elder, do not allow myself to be put on the defensive. The young, no matter how loud they get, have no real desire to humiliate their elders and, if and when they succeed in doing so, are lonely, crushed and miserable, as only the young can be.

Someone my age, for example, may be pleased and proud that Carter has blacks in his Cabinet. A younger person may wonder just what their function is in such a Cabinet. They will be keenly aware, too, that blacks called upon to represent the Republic are, very often, thereby prohibited from representing blacks. A man my age, schooled in adversity and skilled in compromise, may choose not to force the issue of defense spending versus the bleak and criminal misery of the black *and* white populations here, but a younger man may say, out loud, that he will not fight for a country that has *never* fought for him and, further, that the myth and menace of global war are nothing more and nothing less than a coward's means of distracting attention from the real crimes and concerns of this Republic. And I may have to visit him in prison, or suffer with him there—no matter. The irreducible miracle is that we have sustained each other a very long time, and come a long, long way together. We have come to the end of a language and are now about the business of forging a new one. For we have survived, children, the very last white country the world will ever see.

*December 17, 1983*

## From Rags to Rage to Art

*Patricia Vigderman*

IN SEARCH OF OUR MOTHERS' GARDENS: Womanist Prose.
*By Alice Walker*

In the title essay of this collection, Alice Walker looks at black women's experience through the lens of Virginia Woolf's remark, "Anon, who wrote so many poems without signing them, was often a woman." The heritage of black women artists, she suggests, is not anonymous literature but creations like the priceless quilt now hanging in the Smithsonian Institution, made by "an anonymous Black woman in Alabama." The uncorrected galleys I read have a brilliant typographical error: the quilt, they say, is "made of bits and pieces of worthless rage."

The conversion of rags to rage and then to art is a large part of Walker's work. The book's pervasive concern is the question of what it means to be a black Southern woman writer and heiress to all that's implied in those three adjectives. The title essay is about laying claim to that inheritance, and the title itself is quite literal: Walker's mother is so gifted a gardener that to this day perfect strangers driving by her house "ask to stand or walk among my mother's art." This essentially anonymous artistry is, like the quilt from Alabama, an alternative to madness, to the mutilated vision of the slave poet Phillis Wheatley or the blind-souled women in Jean Toomer's novel *Cane*. As the Creator in the Garden, Walker's mother conveys an idea of art that includes the ability to hang on.

The essay was originally a talk, and this image may be more powerful when called up by Walker's own voice: on the printed page it seems somewhat contrived. A much more satisfying treatment of the elder Walker's role in her daughter's creative drama is in an essay called "Beyond the Peacock: The Reconstruction of Flannery O'Connor." Here, Walker describes the trip she and her mother took to visit first the share-farmer shack in which the Walker family lived in 1952 and then

"Andalusia," the country house outside Milledgeville, Georgia, where Flannery O'Connor lived the last thirteen years of her life. The two houses are minutes apart on the same road. The coincidence is important because it was O'Connor's work that made Walker realize she would never be satisfied with a segregated literature. The essay is important because it is when Walker is following her longing for a culture that does not discriminate by race that she is most true to herself.

In "Beyond the Peacock," Walker and her mother stand in the pasture before the rotted-out, hay-filled shack that was once their home, amazed at the beautiful daffodils that now cover the yard. Alice remembers mostly misery: her segregated school, a water moccasin that frightened her, a lost cat. Her mother remembers the landlord who cheated her out of her half of the calves she had raised for him. Then she says, "Well, old house, one good thing you gave us. It was right here that I got my first washing machine!" The ordinariness of her determined optimism intensifies the cruelty of the past.

The dilemma in this essay is how a black Southern writer is to place a white one, given that they stand on opposite sides of that cruelty. "What I feel at the moment of knocking," writes Walker of approaching O'Connor's door, "is fury that someone is paid to take care of her house, though no one lives in it, and that her house still, in fact, stands, while mine . . . is slowly rotting into dust. Her house becomes—in an instant—the symbol of my own disinheritance." And yet she says O'Connor's *Mystery and Manners*, "which is primarily concerned with the moral imperatives of the serious writer of fiction, is the best of its kind I have ever read."

When Walker is balancing that paradox of social injustice and artistic integrity, she is most satisfying. What she admires about O'Connor's fiction, she explains, is that both black and white characters are demythified—"white folks without the magnolia . . . black folks without melons and superior racial patience." Walker describes her mother with that same fidelity to real life. She knows that her mother felt the same anger she herself felt at the door of Andalusia but that in her Christian cosmology, the injustice is neutralized by O'Connor's early and painful death. Walker herself doesn't have five minutes for this outlook, but she is not trying to give her mother mythic meaning here. Rather, she is doing her mother the honor of presenting her as she really is. It is quite natural, then, that her mother should have the last word. As they are leaving, Walker murmurs something about being inspired by the splendor of the peacocks that still strut the lawns of Andalusia. "They'll eat up every bloom you have, if you don't watch out," comments her mother, who sticks to the truths a garden teaches.

Alice Walker has another model, one more important to her than Flannery O'Connor: Zora Neale Hurston, whose name appears in essay after essay. What Hurston offers and what sets her apart from most other celebrities of the Harlem Renaissance (whom she referred to as the "niggerati") is her conviction that Afro-American folk culture is as rich a wellspring for art as any Anglo-American source. "Intellectual lynching" is the name she gave black artists' and critics' emulation of whites, and she repudiated the criticism of bourgeois blacks who found her (very successful) black folk musical *The Great Day* detrimental to the cause of integration. "Fawn as you will," she wrote in 1934. "Roll your eyes in ecstasy and ape [the white man's] every move, but until we have placed something upon his street-corner that is our own, we are right back where we were when they filed our iron collar off."

In spite of her achievements, Hurston died in poverty and was buried in an unmarked grave. Walker's image of that neglected, weed-choked Florida cemetery, the "Garden of the Heavenly Rest," belongs beside the picture of her mother's garden. Indeed, "Looking for Zora," which describes Walker's 1973 trip to find Hurston's grave and put a stone on it, is the real conclusion to Walker's history of the fate of black women artists.

Her account is a collection of anecdotes about Hurston's neighbors, a friend or two and a lively assistant from the funeral home that buried her, who slogs through the crackling, hissing weeds with Walker to help keep up her courage against lurking snakes. The trip left Walker emotionally mute; she leaves the conclusion of the essay to her subject. On whether being black is "a lowdown dirty deal," Hurston wrote, "No, I do not weep at the world—I am too busy sharpening my oyster knife."

Hurston died in 1960, the year Walker's mother bought a television set. That enabled Alice, a high school student, to see Martin Luther King Jr. being hustled into a police wagon in handcuffs. The sight changed her life, focusing in an instant the idea of fighting for one's inheritance. Her essay "Choice: A Tribute to Dr. Martin Luther King, Jr." stresses a freedom that is different from Hurston's self-assured and lonely independence. It's a vision that sees an unmarked grave as a specifically political consequence.

King, she says, gave young Southern blacks the choice of staying home, the choice not to go north to seek their fortune, not to accept disinheritance. Where Hurston saw her black community as irrevocably separate from white culture (and a good thing, too), the black community for Walker has been one engaged in a struggle with white America. An important part of her adult life was spent in the civil rights movement, and her perception of the relationship between America and its black citizens is much more openly angry than Hurston's.

While it gives her great satisfaction to see a black teen-ager happily swimming in the pool of a motel formerly for whites only, her memories of how bitter was the battle to gain that simple acceptance finally drove her from the South. In "Looking to the Side, and Back," she contends that the black community was wrong to talk "only about the bravery, never about the cost," wrong to refuse to deal with any personal damage that did not fit the black self-image or the political morality of the time.

That willingness to cut through the jargon of race relations accounts for her unorthodox demand that black *women's* reality be honored as something in its own right. She has invented the word "womanist" to describe "a black feminist or feminist of color." The nuances of the word include outrageousness, willfullness, seriousness, capableness and wholeness. It connotes an attitude that is antiracist and pleasure-loving. Walker implies that a womanist is deeper in tone than a feminist: "Womanist is to feminist as purple to lavender." Indeed, the very sound of the word is more solid.

Her definition is full of health and hope, a manifesto of what she wants for black women. It is somewhat at odds, however, with many of the most interesting observations in the essays. Walker argues that black women should be free *not* to be strong. The invincible black woman is a staple of American mythology—both black and white— and it is damaging to black women's sense of themselves and to their sense of what they owe black men. In "A Letter to the Editor of *Ms.*," she rejects the quasi-feminist claim that black women are the "only true queens of the universe," and not just for the usual anti-pedestal reasons. Queens, she points out, are bred to know their lineage and history; black women hardly know their own mothers' lives. "I think," she says drily, "we might waive the wearing of a crown until we have at least seriously begun our work."

When Walker sticks to the truths a garden teaches, she is witty, generous and serious. She is at her best in the essays that tell her own story—"Beyond the Peacock," the ones about Hurston, the several tributes to King, the vignettes of ordinary life in the post-movement South, "Beauty: When the Other Dancer Is the Self" (the emotional history of being blind in one eye) and a long 1973 interview. In many of her public pronouncements, though, she seems to be striking atti- tudes. White American writers tend, she writes in "Saving the Life That Is Your Own,"

> to end their books and their characters' hues as if there were no better existence for which to struggle. The gloom of defeat is thick.
>
> By comparison, black writers seem always involved in a moral and/or physical struggle, the result of which is expected to be some kind of larger freedom.

That is nonsense, and her readings of the two books she uses to illus- trate the point (Kate Chopin's *The Awakening* and Hurston's *Their Eyes Were Watching God*) are so cursory as to be dishonest. She quickly moves on to a much easier point: that while Chopin is now a staple of women's literature classes, Hurston is not.

The implausibility of that passage would hardly bear pointing out were it not more than an off-the-cuff reply to an unexpected question from the audience. Walker seems to apply an imperative for dispelling "the gloom of defeat" to her own fiction, to its detriment. Although her Pulitzer Prize-winning *The Color Purple* tells a story of brutality and injustice, it succeeds because the language is so lively, the tale so rich and various that the very pleasure of reading it implies hope—indeed, a "larger freedom." But I stopped believing in both the book and the main character, Celie, every time I felt I was seeing "larger freedom" road signs. When a moral truth has been deliberately placed on the path, the reader is being treated like a fool, and when Celie becomes a mouthpiece for Walker's opinions she becomes a foolish character. By the end of the book she has changed so completely from a helpless, sexually abused peasant into the powerful center of a happy, down-home buzz that the outlines of her character are blurred.

This eagerness to make the womanist point prevents *In Search of Our Mothers' Gardens* from being wholly satisfying. The main problem for a socially conscious artist is to preserve emotional honesty when the situation seems almost to demand excess and posturing. The disappointments of this collection are perhaps an indication of how very difficult that is.

A book review, "*Gifts of Power: The Writings of Rebecca Jackson*," for instance, tells the story of a nineteenth-century black woman whose remarkable spiritual experiences and powers led her ultimately to the Shakers. It's a story that offers Walker the opportunity to discuss issues she cares about: human spiritual life, the lost history of black women, the exclusion of women from community and church leadership. Yet instead of taking up any one of those, she drifts into a tangential argument with the book's editor about whether Jackson could properly be called a lesbian, and if indeed the term lesbian is at all appropriate to describe black woman-bonding, since it probably predates Sappho and, anyway, the symbolism of Lesbos being an island is "far from positive." That all may well be true, but as the conclusion of an essay that promises more serious topics, it's only irritating.

These essays have appeared in a great range of publications: *Conditions, Ms., The Black Scholar, Mother Jones, The New York Times*; many of them were written as talks. As its piecemeal construction implies, *In Search of Our Mothers' Gardens* is not intended as a major statement of either esthetic or political thought. Nevertheless, in many of these pieces Walker avoids the larger and more difficult issues in favor of much smaller, flashy assertions. The book hasn't been assembled with the care lavished on her mother's garden, and some of the promised blooms have been eaten by the peacocks.

*May 23, 1994*

## Among Moses' Bridge-Builders

*Patricia J. Williams*

When *The Nation* asked me to write an essay on the fortieth anniversary of *Brown v. Board of Education,* I felt as though I were being called to the grandest project of my career. This is the case, after all, that shaped my life's possibilities, the case that, like a stone monument, stands for just about all the racial struggles with which this country still grapples. When *The Nation* also suggested that a conversation with the Brown family might be the focal point of such an essay, I actually got nervous. The symbolic significance of the case had definitely made them Icons of the Possible in my mind: Oliver Brown, now deceased, whose name is first in a list of many others and whose name, as a result, became the reference for all subsequent generations of discussion; Leola Brown Montgomery, Oliver Brown's widow; Linda Brown Thompson, the little girl (formerly a teacher for Head Start and now program assistant for the Brown Foundation) on whose behalf Oliver Brown sued; the middle daughter, Terry Brown Tyler; and Cheryl Brown Henderson, the youngest daughter and also an educator.

"Don't make icons of us," was just about the first thing out of Cheryl's mouth, when she finally responded to the gushy messages I left on the answering machine at the Brown Foundation, the organization she founded and heads. But . . . but . . . , I said, distinctly crestfallen.

"It was pure accident that the case bears our name," she continued, with no chance for me to argue about it. "It's just a name, it could have been a lot of people's names. It's not *our* case. Ask us about the Brown Foundation."

The foundation is an organization dedicated to "setting the record straight," as Cheryl Brown Henderson put it. "I'm afraid that a lot of people believe the lawsuit to be something that happened as a very isolated incident, when in fact there were many, many cases that preceded it. We're talking about public school cases that began back in 1849, and, in Kansas, began in 1881." I knew that, of course—"of course" only because teaching the history of civil rights is a big chunk of what I do for a living. I'm even someone who's always complaining that too often the civil rights movement has been too neatly condensed into a few lionized personalities, rather than understood as a historical stream of events. But still—this was different somehow, this was *Brown*, after all, and here I was in the presence of Legend Incarnate and, well, inquiring minds *do* want to know. Of course, I didn't quite put it that way. I just asked them to share the sustained insight and privileged perspective that residing inside the edifice of great moments in social history might bring.

"Our family came to Kansas for the railroad in 1923," said Mrs. Leola Brown patiently, apparently quite used to cutting through the exuberant excesses of questions with no borders, never mind answers. "A lot of the early African-American and Hispanic residents of Topeka came for employment purposes. The headquarters of the Santa Fe railroad were here. There were decent wages and you could be part of a union and have job security, those sorts of things."

"When did you join the N.A.A.C.P.?" I pressed, longing for detail about what, at odd moments, I caught myself thinking of as "our" story. "Were there any significant events in your life that precipitated your involvement in the case against the school board?"

"We joined for no specific incident. It was in 1948 or '49, something like that. There was nothing specific. It was everything. We were discriminated against in all phases of life. We couldn't go to the restaurants or the shows, or if we did, we had to sit in a certain place, we had to go through a certain door to get there. . . ." she trailed off.

"It wasn't only about the schools, you see, it was about all of the things that were against us, all the rejection and neglect, all the things we could not do here."

As Mrs. Leola Brown spoke, describing conditions that affected millions of blacks as well as her family, I understood why her daughters were so insistent on my not making this story into an exceptional one. It was a story that couldn't, shouldn't be made into private property; it was an exemplary story, but far from unique.

My family too joined the N.A.A.C.P. not because of a great event but because of all the ordinary daily grinding little events that made life hard in the aggregate. I knew the back of the bus stories, the peanut gallery stories, the baggage car stories, the having to go to the bathroom in the woods stories—the myriad, mundane, nearly invisible yet monumentally important constraints that circumscribed blacks, and not only in the South.

My father, who grew up in Savannah, Georgia, during the 1920s and '30s, remembers not only the inconveniences but the dangers of being black under Jim Crow. "You had to be careful of white people; you got out of the way, or you'd get hurt, immediately. If you saw a white person coming, you got off the sidewalk. Don't make too much noise. Know which side of the street to walk on. You were always conscious of the difference. The big conversation in all 'colored' homes was just that, color. It affected everybody."

"That's exactly why Brown is indeed 'our' story," advised a friend of mine who, being fifteen or so years older than I, was old enough to have worked for N.A.A.C.P. causes and gone on enough marches to have worn out many pairs of shoes. "The civil rights movement was all about ordinary people who weren't necessarily on the road to Damascus. If some lent their names, others lent their backs, or their expertise or their lives. It was life-threatening work after all, so nobody did it to get their name up in lights; you did it because there was no alternative. Neither fame nor anonymity existed as issues per se—that's come later, as the country seems to have sorted out who it's going to remember and what it will forget. It was about group survival. You were always thinking about what would make it better for the children."

I pressed the Browns about this centrality of segregation in people's lives. Segregation affected most aspects of daily life, they explained, but they noted that the situation in Kansas was not exactly like what was going on in many Southern states. The neighborhood in which the Browns lived, for example, was fully integrated at the time the suit was initiated, and unlike many children even today, Linda Brown, in the wake of the case, was able to finish her education at integrated schools. The Browns describe most of the neighborhoods in Topeka as having been pretty stable over time—although the Browns' old neighborhood and the all-white school that was the object of the suit no longer exist. "The highway has come through." Although Topeka did undergo some of the divisive and segregating effects of urban renewal programs, the Browns say Topeka did not undergo major upheavals during the 1960s, as did most Northern cities where white flight changed "urban centers" into "inner cities" overnight.

How, I asked, does one reconcile the racism that produced the rigid school segregation in Topeka yet permitted people to live side by side? "You have to understand Kansas history," said Cheryl Brown Henderson. "The era that won the state the name of 'Bleeding Kansas' was born out of the battle about whether it would be a slave state or not. . . . When Kansas became a free state, it became a kind of promised land for people of African descent. They started moving in great numbers westward, and out of the South." She described the struggle to integrate schools as well over a hundred years old, typified by such compromises as when "the Kansas legislature in the 1870s enacted a law saying that if you were a community of a certain size, you could have segregated schools, but if you were a small community, and it was not economically feasible to have a school for, say, three children—then you could not segregate on the basis of race. This has always been a place of great contrasts and contradictions."

Kansas is indeed unique in history, but it is not alone in the peculiarity of its contradictory attitudes about race. Perhaps part of the difficulty in reviewing the years since Brown with anything like a hopeful countenance is that we as a nation have continued to underestimate the complicated and multiple forms of prejudice at work in the United States. Segregation did not necessarily bar all forms of

racial mixing; its odd, layered hierarchies of racial attitude were substantially more complicated than that. My grandfather, for example,
was a doctor who owned many of the houses in the neighborhood
where he lived. "Dad's tenants were white, Irish," says my father.
"But I never even thought about where they went to school. We all
lived kind of mixed up, but the whole system made you think so sep-
arately that to this day I don't know where they went to school."
There is an old story that speaks to the profundity of these invisible
norms: Three men in the 1930s South set out to go fishing in a small
boat. They spent the morning in perfectly congenial and lazy conversation. At lunchtime, they all opened their lunchbuckets and proceeded to eat, but not before the two white men put an oar across the
middle of the boat, dividing them from their black companion.

The continuing struggle for racial justice is tied up with the
degree to which segregation and the outright denial of black
humanity have been *naturalized* in our civilization. An aunt of mine
who is very light-skinned tells of a white woman in her office who
had just moved from Mississippi to Massachusetts. "The North is
much more racist than the South," she confided to my aunt. "They
don't give you any credit at all for having white blood." This
unblinking racial ranking is summarized in the thoughts of James Kil-
patrick, who stated the case for Southern resistance in a famous and
impassioned plea:

> For this is what our Northern friends will not comprehend: The
> South, agreeable as it may be to confessing some of its sins and to
> bewailing its more manifest wickednesses, simply does not con-
> cede that at bottom its basic attitude is "infected" or wrong. On
> the contrary, the Southerner rebelliously clings to what seems to
> him the hard core of truth in this whole controversy: *Here and
> now,* in his own communities, in the mid-1960s, the Negro race,
> as a race, plainly is not equal to the white race, as a race; nor, for
> that matter, in the wider world beyond, by the accepted judg-
> ment of ten thousand years, has the Negro race, as a race, *ever*
> been the cultural or intellectual equal of the white race, as a race.
> This we take to be a plain statement of fact, and if we are not

amazed that our Northern antagonists do not accept it as such, we are resentful that they will not even look at the proposition, or hear of it, or inquire into it.

Dealing with the intractability of this sort of twisted social regard is what the years since *Brown* have been all about. Legal remedy after legal remedy has been challenged on the basis of assertions of not being able to "force" people to get along, that "social equality" (or, these days, "market preference") is just not something that can be legally negotiated. One of the attorneys who worked on the original *Brown* case, Columbia University School of Law Professor Jack Greenberg, dismissed these arguments concisely: "You have to wonder," he says, "how it is that *Plessy v. Ferguson*, which made segregation the law for almost sixty years, didn't come in for the same kinds of attacks as 'social engineering.' "

Have you been disappointed by the years since 1954? I asked Mrs. Leola Brown Montgomery. Of course, she said. And then added, "But I don't think that anybody anticipated the country's response. The attorneys, the parents, we didn't really understand the insidious nature of discrimination and to what lengths people would go to not share educational resources: leaving neighborhoods en masse because African-American children could now go to the school in your neighborhood. Not offering the same kinds of programs, or offering a lesser educational program in the same school—I don't think anybody anticipated what we've ended up with. . . . But we're currently still in the midst of the country's response, in my opinion."

Duke University School of Law Professor Jerome Culp has observed that the litigators and activists who worked on *Brown* in the early 1950s assumed at least three things that have not come to pass: (1) that good liberals would stand by their commitment to black equality through the hard times; (2) that blacks and whites could come to some kind of agreement about what was fair and just—that there was a neutral, agreed-upon position we could aspire to; (3) that if you just had enough faith, that if you just wished racism away hard enough, it would disappear.

"Growing up," says my father, "we thought we knew exactly

what integration meant. We would all go to school together; it meant the city would spend the same money on you that it did on the white students. We blacks wouldn't be in some cold isolated school that overlooked the railroad yards; we wouldn't have to get the cast-off, ragged books. We didn't think about the inevitability of a fight about whose version of the Civil War would be taught in that utopic integrated classroom."

The *Brown* decision itself acknowledged the extent to which educational opportunity depended on "intangible considerations" and relied "in large part on 'those qualities which are incapable of objective measurement but which make for greatness.' " Yet shaking the edifice of education in general since 1954 has become vastly more complicated by the influence of television, and the task of learning racial history has been much confounded by the power of mass media.

"We've become a nation of soundbites," says Cheryl Brown Henderson. "That millisecond of time to determine our behavior, whether it's behavior toward another individual, or behavior toward a product we might purchase, or our behavior with regard to what kind of housing or community we want to live in—I really think we allow that millisecond to determine far too much of our lives. When you take something that short and infuse it with a racial stereotypy and no other information is given, the young person looking at that—even the older person who spends most of his time watching television—that's all they know. How can you expect them to believe anything else? They're not going to pick up a book and read any history, do any research, or talk to anybody that may in fact be able to refute the stereotype."

In addition to stereotypes, perhaps the media revolution has exacerbated the very American tendency to romanticize our great moments into nostalgia-fests from which only the extremes of Pollyanna-ish optimism or Malthusian pessimism can be extracted. The Hollywood obsession with individual charismatic personalities diminishes the true heroism of the multiplicity of lives and sacrifices that make for genuine social change. Such portrayals push social movement out of reach, into the mythic—when in fact it emanates from the realm of the solidly and persistently banal. For all the biblical imagery summoned to inspire the will to go on with the civil rights struggle in this country, if the waters have parted at any given moment, perhaps it has been more attributable to all those thousands of busy bridge-builders working hard to keep Moses' back covered—just people, just working and thinking about how it could be different, dreaming big, yet surprised most by the smallest increments, the little things that stun with the realization of the profundity of what has not yet been thought about.

My father muses: "It's funny . . . we talked about race all the time, yet at the same time you never really thought about how it could be different. But after *Brown* I remember it dawning on me that I *could* have gone to the University of Georgia. And people began to talk to you a little differently." The white doctor who treated my family in Boston, where I grew up, "used to treat us in such a completely offhand way. But after *Brown*, he wanted to discuss it with us, he asked questions, what I thought. He wanted my opinion and I suddenly realized that no white person had ever asked what I thought about anything."

Perhaps as people like my father and the doctor have permitted those conversations to become more and more straightforward, the pain of it all, the discomfort, has been accompanied by the shutting down, the mishearing, the turning away from the euphoria of *Brown*. "It has become unexpectedly, but not unpredictably, hard. The same thing will probably have to happen in South Africa," sighs my father.

When Frederick Douglass described his own escape from slavery as a "theft" of "this head" and "these arms" and "these legs," he employed the master's language of property to create the unforgettable paradox of the "owned" erupting into the category of a speaking subject whose "freedom" simultaneously and inextricably marked him as a "thief." That this disruption of the bounds of normative imagining is variously perceived as dangerous as well as liberatory is a tension that has distinguished racial politics in America from the Civil War to this day. Perhaps the legacy of *Brown* is as much tied up with this sense of national imagination as with the pure fact of its legal victory; it sparkled in our heads, it fired our vision of what was possible. Legally it set in motion battles over inclusion, participation and reallocation of resources that are very far from resolved. But in a larger sense it committed us to a conversation about race in which all of us must join—particularly in view of a new rising Global Right.

The fact that this conversation has fallen on hard times is no reason to abandon what has been accomplished. The word games by which the civil rights movement has been stymied—in which "inner city" and "underclass" and "suspect profile" are racial code words, in which "integration" means "assimilation as white," in which black culture means "tribalism," in which affirmative action has been made out to be the exact equivalent of quota systems that discriminated against Jews—these are all dimensions of the enormous snarl this nation has been unraveling, in waves of euphoria and despair, since the Emancipation Proclamation.

We remain charged with the task of getting beyond the stage of halting encounters filled with the superficial temptations of those "my maid says blacks are happy" or "whites are devils" moments. If we could press on to an accounting of the devastating legacy of slavery that lives on as a social crisis that needs generations more of us working to repair—if we could just get to the enormity of that unhappy acknowledgment, then that alone might be the paradoxical source of a genuinely revivifying, rather than a false, optimism.

The most eloquent summary of both the simplicity and the complexity of that common task remains W.E.B. Du Bois's essay "On Being Crazy":

After the theatre, I sought the hotel where I had sent my baggage. The clerk scowled.

"What do you want?" he said.

Rest, I said.

"This is a white hotel," he said.

I looked around. Such a color scheme requires a great deal of cleaning, I said, but I don't know that I object.

"We object," said he.

Then why, I began, but he interrupted.

"We don't keep niggers," he said, "we don't want social equality."

Neither do I, I replied gently, I want a bed.

*October 30, 1995*

## Doing Time, Marking Race

*John Edgar Wideman*

I know far too much about prisons. More than I ever wished to know. From every category of male relative I can name—grandfather, father, son, brother, uncle, nephew, cousin, in-laws—at least one member of my family has been incarcerated. I've researched the genesis of prisons, visited prisons, taught in prisons, written about them, spent a night here and there as a prisoner. Finally, I am a descendant of a special class of immigrants—Africans—for whom arrival in America was a life sentence in the prison of slavery. None of the above is cited because it makes me proud or happy, but I feel I should identify some of the baggage, whether bias or insight, I bring to a discussion of prisons.

The facile notion of incarceration (read apartheid) as a cure for social, economic and political problems has usurped the current national discussion. *Which candidate is tougher on crime* was the dominant issue dramatized in TV ads during the last election campaign. And the beat goes on.

"Tougher" seems to mean which candidate behaves more like the bullies I encountered in junior high school, the guys whose fierce looks, macho words and posturing lorded it over the weakest kids, stealing their lunch money, terrorizing and tormenting them to gain a tough-dude image. Cowards at the core, bad actors mimicking the imagined thugs who keep them awake at night.

What bothered me most about the hysterical, bloodthirsty TV ads during the last election was the absolute certainty of the candidates that the prison cells they promised to construct, the draconian prison terms and prison conditions they would impose if elected, would never confine them or those who voted for them. Ignorance, racism, naiveté couldn't account for this arrogant, finger-pointing certainty. The only way they could be so sure was to know the deck was stacked, know that they enjoyed an immunity. The ones they were promising to lock up and punish, by design, would never be their people. Always somebody else. Somebody other. Not their kind. The fix was in. Without referring explicitly to race or class, the candidates and their audiences understood precisely who the bad guys were and who the bad guys would continue to be, once the candidates assumed power. I recall a sentencing hearing in a courtroom, the angry father (white) of a victim urging a judge (white) to impose upon a young man (black), who'd pleaded guilty, the most severe punishment because "they're not like us, Your Honor."

Honest fear, thoughtful perplexity, a leavening of doubt or hesitancy, the slightest hint, then or now, that what the candidates insinuated about the "other," about criminals and misfits, also implicated them, would be a welcome relief. Instead, the rhetoric continues, Manichean, divisive and absolute, the forces of light doing battle with the forces of darkness.

As an African-American, as a human being, I haven't yet shaken the sense of being personally assaulted by the campaign appeals to the electorate's meanest instincts. Nor have I been able to forgive the success of the tactic.

Sure enough, our country's in deep trouble. Drastic measures are required. But who says we must always begin at the bottom, taking from those who have least? Why heap more punishment on the losers, the tiny majority of lawbreakers who are dumb enough or unlucky enough to get caught and convicted? Building more prisons doesn't decrease crime. Removing federal money from some citizens' hands (the poor) and placing it in others' (the rich) doesn't save the nation billions. Why are patently false cures proclaimed and believed with such passionate conviction?

Why not start at the top? Limit maximum income. Reduce military spending. Wouldn't it be better to be swept from the earth while trying to construct a just society, rather than holding on, holding on, in a fortress erected to preserve unfair privilege? What indefensible attitudes are we assuming toward the least fortunate in our society? Isn't shame the reason we are desperately intent on concealing from ourselves the simple injustice of our actions?

We're compiling a hit list. Retrogressing. Deciding once more it's in the nation's interest to treat some as more equal than others. Belief that America is burdened by incorrigibles—criminals, the poor and untrained, immigrants too different to ever fit in—is an invitation to political leaders who can assure us they have the stomach and clean hands to dispose of surplus people pulling the rest of us down. We're looking to cold-eyed, white-coated technocrats and bottom-line bureaucrats for efficient final solutions. If this sounds paranoid or cartoonish, you must be unaware of facilities such as Pelican Bay in California, already in operation: chilling, high-tech, supermax prisons driving their inmates to madness and worse.

The sad, defeatist work of building prisons, the notion that prison walls will protect us from crime and chaos, are symptomatic of our shortsightedness, our fear of engaging at the root, at the level that demands personal risk and transformation, of confronting the real problems caging us all.

In the guise of outrage at crime and criminals, hard-core racism (though it never left us) is making a strong, loud comeback. It's respectable to tar and feather criminals, to advocate locking them up and throwing away the key. It's not racist to be against crime, even though the archetypal criminal in the media and the public imagination almost always wears "Willie" Horton's face. Gradually, "urban" and "ghetto" have become code words for terrible places where only blacks reside. Prison is rapidly being re-lexified in the same segregated fashion.

For many, the disproportionate number of blacks in prison is not a worrisome issue; the statistics simply fulfill racist prophecy and embody a rational solution to the problem of crime. Powerful evidence, however, suggests racism may condition and thereby determine where the war on drugs is waged most vigorously. A recent study, summarized in *The New York Times* on October 5, indicates that although African-Americans represent about 13 percent of the total population and 13 percent of those who are monthly drug users, they are 35 percent of those arrested for drug possession, 55 percent convicted for possession and 74 percent of the total serving sentences for possession.

We seem doomed to repeat our history. During the nineteenth

century institutions such as prisons, orphanages, asylums and poor-houses developed as instruments of public policy to repair the gaping rents in America's social fabric caused by rapid industrialization and urbanization. Politicians driven by self-interest, hoping to woo busi-nessmen and voters with a quick fix, avoided confrontation with the underlying causes of social instability and blamed the poor. Inborn idleness, irresponsibility, uncontrollable brutish instincts, inferior intelligence, childlike dependence, were attributed to the lower classes. Public policies, focusing on this incorrigible otherness, defined the state's role as custodial, separating and controlling sus-pect populations. State intervention into the lives of the poor neither diminished crime nor alleviated misery but did promote fear and loathing of the victims of chaotic social upheaval.

Today young black men are perceived as the primary agents of social pathology and instability. The cure of more prisons and longer prison terms will be applied to them. They will be the ones confined, stigmatized, scapegoated. Already squeezed out of jobs, education, stable families and communities, they are increasingly at risk as more and more of the street culture they have created, under incredible stress to provide a means of survival, is being criminal-ized (and callously commercialized). To be a man of color of a cer-tain economic class and milieu is equivalent in the public eye to being a criminal.

Prison itself, with its unacceptably large percentage of men and women of color, is being transformed by the street values and street needs of a younger generation of prisoners to mirror the conditions of urban war zones and accommodate a fluid population who know their lives will involve inevitable shuttling between prison and the street. Gang affiliation, drug dealing, the dictates of gang leaders, have replaced the traditional mechanisms that once socialized inmates. Respect for older, wiser heads, the humbling, sobering rites of initiation into a stable prison hierarchy, have lost their power to reinforce the scanty official impetus toward rehabilitation that prison offers. The prison is the street, the street is prison.

If we expand our notion of prison to include the total institution of poverty, enlarge it to embrace metaphorical fetters such as glass ceilings that limit upward mobility for executives of color, two facts become apparent: There is a persistence of racialized thinking that contradicts lip service to a free, democratic society; and for people of color, doing time is only one among many forms of imprisonment legitimized by the concept of race.

The horrors of the prison system, the horrors of racism, depend upon the public's willed ignorance. Both flourish in the darkness of denial. As long as the one-way street of racial integration and the corrosive notion of a melting pot confuse our thinking about national identity and destiny, we'll continue to grope in darkness. We need to be honest with ourselves. Who we are, what kind of country we wish to become, are at issue when we talk about prisons.

*October 30, 1995*

## Different Drummer Please, Marchers!

*Patricia J. Williams*

By the time this is published, I imagine it will be a different world; but imagine if you will, Gentle Reader, a time before the Million Man March on Washington. Imagine trying to imagine what will happen, if whatever has already happened hadn't yet.

I am trying to do just that because I am trying to understand the enormous, even passionate, appeal the very idea of this march has among so many of my friends—black men whose opinions I respect, whose values I admire. I guess I also need to confess that I find that appeal somewhat mystifying because I have nothing but misgivings about any venture organized by either Nation of Islam leader Louis Farrakhan or former N.A.A.C.P. executive director Ben Chavis, never mind the two of them together. From Farrakhan's legendary anti-Semitism to Chavis's legendary sexual transgressions, there have been enough examples of bad judgment, ethnic slurs, extreme misogyny, uncontained homophobia and old-fashioned breach of fiduciary responsibility to make them the media's top Black Leaders Everyone Just Loves to Hate. Add in the media talents of Washington Mayor Marion Barry and the Rev. Al Sharpton, who recently jumped on board the organizational bandwagon, and I start to get extremely anxious.

My anxiety notwithstanding, eighty black religious leaders have declared October 16 a holy day. Both Jesse Jackson and Cornel West have decided to march. Baltimore's thoughtful mayor, Kurt Schmoke, supports the idea of a show of black male "uplift." The Association of Black Psychologists has issued an endorsement of the march as a way to focus on black men's "personal responsibility to arrest self-imposed destructive attitudes, feelings and behavior," and C. DeLores Tucker, head of the National Political Congress of Black Women and crusader against misogynist gangsta rap, has let her approval be known. New York's oldest black-owned paper, *The Amsterdam News*, dismisses critics of the march as those who will "grind their molars into dust."

There are, I realized, a lot of powerful currents swirling underneath this one. So I decided to take a look at the official "Position Statement" of the organizing committee. "We are coming to Washington . . . to repent and atone," it says. Men are urged to come as a way of taking "our place" at the "head of families" and "maintainers" of women and children. Women are urged not to attend, but to "stay at home" while remaining "by our side" and are thanked for their patience in "waiting for us to take up our responsibility." The march will be a day of prayer and petition to "the government" that manufacturing jobs need not be "ceded" to "Third World countries." "The Black community . . . in a partnership with government" can unite to form "the salvation army of the world."

The steely-eyed lawyer in me reviews all this and concludes that this is going to be a public relations nightmare. A National Day of Atonement, as the Position Statement puts it—this is a religious enterprise. Why march on Washington? That's not where God lives, last I heard. This basically fundamentalist platform of isolationism, personal responsibility and women-waiting-at-home sounds somewhere between the scripts of the Promise Keepers (a Christian men's movement) and the Contract With America. And while atonement might be a great idea if it were only for the organizing committee, dragging a million black men with them risks buying into the stereotypification of criminality and deviance as exclusively a "black male thing"—and a pathological thing at that. It starts to sound like a day for black men to forgive themselves for the *stereotype* of themselves, even if in the name of "showing the world who we are." And isn't there a risk that all it will take is one sorry indiscretion, one set of loose lips, for the antihero of the march to assume the Willie Horton Crown of Media Thorns and the march to be declared a riot? Then a million others will be deemed the "just likes" of.

*Yes, of course that will happen,* says a friend who's going. *But that's what happens all the time. It doesn't matter who's in charge. It doesn't matter who says what. It doesn't matter, it doesn't matter. No one sees a difference, nothing makes a difference. Black men are living in a state of despair and distortion. Who cares what the media thinks—this thing could be a communion I need in the worst way.*

It is this kind of passionate hope so many will bring to this event that I hope is not disappointed—this promise of renewal, this potential for affirmation that seems so precariously placed and so bottomlessly expectant. There are friends of mine who would have absolutely nothing to do with the conservative fundamentalism of this platform under any other circumstance who find this call for a coming together irresistible—and they will not argue about it; they do not care to see beyond that Great Coming of togetherness.

And while I understand that longing on many levels—there is a real and dangerous racial crisis facing this nation, and black men are bearing much of the brunt of this country's worst fears and cruelest neglect—I also worry about a "personal responsibility" march, as some of the organizers have called it, on the site of the civil rights marches of the past. The privatizing symbolic catchwords of the day seem to have displaced the broader political battles of the past. If the marches of the past were about all blacks achieving the full benefits of citizenship, this march of atoning black men seems to insist that "We exist," "We are different!" and "We are good!" And there is something about that vision of a march-of-atonement that I find inestimably sad—a loneliness, an absence at the center, no matter how many voices are lifted to testify and no matter how many millions may show up to be seen.

I'll tell you what I'd like to see. If we're going to have a national day of atonement, what a great occasion to extol inclusiveness as the centerpiece. Why not design a march that Bob Packwood could join, marching side by side with Ben Chavis, both apologizing up a storm? Where Rush Limbaugh and Mark Fuhrman could weep for their sins with Marion Barry; where Pat Buchanan and Louis Farrakhan could jump up shouting with the ecumenical power of divine redemption. In which Clinton came down from his mount and atoned for Lani Guinier, while Jesse Helms climbed up out of his burrow and let Clinton appoint her to the Justice Department. In which Charles Murray and Dinesh D'Souza confronted the Black Child Within and had transformational experiences. And it would be good to see Ricki Lake out there atoning too—quietly, if it's not too great a stretch of the imagination. Shoving the cameras away, muttering those words we all so long to hear: "Enough!"

*May 6, 1996*

## A Different Sense of Time

*Nell Irvin Painter*

*The Future of Race.* By Henry Louis Gates Jr. and Cornel West.

Not long ago a colleague of mine was musing over where he and I would have been teaching seventy-five years ago. The University of Chicago, he decided, would have suited us just fine. I demurred. Though he might have had many choices, I wouldn't have been teaching in *any* American university seventy-five years ago. No, I conclude. I wouldn't go back seventy-five years or to any previous time. In fact, I wonder whether I was born a few years too early to take full advantage of opportunities open to educated black women. Aware of old impediments and delighting in the new field of black women's studies, I place my hopes in the future. My sense of time differs from what I find in Henry Louis Gates Jr. and Cornel West's new book, *The Future of the Race*.

The title of Gates and West's book evokes nineteenth- and early-twentieth-century works: Martin Delany's *Past, Present and Future of the Negro Race* (1854), William Hannibal Thomas's *The American Negro: What He Was, What He Is, and What He May Become* (1901), I. Garland Penn's *The United Negro: His Problems and His Progress* (1902), Pauline Hopkins's *A Primer of Facts Pertaining to the Early Greatness of the African Race and the Possibility of Restoration by Its Descendants* (1905) and, of course, W.E.B. Du Bois's 1940 autobiography *Dusk of Dawn*, with its anthropomorphic subtitle: *An Essay Toward an Autobiography of a Race Concept*.

Within all these titles lie two assumptions no longer so openly embraced: that it is possible to speak of African-Americans in the singular—as what used to be called "the Negro" and now most often appears as "the black community"—and that the authors in question possess authority to speak for the whole African-American race. Gates and West, two of our leading black intellectuals, cast themselves as the grandchildren of what Du Bois called the Talented Tenth—perhaps, with their Du Boisian Vandyke beards and their Du Boisian three-piece suits, the grandsons of Du Bois himself. Certainly they are taking upon themselves the Talented Tenth's early-twentieth-century responsibility to lead the race.

Who is the Talented Tenth? This time-bound phrase comes from Du Bois's 1903 essay, "The Negro Problem," quoted in the Appendix of *The Future of the Race*, and begins: "The Negro race, like all races, is going to be saved by its exceptional men." These exceptional men—and Du Bois did mean *men*—would "guide the Mass away from the contamination and death of the Worst." The Talented Tenth would shoulder the task of uplifting the race without succumbing to money-grubbing selfishness; their formal education signified their intelligence and enlightened character. In 1903, the Talented Tenth was broad-minded and big-hearted by definition.

The passage of forty-five years diminished Du Bois's assurance. By 1948 he had revised his appraisal, and that revision also appears in the Appendix. He confessed the error of his assumption that altruism flowed automatically from higher education. The Best Men had not become the best of men. He lamented that the Talented Tenth had mostly produced self-indulgent egotists who turned their training toward personal advancement. Meanwhile, Du Bois had been learning to respect the masses from reading Marx. Nonetheless, he still cherished a hope that a new, self-sacrificing Talented Tenth of internationally minded men—still men—would ally African-Americans to the peoples of the Third World and uplift the colored masses universally.

Gates and West, who teach at Du Bois's own Harvard University, accept his challenge with all its Victorian mission of uplift. Although they announce their essays as the fruit of long conversations in Cambridge, they do not enter into dialogue. Rather, this book provides a remarkable contrast of the two men's idioms.

Gates's subject matter is disillusionment and loss, yet the tone of his essay is relaxed and autobiographical, taking up where he left off in his highly praised 1994 memoir, *Colored People*. We learn that as an undergraduate at Yale in the late sixties and early seventies, his idols were radical black upperclassmen Glenn DeChabert and Armstead Robinson. Both were from middle-class families and lived useful lives, but in Gates's estimation they failed to realize their wondrous potential. Both died in their 40s, DeChabert a heavy smoker and Robinson stressed and overweight. For Gates, DeChabert and Robinson serve as symbols of the waste of black Yale men through madness, suicide and murder.

Among his collegiate memories Gates threads current social science data reflecting the tragedy of black life at the end of the twentieth century. Stuck in chronic poverty, the one-third of U.S. blacks who belong to the underclass are desperate and self-destructive. Gates's "Parable of the Talents" casts middle- and underclass blacks as the servants in the book of Matthew, in which "unto every one that hath shall be given, and he shall have abundance; but from him that hath not shall be taken away even that which he hath." Weeping and gnashing their teeth, the black poor have been cast into outer darkness, their paltry store of money taken from them and bestowed upon blacks of privilege. This exchange Gates interprets as dialectical.

For the one-third of American blacks who are middle class, he says, abundance has not yielded contentment. (The other one-third is not mentioned.) Instead, the consequences of their affluence are hopelessness and misery. Even the renaissance of black arts and artists that began around 1987 fails to compensate for the vicious political economy of our time. Gates believes that black people need a new kind of political leadership, which paradoxically must de-emphasize the notion of such a thing as black America.

In the end, even hard evidence that the black poor are bad off and well-off blacks are wretched doesn't sour Gates's survival. At Yale, he refused to play identity games, emerging from the crucible of black power with his humanity intact. Now he feels lucky to be the servant with eleven talents, wondering only occasionally why he is still here and flourishing and his heroes are not.

West's essay, at odds with his personal warmth and engagement, is downright gloomy. His title—"Black Strivings in a Twilight Civilization"—owes as much to the French Catholic philosopher Jacques Maritain's 1939 *Twilight of Civilization* as to Du Bois's concern with racial ambition. Where Gates is autobiographical and empathetic, referring only occasionally to Du Bois, West thrice in his opening pages indicts his intellectual grandfather for failing to immerse himself in everyday blackness.

This fault comes at the beginning of a litany of weakness: Du Bois had Enlightenment ideals; Du Bois cherished Victorian values; Du Bois was an optimist, squarely within the U.S. tradition. Du Bois's views are antiquated, a jumble of "glib theodicy, weak allegory, and superficial symbolism." Tainted by patriarchy, his ideal of the Talented Tenth's mission now requires complete reformulation. Du Bois also failed intellectually by not engaging Russian pre-revolutionary thinkers and the writing of Central European Jews between the two world wars. Tolstoy, Chekhov and Kafka knew better than to place their faith in Enlightenment or Victorian values. They resisted the temptation of optimism.

Despite all his failings, says West, Du Bois is still the best black intellectual ancestor we have, the crucial starting point, "the brook of fire through which we all must pass in order to gain access to the intellectual and political weaponry needed to sustain the radical democratic tradition in our time." But because he "falls short of the mark," Du Bois the (grand)father must be, if not slain, then laid aside.

In Du Bois's place, West elevates several other black artists and public intellectuals. Louis Armstrong, Duke Ellington, John Coltrane, Sarah Vaughan, Toni Morrison and Richard Wright offer antidotes to black anguish. For West, being black is inherently tragic, for others see our bodies as abominable and our ideas as debased, while our pain remains unnamed and invisible. We struggle to resist madness and suicide from within a racial culture that must contend perpetually with rage. West finds that in their pessimism about the United States, black nationalists such as Maulana Karenga, Imamu Amiri Baraka and Haki Madhubuti may discern our racial condition more clearly than black academics.

I am fascinated by West's apocalyptic tone. Where Gates turns to the New Testament book of Matthew, West shares the imagery of the Old Testament book of Daniel and borrows the title of a lecture delivered on the eve of the Second World War. He finds our times, too, full of portent:

> Public life deteriorates due to class polarization, racial balkanization, and especially a predatory market culture. With the vast erosion of civil networks that nurture and care for citizens . . . and with what might be called the gangsterization of everyday life, characterized by the escalating fear of violent attack, vicious assault, or cruel insult, we are witnessing a pervasive cultural decay in American civilization. . . . Increasing suicides and homicides, alcoholism and drug addiction, distrust and disloyalty, coldheartedness and mean-spiritedness . . . cheap sexual thrills

and cowardly patriarchal violence are still other symptoms of this decay.

In so grim an era, West concludes, only a multiclass, multiracial alliance can prevent the installation of a "homespun brand of authoritarian democracy." Lacking so ambitious and unlikely a national initiative, a Talented Tenth now consisting of *nouveaux riches* is intoxicated by empty pleasures. The heroic, prophetic few may strive toward the alliance that would deliver us, but their unpleasant truths will not pierce the hedonism of their fellows. West leaves us peering into the abyss.

For both Gates and West, the future of the race looks dispiriting, as, perhaps, any such investigation of the perpetually poorest racial-ethnic group in the country is likely to suggest, and particularly if Du Bois becomes the embodiment of the race. Over the course of his long life, well-educated and economically middle-class Du Bois sought a worthy role within a race oppressed by poverty, discrimination and lack of education. Toward the end of his life he gave up hope of amelioration and went into exile in West Africa. He died in 1963 in the early years of the civil rights revolution.

Du Bois never saw the enactment of the Civil Rights Act of 1964 and the age of affirmative action, which provided unprecedented opportunities to men like Gates and West. Du Bois died before the growth of the largest African-American middle class in history. He also died long before the invention of black women's studies, whose tenor often varies from what black men have to say.

As someone who finds opportunity as well as apprehension in contemporary America, I suspect that the difference between my hopeful hope and Gates's and West's unhopeful hope is gendered. While black women scholars write critically of the work of other black men and women, for the most part we embrace rather than censure our biological and intellectual foremothers, as in books like Alice Walker's *In Search of Our Mothers' Gardens* (1983) and Patricia Hill Collins's *Black Feminist Thought: Knowledge, Consciousness, and the Politics of Empowerment* (1990) and articles like Elsa Barkley Brown's

"Afro-American Women's Quilting: A Framework for Conceptualizing and Teaching African-American Women's History" in *SIGNS* (Summer 1989). We know our opportunities appealed only yesterday. As a result of having flourished during the late twentieth century, black women's studies is likely to find more grounds for hope in the future of the race than does *The Future of the Race.*

*January 26, 1998*

## Shooting Women

*John Leonard*

*Paradise.* by Toni Morrison.

So abundant, even prodigal, is Toni Morrison's first new novel since her Nobel Prize, so symphonic, light-struck and sheer, as if each page had been rubbed transparent, and so much the splendid sister of *Beloved*—she has even gone back to Brazil, not this time to see the three-spoke slave collar and the iron mouth-bit but to check out candomblé—that I realize I've been holding my breath since December 1993. After such levitation, weren't all of us in for a fall? Who knew she'd use the prize as a kite instead of a wheelbarrow?

And I realize I've been holding my breath even on those occasions—under a tent at Caramoor, once in a cathedral—to which I've been invited as a designated partisan, after which I'm guaranteed a standing ovation because, of course, I'm followed by the laureate, who reads from her novel in progress, which begins: "They shoot the white girl first." All week long in Stockholm, after the embassy lunch and the postage stamp with her face on it, before the concert and the banquet, between madrigals and snowflakes and candle flames and the joy ride in the Volvo limo behind a police escort to the great halls and the grand ballrooms and the singing waiters and the reindeer steak, I had thought of Pecola, pregnant with her father's baby, believing that if only she had blue eyes she'd be loved as much as Bojangles had loved Shirley Temple. And of Sula, who, when she loved a man, rubbed the black off his bones down to gold leaf, then scraped away the gold to discover alabaster, then tapped with a hammer at the alabaster till it cracked like ice, and what you felt was fertile loam. And of Milkman in *Song of Solomon*, who went south from Detroit to a ruined plantation and a cave of the dead, who learned from blue silk wings, red velvet rose petals, a children's riddle song and a bag of human bones not only his own true name but also how to fly . . . all the way back to Africa. And of the horseback ghosts of the blind slaves in *Tar Baby*, where Caliban got another chance against Prospero. And of Sethe in *Beloved* like a black Medea with a handsaw, and Denver, who swallowed her sister's blood, and Beloved swimming up from blue water to eat all the sugar in the world: *Beloved*, that ghost story, mother epic, folk fable, fairy-tale incantation of lost children, men like centaurs, lunatic history and babies offered up like hummingbirds to shameful gods. Where had it been hiding, this book we'd always needed? Who now can picture our literature in its absence, between Whitman and Twain, the Other in Faulkner and Flannery O'Connor? Before *Beloved*, our canon was wounded, incomplete. Until *Beloved*, our imagination of America had a heart-sized hole in it big enough to die from, as if we'd never seen black boys "hanging from the most beautiful sycamore trees in the world." And, finally, *Jazz*: as if Sidney Bechet had met the Archduke Trio or Ellington gone baroque; a novel that wrote itself by talking to us, a story that confided: "I love the way you hold me, how close you let me be to you. I like your fingers on and on, lifting, turning. I have watched your face for a long time now, and missed your eyes when you went away from me. . . . Look, look. Look where your hands are. Now."

After her dispossessions and her hauntings, her butter cakes and baby ghosts, her blade of blackbirds and her graveyard loves, Not Doctor Street and No Mercy Hospital and all those maple syrup men "with the long-distance eyes": *Just look where she was now*. We stood at our banquet tables in Stockholm's city hall, in white tie and ball gowns and trepidation. A trumpet fanfare sounded. Above us, past a gilded balustrade, the processional began. The winner of the prize came down the marble steps at last, on the arm of the King of Sweden. Never mind that I am pale and I am male. She'd taught me to imagine the lost history of her people, to read the signs of love and work and nightmare passage and redemptive music, to hear the deepest chords of exile. I was proud to be a citizen of whatever country Toni Morrison came from. And that night she gave lessons to the noble rot of Europe on what majesty really looks like.

All of this—up in the air, at risk, dancing on the vaulted ceiling.

"They shoot the white girl first." In her lecture to the Swedish Academy, she had spoken against the punishing speech of the organs of obedience, used to "sanction ignorance and preserve privilege"; against the "obscuring" and "oppressive" language of state, the "calcified language of the academy," the "faux-language of the mindless media," the "policing languages" of "racist mastery" and the "seductive, mutant language designed to throttle women, to pack their throats like pâté-producing geese with their own unsayable, transgressive words." Rather than these obscenities, she proposed a tongue that "arcs toward the place where meaning may lie." Word-work is sublime, she said, "because it is generative; it makes the meaning that secures our difference, our human difference." Death may be the meaning of life, but language is its measure. Language alone "protects us from the scariness of things with no names. Language alone is meditation." Meditating, she'd found brave words like "poise," "light," "wisdom," "deference," "generosity," "felicity" and "trust."

To these, we must now add "solace." Like Schopenhauer and the sorrow songs, *Paradise* seeks consolation. Part history and part Dreamtime, part opera, part Matisse, it would be surpassing and transcendent if only for the notion of a "Disallowing." But its rainbow parabola also includes Reconstruction and Trails of Tears, Vietnam and civil rights, patriarchy and ancestor worship, abduction and sanctuary, migration and abandonment, sex and ghosts. Considering degrees of blackness, it will raise a ruckus and rewrite God. The Academicians might as well retire their prize.

• • •

*Bodacious black Eves unredeemed by Mary, they are like panicked does leaping toward a sun that has finished burning off the mist and now pours its holy oil over the hides of game.*

*God at their side, the men take aim. For Ruby.*        (Paradise)

In a house shaped like a cartridge, in a state shaped like a gun, the fathers and sons of the nearby all-black town of Ruby shoot down running women as if they were deer. *They shoot the white girl first.* Not the least of many mysteries in *Paradise* is how hard it is to figure out which of the five women attacked by a fearful lynching party in a former convent in a godforsaken Oklahoma in the seventies is, in fact, white. We do know the lynchers are "blue-black people," called "8-rock" after coal at the deepest level of the mines. To understand how it happened—the act of violence at the heart of every Morrison novel, the wound that will not heal—we must first know the stories of the convent and the town, then the dreams of the players and finally the template's design. We get all three simultaneously, in flashes of lyric lightning; in raptures, seizures or eruptions of vol- canic consciousness ("You thought we were hot lava and when they broke us down into sand, you ran!"); and in "the cold serenity of God's wrath."

The "big stone house in the middle of nothing" began as an embezzler's mansion, with lurid appointments of nude Venus stat- uary, nipple-tipped doorknobs and vagina-shaped alabaster ashtrays. After this Gatsby's imprisonment, it was taken over by nuns and turned into Christ the King School for Native Girls, most of whom would run away from the God who despised them. But the nuns brought with them their own luridities, including an etching of St. Catherine of Siena, on her knees, offering up a plate of breasts. And when the last nun died—leaving behind only Consolata, the child they'd stolen decades ago from Rio's slums—the convent became, without even thinking about it, a sanctuary for young women orphaned or broken on history's wheel, a safehouse for the throw- away, castaway female children of the sixties and seventies, on the road and looking to hide from angry fathers, abusive husbands, dead babies, boyfriends in Attica, rapists, Vietnam, Watergate, black water and little boys on protest marches "spitting blood into their hands so as not to ruin their shoes."

Something will happen in 1976 to this haphazard, ad hoc community of "women who chose their own company," these wild-thing Sulas—to Consolata in the cellar, with her wine bottle and her bat vision; to Seneca in the bathtub, the "queen of scars," making thin red slits in her skin with a safety pin; to Mavis, who hears her asphyxiated twins laughing in the dark; to Gigi/Grace, who seeks buried treasure; to Pallas/Divine, who could be carrying a lamb, a baby or a jaguar. They are suddenly full of "loud dreaming." They chalk their bodies on the basement floor. They shave their heads and dance like holy women in the hot rain: *If you have a place that you should be in and somebody who loves you waiting there, then go. If not stay here and follow me. Someone could want to meet you.*

And the nearby town: ah, Ruby. Although Morrison doesn't say so, the ancients believed that rubies were an antidote to poison, warded off plague, banished grief and divested the mind from evil thoughts. A "perfect ruby" was the philosophers' stone of the alchemists. We may also remember Dorothy's slippers in *The Wizard of Oz*. Ruby, Oklahoma, is likewise a refuge, as well as a fortress, a Beulah, Erewhon and Shangri-La, not to mention the promised land of Canaan, and the last stop of a long line that began with the passage from Africa, that included landfall, slavery and civil war, Emancipation and Reconstruction—a proud community of freedmen, of gunsmiths, seamstresses, lacemakers, cobblers, ironmongers and masons:

> They were extraordinary. They had served, picked, plowed and traded in Louisiana since 1755, when it included Mississippi; and when it was divided into states they had helped govern both from 1868 to 1875, after which they had been reduced to field labor. . . . They had denied each other nothing, bowed to no one, knelt only to their Maker.

In 1890, armed with advertisements of cheap land for homesteading—at the expense, of course, of the Choctaw, Creek and Arapaho who happened to live there—they "took that history, those years, each other and their uncorruptible worthiness" and walked to Oklahoma, fifteen families looking for a place to build their communal kitchen, to inscribe on this brick altar of an Oven a ferocious prophecy ("Beware the Furrow of His Brow"), seed their fields and their women and make a home they called Haven—one of many all-black towns in the territory of the time, like Taft, Nicodemus, Langston City and Mound Bayou. Following a specter into the wilderness, they had endured black-skinned bandits, "time-sharing shoes," rejection by poor whites and rich Choctaw, yard-dog attacks and the jeers of prostitutes. What they hadn't prepared for—a humiliation that more than rankled, that "threatened to crack open their bones"—was the "contemptuous dismissal" they received from Negro towns already built. This was the infamous "Disallowing." And the reason for it is the secret of Ruby, which is where nine of these families went next, in 1949, after the men came home from war to Haven, to find America unchanged: "Out There where your children were sport, your women quarry, and where your very person could be annulled." Disallowed like the ex-slaves, the ex-soldiers dismantled their Oven, shouldered their guns, pulled up their stakes and struck out again. For Ruby.

Prosperous Ruby: wide streets, pastel houses, enormous lawns, many churches (if only a single bank) and flower gardens "snowed with butterflies,"; household appliances that "pumped, hummed, sucked, purred, whispered and flowed"; Kelvinators as well as John Deere, Philco as well as Body by Fisher. No diner, no gas station, no movie house or public phone, no hospital or police, no criminals and no jail, no "slack or sloven woman," nor, of course, any whites. "Here freedom was a test administered by the natural world that a man had to take for himself every day. And if he passed enough tests long enough, he was  king." It was as if Booker T. Washington had gone to bourgeois heaven, without having to die first. Because nobody ever dies in Ruby. That's the deal they've made with God, the guy with the Furrowed Brow. It's payback for The Disallowing.

I'll explain The Disallowing in a minute. But you should know that something is also happening in Ruby. A new reverend, a veteran of the civil rights movement, messes with the minds of the children. (He actually thinks that "a community with no politics is doomed to pop like Georgia fatwood.") Somebody paints, on their sacred Oven, a jet-black fist with red fingernails. Not only do daughters refuse to get out of bed, and brides disappear on their honeymoons, but the women of Ruby begin to question the Fathers, who get angrier and noisier: *They dug the clay—not you. They carried the hod—not you. They mixed the mortar—not a one of you. They made good strong brick for that oven when their own shelter was sticks and sod. You understand what I'm telling you? . . . Act short with me all you want, you in long trouble if you think you can disrespect a row you never hoed.* Naturally, the convent women will be blamed. Hadn't they shown up at a wedding reception to which they should never have been invited in the first place, "looking like go-go girls: pink shorts, see-through skirts; painted eyes, no lipstick; obviously no underwear; no stockings"? Haven't our own women, who can't drive, been seen on foot on the road going to or coming from secret visits there—for vegetables, for pies and maybe even for abortions? "The stallions were fighting about who controlled the mares and their foals," thinks Billie Delia, who as a child rode bare-bottomed on a horse until they reviled her for it. Graven idols, black arts, narcotic herbs, lesbian sex!

Besides—"out here under skies so star-packed it was disgraceful; out here where the wind handled you like a man"—the women of the convent are not 8-rock.

*For ten generations they had believed the division they fought to close was free against slave and rich against poor. Usually, but not always, white against black. Now they saw a new separation: light-skinned against black. . . . The sign of racial purity they had taken for granted had become a stain. The scattering that alarmed Zechariah because he believed it would deplete them was now an even more dangerous level of evil, for if they broke apart and were disvalued by the impure, then, certain as death, those ten generations would disturb their children's peace throughout eternity.*

• • •

The fifteen families on their way to the promised land were Disallowed by "fair-skinned colored men," "shooed away" by "blue-eyed, gray-eyed yellowmen in good suits," because they were *too black*: so black they must be trashy. And so they were bound "by the enormity of what had happened to them. Their horror of whites was convulsive but abstract. They saved the clarity of their hatred for the men who had insulted them in ways too confounding for language." What this meant for Haven and Ruby was that anyone marrying outside the coal-black 8-rock bloodlines, "tampering" with the gene pool, was an outcast, no longer welcome in a community "as tight as wax," no longer even represented in a Christmas schoolroom reenactment of the Nativity that somehow hybridized the birth of Christ with the trek story and the creation myth of the 8-rock forefathers. So what if all those generations kept going "just to end up narrow as bale wire"? In Ruby, nobody dies.

Until they do. And even then, at least in *Paradise*, they don't. Because the midwife Lone is there to teach Consolata how to raise the dead. And Sloane's boys, who died in Vietnam, are as likely to show up leaning on her Kelvinator as Mavis's twins, who died in a mint-green Cadillac, will be heard laughing in the convent dark. And Dovey has a "Friend," who may be the apparition that led the fifteen families to their Haven, who visits her in the garden on his way to someplace else. And the fire-ruined house in the wilderness where Deacon meets his secret love is full of ash people, fishmen, nether shapes and a girl with butterfly wings three feet long. And in the meadow where the convent women run from the guns of Ruby, there is a door. And on the other side of the door is solace and Piedade, who will bathe them in emerald water and bring shepherds with colored birds on their shoulders "down from the mountains to remember their lives in her songs."

Piedade; Pietà. Consolata; consolation. Hunted; haunted. Convent, covenant and coven. Morrison names: Seneca, Divine, Elder, Drum, Juvenal, Easter, Royal, Pious, Rector, Little Mirth, Flood, Fairy, Brood, Praise, Pryor, Apollo, Faustine, Chaste, Hope and Lovely. She evokes: late melon and roast lamb, wild poppies and river vine, burnt lavender and broken babies; cherubim and body bags. And she redeems: There is a ghost for every family secret and every horror in history, and the language to forgive them. If we knew how she did it, we'd have literary theory instead of world radiance. I was holding my breath, and she took it away.

## PART TWO

# REPORTERS

*February 14, 1867*

## The Freedmen

We notice in another place the action of the legislature of this State upon the question, Shall or shall not colored men be allowed to vote for delegates to the State convention?

—A bill has passed the Pennsylvania Senate, and is pretty certain to pass the House, "stamping out" the practice of excluding colored passengers from the public conveyances simply on account of their color.

—The Maine House has refused to agree with the Senate in so amending the law as to permit white persons to intermarry with negroes, Indians, or mulattoes. The vote was: yeas, 45, nays, 76.

—The Tennessee Legislature has almost adopted a bill enfranchising the blacks of that State—"the greatest victory since the war began," said Senator Fowler.

—The bestowal of suffrage on the colored citizens of the District, and the evident determination of Congress to secure them in the exercise of that right, have wrought some marvellous changes in Georgetown and Washington. Officials who recently were conspicuous in devising means to evade the several acts of Congress compelling education to be provided for blacks as for whites, since both were taxed for school purposes, now calculate nervously their chances at the next election, and reveal an admirable solicitude for the intelligence of their constituents. The Georgetown election takes place on Monday, the 25th; the Washington some time in June, we believe. Both will be watched with uncommon interest.

—The Maryland House of Delegates refused the use of their hall to Gen. Howard and Judge Bond, to deliver a lecture in aid and in explanation of the objects of the Baltimore Association for the Improvement of the Colored People, but gave the desired permission to the General alone. Never would Mr. Representative Clark, the "proud" mover of the amendment (all his own), "consent that Judge Bond, or any other Marylander who advocated the social and political equality of the black race, should have the use" of the chamber. Mr.

Nelson wanted to know whether if negroes applied for admittance they would be let in; a kind of irony in which the chevaliers of slavery and color-prejudice have never been excelled.

—On the 6th inst. the Delaware House did two notable things: rejected the Constitutional Amendment, and defeated a bill to allow negroes to testify, and to make the same penalties applicable to black and white criminals without distinction.

—Gov. Cummings, of Colorado, has labored faithfully with the legislature of that Territory to procure equal rights for the colored population. His message of Dec. 13 closed with an earnest appeal on this subject, but it was disregarded. An act of March 11, 1864, had disfranchised all negroes and mulattoes, and last month, in spite of the Governor's veto, these classes were excluded from the jury-box also.

—Both houses of the Missouri Legislature are agreed in proposing such an amendment of the State convention as shall do away with distinctions of color.

—The City Council of Baltimore has appropriated $20,000 to the colored schools of that city.

—Gen. Howard has notified the agents of the Bureau that they are to exact no fees for their services between planters and freedmen in the matter of contracts. These, he recommends, should always be in writing.

—The colored mistress of a man in Louisville was poisoned by him on the 7th inst. The excuse which prevailed with the justice before whom he was brought, and who at once released him, was "that he was afraid the girl would tell his wife that she was with child by him!"

—The omnipresent "regulators" have appeared in the neighborhood of Wilmington, N.C. Their plunder was horseflesh, and their victims negroes.

—Inspector-General Sewell is engaged in Virginia, transferring the unsettled freedmen to homes in the North and West, when no homes can be found for them in the State itself.

—Fifty-four contracts were made by freed people in Kentucky during the month of December. The average wages of men were $16.41 and of women $8.50, monthly, besides rations and quarters as usual.

*May 16, 1867*

## Land for the Landless

Mr. [Charles] Sumner gave expression in the Senate, two months ago or more, to the opinion that the grant of "a piece of land" to each colored head of a family "was necessary to conclude the glorious work of emancipation." In answer to enquiries as to where "the piece of land" was to come from, he said it might come from land sold for taxes, and might *have* come out of the property of applicants for pardon as a condition of the pardon. The exact size of "the piece of land" was not settled by Mr. Sumner. This important detail, as well as we can make out, was left to Mr. Phillips, who has decided that the superficial area of the farm which each negro head of a family ought to have, in order to complete the work of emancipation, is forty acres. Mr. [Wendel] Phillips, as might be expected, is not troubled with Mr. Sumner's doubts about where the land ought to be got. He has determined offhand, and with a confidence which makes the difficulty that has been found in governing the world perfectly incomprehensible, that the required number of forty-acre farms ought to be secured by wholesale confiscation of rebel property. But even Mr. Phillips does not seem to have given the subject all the attention it merits; for there was not a word said about it at the last meeting of the Anti-Slavery Association until, towards the close, Colonel Higginson delivered himself of his views upon it, which seems to have wakened Mr. Phillips up to a sense of his neglect, for he drew a confiscation resolution on the spot, and it was passed, of course, without a moment's delay. Whether Mr. Sumner originated the idea or not, it is certain that it has made considerable progress, and, as might be expected, finds great favor amongst the Southern Radicals, and is now a topic at loyalist meetings. At the Hunnicutt convention, a few weeks ago, it was received with enthusiasm; and if the great body of the freedmen throughout the South are not greatly taken by it when it is urged upon their attention, it will show that they surpass in wisdom and self-restraint and honesty any landless class that has ever yet appeared in history. The Southern whites already begin to be considerably alarmed by it, especially in the States in which the blacks are in the majority, and Governor Perry uses it freely, and we may be sure others will do the same, to dissuade the white population from voting for a convention under the Reconstruction act. The amount of mischief which the agitation of the scheme may do, either in postponing reconstruction or preventing the great body of the late rebels from taking part in it is, we think, incalculable. The argument of the advocates of the confiscation scheme is substantially this: Land is necessary to complete the glorious work of emancipation—forty acres, or thereabouts, for each head of a family; in most States the whites take every pains to prevent negroes acquiring land, and will not sell it even to those who are able to purchase it; the Government does not own any land in the rebel States, or not enough; it is, therefore, right and expedient to seize the land of persons who have taken part in the rebellion or aided it—that is, of the entire landholding class—and divide it amongst the poor, both black and white.

Now, we totally deny the assumption that the distribution of other people's land to the negroes is necessary to complete the work of emancipation. We admit that farmers make the best citizens of a republic, and that the possession of land does exercise a conservative and elevating influence on character, but so does the possession of railroad stock or Government bonds or good clothes. But there is no mysterious virtue in land which makes the manner in which it is acquired of no consequence; like everything else, whether it will prove a blessing or a curse to the holder depends on how he gets it. If he has inherited it from an honest father, as most of our farmers have, or has bought it with the proceeds of honest industry, it is pretty sure to prove a blessing. If he has got it by gambling, swindling, or plunder, it will prove a curse. In this respect it differs in no degree from gold or any other kind of property. A large fortune amassed by hard work and upright dealing ought to, and in most cases does, improve the character of its owner, and cannot be regarded, on the whole, as anything but a benefit for him and all connected with him. A large fortune acquired by cheating, gambling, or robbery is almost sure, if not squandered in riotous living, to kill the soul of him who makes it—to render all labor irksome to him, all gains slowly acquired seem not worth having and patience and scrupulousness seem marks of imbecility. This is in fact one of the oldest and most familiar truths in the world—a truth which every generation in every country sees illustrated every day. Farms taken from the rightful owners by the strong hand of power as a piece of political vengeance wreaked without the intervention of courts of justice, in defiance of the forms of law and to the ruin of the innocent and helpless, have never, we are glad to say, brought anything to the takers but political and moral blight and damnation. No community built up in this way ever enjoyed its booty, or ever held it without being depraved by it. This mode of political propagandism has been tried by the English in Ireland, by the Turks in Turkey, by the Spaniards in America, and it has in every case debauched those who tried it. At the South the white has for two hundred years robbed the black, and he is atoning for it to-day in sackcloth and ashes; if we now set the black to rob the white, we may be sure that like retribution will speedily follow. The negro is just entering on free life, and if he is fit to vote, as we believe he is if evil-minded demagogues will let him alone, he is also fit to win a farm for himself as a poor white man has to win it. If it be deemed desirable that he should have land without waiting to earn it, it ought to be given him out of Government lands, and it would be better for the nation to spend five hundred millions in settling him on them rather than allow or encourage him to use his ballot for the purpose of helping himself to his neighbor's goods.

Nor does the proposal to allow the poor whites to share with him in the fruits of confiscation deprive the scheme of one particle of its repulsiveness. Equality is a good thing, but there are certain transactions which it cannot redeem. A division of rich men's land amongst the landless, as the result of a triumph at the polls, would give a shock to our whole social and political system from which it would hardly recover without the loss of liberty. Every election would thenceforward threaten property, and men of property, we may be sure, would find, as they have found under similar circumstances in all countries, the means of protecting themselves—but not through constitutional government.

What the negroes want is education. Let us vote millions for schools, tens of millions for books and papers, but not one cent for gifts or largesses. No man in America has any right to anything which he has not honestly earned, or which the lawful owner has not thought proper to give him. We do not want to see reproduced, in the middle of the nineteenth century and in a Christian republic, the depraved and worthless mob who, in the declining days of Rome, purchased with their votes the privilege of living in idleness on the spoil of the public enemy. We are thus earnest in calling attention to this matter because there are a hundred indications that the talk of confiscation is already unsettling the minds of the negroes, turning their steps away from the paths of peaceful industry, and teaching them to look for comfort and independence in the wilds of political intrigue. If the ballot and education are not sufficient to secure their elevation, other means must be tried; but the Northern public cannot one minute too soon silence or rebuke those who seek to place organized plunder amongst these means. A negro farmer, squatted on his forty acres of confiscated land, with the former owner, or the children of the former owner, living around him, hatred in their hearts and curses on their lips, would be one of the most pitiable objects in creation. He would never lie down at night with the certainty of seeing the morning sun; never leave his home with the certainty of re-entering it. There are already plenty of barbarizing influences at work in Southern society, influences which it will for years take the whole force of Northern civilization to combat. A forcible redivision of lands would create another and a more powerful one than any, and one which the growth of knowledge would do nothing to weaken, for hatred of the spoiler is, perhaps, the only one of the passions which civilization, instead of checking, stimulates. The freedmen and loyalists are about in all the States to take part in framing constitutions, and if they do not regulate the landlords and laws of landlord and tenant in such a way as to facilitate the acquisition and retention of homes by poor men, they will prove more foolish or shortsighted than we take them to be.

*May 28, 1874*

## Open Letter to Gen. Grant

The negro ex-Senator from Mississippi, Mr. Revels, has written an open letter to General Grant "concerning the situation." Since Reconstruction, he says, the people of his race in Mississippi have been "enslaved in mind by unprincipled adventurers," who were willing to "stoop to anything" to get power. The negroes were "naturally" Republicans, but, "as they grow older in freedom, so do they in wisdom"; and so, on finding out that they were being used as mere tools," a great portion of them determined, by "casting their ballots against these unprincipled adventurers," to overthrow them; that the negroes were told that they must vote for men "notoriously corrupt and dishonest" because the salvation of the "party depended upon it"; and that any man who scratched his ticket was not a Republican. It was to "defeat this policy," he continues, that at the late election men united, "irrespective of race or party affiliation," and "voted together against men known to be incompetent and dishonest." The colored masses in Mississippi, he says, are unwilling to recognize these rascally officials as Republicans, as they "do not believe that Republicanism means corruption, theft, and embezzlement." These three offences, however, have been "prevalent" among the office-holders; and "to them must be attributed the defeat of the Republican party [in Mississippi], if defeat there was." Mr. Revels looks upon it as "an uprising of the people, the whole people, to crush out corrupt rings and men from power." He says also that the bitterness and hate between the races have been almost "obliterated" in Mississippi, and would have been entirely wiped out but for the efforts of these "unprincipled men" to keep it alive for their own purposes. This account of the matter, as it comes from a negro, can hardly be pooh-poohed as a "rebel lie." We hope it will be brought to Mr. Morton's attention.

*April 19, 1894*

## The Situation in South Carolina.

To the Editor of *The Nation*:

Sir: South Carolina may be described as a one-city State. That city is Charleston. Columbia, although the capital on account of its central site, is comparatively a small place (12,000 inhabitants), has very few if any manufacturing interests, and does not possess any trade worth the name except that which is purely local. The other towns in the State are little more than country villages; the largest being Spartan-burg (9,000), Beaufort (5,000), and Greenville (5,000).

Charleston is a very old and a very opulent city—one of the richest cities for its size in the United States. It has about 60,000 inhab-itants, 30,000 of whom are negroes. It has a large trade with South Carolina and neighboring States, and ships its phosphates and cotton all over the United States and direct to England. The wholesale gro-cery business finds there a very important centre. There are also a number of wealthy cotton and rice factors. The business which has been extremely profitable in Charleston for years past, mainly as an adjunct of the corner grocery-stores, has been the liquor business with negroes. Most of the corner grocery-stores in Charleston had, up to the 1st of July last, a groggery annex. The negro, while he is an excel-lent and capable workman, is also a hopeless spendthrift. So it hap-pened that a large proportion of his wages found their way every Saturday night into the hands of the corner grocer, who had been trusting him through the week for his groceries and liquors. This liquor trade was morally all wrong, encouraging as it did, in the most illiterate and unbridled element of the population, a taste for the unlimited consumption of strong drink. But the trade was carried on honestly and in an orderly manner, and open drunkenness was not any more noticeable in Charleston among the negroes than among the lower classes in Northern cities.

When the dispensary law went into effect on July 1, 1893, all this liquor business was wiped out in one day. All the corner groggeries became a thing of the past, and all the East Bay Street wholesale houses closed their doors. One East Bay firm of wholesale grocers and liquor-dealers disposed of some $100,000 worth of choice wines and liquors at public sale on the 29th and 30th of June, 1893. It was not possible that their means of livelihood should be thus swept away from so many of the citizens of Charleston and elsewhere throughout the State at one fell blow without creating bad blood between the liquor-dealers and the executive which had thus ruined their trade. Most of them, however, left Charleston and the State, and began business over again elsewhere.

But there were far more vital grounds of antagonism between the Governor and his Populist party and what he styles the "Bourbon" element, or prevalent "oligarchy," which means the wealthy, intellectual, and aristocratic classes. I am a Northern man by birth and instinct, but I have lived a great deal in the South of late years, and I am anxious that the intelligent classes here should understand exactly how the old, ante-bellum Southern element is now handicapped, and how it feels. It will be necessary to make very plain statements where so much misunderstanding exists, but I will try to explain the situation without hurting any one's sensibilities intentionally. The Populist party in South Carolina is largely composed of "Farmers' Alliance" men. This class as a whole is averse to hard work and keenly jealous of those who possess a larger share of this world's goods than do they. I have traversed the State of South Carolina again and again, on its trains, and have always been amazed to notice the great multitude of white men (mainly farmers from appearance) congregated at the depots. This concourse had, apparently, come together, not to board the tram (for the bulk of patrons of Southern local trains are negroes), but simply to kill time and enjoy a better opportunity for the pleasant interchange of ideas. The Populists of South Carolina are famous talkers. They are unusually intelligent for their surroundings, are extremely clever at finance, and no doubt *able* to make themselves felt in almost any profession or branch of trade; *but they will not work.* Everything is done for them by the negro laborers.

These men are mainly descendants of the ante-bellum Southern planter (with some admixture of "carpet-bagging" stock); and, shorn of their property in the shape of negroes, and hence of their means, have never been able to readjust themselves to the changed condition of affairs. Prevented from providing themselves with the luxuries or accomplishments of life, they have preserved the pride, but lost the cultivation and well-to-do appearance, of their parents. They have certainly never been able to bring themselves, with any assiduity, to the day-in-and-day-out drudgery of work. Out of this class has Benjamin R. Tillman sprung. He and his fellow Populists have developed a deep and enduring hatred of the rich and aristocratic class, and as this class is chiefly to be found in Charleston, Charleston is hated by the Populists of South Carolina. Gov. Tillman, before his election, threatened to make Charleston "whistle" if he got into power. And the minute he was elected he proceeded to put his threat into execution. The first descent of his constables was made upon Charleston. The circumstances attending their raid were such as to drive into fury even those who were "as patient as sheep." Private houses were entered in the pretended search for liquors, the contents of trucks and bureau-drawers strewn on the floor, and, in one case, the sheets and blankets torn off a bed in which a man's sick wife was lying.

The people of Charleston, though exasperated beyond all endurance, acted upon this occasion with firmness and great self-control. They acted just as one would hope that people of good repute, extensive cultivation, and great common sense would act. They protested firmly against the lawless employment of executive power, but did not allow themselves to be driven into the unthinking frenzy of bloodshed and retaliation which Tillman expected. Since then he has tried all expedients, but in vain, with the idea of getting the "Bourbon" classes to retaliate, and so throw themselves into his clutches. At the time when some negroes were lynched in the interior of the State, he endeavored to transfer St. Julien Jervey, the district attorney of Charleston, out of his own district and into that where the lynching had occurred (Edgefield, I think it was), that he might act as prosecuting attorney, and suffer the odium which the prosecution of the murderers would locally create. As the Populist class is in the great majority, and can prolong the present crisis indefinitely, it may finally succeed in goading the long suffering Bourbons into mad retaliation. The better class of the citizens of South Carolina thus stand in great need of sympathy and support from the orderly and intelligent portion of Northern communities.

M.D.
Philadelphia, April 9, 1894

*November 17, 1898*

## The Race Riots in North Carolina

To the Editor of *The Nation*:

Sir: When will the national conscience be sufficiently aroused to put an end to lynchings and race riots? These lawless outbreaks of anarchy are becoming so frequent in a large part of the Union as to endanger the stability of republican institutions. The lynchers are invariably white mobs, composed of the "best citizens," who commit, with impunity, acts of violence. These self-appointed committees of public safety burst open the doors of jails, overpower sheriffs and guards, seize negroes held for crime, and, having deprived them of their inalienable right to a fair, impartial trial, shoot, slaughter, and hang them without delay.

It is evident that, in many portions of our country, individual liberty does not exist. Of the numerous illustrations that might be given to prove the truth of this statement, none is more striking than the recent riots and bloodshed in Wilmington, N.C. A few days ago there was a bloody riot in its streets, and the office of a colored newspaper was wrecked and set on fire. According to the Associated Press dispatches, the offence of the proprietors of that paper was their refusal to comply with the demands of a committee of business men who notified them to suspend publication by a certain fixed time. The result was a riot and reign of terror, until cooler counsels prevailed and the semblance of order was restored. The following night a big lynching party was proposed to kill six negroes in jail, but, a new Mayor having been appointed who possessed some backbone, this scheme was nipped in the bud, and a fresh crime against freedom and the rights of humanity prevented by deporting the negro prisoners and some other characters, white and black, said to be dangerous.

Are the people of the United States prepared to tolerate for ever the pernicious actions of law-breakers, composed of the "best elements of society," who slaughter, without fear of punishment, their fellow-creatures, suppress the right of free speech and press, set fire to the homes of obnoxious colored officials, endanger the lives of innocent families, and trample under foot the laws and Constitution of their country?

We Americans have no right to call ourselves enlightened and civilized so long as we permit such outrages to occur. Even Mexico can deal effectively with lynchers, no matter from what rank of society they spring. The energetic Government of that country meted swift justice upon same miscreants who attempted to lynch the would-be assassins of President Porfirio Diaz, and, if the writer's memory is not at fault, executed some of them. What a magnificent illustration her rulers gave that they were determined, at all costs, to secure to criminals guilty of high treason the sacred guarantees of justice.

F.M. Noa.

Geneva, N.Y., November 12, 1898

*August 29, 1907*

# France and Morocco

The situation at Casablanca and in the interior has entered on a phase which, European opinion almost unanimously holds, leads inevitably to a war of conquest and occupation by France. The initial attack on the port town by natives may have been caused partly by the desire for loot; but brigands do not sit down to besiege a European army equipped with machine guns, nor do they charge with fanatical courage in the face of shell fire, except under the impulse of a higher and more unifying principle than mere robbery. Taken in conjunction with the general anti-foreign ferment throughout the region and the appearance of pretenders and prophets, the fighting at Casablanca seems to have been the first striking episode of the Holy War that has so long been expected in North African Islam, and especially in Morocco. Europe seems to be taking it for granted, and with good reason, that France will be free from international interference if near events, as interpreted by herself largely, should necessitate the practical abandonment of the agreement with Germany framed with such care at Algeciras a year and a half ago. The questions that arouse interest at present are how difficult France is likely to find the work that has been cut out for her and whether, having got through with it, she will think it worth while.

That a war of conquest in Morocco would be an enterprise of years and large expenditure, is obvious. At the same time, there is no reason to doubt the ultimate result. The Holy War, like the Yellow Peril, has been endowed with exaggerated danger for the Western mind. Experience has yet to show that religious fanaticism of the most exalted kind is proof against magazine rifles and machine guns, in the long run; the process of subjugation may continue for ten years or for thirty, and it may be interrupted by unpleasant incidents like the decimation of Hicks Pasha's army in the Sudan, or France's own affair with the Chinese in Tonkin, but it would be denying the entire course of history to assume seriously that in a conflict sharply drawn between Europe and the Orient, barbarism could hope for victory.

Whatever danger or discomfiture has come to any one Christian Power from Holy Wars and Yellow Perils can be accounted for by the precious aid and comfort which Islam or Asia has received from other Christian Powers.

Assuming the reduction of Morocco as an accomplished fact, many political experts, like the author of a penetrating article in the London *Nation*, see little profit that would accrue to the French people from adding Morocco to their North African domains. The argument is that the French are the "unexpanding" race, and that colonialism with them must be mainly an artificially stimulated movement, cherished by a comparatively small section of the country. It may be admitted that the entire prevalent conception of colony-grabbing for the sake of that fetich "expansion" is ignoble and in the last resort economically unsound. But in the game as it is being played by the Powers, France has by no means acquitted herself badly, in spite of a general impression to the contrary. Her Indo-China possessions are making unmistakable progress, and her West African colonies are being developed with fair speed, considering the difficulties of the task. The essential point, however, is that Morocco, like Algiers, would scarcely constitute a colony in the proper sense, situated as it would be only across the breadth of the Mediterranean Sea from the suzerain country. Frenchmen, it is true, do not choose to emigrate, as do England's teeming younger sons. Yet Algeria's population of five millions contains nearly three hundred thousand Frenchmen, whereas India, with her three hundred millions, is held for Great Britain by less than one hundred thousand Englishmen. Not only does this comparison favor France but French expansionists can also urge that of Algeria's foreign commerce of 620,000,000 francs, France controls 80 per cent.

To a large party in France, a serious attempt to solve the Moroccan question will appeal because of the stimulus which the responsibility may be expected to impart to the national life. A campaign in Morocco would be almost worth while if it could convince people once for all of the stability of the Third Republic. The correspondent of the New York *Evening Post* in Paris has recently pointed out that the constantly growing victories of the present government *bloc* in the elections of the last six or seven years should leave no doubt of the weakness of the various anti-republican factions in the country and in Parliament. Yet the Nationalist and Monarchist plotters have been able to keep the nation in a continuous state of fret and anxious heart searching. Are our institutions stable? Can the army be relied upon? Is the young generation utterly gone to the dogs by the way of decadentism and absinthe, or is there health left in us to maintain the old national ideals? If decrepit dynasties have been able to keep themselves erect through foreign adventure, the republic may find at least one item of profit in an enterprise that would keep most of its hotheads out of worse trouble.

*June 11, 1903*

## Book Review

*The Souls of Black Folk:* **Essays and Sketches by W. E. Burghardt Du Bois.**

Mr. Du Bois has written a profoundly interesting and affecting book, remarkable as a piece of literature apart from its inner significance. The negrophobist will remind us that Mr. Du Bois is not so black as he has painted himself, and will credit to the white blood in his veins the power and beauty of his book. But the fact is, that the features of Mr. Du Bois's mind are negro features to a degree that those of his face are not. They are the sensibility, the tenderness, the "avenues to God hid from men of Northern brain," which Emerson divined in the black people. The bar of music from one "Sorrow Song" or another which stands at the head of each chapter is a hint (unintended) that what follows is that strain writ large, that Mr. Du Bois's thought and expression are highly characteristic of his people, are cultivated varieties of those emotional and imaginative qualities which are the prevailing traits of the uncultivated negro mind. Hence one more argument for that higher education of the negro for which Mr. Du Bois so eloquently pleads. Such education of ten thousand negroes would be justified by one product like this.

The book will come as a surprise to some persons who have heard Mr. Du Bois speak upon his people's character and destiny, and, finding him coldly intellectual, have not been at all prepared for the emotion and the passion throbbing here in every chapter, almost every page. It is almost intolerably sad. "Bone of the bone and flesh of the flesh of them that live within the veil," the writer manifests throughout an aching sense of the wrongs done to his people, heretofore and still. But those will greatly misconceive who think that we have here merely an outburst of emotion. Back of this there is careful knowledge of past and present conditions in the South, clear insight into their meanings, a firm intellectual apprehension of their tendency, which is something to be reckoned with by every citizen who has at heart the welfare of his country, inseparable from the welfare of the colored people. The perfervid rhetoric will seem extravagant to the dull and cold, but, though it sometimes obscures what it would fain illuminate, it is the writer's individual form, it is not the substance of his protestation, which is compact of intellectual seriousness and moral truth.

The initial chapter is of a general character, setting forth the spiritual strivings of the negro—to be at once a negro and an American; "to be a co-worker in the kingdom of culture, to escape both death and isolation; to use his best powers and his latent genius," which have heretofore been wasted, dispersed, and forgotten. A second chapter takes more definite shape, telling the story of emancipation, what it meant to the blacks, and what happened to the days of the carpet-bagger and his co-adjutors in the Reconstruction period. The emphasis is on the Freedmen's Bureau, whose merits and demerits are considered in an impartial manner. There is an eloquent tribute to "the crusade of the New England schoolma'am" in the South, which in one year gave instruction to more than one hundred thousand blacks. There is a fit rebuke for the cheap nonsense, of which we hear so much, concerning the enfranchisement of the negro. There was no choice, we are very properly assured, between full and restricted suffrage; only a choice between suffrage and a new form of slavery. It is conceded that a race-feud was the inevitable consequence of the choice the North was forced to make.

But the most concrete chapter in Mr. Du Bois's book is the third, "Of Mr. Booker T. Washington and Others." Mr. Washington's ascendancy is designated as "the most striking thing in the history of the American negro since 1876." Entertained with unlimited energy, enthusiasm, and faith, his programme "startled and won the applause of the South, interested and won the admiration of the North, and, after a confused murmur of protest, it silenced if it did not convert the negroes themselves." The merits of that programme are detailed with warm appreciation, while at the same time a criticism is made upon it so thoughtfully conceived that it deserves the attention of Mr. Washington's best friends and the best friends of the negro and the white people of the South. The criticism will be resented with bitterness by those for whom Washington's attraction is the concessions they suppose him to have made, and with hardly less by many who are convinced that he has solved the race problem in a completely successful manner. There are those who seem to regard any criticism of his programme as only a less malignant form of lese-majesty than criticism of the war programme of a President. But he is strong and wise enough to welcome any honest difference from his own views and aims. The criticism is that Mr. Washington asks the negro to surrender, at least for the present, political power, insistence on civil rights, the higher education. Advocated for fifteen years, triumphant for ten, this policy has coincided with the disfranchisement of the negro, his relegation to a civil status of distinct inferiority, the impoverishment of institutions devoted to the negro's higher education. That here is not merely coincidence, but effect, is Mr. Du Bois's contention. Also, that Mr. Washington's desired ends cannot be reached without important additions to his means: the negro may not hope to be a successful business man and property owner without political rights, to be thrifty and self-respecting, while consenting to civic inferiority, to secure good common-school and industrial training without institutions of higher learning. "Tuskegee itself could not remain open a day were it not for teachers trained in negro colleges; or trained by their graduates."

It is not so clear to us as it is to Mr. Du Bois that Mr. Washington has made the base concessions here ascribed to him. We recall passages in his books and speeches and letters that point a different moral. We recall his protests sent to the disfranchising conventions in Alabama and Louisiana. It may be that of late he has become more subdued than formerly to those he has worked with, some of whom have the habit of giving his programme the color of their own exaggerated caution and timidity. Then, too, Mr. Du Bois, while acknowledging that Mr. Washington's programme is provisional, does not make this acknowledgment with sufficient emphasis. But this third chapter as a whole, and the expansion of its prominent details in the succeeding chapters, deserve the carefullest consideration. Their large intelligence and their lofty temper demand for them an appreciation as generous as the spirit in which they are conceived.

Where all is good, it is invidious to select, but the chapters "On the Training of Black Men" and "Of the Sons of Master and Man" merit, perhaps, particular attention. The pathos of the chapter called "The Passing of the First Born" is immeasurably deep. It will appeal to all who have a human heart. It tells the story of a baby's life and death, the joy his coming meant; the "awful gladness" when he died: "Not dead, but escaped; not bond, but free." Clearly the burden of Mr. Du Bois's complaint, not explicitly, but implicitly at every turn, is made more grievous by the denial of social equality to himself and his people. In the urgency of this note is there not possibly a lack of the profoundest self-respect? If Mr. Du Bois can sit with Shakspere and Plato, and they do not wince at his complexion, why should he care so much for the contempt of Col. Carter of Cartersville? Why not trample on it with a deeper pride? A society based on money values may reject such a man as scornfully as one based on the tradition of slavery, but a society based upon character and culture will always welcome him though he were blacker than the ace of spades, not as showing him a favor, but as anxious to avail itself of his ability.

*February 18, 1915*

# The Higher Education of the Negro.

*Oswald Garrison Villard*

The bestowal of the first Spingarn medal—an admirably planned prize, to be awarded annually to the colored man or woman who has rendered the greatest service to the colored race—upon Prof. Ernest E. Just, a young scientist and professor in the Howard University Medical School, is certain to attract widespread attention. The committee, of which Mr. Taft is a member, did not find the choice an easy one, there being a number of possibilities from whom to select. That the recipient should be a scientist rather than an inventor, or a leader in farming or banking, will doubtless surprise many people, as it will put to their trumps those who continue to maintain that the negro is incapable of the higher education. Professor Just, be it noted, is but thirty-one years of age; yet he has already attracted the attention of scientists of repute, his original work in physiology, biology, and zoology having been heartily commended by no less an authority than Prof. Jacques Loeb.

Plainly this is just the type of man the Spingarn medal ought to distinguish—a colored man who is proving the capability of the race, and is also ready to make sacrifices for the benefit of his people. It has been a distinct weakness of the race in its struggle upward from slavery that it has often lacked solidarity and a readiness to contribute to the welfare of the whole. That this is now a rapidly passing condition there are plenty of instances besides this one of Professor Just to prove. Indeed, the support given to the National Association for the Advancement of Colored People, in whose hands Professor Spingarn has placed the award of the medal, is a remarkable case in point. That organization has taken radical and unpopular ground; time-servers in both races have shunned it as if it were something unworthy, instead of a manly and straightforward effort to preserve to the colored people their civil and political rights as guaranteed by the Constitution. Yet the Association has flourished, spread over the country, and made a reputation for itself as a guardian of the colored people's liberties, largely as a result of the efforts and financial sacrifices of the negroes themselves.

It is, of course, true that Professor Just is not the only colored man to do scientific work of a high order, nor the only colored teacher ready to labor for a pittance in order to aid the education of his people. But the honor bestowed upon him is worthwhile merely if it recalls to public attention once more the fact that no one can measure the contributions colored Americans are certain to make to our common civilization, and not merely in the fields in which lie their peculiar talents. It was a colored physician who first ventured an operation on the living human heart; a colored painter is in the front rank of his art as the delineator of Biblical scenes; no composer of recent years won greater honors than Coleridge-Taylor, the negro. Any policy, therefore, which should limit the education and the opportunities of the race must result in a grave loss to humanity as a whole.

No policy could be more erroneous. In the first place, for the exceptional man there must always be the opportunity to rise just as far as his genius will carry him; in the second, if a great mass of people is to be uplifted, they must have leaders of their own fitted to command because of their intellectual powers and their specially advanced training. They must have intelligent and well-taught clergymen, teachers, physicians, and lawyers, to say nothing of the other professions and of the need of skilled insurance-company managers, bankers, etc. These are not often to be obtained from the common schools, particularly if these schools are mere pretences, not schools, as are so many in the Southern States. This need has recently been well expressed in the first report of the General Education Board, where it is pointed out that if "primary and secondary negro schools are to have good teachers, principals, and supervisors, provision must be made for the higher training of these instructors and supervisors." At the same time the report points out that the "mere attempt to deliver the traditional college curriculum to the negro does not constitute a higher education," and urges the establishment of college curricula, which shall be adapted from time to time to the needs, environment, and capacity of the negro student. With this we are in the main heartily agreed, and in so far as the opposition to the higher education of the negro is based on a belief that subjects are taught him which can have no practical value for him, this programme would properly meet the objection.

For the exceptional man of Professor Just's type no one ought, however, to fence in any field of learning. He should be free to roam where'er he will in our choicest educational pastures. Anything else would spell folly and, what is worse, a gross national injustice which would merely have to be stated to carry its own condemnation.

*May 18, 1916*

## Injustice Accorded to Black Soldiers

In the forefront of the pursuit of Villa have been the colored soldiers of the Tenth Cavalry and Twenty-fourth Infantry. The Philadelphia *Tribune*, a newspaper edited by colored men, prints a picture of one of these soldiers over the caption, "The flag he is fighting to protect does not protect his kith or kin." What are these soldiers to say to the news from Waco, as they are told that they must risk their lives to destroy those of the Mexican bandits? What are they to say when they learn that Congress, while increasing the army by more than 100 per cent, is not providing for a single additional colored regiment, and the War Department holds that it cannot designate one to be composed of colored soldiers without Congressional authority? They know that the four colored regiments are filled to overflowing; that they are the easiest regiments to recruit; that the effort to recruit white soldiers is almost a failure; that their record as soldiers proves them to be of the best material the United States has. What are they to think of all of this and of the fact that the South's opposition to a Federal volunteer army is in part due to its refusal to permit colored men to serve in the militia?

*June 22, 1916*

## Lynching Defended

To the Editor of *The Nation*:

Sir: A recent editorial in *The Nation* concerning the burning of a negro in Waco, Tex., for murder and rape on a white woman leads me to write you this letter for publication. Let me say, however, that your editorial was not that wild denunciation that one so often sees in our Northern papers against lynching.

I was born in New York, educated in a Middle Western college. I never crossed the Mason and Dixon line till I was twenty-eight years old. During this time I thought Southern people who lynched and burned negroes for rape were barbarians, and deserved the same torture they dealt to the negroes. To date I have been living in the South fifteen years; and now I'm a convert. I have found that the average Southern man knows more about the North than the Northern man does about the South. There are reasons for this: The North is richer and greater in many respects than the South, and when a man of the South has the time and means to travel he goes North. The Northern man goes abroad. Look up the enrollment of students by States in our Northern colleges. You will find students from Southern States in surprisingly great numbers, especially graduates. Apply a similar test to the Southern colleges; many excellent institutions do not have a single student from the North. Southern merchants, bankers, educators, and even farmers and other business men, spend from a few weeks to a number of years up North. The same percentage of Northern people does not thus become acquainted with the South by visiting it.

I say I am a convert in reference to the negro question. I have lived in the North among negroes, but they were of the better class; they were more intelligent and refined than those of the South. Their superiority was due, in the main, to two factors, viz (1) they were, to begin with, the thriftiest, most moral and intelligent, of the Southern negroes that had moved from the South, or the descendants of such, and (2) they were so few in number that they were swept by the current of the Northern will and social pressure. Since I had never heard of a case of rape on a white woman in our community, I thought the negroes and whites of the South ought to get along equally as well. But circumstances are far different in these two sections. In many sections of the South negroes greatly outnumber the whites. When such is the case, negroes are inclined to be troublesome and insolent to the whites. I got a taste of this contempt for white minority some years ago in a South Carolina town, where I had frequently gone as a travelling salesman. I walked in company with two other white men to a commissary store in the suburbs. On the way out we met a large negro that I had often seen about the commissary. He politely gave us half the sidewalk, and spoke to us. An hour later I returned alone, and met the same negro and a companion. The former tilted his head proudly into the air, and, whistling a brazen tune, jostled me from the walk.

It may be bad to lynch, but is it not far worse for a dehumanized fiend, swelling with bestial lust, to lay his cursed hands on a pure, defenceless woman to satisfy his animal nature? Mr. Editor, you have never had a sister, a wife, or a child outraged by a beast who has all the privileges of respectable men.

Think how you would act and feel if the life, and that which is a thousand times more sacred than life, of your dearest one were forever blasted at the hands of the Southern woman's worst enemy. Five years ago I beheld a sight the like of which I hope I may never live to see again. A doctor friend asked me to go with him to a country home; for I might be of service. An honest-faced, intelligent young farmer met us at the gate. Tears were streaming down his cheeks, and he was suffering great anguish of mind and heart. In the house his beautiful wife lay a writhing, groaning mass on the bed. The shock was too much for her. After medical attention, she somewhat regained herself, but only to think of her poor baby—for the outraged girl was only eleven. The wife and mother cried, begged wildly for help, caressed her husband, and worked herself into a feverish exhaustion. In the little girl's room we beheld on the bed the body of a murdered child, with golden hair, tangled and clotted with her own dying blood. A grewsome cut on her left cheek yawned to the bone. Her throat was black and swollen from the strangler's hand. Two of her front teeth were broken off. The most horrible sight cannot be spoken for print, but the child was eleven, and the negro a large man of twenty-five, and he resorted to laceration with a knife. This is by no means an exaggerated case. There are others equally as bad.

If that had been your only child that had been raped and murdered by a trusted farm hand, and he had been lynched that night by your neighbors—would you have sat down next day and written an editorial against *lynching*, or against *raping*? 'Tis exceedingly strange that whenever a negro is lynched for rape, our Northern papers are filled with editorials about the awful crime of lynching. Yet I have never read one editorial protest against the rape fiend. Your silence on the thing would indicate that the life and character of a pure woman are not so sacred as the life of a vulture that preys upon the vitals of society.

Some people seem to think lynching is for the negro alone. He happens to select premeditatedly his manner of dying. Let the white man commit rape, and he will meet a like fate. I believe that the sacredness of woman is so divine that whoever seeks to outrage her deserves a punishment more awful than that accorded to a common murderer. Just as the carcass of a pirate dangling from the arm of a ship was a warning example to other men of piratical intentions, so is the lynched rape fiend a warning sign to those who think they may tamper with the character of a woman. The righteous indignation of a community in speedily and awfully punishing the heinous crime is not to be too hastily criticized by those who do not know conditions, and who have never felt the pangs of hell in having a loved one ruined.

Let us be honest and unprejudiced. The Southern people are actually human beings. They are from the same stock and race as the Northern people. Let your criticism be constructive, and not condemning. Devise plans to prevent the negro from causing the South to wreak vengeance on him, and then black bodies hanging from telephone poles will be as rare as dead pirates hanging from the yardarms of present-day ships. Lynching is a horrible disease. Remove the cause, and the disease disappears. Try to feel and think in your time about the negro situation in the South as the great Lincoln did in his time, when he said: "I have no prejudice against the Southern people. They are just what we would be in their situation."

J.T. Winston.
Bryan, Tex, May 26.

[No one in the North has the slightest sympathy with the perpetrators of these unspeakable crimes, whether white or black. The obvious condemnation of lynching is that it is extra-legal, and is readily extended from rape to other less serious crimes, frequently on inadequate grounds of suspicion. ED. THE NATION.]

*August 30, 1917*

## Mutiny Condemned

As no provocation could justify the crimes committed by mutinous negro soldiers at Houston, Texas, so no condemnation of their conduct can be too severe. It may be that the local authorities were not wholly blameless, and that the commanding officers were at fault in not foreseeing the trouble and taking steps to guard against it. But nothing can really palliate the offence of the soldiers. They were false to their uniform; they were false to their race. In one sense, this is the most deplorable aspect of the whole riotous outbreak. It will play straight into the hands of men like Senator Vardaman who have been saying that it was dangerous to draft colored men into the army. And the feeling against having colored troops encamped in the South will be intensified. The grievous harm which they might do to their own people should have been all along in the mind of the colored soldiers, and made them doubly circumspect. They were under special obligation, in addition to their military oath, to conduct themselves so as not to bring reproach upon the negroes as a whole, of whom they were in a sort representatives. Their criminal outrage will tend to make people forget the good work done by other negro soldiers. After the rigid investigation which the War Department has ordered, the men found guilty should receive the severest punishment. As for the general army policy affecting colored troops, we are glad to see that Secretary Baker appears to intend no change in his recent orders.

*August 18, 1926*

## Garvey: A Mass Leader

*E. Franklin Frazier*

The Garvey movement is a crowd movement essentially different from any other social phenomenon among Negroes. For the most part American Negroes have sought self-magnification in fraternal orders and the church. But these organizations have failed to give that support to the Negro's ego-consciousness which the white masses find in membership in a political community, or on a smaller scale in Kiwanis clubs and the Ku Klux Klan. In a certain sense Garvey's followers form the black Klan of America.

The reason for Garvey's success in welding the Negroes into a crowd movement becomes apparent when we compare his methods and aims with those of other leaders. Take, for example, the leadership of Booker Washington. Washington could not be considered a leader of the masses of Negroes, for his program commended itself chiefly to white people and those Negroes who prided themselves on their opportunism. There was nothing popularly heroic or inspiring in his program to captivate the imagination of the average Negro. In fact the Negro was admonished to play an inglorious role. Certain other outstanding efforts among Negroes have failed to attract the masses because they have lacked the characteristics which have distinguished the Garvey movement. It is only necessary to mention such an organization as the National Urban League and its leadership to realize that so reasoned a program of social adjustment is lacking in everything that appeals to the crowd. The leadership of Dr. Du Bois has been too intellectual to satisfy the mob. Even his glorification of the Negro has been in terms which escape the black masses. The Pan-African Congress which he has promoted, while supporting to some extent the boasted aims of Garvey, has failed to stir any considerable number of American Negroes. The National Association for the Advancement of Colored People, which has fought uncompromisingly for equality for the Negro, has never secured, except locally and occasionally, the support of the masses. It has lacked the dramatic element.

The status of Negroes in American life makes it easy for a crowd movement to be initiated among them. In America the Negro is repressed and an outcast. Some people are inclined to feel that this repression is only felt by cultured Negroes. As a matter of fact many of them can find satisfaction in the intellectual and spiritual things of life and do not need the support to their personalities that the average man requires. The average Negro, like other mediocre people, must be fed upon empty and silly fictions in order that life may be bearable. In the South the most insignificant white man is made of supreme worth simply by the fact of his color, not to mention the added support he receives from the Kiwanis or the Klan.

Garvey came to America at a time when all groups were asserting themselves. Many American Negroes have belittled his influence on the ground that he is a West Indian. It has been said that Garvey was only able to attract the support of his fellow-countrymen. The truth is that Garvey aroused the Negroes of Georgia as much as those of New York, except where the black preacher discouraged anything that threatened his income, or where white domination smothered every earthly hope. Moreover, this prejudice against the West Indian Negro loses sight of the contribution of the West Indian to the American Negro. The West Indian who has been ruled by a small minority instead of being oppressed by the majority, is more worldly in his outlook. He has been successful in business. He does not need the lodge, with its promise of an imposing funeral, or the church, with its hope of a heavenly abode as an escape from a sense of inferiority. By his example he has given the American Negro an earthly goal.

Garvey went even further. He not only promised the despised Negro a paradise on earth, but he made the Negro an important person in his immediate environment. He invented honors and social distinctions and converted every social invention to his use in his effort to make his followers feel important. While everyone was not a "Knight" or "Sir" all his followers were "Fellow-men of the Negro Race." Even more concrete distinctions were open to all. The women were organized into Black Cross Nurses, and the men became uniformed members of the vanguard of the Great African Army. A uniformed member of a Negro lodge paled in significance beside a soldier of the Army of Africa. A Negro might be a porter during the day, taking his orders from white men but he was an officer in the black army when it assembled at night in Liberty Hall. Many a Negro went about his work singing in his heart that he was a member of the great army marching to "heights of achievements." And even in basing his program upon fantastic claims of empire, Garvey always impressed his followers that his promise was more realistic than that of those who were constantly arguing for the theoretical rights of the Negro. In the *Negro World* for October 18, 1924, he warned his followers that

> Those who try to ridicule the idea that America is a white man's country are going to find themselves sadly disappointed one of these days, homeless, shelterless, and unprovided for. Some of us do harp on our constitutional rights, which sounds reasonable in the righteous interpretation thereof, but we are forgetting that righteousness is alien to the world and that sin and materialism now triumph, and for material glory and honor and selfishness man will slay his brother. And in the knowledge of this, is the Negro still so foolish as to believe that the majority of other races are going to be so unfair and unjust to themselves as to yield to weaker peoples that which they themselves desire?

And after all this is essentially what most Negroes believe in spite of the celebrated faith of the Negro in America.

A closer examination of the ideals and symbols which Garvey always held up before his followers shows his mastery of the technique of creating and holding crowds. The Negro group becomes idealized. Therefore he declares he is as strongly against race-intermixture as a Ku Kluxer. He believes in a "pure black race just as all self-respecting whites believe in a pure white race." According to Garvey, civilization is about to fall and the Negro is called upon "to evolve a national ideal, based upon freedom, human liberty, and true democracy." The "redemption of Africa" is the regaining of a lost paradise. It is always almost at hand.

This belief has served the same purpose as does the myth of the general strike in the syndicalist movement. Garvey, who is dealing with people imbued with religious feeling, endows the redemption of Africa with the mystery of the regeneration of mankind. He said on one occasion: "No one knows when the hour of Africa's redemption cometh. It is in the wind. It is coming one day like a storm. It will be here. When that day comes, all Africa will stand together."

Garvey gave the crowd that followed him victims to vent their hatred upon, just as the evangelist turns the hatred of his followers upon the Devil. Every rabble must find someone to blame for its woes. The Negro who is poor, ignorant, and weak naturally wants to place the blame on anything except his own incapacity. Therefore Garvey was always attributing the misfortunes of the Negro group to traitors and enemies. Although the identity of these "traitors" and "enemies" was often obscure, as a rule they turned out to be Negro intellectuals. The cause for such animosity against this class of Negroes is apparent when we remember that Garvey himself lacks formal education.

Garvey who was well acquainted with the tremendous influence of religion in the life of the Negro, proved himself matchless in assimilating his own program to the religious experience of the Negro. Christmas, with its association of the lowly birth of Jesus, became symbolic of the Negro's birth among the nations of the world. Easter became the symbol of the resurrection of an oppressed and crucified race. Such naive symbolism easily kindled enthusiasm among his followers. At other times Garvey made his own situation appear similar to that of Jesus. Just as the Jews incited the Roman authorities against Jesus, other Negro leaders were making the United States authorities persecute him.

Most discussions of the Garvey movement have been concerned with the feasibility of his schemes and the legal aspects of the charge which brought him finally to the Atlanta Federal Prison. It is idle to attempt to apply to the schemes that attract crowds the test of reasonableness. Even experience fails to teach a crowd anything, for the crowd satisfies its vanity and longing in the beliefs it holds. Nor is it surprising to find Garvey's followers regarding his imprisonment at present as martyrdom for the cause he represents, although the technical charge on which he was convicted is only indirectly related to his program. But Garvey has not failed to exploit his imprisonment. He knows that the average man is impressed if anyone suffers. Upon his arrest he gave out the following statement: "There has never been a movement where the Leader has not suffered for the Cause, and not received the ingratitude of the people. I, like the rest, am prepared for the consequence." As he entered the prison in Atlanta he sent a message to his followers which appeared in his paper, the *Negro World*, for February 14, 1925. He paints himself as a sufferer for his group and blames his lot on a group of plotters. In commending his wife to the care of his followers he says: "All I have, I have given to you. I have sacrificed my home and my loving wife for you. I intrust her to your charge, to protect and defend in my absence. She is the bravest little woman I know." Such pathos he knew the mob could not resist, and the final word he sent to his supporters under the caption, "If I Die in Atlanta," with its apocalyptic message, raises him above mortals. He bade them "Look for me in the whirlwind or the storm, look for me all around you, for, with God's grace, I shall come and bring with me the countless millions of black slaves who have died in America and the West Indies and the millions in Africa to aid you in the fight for liberty, freedom, and life."

Since his imprisonment Garvey has continued to send his weekly message on the front of his paper to his followers warning them against their enemies and exhorting them to remain faithful to him in his suffering. It is uncritical to regard Garvey as a common swindler who has sought simply to enrich himself, when the evidence seems to place him among those so-called cranks who refuse to deal realistically with life. He has the distinction of initiating the first real mass movement among American Negroes.

*January 30, 1935*

## Issues and Men
### Walking Through Race Prejudice

*Oswald Garrison Villard*

A simple news item in the New York dailies the other day gave me a real thrill. It read as follows: "Twenty-nine sergeants today were promoted to lieutenants by Police Commissioner Lewis J. Valentine. Among them was Samuel J. Battle, a Negro, the first of his race to rise above the rank of patrolman." It took my mind back a long time, to the days of the founding of the National Association for the Advancement of Colored People, and the demand of some of us who were associated in that undertaking that Negroes be appointed to the police force of New York City. Of course we were looked upon as crazy people. It had never been done and it couldn't be done. You could not mix the two races. Had we forgotten that policemen sleep and at times eat in police stations, and that you could not expect white policemen to associate in that way with colored men? Policing the city was a white man's privilege, and while you might find a colored man who had the physical courage necessary for the job, you could not find one with the brains and the judgment necessary in some of the dangerous situations which arise in a policeman's life, and of course it was inconceivable that a colored man should have the right to give orders to white men. Vainly we pointed out that the men best fitted to deal with Negroes were men of their own race; that as Italian detectives were put on the force to deal with Italian criminals and Russians to deal with Russians, so colored police would not only understand colored people better, but actually get greater obedience and cooperation from them than would white.

Well, time passed. Negroes took the civil-service examination for patrolmen but were usually found ineligible or skipped on the list for promotion. Finally one man, Samuel J. Battle, came along who stood so high in his examinations that it was impossible to pass him over, and besides there was a police commissioner in office who was willing that the experiment should be tried. He was appointed and assigned to a station house—and went through hell. He did encounter race prejudice—lots of it. Had he been a colored cadet at West Point he could not have been tried more severely. Whether he was inspired by the fact that he was a pioneer for his race or not, he stuck it out and won the respect and regard of the men who had started out by yielding to senseless prejudice without stopping to reason about it. Today there are no less than 125 Negroes in the Police Department doing entirely satisfactory work. Battle was the first to be promoted to sergeant, but another Negro, Dr. Louis T. Wright, has been for years a police surgeon, having the rank now of inspector. The white policemen are very happy to have his services. He was the second Negro medical man to be elected to the College of Surgeons; at a dinner given to him in recognition of this the chief surgeon of the Police Department testified in highest terms to Dr. Wright's worth as a physician and a man. But, of course, it couldn't be done before it was attempted. Oil and water wouldn't mix, and white men would never submit to close association with Negroes or to examination by a colored physician.

In the Fire Department of New York City the captain of Engine Company 55 is Wesley Williams. He, too, is a colored man—no doubt about that—and he is today commanding the very same company which he joined years ago as a lowest-grade fireman. He, too, was told that he could not last, that he wouldn't be allowed to sleep in the dormitory with the white men. He attended strictly to his business; he took with a smile the tricks played upon him in the hope of shaking his nerve and getting him to resign; he worked his way up steadily through every grade, serving always with this same company which he now commands. The white men under him who know his worth are happy to serve under him, and the Fire Commissioner went out of his way, when Wesley Williams was promoted, to call attention to the fact that he was the first colored man to reach this rank, and that he was considered one of the ablest officers in the department. It couldn't be done!

All this reminds me of the old Eastern fable of the traveler who came to a narrow defile and found his way blocked by an obstacle. He tried to surmount it and could not. He tried to go around either side and failed. He tried to go under it, but that was impossible. Finally, after much delay and doubt—he walked right through it and found that it wasn't an obstacle after all. So it is with many manifestations of race prejudice. Years ago in New York City the Cosmopolitan Club gave a dinner to which some of us were invited to discuss the lot of the Negro in New York. Of course some Negroes were asked. How could we discuss the Negro problem adequately without getting their point of view? A drunken Hearst reporter attended and the next day there were tremendous headlines. Leering, vicious-looking Negroes were portrayed by staff artists as sitting next to white women; and the whole undertaking was pictured as a move for miscegenation. The Associated Press sent the story all over the country, with the result that those of us whose names were mentioned, both men and women, received letters of abuse and obscenity from half the states in the Union, and the good old New York *Times*, true to its Southern owner-ship, solemnly warned us that we were countenancing something that must never be in America.

Well, a couple of years ago I attended a dinner here in a leading hotel in honor of a British lieutenant general, given by a group of entirely conservative persons interested in Southern education. Half the people in the room were Negroes and half whites, but this fact was never referred to in the accounts of the dinner. White people and colored people frequent the same night clubs and restaurants in Harlem, there is free and open association between literary men and women and artists of both races, yet the Republic still stands, the heavens have not fallen, and in its own opinion the Anglo-Saxon race is as sacredly virile as ever.

*September 26, 1942*

## Fighting for White Folks?

*Horace R. Cayton*

Any discussion of the problem of Negro morale must start with the paradoxical role which the Negro plays in American life. The position of the Negro in the social structure of the country varies from region to region. In the deep South he is a member of a caste whose status is scarcely in harmony with democratic theory; in the urban North he is set apart to the extent that he usually does not participate in white social activities and a ceiling is placed upon his opportunities to compete in economic and political life. In the North the Negro does enjoy, however, some of the rights, privileges, and protection of the law in common with white citizens. The major difference between the North and the South is that in the deep South the present social order depends upon the subordination of the Negro, while in the North he is an incidental minority problem.

The subordination of persons in a society because of race, religion, or culture is of course nothing new. Many societies, that of India, for example, have existed for centuries under a system in which a person's position is determined at birth. These societies have usually assigned people to a higher or lower position on the basis of certain absolute values. Thus in India when the caste system operated effectively, it did so because the religion which regulated society was accepted by both the higher and the lower groups. The paradox of the Negro in America is that he has a relatively fixed, caste-like status in a society based upon the political principle of democracy.

The slave Negro was not included in the democratic tradition. He was not permitted to be a part of the social and cultural democracy of the new nation born in 1776. This forced cultural isolation prevented the Negro then from identifying himself with the whole society and continued to prevent him, even after his emancipation, from entering that society on an equal footing with the whites. With his increased education and the increased social consciousness of white persons, he has, of course, come to share more and more in the fruits of citizenship.

On the other hand, the Negro's conception of himself and his expectations from the total society have always been in advance of what the social structure would permit. The more educated Negroes have been keenly aware of the contradiction between democracy and racialism. Each increment in education, each rise in status, has brought home to Negroes the discrepancy between these two forces in American life and as a result has heightened the racial consciousness of the group as a whole and produced frustration, cynicism, and bitterness in many individuals.

This situation has fundamental implications for the problem of morale among Negroes. One of the prime factors in morale is the identification of the individual with the collective enterprise. Having been denied many of the rights and privileges of American citizenship, Negroes are not now psychologically prepared to accept responsibility for the acts of the collective society from which they have always felt isolated. Their attitude is illustrated by the story of the old share-cropper who came to the "Big House" to get his ration of corn meal and fat-back. After receiving his supplies, and just before leaving, he looked at the plantation owner and said, "By the way, Captain, I hear the Japs done declared war on you white folks!" Then there is the story of a small Negro community in the backwoods of Mississippi, none of whose inhabitants could read or write. Not knowing much about the war and being timid about asking white people to explain it, they sent one of their men to a nearby town to see if he could discover, without asking direct questions, what it was all about. After standing around all day and hearing many references to the attempted rape of Hawaii, he returned to his community and reported that Uncle Sam and the Japs were fighting about an "old whore" called Pearl Harbor. This feeling of being alien, of being isolated from the interests of the total society, can be noted among all classes of Negroes. Even those who are more aware of the international issues of the World War share, nevertheless, a deep-seated resentment against their cultural isolation.

Not many Negroes have any strong conviction that the present struggle will improve their status, and without such a conviction morale is necessarily low. As Professor Louis Wirth, the University of

Chicago sociologist, has pointed out, "to make great sacrifices willingly a group must have an unambiguous cause for which to struggle. They must be imbued with the feeling that their cause is right, that something desirable will result or something undesirable will be abolished through their collective action." Even the war effort has been marked by many specific instances of discrimination—segregation in the armed forces, segregation of Negro blood in the Red Cross blood banks, the shooting and killing of Negro soldiers in uniform by military and civilian police, and especially the discrimination against Negroes in defense industries. All these things contribute to the disaffection of the Negro toward the war effort. He compares them constantly with the avowed objectives of the war and recalls his own disillusionment with the results of the First World War. As a matter of fact, in many regions the more frequently the slogans of democracy are raised for the general population the lower falls Negro morale. The general bitterness was summed up by a young Negro who, on being inducted into the army, said, "Just carve on my tombstone, 'Here lies a black man killed fighting a yellow man for the protection of a white man.'" Another Negro boy expressed the same feeling when he said he was going to get his eyes slanted so that the next time a white man shoved him around he could fight back.

Such statements reveal the resentment which has been generated by the Negro's isolation and indicate his lack of identification with the purposes and privileges of the majority group, his growing tendency toward psychological identification with other non-white people, and his hope for a change. The growing identification of the American Negro with non-white people all over the world is no figment of Nazi propaganda. A recent issue of a Negro weekly contained five articles and an editorial on colored people outside of America. One article was on the African trade unions in South Africa; two were on the Indian situation; one was on Churchill's statement that the Atlantic Charter was not to be applied to colonies held by the United Nations; and one was on Negroes in South America. It may seem odd to hear India discussed in poolrooms on South State Street in Chicago, but India and the possibility of the Indians obtaining their freedom from England by any means have captured the imagination of the American Negro. The feeling throughout the colored world is that there is going to be a change in the status of non-white people, and there is little fear that the change could be for the worse. Whereas for years Negroes have felt that their position was isolated and unalterable, some of them are now beginning to feel that dark people throughout the world will soon be on the march.

The real danger does not lie in the agitation of some Negro leaders or in the very vocal Negro press. In the main Negroes in the United States are a disorganized, leaderless group. The N.A.A.C.P. is made up of a handful of Negro intellectuals and professionals and has no mass following. The church has lost its control over the majority of the urban Negro population. But inspired by the feeling that a change in status for the Negro is imminent, black America is ready for a nationalistic movement such as Garvey's when the right demagogic leadership presents itself.* In such a contingency the present leaders, even though they were convinced that all demands should be held in abeyance for the duration and were willing to preach this to the Negro masses, would be incapable of exercising any real control over the masses.

Last year, in an article in *Opportunity*, the writer made the following prophecy concerning the problem of building Negro morale:

> The problem of maintaining Negro morale will increase in importance as we move closer to the actual war situation. It will doubtless be met by the development of propaganda rather than by any fundamental attempt to change the Negro's social and economic position. . . . The attempt to propagandize the Negro will be fumbling. It will be fumbling because, to my notion, it has not been necessary before for Americans to spend much time and energy meeting the discontent of a large racial minority.

This prediction has been pretty well carried out. Some concrete gains for the Negro are on record—the appointment of the President's Com-

---

* There has been a revival of the Universal Negro Improvement Association, the old Garvey movement, which focused the attention of several million Negroes on a program glorifying the colored races. Its recent national convention, the first for several years, held in Cleveland in August, was attended by more than 400 delegates. This was the largest convention since the peak of the movement. Considerable attention was given to the application of the Atlantic Charter to Africa.

mittee on Fair Employment Practices, the establishment of an aviation unit at Tuskegee and of a naval unit at the Great Lakes Training Station (though they are Jim Crow). These achievements, however, have not done much to improve Negro morale, for traditional American race feeling, plus the fact that the national Administration is supported in its foreign policy by a Congress controlled by Southern politicians, has not only maintained the Southern pattern of rigid segregation but extended it to many fields of social life in the North. Rules of segregation have frequently been enforced as a war emergency where they did not obtain in civilian life before the war.

In the armed forces and to a large extent in industry the Administration has taken the position that a relaxation of the color line would destroy the morale of the majority group. What might be considered the realistic white point of view was expressed in a letter from William A. Krauss, published in *Common Sense* last June. Replying to an article by A. Clayton Powell, Mr. Krauss wrote:

> I think that very few white Americans are made happy by the knowledge that they—the majority—are discriminating against a Negro minority. They will agree up to the hilt with Mr. Powell that the condition is lamentable, but they will not agree to what he seems to be driving at: that is, free, full, and cheerful social equality for the American Negro.
>
> Full social acceptance of the Negro is an idea that simply doesn't occur to the white majority. And social acceptance means far more, of course, than having the Negro in for dinner or inviting him to join the club. . . . Whether in a model world or model army this should or should not be so is, obviously, unprofitable for me or for Mr. Powell to argue—the fact is that in the United States today it is so. It cannot be otherwise, it will not be otherwise, while the majority see the Negro as different.

The very acts which will insure morale for one group may, it is thought, destroy it for another. A large group of white persons in America do not wish to change the position of the Negro. Just as there is a feeling in the non-white world that things are changing, that this is the time to press for gains, so there is a feeling among whites that their position of dominance is being challenged and that they must resist any encroachment on their prerogatives. The problem of building Negro morale, therefore, is one of maintaining the color line—which is considered necessary for the morale of white soldiers, workers, and civilians— while appeasing the rising Negro public opinion with verbal and token gains whenever the tension becomes too great. This difficult task is complicated by the conflict between those who wish to stimulate Negroes from coast to coast to demand complete equality now and those who suggest the organization of a League to Maintain White Supremacy. Propaganda to raise Negro morale has had little success during the past year. Most of the federal propaganda agencies have been too much in fear of a reactionary, Southern-dominated Congress to devise any adequate approach to the problem. The old Office of Facts and Figures, in order to stimulate Negro morale, produced an all-Negro movie short showing a Negro labor battalion singing while they marched and worked. The film simply antagonized Negroes, since it showed them as laborers rather than fighters, conformed to the stereotype of singing Negroes, and emphasized their Jim Crow position in the army. It would have been much better for Negro morale if the film had not been made. Another federal agency worked on a deluxe and expensive edition of a book about the American Negro, illustrated with color photography, designed to counteract the Japanese propaganda that democracy necessarily means white supremacy. The book, however, could not be circulated in the United States because it might offend Southern Congressmen.

The need for more skilful propaganda and more effective action becomes imperative as the position of the American Negro in American democracy gains global importance. There is a close relationship between the interracial tensions within the United Nations and the course of international events. The present crisis in India is raising the expectations of American Negroes. On the other hand, every bid for status by the non-white people of the United Nations—and every military victory of the Japanese—evokes among the majority group the response of fear and the determination to keep down the dark races.

The problem of the American Negro might be met by force if the

Negroes' insistence on equal participation exceeded the willingness of the total society to grant these demands, but in using force the United States, and in fact the United Nations, would lose one of their most powerful weapons—the loyalty of the peoples seeking freedom, regardless of color. Under these circumstances it is difficult to conceive how this country can deal with growing Negro claims without planning a program of concessions. It is true that in the daily press and on the air the Negro is getting more attention than he has enjoyed since the old Abolitionist days. And there is a growing awareness on the part of labor that the Negro problem requires action. In normal conditions all these things would be considered gains for the Negro. But they are sporadic and unintegrated and are insufficient to counteract the apparent inability of the government to set up a comprehensive plan.

Any real change in the morale of Negroes will come only with a real change in the position of the Negro in the social structure of the country. Such a change will involve, especially in the South, a complete revamping of the social relations between the races. That is something which this country will not voluntarily undertake. Unless we are to maintain a society which Edwin Embree has described as "half Nazi, half democrat," the government must intervene with a rational plan. The shape of things to come—the new pattern of race relations—will be worked out on a global basis and will necessitate tremendous internal changes in many countries.

*February 24, 1945*

## Radical Dialectic: Missouri Style

*Carey McWilliams*

In December, 1938, the United States Supreme Court ruled that Missouri must either admit Lloyd Gaines, a Negro, to the law school of the University of Missouri or provide, within the state, educational facilities equal in every respect to those available at the state university. The state court made a similar ruling in 1940 on the application of Lucille Bluford to attend the school of journalism at the University of Missouri.

The implications of the two decisions not only for the border state of Missouri but for the entire South were immediately recognized. The leading Southern newspapers expressed the view that there was no point in trying to evade them and that "skeleton graduate courses" for Negroes would eventually have to be established in all state universities. "Time," said the Raleigh, Missouri, *News-Observer*, "has moved under our feet."

The smallest law school in the world is now functioning at 4300 Ferdinand Street, in the heart of the Negro district of St. Louis. It is the law school which Lincoln University, the state-supported Negro university, set up in 1939 in response to the mandate of the Supreme Court in the Gaines case. Seven students are enrolled—four in the first year, three in the senior year. The all-Negro faculty consists of three full-time instructors, one part-time instructor, and a librarian; there is also a clerical and secretarial staff. The school is housed in a building that would accommodate six or seven hundred students. Enrolment cannot be increased by the admission of white students, for this would be contrary to existing constitutional and statutory provisions, and it is doubtful whether even Japanese American evacuees from the West Coast could be admitted if any applied. Four of the present students are from St. Louis, one from the District of Columbia, one from South Carolina, and one from Louisiana.

In part the low attendance is due to the war, for thirty-four students were enrolled in 1939 and thirty in 1940, 1941, and 1942. The school was closed in 1943 for lack of "properly accredited" students—it is rumored that the failure to approve the credentials of applicants that year was part of a scheme to close the school altogether. There are only two Negro law schools in the country, the other being at Howard University, and Negro students throughout the South have written to Lincoln expressing an interest in attending the law school after the war. A number of Negro soldiers have also indicated their desire to enrol.

It is possible, therefore, that the law school may later become largely self-supporting. To the extent that it does, however, the principle of segregation will become more firmly established. For as the institution and its faculty expand, a new set of vested interests will be created. At present it costs the state more than $2,500 per year, per pupil, to maintain this Jim Crow institution, while the cost of sending students through the regular law school at the University of Missouri is but a fraction of this amount. Credit must be given the state for its compliance with the letter, if not the spirit, of the decision in the Gaines case. The law school is a first-rate institution. It has been approved by the Missouri Board of Bar Examiners and by the Association of American Law Schools. It boasts a law library of 31,000 volumes, one of the three largest law-school libraries in the South; its instructors are thoroughly competent, and its graduates have been readily admitted to the bar.

On the campus of Lincoln University at Jefferson City may be found the nation's most unique school of journalism, created in response to the decision in the Bluford case. Again the state has technically complied with the law. The school is housed in an attractive building; it has a workable library; it receives a large number of newspapers; it has a good print shop; the faculty is excellent; and the students get practical experience in editing a weekly newspaper. When it was first established, the faculty of the school of journalism of the state university at Columbia motored over to Lincoln three times a week to conduct classes, but the school now has a resident, full-time all-Negro faculty. About twelve students are enrolled. I visited a classroom large enough for forty or fifty students in which an instructor sat behind a desk with one student in front of him. It is possible that Negro students in the law and journalism schools are actually getting better instruction—certainly more individual attention—than they would at Columbia. The loneliness, however, for faculty and students, must be acute at times.

It is interesting to note that this ridiculous situation is not looked on with approval by the students at the University of Missouri. When the Lincoln Law School was opened in 1939, white students from Eden Seminary (Washington University) and from the state university established a picket line around the premises and carried placards with such inscriptions as "Old Jim Crow Is Dead" and "Smoke in St. Louis Is Bad—Prejudice Is Worse." In a poll taken at the University of Missouri last spring 60 per cent of the students favored the admission of Negroes to all divisions of the university—and 70 per cent favored their admission to the professional schools. When the University of Missouri and the University of Iowa debated the question "Should Negroes be admitted to the state universities?" Missouri upheld the negative with some reluctance. After the debate a vote was taken among the students present. The result was 216 for the affirmative, 93 opposed.

Recently a delegation of white girls from the University of Missouri appeared on the campus of Lincoln University to interview some of the Negro girls. They asked three questions: (1) Would you be interested in attending the Missouri University School of journalism if Negroes were admitted? (2) Would you expect to live in the same dormitories and belong to the same sororities? (3) Would you expect to date the white fellows on the campus? To each of these questions they received emphatic affirmative answers. The curious young ladies from Columbia seemed not merely satisfied but actually pleased by the answers. One of the delegates, a Jewish girl, said that the answers to the second and third questions had given her some new ideas.

The Missouri pattern of race relations was further complicated when St. Louis University decided last spring to open all its courses to Negro students. At present seventy-seven Negroes are in attendance. Contrary to the predictions of disaster, the non-Negro enrollment, despite the war, has increased 17 per cent since Negroes were admitted; the enrollment of white women has increased from 2,122 to 2,656. There has been no trouble in classrooms or on the campus, and white parents have withdrawn neither their children nor their financial support.

An interesting story lies behind the opening of St. Louis University to Negroes. Over a year ago, in the face of opposition from the hierarchy, notably from the Archbishop of St. Louis, some of the Jesuit instructors at the university began a campaign to force the admission of Negroes. Their efforts reached a climax in February, 1944, when Father Claude H. Heithaus, assistant professor of classical archaeology, delivered a militant sermon on race prejudice at the students' mass in University Church. "Ignorance," he said, "is the school of race prejudice, and provincialism is its tutor. Its memory is stuffed with lies and its mind is warped by emotionalism. Pride is its book and snobbery is its pen. All the hatreds and fears, all the cruelties and prejudices, of childhood are perpetuated by it. It blinds the intellect and it hardens the heart. Its wisdom is wonderful and fearful; for it never learns what is true, and it never forgets what is false." At the close of this memorable sermon—which should be required reading for all Catholics—Father Heithaus made a dramatic appeal to the students. "For the wrongs that have been done to the Mystical Body of Christ through the wronging of its colored members, we owe the suffering Christ an act of public reparation. Let us make it now. Will you please rise? Now repeat this prayer after me. 'Lord Jesus, we are sorry and ashamed for all the wrongs that white men have done to Your colored children. We are firmly resolved never again to have any part in them, and to do everything in our power to prevent them. Amen.' " The entire congregation rose in response to the appeal and repeated the prayer. Copies of the sermon had been printed in advance of its delivery so that no subsequent pressure, however powerful, could force a retraction. The St. Louis *Post-Dispatch* gave it wide publicity. The profound impression made by Father Heithaus on the Catholic community left the hierarchy no alternative to opening the doors of the university to Negroes.

The action of St. Louis University, with its attendant success, has placed both the University of Missouri and Washington University (largely Protestant-supported) in an extremely embarrassing position. The embarrassment is only enhanced by the curious circumstance that both institutions, while denying admission to Negroes, offer no objection to Japanese Americans. A dozen or so Japanese Americans are enrolled in the various professional schools of Washington University. Sooner or later the absurdity of separate professional schools—emphasized by the successful experiment at St. Louis University—is bound to bring about changes in policy at both Washington and Missouri. What is the University of Missouri going to do when a Negro applies for admission to its school of medicine or its school of mines? In either case, technical compliance, after the current pattern, would involve an expenditure of several million dollars. Fortunately, the people of Missouri will vote on a new constitution this month. Under Article IX of the proposed draft, the legislature could provide, if it wished, for non-segregated schools.

Characterized by one Southern newspaper as "a pebble dropped into a calm pool," the Gaines decision has set in motion a series of events which must ultimately culminate in the abolition of segregation in state-supported professional schools throughout the South.

*May 5, 1951*

## Death for Association

*Mary Mostert*

On May 8 Willie McGee will die in the electric chair for the alleged rape of a white woman in Laurel, Mississippi. He has had three trials, but a great many people, white and Negro, still feel that Willie McGee was accused of one thing and found guilty of something entirely different. The facts in the case have long since been buried in a political-racial mud-slinging contest. After the Civil Rights Congress, a so-called Communist-front organization, took up the fight, people seemed no longer to care about any evidence presented by either prosecution or defense.

What actually are the facts? On November 2, 1945, according to the prosecution, Willie McGee entered the woman's house in the dead of night and raped her. McGee's fingerprints in the room and the woman's statement were apparently the main support of the prosecution's case. It was established that the woman's husband and children were asleep in the adjoining room; the woman did not call out because she did not want to wake the children. The defense maintains that there was an entirely voluntary relationship between Willie and the woman for more than three years. The woman was supposed to have sent McGee a note asking him for a date when she was buying gasoline at the filling station where he worked. McGee states he complied with her wishes but finally decided to break off the affair and be faithful to his wife and four children. According to the defense, the woman never underwent a medical examination in order to establish rape.

Many questions are left unanswered by both sides, but certainly there seems pitifully little evidence to warrant taking a man's life. Probably no one except those directly involved will ever know the true story. Most people seem to think that McGee is not guilty of rape but at worst of seduction, perhaps with the woman doing the seducing. Of course in the minds of professional Southerners there is no such thing as a voluntary sex relation between a Negro man and a white woman—any relation at all, to them, is rape.

In spite of the strong feeling about the case, individuals and organizations that are usually vitally interested in such matters have had little to say. A Negro leader has explained why: "This case would warrant the support of the general public, but because the Communists are connected with it, the people are afraid to say anything." A white newspaperman has written: "Communist support has just about sent McGee to the chair. Governor Wright is a very stubborn man, and now he is determined to see McGee burn." The fact that many non-Communists also believe McGee innocent has been conveniently ignored.

The frightening thing about the Willie McGee case is not that a man has been sentenced to die for a crime which he may not have committed. It is not that McGee, by flouting a color taboo, brought down on himself the unequal justice of an unfair, undemocratic system. It is not that no white man has ever been executed in Mississippi for the crime for which McGee will die; or that if the man had been white and the woman black, the case would probably never have got into the courts. The new and most dangerous element is the conviction by association. As one Mississippian put it, "I don't think McGee is guilty of rape, but since he is hooked up with the Communists I don't think he ought to be given another trial." Willie McGee was convicted because he was black and supported by Communists, not on any conclusive evidence.

Editorials in the white press say that anyone who "assists the Communists in trying to save Willie McGee helps the Communist cause." They do not speak of the guilt or innocence of the man. According to a prominant Negro editor, many Negroes, feeling frustrated, unsettled, and confused by such treatment, fall "easy prey to Communist propaganda."

The life or death of Willie McGee, for all practical purposes, is no longer an issue, but the trial has left bitterness and restlessness in the Negro community which will long remain as issues. Negro leaders who for many years have worked for better understanding between the races believe that the Negroes are more unhappy over their position than ever before. The case of Willie McGee has left an ugly scar.

What are we doing to ourselves? In a hysterical attempt to stamp out communism are we creating the very conditions on which communism thrives? Are we completely ignoring our own basic principles and allowing our courts to pass judgment on the basis of race, color, lawyers employed, religious or political affiliation? Now is the time that we should show the world, our minority groups, and especially ourselves that we have some faith in our democracy. By refusing men like Willie McGee fair trial because of their race or their political association, we do not stop communism, we promote it.

*July 7, 1956*

## The New Negro

*E. Franklin Frazier*

Thirty years ago a New Negro made his appearance in the North, following closely upon the mass migrations of Negroes from the South during and following World War I. His emergence was marked by race riots in which he resisted violence with violence. On the spiritual plane, the emergence was heralded by an artistic and literary renaissance in which the Negro made a new evaluation of his experience in America.

Today a New Negro is emerging in the South. So far, no race riots have marked the event nor are there any indications—yet—that the new spirit among Southern Negroes will produce an artistic and literary renaissance. Nevertheless, there are indications all over the South that the Negro is no longer afraid to face the white man and say frankly that he wants equality and an end to segregation.

Nothing so dramatizes the difference between old and new attitudes of the Negro in the South as the contrast between the dignity and courage of Autherine Lucy and the reported attitude of her parents. According to the New York *Times*, Miss Lucy's father said, with reference to her behavior: "We raised ten head of children, nine of them still living and every one of them was taught to stay their distance from white folks, but to give them all their respect. If Autherine has changed from this, she didn't get her new ideas from home."

The boycott of buses in Montgomery, which began as a spontaneous mass movement against discrimination and segregation, has revealed how deep and how widespread is the new spirit. Despite violence and threats of violence the Negro continues his fight to exercise the right to vote. Negro college students are for the first time showing a militant spirit in regard to segregation and discrimination. The autocratic administrations of Negro colleges, especially state schools, have taught humility and acceptance of existing racial patterns; as a consequence, their graduates have been on the whole apathetic toward the race problem. Therefore, Negroes as well as the white controllers of Negro education were startled when the students at the South Carolina State College for Negroes went on strike because state officials threatened to investigate the affiliations of the faculty and student body with the National Association for the Advancement of Colored People. The leader of the students was expelled and the students went back to classes under threat from the Negro administration; they refused, nevertheless, to eat bread supplied from a bakery owned by a member of the White Citizens

Council. More recently, at the State College for Negroes in Tallahassee, Florida, the students struck against the bus company after two female students were arrested for defying segregation regulations.

Whatever may have been the real feelings of Miss Lucy's father, his statement contains a significant observation—namely, that she did not acquire her new ideas at home. The new spirit of the Southern Negroes is a radical break from the traditional pattern of race relations. The old pattern had its roots in a rural society, and, just as the emergence of the New Negro in the North was due to the flight of the Negro from feudal America, so the emergence of the New Negro in the South is primarily the result of the movement of Negroes to cities.

The urbanization of southern Negroes has resulted, first, in a marked change in their occupations. At present, only about a third of the Negroes in the South gain their living from agriculture. Negro workers have not been assimilated into manufacturing, trade and service industries to the same extent as white workers; and many Negroes who have migrated to the southern cities have been forced to move a second time and seek a living outside the South. Nevertheless, because of conditions in southern agriculture, Negroes continue to move into southern cities and those who find work get a new outlook on life as industrial workers. Although Negroes are still kept, on the whole, to unskilled occupations, they receive much higher wages in industry than they did from agriculture. In 1949 the median income of urban Negro workers was twice that of Negro farmers, including owners, renters and laborers, and today the median income of urban Negroes is between three and four times that of rural Negroes. Moreover, although the median income of Negro families in southern cities is only 56 per cent that of white families, this represents an increase during the past six or seven years.

This improvement in the Negro's economic status has had several important effects upon his conception of himself and of his position in the South. He has a greater sense of security and he is in a better position to contribute money to the fight for equality in American life. This shows, for example, in the tremendous growth of NAACP membership in the South. The Negro can now buy those things—radios, televisions, newspapers and magazines—which symbolize a middle-class standard of living and are indicative of his new orientation to the world. The Negro middle class in the South has grown considerably, due largely to the increase in the number of Negro teachers and other professional and white collar workers as well as skilled workers.

The social consequences of urbanization, even more than the economic, helped to bring about profound changes in the Negro's attitude towards his place in southern society. First among these social consequences has been the improvement in his educational facilities. Undoubtedly the Supreme Court desegregation decisions were responsible for some of the recent improvements. But this development was already under way before the decisions, notably during the period of rapid industrialization of the South between 1940 and 1952 when the region's per capita income increased over 200 per cent. The improvement in Negro education was reflected in the reduction of the disparity between the per capita expenditure for the instruction of white and Negro children; in the increase in school attendance at all levels, especially at the secondary level; in the equalization of Negro and white teachers' salaries (except in Mississippi and South Carolina) and in new buildings and other facilities for Negroes.

The influence of formal education in bringing about a new spirit among southern Negroes is only one of a number of factors which have been breaking down their social and mental isolation. In the larger southern cites, relations between whites and Negroes have necessarily undergone changes. For example, in the country store or small-town bank, the Negro is generally expected to observe the "etiquette of race relations" and wait until white people are served. But in the large-city chain stores the customer, who has no status because of race, takes his turn in line. One of the reasons for the present racial tensions in regard to transportation in southern cities is that there is an attempt to maintain a caste relationship in an area of social relations that has become highly mobile and secular.

The effect of mere physical mobility upon Negro attitudes should not be overlooked. Thousands of southern Negroes, rural as well as urban, are moving about the country more than at any time in their history. They see Negroes occupying positions and enjoying rights which were undreamed of a few decades ago. Moreover, they themselves are treated with greater respect when they leave the South. This physical mobility has been increased by the military draft. But military service has done more; it has given the Negro a new conception of his role and his rights as an American citizen. This effect is heightened when the Negro serves in an "integrated" army unit. Men with military experience have often taken the lead in demanding the Negro's right to the ballot. It is perhaps not an accident that the recognized leader of the bus boycott in Montgomery, Alabama, is a minister who served in the armed forces.

Thus the appearance of a New Negro in the South is due primarily to the breakdown of the social and mental isolation in which the Negro people have lived. In a short story which appeared during the Negro renaissance in Harlem, Rudolph Fisher portrayed the astonishment of a Negro migrant from the South who could hardly believe his eyes when he saw a Negro policeman. There are few southern Negroes today who would be astonished at the sight. If they have not seen a Negro policeman in the South, they have become accustomed to seeing him on the screen or on television. Again, the increasing literacy of southern Negroes, resulting from their better education, furnishes another escape from their former mental isolation. Now they can read newspapers and magazines—especially the Negro publications, most of which are located outside the South. These publications constantly play up the Negro's fight for equality, the victories which he has won and the achievements of Negroes everywhere.

The new conception which the southern Negro is acquiring of himself and his place in American life as the result of urbanization is being fostered by the dominant forces in our changing society. Although the growth of labor unions in the South has been retarded by the racial situation, Negro workers are acquiring a new grasp of their relationship to industry through the efforts of the more progressive unions. The present battle for civil rights, which has a special meaning for southern Negroes, is giving his own battle for equality a new orientation. Moreover, southern Negroes are becoming aware of the struggle of the colored colonial peoples for self-determination and the leaders, at least, are to some extent identifying their own struggle with the larger one.

This new awareness of the social and economic forces in American life as well as in the world at large is the mark of the New Negro in the South. And the attitude of the New Negro is perhaps best expressed in the response of a Negro farmer in South Carolina who had been subjected to economic pressure: "We don't scare any more."

*October 27, 1956*

## Which Way Harlem?
### Unity on a Key Issue

*John O'Kearney*

The country approaches its Presidential elections in postures of fantasy. Eisenhower's Republicans and Stevenson's Democrats contend for ballots on jerry-built platforms of Peace and Prosperity, or More Peace and More Prosperity, pretending to be unaware that men of good will in millions are rising to assert that government must recognize and act upon the fact that the issue of our time is civil rights.

*The Nation* set out to enquire what effect the struggle over the Supreme Court's racial segregation order of 1954 is having among the Negroes of the North, specifically in Harlem. Has the incidence of mob violence against integration in the South stirred New York's Negroes to extraordinary political consciousness? Does the Negro, normally neither more nor less political-minded than most of his white fellow citizens, today merit the special concern of both major parties because of "apathy"?

On such issues as the two parties have been able to contrive for public debate, I found the people of Harlem as apathetic as any practical observer would expect. Political interest varies in Harlem as it varies everywhere among the several economic classes. The wretchedly poor are too busy scratching to care about anything else but the prospects of relief from their immediate, clinging wretchedness. The middle group strops its political mind upon the pros and cons of: What's in it for me? Who'll build new schools, hospitals and housing projects? Who's for more pay and broadened opportunity for better jobs? Who's for a non-discriminatory sharing of the city payroll, for cracking down on gouging landlords, for cleaner, safer streets and regular garbage collections? And the upper crust is just sufficiently ill-informed about the processes of political economy to be genuinely perplexed by the opposing claims of office seekers that their machine alone is fit to insure domestic tranquility and to promote the general welfare. The Negro upper crust, like the white, does not know quite how far at sea it is, and is wary about rocking the boat.

Insofar as the Republicans claim credit for peace and prosperity, insofar as the Democrats claim that they could make the one more certain and the other more full, the people of Harlem are apathetic, indeed; but they are in no likelihood of falling into a coma.

In the apartment of a Harlem family, the elderly widowed mother of four children quietly discussed the broad issues as Negroes see them. This woman was a postmistress in the South thirty years ago. Her husband had been a school teacher. "We're not looking for anything that would be wrong," she said, "only for what's right. The Constitution says we have the right to vote. In many parts of the South we either can't vote or we can vote only for people who wish us no good." On the issue of school integration, she said she favors the use of force as it was used at Clinton, Tennessee—the force of law sufficient to forestall violence and mob-inspired bloodshed, a force to keep the peace and yet to make the law the law. To this woman's son, a highly educated, dedicated worker for Negro rights, effectively organized political action could well be the answer. "The Negro is a *peculiar* person," he said. "He wants to be an American citizen. He doesn't wish to break the law—even to gain his rights."

The Negro, 15,000,000 of him throughout the country, each wanting equality of opportunity as one of his civil rights, is constantly aware that in this prosperous national household his victuals are mainly the left-overs from the white man's plate; that if and when—as is not inconceivable—there are portents of the larder's going bare, he'll be back to grubbing for crumbs beneath the white man's table. Of course, things aren't quite as bad as they used to be; there was a time in Harlem, before the riots of 1943, when the whole length of 125th Street, the area's main thoroughfare, running from river to river across Manhattan Island, had no more than a handful of Negro-owned shops manned by Negro workers. Boycotts and a day of violence have changed that. City jobs as policemen, firemen, teachers, clerks, have opened to the Negro. He drives buses and runs subway trains, and there are scores of other jobs, formerly in the white man's preserve, now available to him. Wars have forced changes upon the pattern of race relations—wars and the National Association for the Advancement of Colored People. The gates are opening, but the walls of the ghetto are far from down in this Year of Emancipation, XCIII.

Almost a century has gone since Lincoln's proclamation, since enactment of the Fourteenth Amendment, but in substance the complaint concerning the deprivation of civil rights is valid still. Here and there, in this little thing or that, says the Negro, changes for the better have occurred, but over the whole nation, North as well as South, the opprobrious name of "nigger" is still uttered in condescension or in hate, testifying to the unreadiness of most whites to grant anything to the Negro out of right. What the Negro has gained since Reconstruction, he has gained through pressure of one kind or another. Recognition of this fact is spreading over the whole Negro community. "We have come," said a Negro trade-union leader, "to the brink of the lack of fear. The rank-and-file are saying: 'Whatever comes, we'll face it.' The time has come to complete the Civil War."

In Harlem, as in Negro communities elsewhere, forces are rallying in support of those on the combat fronts in the struggle for civil rights. The Montgomery bus boycott got immediate advisory and financial aid. Northern Negro leaders are in close touch with the tense situation in Birmingham, where the NAACP is under fire and Negroes, fearful of Ku Klux Klan and White Citizens Council outrages, have barricaded their homes and carry shotguns with them in their cars. Money, food and clothing have been raised in Harlem for the past three years for Negroes of Clarendon County, South Carolina, whose action in seeking a U.S. Supreme Court ruling on integration brought down upon them White Council economic sanctions that have driven many to the edge of starvation. (White landlords previously content to get their rent in harvest fields are now demanding cash; so are the country stores which from time immemorial have been selling to farmers on credit.)

It is told of the 1943 riots that, as Harlemites ranged through the streets smashing store fronts and pillaging, Chinese laundrymen pasted crude placards on their windows, reading: "Me colored too"; and that the signs saved them. That bond of "me colored too" is the key to Harlem thought and action even more surely now than it was then. Ultimately the Negro will be content with nothing less than all that was promised to him, *as a citizen*, by Article IV of the Constitution, which declared that "The citizens of each State shall be entitled to all the privileges and immunities of citizens in the several states."

A sentient understanding of the spurious grounds of the white man's prejudice is now coming to the Negro almost in his cradle. Illustration: In a Harlem classroom, Negro children of nine and ten discuss current events. A girl refers to a newspaper story of a *white* woman jailed in Baltimore because she had borne a child by a Negro. There is something incomprehensible about this. Apparently the tables have been turned upside down. Is it not always the Negro who gets hit by the police? A classmate offers an explanation. The police did not go after the Negro man in this case, he says, because it was taken for granted that he was ignorant, irresponsible, "couldn't know any better" than to have broken the law. Wide-eyed nodding heads accept this interpretation of the white man's thinking as indubitably correct.

Attending this understanding of erratic prejudice is a growing pride in the achievements of the colored world abroad. Teachers report their pupils intense interest (however fragmentary their knowledge) in the affairs of Egypt, black Africa, India, Indonesia and China—an interest awakened by the talk of adults at home. The grownups, indignant about—sometimes contemptuous of—federal sufferance of the efforts of White Citizens Council mobs and of state legislatures to flout the integration order, are finding a patch of comfort in "colored" Egypt's seizure of the Suez Canal. And in candid discussions in private homes, and even in barrooms and quiet shops, one often notes outspoken sympathy for Soviet Russia. As one man put it: "Only in Russia, among white nations, can a black man walk in the streets with people who don't make a point of being white."

Harlemites would give India unstinted aid, firm in the belief that it would be used for the good of common folk. They would have Communist China in the United Nations, and have Washington grant her full recognition; for, said a spokesman, "It's absurd to attempt to isolate 600,000,000 people, foolish not to trade with them; and above all, *with us it's a matter of color!*"

This avowed sense of unity with peoples of all shades of color (except, for the moment, with the white man's pink) should be sufficient to convince the European-American that his Afro-American fellow citizens are capable of taking powerful and coherent political action. "There is nothing," said one, "that happens in the South that does not in a measure happen to all of us." And yet another Harlemite, this one a middle-aged woman, said of her neighbors: "Every time something goes wrong down South, it fills 'em up. They're jus' waitin' . . . jus' waitin'."

In not more than two Negroes out of scores did I find aggressive hostility to the white man. One of these calmly said that he had had the treasonable wish that Japan would beat us in World War II. The other, a man met in the street who said he was a teacher, uncovered his hostility by spitting scorn on the notion that race differences exist at all—even as a concept for the convenience of ethnographers. A third man, a gentleman and a scholar, plated with a stoic humor, said he was at a loss to know how to deal with the European-American. The white American's capacity for being un-Christian, he said, could not be measured, nor the depth of his bigotry fathomed; he pursues his bigoted way with a "ferocity" that leads one to the conclusion—against the dictates of reason—"that there must be something biologically wrong with him." "If this be true," my acquaintance said, laughing, "it would be a sort of reversal of our respective positions."

This third man's judgment is harsh, but it's been heard before. Frederick Douglass, Negro fighter for freedom, was invited to address the citizenry of his home town of Rochester on July 4, 1852. "What to the slave is the Fourth of July?" he asked, and ended his address:

> Go where you may, search where you will, roam through all the monarchies and despotisms of the Old World, travel through South America, search out every abuse, and when you have found the last, lay your facts by the side of the everyday practices of this nation, and you will say with me that, for revolting barbarity and shameless hypocrisy, America reigns without a rival.
>
> The citizens erected a monument to his memory.

The struggle is no longer a struggle of slaves in chains under the whip, but so long as the Negro has been denied the civil rights that were not his rights because he was a slave, but ought to have become his rights as a freed man, he is shackled still. What in Harlem is he going to do about it, come Election Day next month?

In 1952, Harlem voted for Stevenson by four to one, largely because the Democratic machine has controlled the vote there since 1932. This year, independent Negro observers predict a shift, but they differ on its direction. One school says that 8 to 12 per cent of the Democratic Negro vote will go GOP, not because Eisenhower is gaining favor over Stevenson, but because the Negro wants to elect a Republican Senate which would get rid of Senator Eastland of Mississippi as chairman of the Judiciary Committee. This view holds that the Negroes want a GOP victory even at the cost of delaying the retirement of FBI chief J. Edgar Hoover, who in Harlem opinion would be better employed in chasing down racist rabble-rousers than in pursuing Communists—"those horsemen without a horse."

The other school thinks the shift will be the other way because Negroes have come to believe that a Stevenson in the White House would be "more amenable" than an Eisenhower. An executive of the Brotherhood of Sleeping Car Porters, a union which has influence considerably out of proportion to its 18,000 membership, put it this way: "The Negro has been disaffected by the GOP. We cannot have confidence in our president. Responsible groups could always get in to talk with Franklin Roosevelt—and with Truman. For three years, responsible groups in convention have asked to meet with the President. On four occasions he sent liaison officers to find out why, but nothing ever happened. Stevenson, we feel, would be more approachable."

So go the analyses. Meanwhile Negroes of both major parties have carried on an intensive registration campaign aimed at getting out 2,000,000 new Negro voters on November 6. They have 6,000,000 potential voters in the whole field, about 40 per cent of whom cast ballots in 1952.

In Harlem itself, young men and women formed an Independent Citizens Committee for Encouragement of Registration. This group, so the thinking goes, may become the core of partisan action in 1960, an instrument for electing a citizens' candidate to Congress. But there is no intention of forming a permanent Negro Party. This the Negro abjures. He does not want separate political strength. He wants integration, political assimilation, identity with the white man's established parties. He wants his civil rights.

*August 6, 1960*

## Finishing School for Pickets

*Howard Zinn*

*Atlanta, Ga.*
One quiet afternoon some weeks ago, with the dogwood on the Spelman College campus newly bloomed and the grass close-cropped and fragrant, an attractive, tawny-skinned girl crossed the lawn to her dormitory to put a notice on the bulletin board. It read: Young Ladies Who Can Picket Please Sign Below.

The notice revealed, in its own quaint language, that within the dramatic revolt of Negro college students in the South today another phenomenon has been developing. This is the upsurge of the young, educated Negro woman against the generations-old advice of her elders: be nice, be well-mannered and ladylike, don't speak loudly, and don't get into trouble. On the campus of the nation's leading college for Negro young women—pious, sedate, encrusted with the traditions of gentility and moderation—these exhortations, for the first time, are being firmly rejected.

Spelman College girls are still "nice," but not enough to keep them from walking up and down, carrying picket signs, in front of two supermarkets in the heart of Atlanta. They are well-mannered, but this is somewhat tempered by a recent declaration that they will use every method short of violence to end segregation. As for staying out of trouble, they were doing fine until this spring, when fourteen of them were arrested and jailed by Atlanta police. The staid New England women missionaries who helped found Spelman College back in the 1880s would probably be distressed at this turn of events, and present-day conservatives in the administration and faculty are rather upset. But respectability is no longer respectable among young Negro women attending college today.

"You can always tell a Spelman girl," alumni and friends of the college have boasted for years. The "Spelman girl" walked gracefully, talked properly, went to church every Sunday, poured tea elegantly and, in general, had all the attributes of the product of a fine finishing school. If intellect and talent and social consciousness happened to develop also, they were, to an alarming extent, by-products.

This is changing. It would be an exaggeration to say: "You can always tell a Spelman girl—she's under arrest." But the statement has a measure of truth. Spelman girls have participated strongly in all of the major actions undertaken by students of the Atlanta University Center* in recent months. They have also added a few touches of their

* The Atlanta University Center is a loose federation of six privately supported Negro colleges in Atlanta: Morehouse College for men, Spelman College for women, Clark College, Morris College, Atlanta University (the graduate school), and the Interdenominational Theological Center. Spelman gets its name from the mother-in-law of John D. Rockefeller. The elder Rockefeller's money put Spelman on its feet.

own and made white Atlanta, long proud that its nice Negro college girls were staying "in their place," take startled notice. A few weeks ago a Spelman student, riding downtown on the bus, took a seat up front. (This is still a daring maneuver, for in spite of a court decision desegregating the buses, most Negroes stay in the rear.) The bus driver muttered something unpleasant, and a white woman sitting nearby waved her hand and said, "Oh, she's prob'ly goin' downtown to start another one o' them demonstrations."

The reputedly sweet and gentle Spelman girls were causing trouble even before the recent wave of sit-ins cracked the wall of legalism in the structure of desegregation strategy. Three years ago, they aroused the somnolent Georgia Legislature into near-panic by attempting to sit in the white section of the gallery. They were finally shunted into the colored area, but returned for the next legislative session. This time they refused to sit segregated and remained on their feet, in a pioneering show of non-violent resistance, until ordered out of the chamber.

The massive, twelve-foot stone wall, barbed-wire fence and magnolia trees that encircle the Spelman campus have always formed a kind of chastity belt around the student body, not only confining young women to a semi-monastic life in order to uphold the ruling matriarchs' conception of Christian morality, but "protecting" the students from contact with the cruel outside world of segregation. Inside the domain of the Atlanta University Center, with its interracial faculty, occasional white students and frequent white visitors, there flourished a microcosm of the future, where racial barriers did not exist and one could almost forget this was the deep South. But this insulation, while protecting the University Center's island of integration, also kept the city of Atlanta for many years from feeling the barbed resentment of Negro students against segregation. Spelman girls, more sheltered than women at the other colleges, were among the first to leave the island and to begin causing little flurries of alarm in the segregated world outside.

Even before bus segregation in the city was declared illegal, some Spelman girls rode up front and withstood the glares and threats of fellow passengers and the abuse of the bus driver. Once, a white man pulled a knife from his pocket and waved it at a Spelman sophomore sitting opposite him in a front seat. She continued to sit there until she came to her stop, and then got off. Spelman students, along with others, showed up in the main Atlanta library in sufficient numbers last year to worry the city administration into a decision to admit Negroes there. The girls spent hours between classes at the county courthouse, urging Negroes to register for voting. They made a survey of the Atlanta airport in connection with a suit to desegregate the airport restaurant, and a Spelman student took the witness stand at the trial to help win the case.

Such activities may bring bewilderment to the conservative matriarchy which has played a dominant role in the college's history, but they are nothing short of infuriating to the officialdom of the State of Georgia, ensconced inside the gold-domed Capitol just a few minutes' drive from the Negro colleges of the Atlanta University Center. Georgia's bespectacled but still near-sighted Governor Vandiver, who resembles a pleasant and studious junior executive until he begins to speak, began his current burst of hysteria when student leaders at the six Negro colleges put their heads together and produced a remarkable document which was placed as a full-page ad in the Atlanta newspapers on March 9 (and reprinted by *The Nation* on April 2). The document, entitled "An Appeal for Human Rights," catalogued Negro grievances with irritating specificity and promised to "use every legal and non-violent means at our disposal" to end segregation. Vandiver's reaction was immediate: the appeal was "anti-American" and "obviously not written by students." Furthermore, the Governor said: "It did not sound like it was prepared in any Georgia school or college; nor, in fact, did it read like it was written in this country." Actually, a Spelman student had written the first rough draft, and student leaders from the other five colleges collaborated in preparing the finished product.

On the sixth day after publication of the appeal, at 11:30 on a Tuesday morning, several hundred students from the Atlanta University Center staged one of the South's most carefully planned and efficiently executed sit-in demonstrations at ten different eating places, including restaurants in the State Capitol, the county courthouse and City Hall. Among the demonstrators were several carloads of Spelman students, riding into town that morning without the knowledge of deans or presidents or faculty, to participate in the sit-ins, tangle with the police and end up in prison.

Of the seventy-seven students arrested, fourteen were Spelmanites; and all but one of the fourteen were girls from the deep South, from places like Bennettsville, South Carolina; Bainbridge, Georgia; Ocala, Florida—the Faulknerian small towns of traditional Negro submissiveness.

The Atlanta *Constitution* and the *Journal* noted the remarkable discipline and orderliness of the demonstration. Perhaps their training came in handy; in prison, Spelman girls were perfect ladies. A Spelman honor student sat behind bars quietly reading C.S. Lewis' *The Screwtape Letters*, while flashbulbs popped around her.

The State of Georgia, however, reacted with a special vindictiveness. To the seventy-seven sit-inners, the Fulton County prosecutor has added the names of the six students who wrote and signed "An Appeal for Human Rights." All eighty-three are facing triple charges of breaching the peace, intimidating restaurant owners and refusing to leave the premises, the penalties for which add up to nine years in prison and $6,000 in fines. The use of "conspiracy" charges to tie all eighty-three students to each of the ten eating places creates a theoretical possibility of ninety-year sentences. Nothing is fantastic in this state.

On May 17, to commemorate the 1954 Supreme Court decision, over a thousand students marched through downtown Atlanta to a mass meeting at the Wheat Street Baptist Church, while a hundred hastily summoned state troopers guarded the Capitol a few blocks away with guns, billy clubs and tear gas. The students were heavily armed with books and songs, and when they were assembled in the church sang, "That Old Ne-gro, He Ain't What He Used to Be!"

What is the source of this new spirit which has angered the state administration and unsettled the old guardians of genteel passivity?

There is something fundamental at work which is setting free for the first time the anger pent up in generations of quiet, well-bred Negro college women, not only at Spelman College, but at Fisk, Bennett, Alabama State and other institutions throughout the South. The same warm currents which are loosening the ice-blocks of the *status quo* throughout the world are drifting into the South and mingling with local eddies of discontent. What has been called a global "revolution in expectations" rises also in the hearts and minds of Southern Negroes.

Expanding international contacts are reaching even into small Southern colleges. The arrested Spelman girl from Bennettsville, South Carolina, spent last year in Geneva studying international relations, and spent the summer in Soviet Russia. The Atlanta student who helped draft the appeal has just returned from a year of studying music in Paris. Last September, two young African women, under the auspices of the militant Tom Mboya, flew in from Kenya to enroll at Spelman. The tame-sounding phrase "cultural exchange" may have revolutionary political implications.

Like many Negro campuses in the South, Spelman is losing its provincial air. This spring, the first white students came—five girls from Midwestern colleges who are the advance guard of a long-term exchange program. In the past few months there has been a sudden burgeoning of contact, both intellectual and social, with students from the half-dozen white colleges in Atlanta. Liberal Southern whites have joined the faculties of Spelman and Morehouse colleges. This growing interracial contact is helping to break down the mixture of awe-suspicion-hostility with which deep-South Negroes generally regard whites. And for Spelman, unexpressed but obvious pressure to adopt the manners and courtesies of white middle-class society breaks down as Spelman girls get a close look at how whites really behave.

The new Spelman girl is having an effect on faculty and administrators. Many who were distressed and critical when they first learned their sweet young things were sitting behind bars, later joined in the applause of the Negro community and the nation at large. Spelman's President Albert Manley, who inherited the traditions of conservatism and moderation when he took the helm seven years ago, has responded with cautious but increasing encouragement to the boldness of his young women. At the college commencement exercises this year, Manley startled the audience by departing from the printed program and the parade of parting platitudes with a vigorous statement of congratulations to the senior class for breaking the "docile generation" label with its sit-ins, demonstrations and picketing.

Four years ago, a girl in my Western Civilization course spoke candidly and bitterly about her situation and that of her classmates. "When I was little," she said, "my mother told me: remember, you've got two strikes against you—you're colored, and you're a woman; one more strike and you're out—so be careful." The student continued: "That's the trouble with all these Spelman girls. They're careful. They hardly utter a peep. They do everything right, and obey the rules, and they'll be fine ladies some day. But I don't want to be that kind of a lady. I'm leaving at the end of the semester and going back up North."

I don't know where that student is today. She would have graduated with this class on Commencement Day, with students who marched and picketed and sat-in and were arrested, and will soon come up for trial. I wish she had stayed to see.

*March 3, 1962*

## Report on Civil Rights
### Fumbling on the New Frontier

*Martin Luther King, Jr.*

*In our issue of Feb. 4, 1961, the Reverend Martin Luther King, Jr., outlined a program on civil rights which he thought the newly installed*

*Kennedy Administration might fruitfully follow. The title was "Equality Now: The President Has the Power"; the thesis, that faster progress toward racial equality could be made by the exercise of existing Executive authority than through Congress where, in the last analysis, the Dixiecrats wield decisive power.*

*Mr. King's original article was projected as the first of a series of annual reviews by him of the fight for racial equality. In the following article, the year 1961 comes under scrutiny. It goes without saying that the American Negro has no more knowledgeable or influential spokesman than this Southern clergyman, who rose to national prominence during the historic Montgomery bus boycott and is now President of the Southern Christian Leadership Conference.*

—EDITORS.

The Kennedy Administration in 1961 waged an essentially cautious and defensive struggle for civil rights against an unyielding adversary. As the year unfolded, Executive initiative became increasingly feeble, and the chilling prospect emerged of a general Administration retreat. In backing away from an Executive Order to end discrimination in housing, the President did more to undermine confidence in his intentions than could be offset by a series of smaller accomplishments during the year. He has begun 1962 with a show of renewed aggressiveness; one can only hope that it will be sustained.

In any case, it is clear that the vigorous young men of this Administration have displayed a certain *élan* in the attention they give to civil-rights issues. Undaunted by Southern backwardness and customs, they conceived and launched some imaginative and bold forays. It is also clear that this Administration has reached out more creatively than its predecessors to blaze some new trails, notably in the sensitive areas of voting and registration. Moreover, President Kennedy has appointed more Negroes to key government posts than has any previous administration. One Executive Order has been issued which, if vigorously enforced, will go a long, long way toward eliminating employment discrimination in federal agencies and in industries where government contracts are involved. So it is obvious that the Kennedy Administration has to its credit some constructive and praiseworthy achievements.

With regard to civil rights, then, it would be profoundly wrong to take an extreme position either way when viewing the Administration. While the President has not yet earned unqualified confidence and support, neither has he earned rejection and withdrawal of support. Perhaps his earnestness of attitude, fed with the vitamins of mass action, may yet grow into passionate purpose. The civil-rights movement must remain critical and flexible, watchful and active.

It is fortunate that the initiatives that President Kennedy has directed toward the reduction of international tensions present no contradictions with respect to civil rights. The Administration need have no fear that the white South will punish it for its desegregation attitudes by withholding support for a new foreign policy. While white and Negro Southerners have not yet mastered the art of living together in a relaxed society of brotherhood, they are united in the desire to remain alive. Indeed, Negroes *need* an international *détente*, because in a period of tensions and crisis their needs are easily forgotten, and a political rigidity grips the nation that sharply inhibits social change.

The year 1961 was characterized by inadequacy and incompleteness in the civil-rights field. It is not only that the Administration too often retreated in haste from a battlefield which it has proclaimed a field of honor, but—more significantly—its basic strategic goals have been narrowed. Its efforts have been directed toward limited accomplishments in a number of areas, affecting few individuals and altering old patterns only superficially. Changes in depth and breadth are not yet in sight, nor has there been a commitment of resources adequate to enforce extensive change. It is a melancholy fact that the Administration is aggressively driving only toward the limited goal of token integration.

It is important to understand the perspective from which this criticism develops. The paradox of laudable, limited progress on the one hand, and frustrating insufficiency of progress on the other, is understandable if it is realized that the civil-rights struggle can be viewed from two quite dissimilar perspectives. Many people of good will accept the achievement of steady advances, even when fractional. They feel simple addition must eventually accumulate a totality of social gains which will answer the problem. Others, however, viewing the task from the long perspective of history, are less sanguine. They are aware that the struggle being waged is against an opposition capable of the most tenacious resistance, either actively or through inertia. Such forces are not overcome by simple pressures, but only through massive exertion. This is a law not alone of physics, but of society as well.

To illustrate, it is not practical to integrate buses, and then over an extended period of time expect to add another gain, and then another and another. Unfortunately, resistance stiffens after each limited victory; inertia sets in, and the forward movement not only slows down, but is often reversed entirely. What is required to maintain gains is an initial sweep of positive action so far-reaching that it immobilizes and weakens the adversary, thus depriving him of his power to retaliate. Simultaneously, in order that public officials are not left free to circumvent the law by local devices, an extensive campaign to put the franchise in the hands of Negroes must be conducted. These programs, in turn, require for their success that a corps of responsible leaders be trained and developed—that ample legal defense skills and financial resources be available. In short, what is required is massive social mobilization uniting the strength of individuals, organizations, government, press and schools.

It is clear that to date no Administration has grasped the problem in this total sense and committed the varieties of weaponry required for constructive action on so broad a scale.

Beyond this, the American Negro is impelled by psychological motives not fully understood even by his white allies. Every Negro, regardless of his educational or cultural level, carries the burden of centuries of depravation and inferior status. The burden is with him every waking moment of his life—and often, through his dreams, dominates his sleeping moments as well. It diminishes his confidence and belittles his achievements. He is tormented by the overwhelming task of catching up. This problem sharpens to a razor edge when he confronts a new struggle and is aware of the pitiful inadequacy of his resources.

When the nation feels threatened by war, a military budget of some $50 billion is freely spent each year to achieve security. Not even $1 billion a year is spent by government on behalf of 20,000,000 Negroes seeking to defend themselves from the persistent attack on their rights. When Negroes look from their overworked, under-manned civil-rights organizations to their government, they see in Washington only a tiny bureau, equally undermanned and over-worked, hopelessly incapable of doing what is necessary. They cannot feel certain that progress is over tomorrow's horizon, or even that the government has any real understanding of the dimensions of their problems.

Their sense of inadequacy is further heightened when they look at Africa and Asia and see with envy the bursting of age-old bonds in societies still partially at a tribal level, but ablaze with modern vitality and creativity. An Alliance for Progress for South America, to cost $20 billion, is forward-looking and necessary. An Alliance for Progress for the turbulent South is equally necessary. From this perspective, the New Frontier is unfortunately not new enough; and the Frontier is set too close to the rear.

In the year that has just passed, certain significant developments occurred in the South that are worthy of comment. Despite tor-menting handicaps, Negroes moved from sporadic, limited actions to broad-scale activities different in kind and degree from anything done in the past. City after city was swept by boycotts, sit-ins, freedom rides and registration campaigns. A new spirit was manifest in the Negro's willingness to demonstrate in the streets of communities in which, by tradition, he was supposed to step aside when a white man strode toward him.

The change in spirit was even more dramatically exemplified by the Negroes' willingness, in communities such as Albany, Georgia, to endure mass jailing. Words cannot express the exultation felt by the individual as he finds himself, with hundreds of his fellows, behind prison bars for a cause he knows is just. This exultation has been felt by businessmen, workers, teachers, ministers, housewives, house-maids—in ages ranging from the early teens to the seventies. Signifi-cantly, these people were not gathered from across the nation; all were local residents, except for a few "outsiders" and "aliens"—including this writer, who is from far-off Atlanta, Georgia.

To the depth of these movements was added breadth when areas such as Mississippi and rural Georgia, hitherto quiescent, were churned into turbulence by registration campaigns and freedom rides.

Thus 1961 saw the Negro moving relentlessly forward against an opposition that was occasionally reasonable, but unfortunately more often, vicious. It was a year of the victory of the nonviolent method: though blood flowed, not one drop was drawn by a Negro from his adversary. Yet the victories were scored by the victims, not by the vio-lent mobs.

These highlights are cited to illustrate that Negroes, despite short-comings and a flood of unresolved problems, were spiritedly meeting their obligation to act.

It is against this backdrop that the inquiry into the experience of 1961 turns us again to the Administration and its responsibilities. At the beginning of the year, the cautious approach of the Administra-tion turned a possible spectacular victory into a tragic defeat. A move was made in the Senate to end the two-thirds cloture rule—the leg-islative incinerator that burns into ashes all civil-rights bills. At the cli-mactic moment, the Administration remained mute instead of carrying out its pledge of active leadership. Even so, the measure was defeated by a narrow 50–46 vote. No one doubts that had the Admin-istration spoken, a historic victory would have resulted.

The Administration then brought forth a plan to substitute Executive orders for legislative programs. The most challenging order, to end discrimination in federal housing, while no adequate substitute for the many legislative acts promised in campaign platforms and speeches, nevertheless was alluring, and pressure abated for Congressional action. The year passed and the President fumbled. By the close of the year, a new concept was adopted: the President now wished to "move ahead in a way which will maintain a consensus." According to Washington observers, this concept derived from the President's concern that his legislative programs in other areas, notably his trade program, might suffer at the hands of key Southern Congressmen—if he moved "too fast" on civil rights.

For years, Abraham Lincoln resisted signing the Emancipation Proclamation because he feared to alienate the slaveholders in the border states. But the imperatives of the Civil War required that slavery be ended, and he finally signed the document and won the war, preserved the nation, and gave America its greatest hour of moral glory. President Kennedy may be tormented by a similar dilemma, and may well be compelled to make an equally fateful decision—one which, if correct, could be found a century later to have made the nation greater and the man more memorable.

Though one can respect the urgency of trade legislation to facilitate competition with the European Common Market, the 20 million Americans who have waited 300 years to be able to compete as human beings in the market place at home have the right to question whether, this year, trade agreements are more important than their long-postponed freedom. Should Americans favor the winning of the welfare and trade programs in Congress at the cost of the Negro citizen's elementary rights?

Are we seeking our national purpose in the spirit of Thomas Jefferson, who said: "All men are created equal . . . endowed with certain inalienable rights. . . . Among these are life, liberty and the pursuit of happiness"? Or are we pursuing the national purpose proclaimed by Calvin Coolidge, who said: "The business of America is business"?

It may be an electrifying act to shelve trade bills for human-rights legislation because it has never been done before. Perhaps that alone is reason enough to do it.

Even apart from morality, practical considerations require a different course. The defensive posture of the President against adversaries seasoned in the art of combat, and older than the nation itself, will increase his impotence, not release his strength. They have already paralyzed his Executive power by holding hostage his legislative program. If he cannot break out of this prison, he will be unable either to influence legislation or use his Executive powers, and in this confinement he may become a tragically helpless figure.

Impotence at a moment of kaleidoscopic world change is even worse than error. The President is seeking compromises acceptable to his jailers, but they would rather paralyze him than accept compromises. It is deeply significant that the activities of the ultra-right-wing organizations are aimed principally at the President, and that the one issue uniting all the disparate rightist groups is their virulent opposition to civil rights. He has already challenged them, boldly, but holding to the offensive on civil rights is part of the challenge.

The President and the Administration are impressively popular. The President will have to take his fight to the people, who trust him. He must now trust *them*. He can be confident that correct policy, sound issues and an aroused people are a fortress mightier than a hundred reactionary committee chairmen. An illustrious predecessor, Franklin Roosevelt, relied more on the weight of the people than on maneuvering in Congressional cloakrooms.

If the President acts, his leadership will communicate strength to waiting millions. Firm, decisive direction from him will galvanize the forces that can turn a program into an actuality. "Nothing in the world is stronger," Victor Hugo said, "than an idea whose time has come." The nation is ready and eager for bold leadership in civil rights. This is evident in the scope and quality of the actions that were conducted last year even in the absence of sustained, strong, national leadership.

The opportunity is not yet lost, nor has the sincerity of the Administration been irrevocably discredited. But the clock of history is nearing the midnight hour and an upsurge in governmental activity is an inescapable necessity. The Negro in 1962—almost one hundred years after slavery's demise—justifiably looks to government for comprehensive, vital programs which will change the totality of his life.

Civil rights will continue for many decades to remain a political football unless the national government abandons the traditional piecemeal approach and constructs a long-term plan. India and other underdeveloped nations, confronting the monumental challenge to liquidate centuries of backwardness, have relied upon detailed plans of two years, four years, six years. The plans define the specific steps to be taken by stages which will lift the nation into a new era. We are not strangers to such conceptions. The President has proposed a ten-year plan to put a man on the moon. We do not yet have a plan to put a Negro in the State Legislature of Alabama.

The development of a plan for the nation-wide and complete realization of civil rights would accomplish several purposes. It would affirm that the nation is committed to solve the problem within a stated period of time; it would establish that the full resources of government would be available to that end, whatever the cost. (In this connection, it is well to remember that our country built its foundations on a common economy based on two centuries of virtually unpaid labor by millions of Negroes.) Finally, a plan would enable the nation to assess progress from time to time, and would declare to those who dream that segregation and discrimination can still be preserved that they must begin to live with the realities of the twentieth century.

*September 14, 1963*

## Rise of the Negro Militant

*Hoyt W. Fuller*

*Chicago*
At the time that Louis E. Lomax's *Harper's* article, "The Negro Revolt Against the Negro Leadership Class," appeared back in 1960, only a few people—black or white—envisioned any imminent upheaval in

the ranks of Negro leaders. Today, it is rather freely charged that the NAACP, for example, until recently was almost as much a Negro status organization as it was a battler for equal rights. But this kind of talk would have seemed blasphemous only a short time ago. With a speed matching the tempo of the general assault against segregation, Negroes of all social and economic strata are coming to realize the correctness of Mr. Lomax's contention that the entrenched Negro leadership class—largely, the upper-middle class—is equally a target of the current Negro revolt.

Perhaps nowhere in the nation is the revolt against the Negro leadership class so dramatic and—to the growing number of erstwhile associates of that class—so welcome as in Chicago. There is a certain logic in this: no other American city can match Chicago in the qualitative depths to which its Negro leadership has descended. In all fairness, it must be stated that a substantial minority of middle-class Negroes here have long opposed the Negro elements in the city's powerful Democratic political machine. Protest votes are regularly cast for Republicans in South Side wards; but they are cast with the prior knowledge that, against the machine's formidable efficiency, the gesture is foredoomed to failure. Considering the machine's effectiveness, Negro politicians here—for the present, at any rate—have little reason to fear the Negro revolt. However, other members of the Negro leadership class are discovering that they are, indeed, vulnerable.

The first of these leaders to suffer the arrows of the aroused Negro public was Mrs. Wendell E. Green, widow of a circuit judge and—until last May—the only Negro member of the city's school board. For several years, under the leadership of the Chicago Urban League's dynamic executive secretary, Edwin C. Berry, segments of the Negro community have been engaged in running skirmishes with School Superintendent Benjamin Willis and the school board over the issue of *de facto* and contrived segregation in the schools. The superintendent has been little inclined to entertain the Negroes' complaints, and the board generally has supported him. What sympathy the Negro groups received from the board came, almost invariably, from Raymond W. Pasnick, who is white. Mrs. Green either supported Superintendent Willis or was silent. (There exists a parallel situation in the City Council. The half-dozen Negro Aldermen, all Democrats, are contemptuously referred to as "The Silent Six." It is white Alderman Leon Despres who persistently speaks out in behalf of the Negro community and who, because of it, is frequently attacked by his Negro colleagues.)

Criticism of Mrs. Green had smoldered for several months before it fiscally exploded last spring. The breaking point arrived when it was revealed that Mrs. Green, alone of the eleven board members, had expressed reservations on the appointment of Robert J. Havighurst, an outspoken white, liberal educator, to head a long-delayed survey of the public-school system. (Other board members undoubtedly opposed the appointment, but reserved comment.) Certain individuals and organizations, notably the American Legion, objected to Dr. Havighurst on the grounds that he had associated with left-wing organizations. Mrs. Green, in newspaper reports, disapproved of the educator's proposals for regional high schools and requested the first of several postponements on voting on his appointment. She was also active in urging subsequent deferments on one pretext or another.

Various Negro pressure groups apparently had urged Mrs. Green to become more aggressive in behalf of integrated schools, but to little avail. When, early in May, she appeared at the Dulles Elementary School to address the PTA, she was met by organized demonstrations. Later, when it was learned that she would address the graduating class of the all-Negro Dunbar Vocational High School (on an invitation extended seven months earlier), several predominantly Negro groups announced they would be on hand for a "peaceful protest," charging the Negro board member with "support of Jim Crow education, support of second-rate education, an attempt to sabotage the survey of Chicago's schools, and misrepresenting her office." The protesting groups included the NAACP and CORE as well as the Negro American Labor Council, Teachers for Integrated Schools and Independent Democrats for Political Progress.

On the evening of the commencement ceremonies, some 900 pickets ringed the high school long before Mrs. Green's arrival. When

Principal Joseph J. Dixon introduced the guest speaker, about 200 persons in the audience arose and walked out. Mrs. Green proceeded to deliver her address; after she sat down, those who had walked out returned to the auditorium. Through it all, Mrs. Green retained a remarkable dignity and composure, but it was clear that the experience had bewildered and badly upset her.

One of Mrs. Green's severest critics was Charles H. Jones, Jr., spokesman for the Chicago Area Friends of the Student Non-Violent Coordinating Committee (SNCC), who insisted that she should resign from the school board. "She has refused to recognize the necessity that Negroes must be unshackled and let out of the ghettos," he said. In a statement released prior to the Dunbar Vocational High School protest, Jones said that the protesting organizations had "tried repeatedly during the period Mrs. Green has been a member of the Chicago Board of Education to treat her with all the respect and courtesy due a member of this important body, being ever mindful of her age [she is over sixty] and her sex. This respectful treatment has been met repeatedly with hostility, disdain and non-cooperation. We are sick at heart that this public protest is necessary, but in the last half of the twentieth century—one hundred years after Emancipation—when this nation's children, generation after generation, have been marred and maimed by second-class treatment, we can no longer allow false representation of Negroes to go unchallenged."

But the more telling portent for Mrs. Green and for Negro leaders of her persuasion was contained in a statement Jones made later to a reporter. Mrs. Green, he charged, "has no psychological or emotional identity with the Negro community." In an amplification of this proposition, a rebel NAACP leader aimed this broadside: "You know, in the past, so many elite Negroes received appointments and honors—and considerable status and income—as representatives of the Negro community when they actually made every effort to cut themselves off from the true Negro community. They were too busy being like white people and trying to persuade white people that they were different from the Negro masses. Literally carbon copies of white people, you know. It was self-degrading, and it is no wonder white people despise them. Well, it's not going to be like that any more, either outside the NAACP or inside it. The leaders must be with the people—or else."

Less than two weeks after Mrs. Green's experience, Mayor Richard J. Daley and the Rev. Joseph H. Jackson underwent similar ones at the hands of the outraged young civil-rights activists. Both were shouted off the platform when they attempted to address an NAACP mass meeting following a parade on July 4. Despite official denials by the top level of the NAACP hierarchy, the Young Turks of that organization are known to have been very much in league with the fomenters of the protest against the two speakers. They wanted both the Mayor and the minister to know that soft-treading on the issue of equal rights had been relegated to history. And they wanted the NAACP brass to know that apologies were not in order.

By the middle of July, the campaign against school segregation intensified to the point where violence flared, and the CORE sponsors of the drive were no longer effectively in control. The newspapers pointed accusing fingers and made dire warnings, and the police moved in to make arrests and restore a kind of order. One day Alderman Charles Chew, a Negro who had been elected as an "independent" Democrat, showed up among the pickets outside the Board of Education offices downtown. And then, the following day, a truly strange event took place. Alderman Claude W. B. Holman announced that he and the other four available Negro Aldermen (one was on vacation) were sponsoring a "monster" civil-rights rally on August 5. On the same day, it was also learned, some sixteen civil-rights groups had organized the Coordinating Council of Community Organizations (CCCO) and had set a huge conference on civil rights without notifying or inviting any of the Negro Aldermen. (Later in August, four of these Aldermen arranged a meeting with School Board President Clair M. Roddewig without notifying or inviting Alderman Chew.)

Noting the Negro Aldermen's belated attempt to get on the band wagon, the Rev. Arthur M. Brazier, a militant Negro leader and head of CCCO, said wryly: "The Aldermen have begun to get the message that the Negro people are not satisfied with the way the councilmen have been conducting themselves."

*May 4, 1964*

## Wallace in Indiana

*Gordon Englehart*

*Indianapolis*

Not since rebel raider John Hunt Morgan jumped the Ohio River near Corydon 101 years ago and galloped toward Cincinnati has an Alabamian cut such a swath across Indiana. This spring's invader, Governor George C. Wallace, is—like his gray-clad forebear— spurring a States'-rights horse into combat against an enemy he identifies as the federal government. He is one of five candidates in the Indiana Democratic Presidential preferential primary May 5.

Wallace isn't, of course, a serious Presidential candidate. His announced broad goal is to "conservatize" both parties into curbing or trimming back "the omnipotent rush and grasp for power in Washington." His immediate target is what he calls the civil-wrongs bill now pending in the U.S. Senate. "You have a good opportunity to kill this bill by voting for me," he tells Hoosiers.

Wallace is not expected to defeat Indiana Governor Matthew E. Welsh, a favorite-son candidate running in the primaries to hold the Indiana delegation for President Johnson. But Welsh, other Democratic Party officials, and Indiana church leaders are worried that Wallace will poll an impressive number of votes. "He's known, he will be well financed and he is riding the crest of an emotional issue," Welsh said before Wallace arrived. Welsh recalled that another such issue— anti-Catholicism—was potent enough in Indiana in the 1960 primary to hand political unknowns Lar Daly and John H. Latham 82,000 votes compared to 351,000 for John F. Kennedy. Daly, the America-Firster from Chicago, and Latham, a retired pipe fitter from Rockville, Ind., are candidates again this year. The fifth hopeful is one Faye (Fifi) Carpenter-Swain, a Cincinnati blonde who wears a wrist watch around her ankle.

Wallace beamed confidence as he arrived in Indianapolis, April 14, fresh from the Wisconsin primary where he had bagged a surprising third of the votes. "Governor Reynolds said it would be a catastrophe if I got 100,000 votes," he chortled. "Well, I got 264,000, so there must have been three catastrophes in Wisconsin." Wallace cannily refused to speculate on his Indiana vote. "If we get any votes at all, we have won," he said. "If I get any significant vote, it will not only shake the eye teeth of the liberals in both parties, it will make them drop out."

Wallace arrived in style—in an Alabama state plane decorated with a Confederate flag and the slogan, "Stand up for America." He was accompanied by three husky, cool-eyed Alabama state highway patrolmen, and by his executive secretary, Earl Morgan. Press, radio and television newsmen gave the arrival full treatment. Next morning, about twenty-five members of the National Association for the Advancement of Colored People and the Indianapolis Social Action Council obligingly drew more attention to the visitor by picketing outside the Claypool Hotel. The 45-year-old Governor showed up for a packed press conference in a dark blue suit and white shirt with tab collar and French cuffs. On his left hand a heavy Masonic ring nestled up to a gold wedding band.

Wallace is short—5 feet 7—but still about as trim as when he was the 1936 Golden Gloves bantamweight champion of Alabama. Dark brown hair is slicked back neatly above a heavy-browed, slightly bull-doggish face. At the press conference and in later Indiana appearances, Wallace played the perfect Southern gentleman. There was no red-neck ranting. He spoke rapidly, fluently, persuasively, quietly, with a pleasing accent. He displayed a quick wit, and proved imperturbable under the most hostile questioning.

A churchman later said he now believes reports of "the man's dexterity in confusing and embarrassing even the most adroit debaters." A Republican leader says no Hoosier politician of either party can touch him as a public speaker. "The word for him is slick," the Indianapolis *Times* commented editorially. As he did with Wisconsin's Governor, Wallace carefully praised Welsh as a high-type man for whom he has the greatest regard—and then challenged him to a television and radio debate. "I am not interested," was Welsh's first reaction. Later, however, when Wallace moved out to Butler University, the normally even-tempered Welsh cut loose with the most vitriolic statement of his political career:

> This is the man who was the mortal enemy of President John F. Kennedy.
>
> This is the man who tolerated the presence of billboards in his state, before the assassination, which demanded "K.O. the Kennedys."
>
> This is the man whose beliefs were responsible for the deaths of innocent children in the bombing of a Sunday-School class in a Montgomery church [Welsh meant Birmingham].
>
> This is the man who stood by while dogs were set upon human beings and tire hoses were turned on groups of peaceful demonstrators.
>
> This is the man who is trying to destroy the political system of the United States as we know it and who seeks to discredit President Lyndon B. Johnson.
>
> This is the man who flies the Confederate flag over the Statehouse in Alabama in place of the Stars and Stripes.

"I made the statement because I wanted Democrats generally to know that this is not going to be a polite tea party," Welsh said later. Wallace mildly replied, "He has a right to his own opinions."

According to Welsh, civil rights is no issue in Indiana because the state already has a law stronger in most respects than the federal bill. The only issue is human decency. "And we in Indiana have written our record in . . . quiet progress."

The 1960 census lists about 274,000 Negroes in Indiana—nearly 6 per cent of the population. The two big clusters are in Indianapolis (20 per cent of its population) and Gary (38 per cent). In 1949, the legislature passed a law ending segregation in schools. The 1961 legislature approved a fair-employment-practices law. The 1963 legislature added public-accommodations and education to its coverage and gave a state Civil Rights Commission enforcement powers. Only housing is not now covered.

Welsh, a lame-duck governor in his final year of office, is a 51-

year-old attorney, from a prominent Vincennes family. He is a former State Representative, State Senator and U.S. District Attorney. He is an honest, hard-working and able administrator—gracious in manner, and a button-down-collar patrician in appearance. But he is a dull speaker, and even he admits that he has collected a lot of "barnacles" in three years in the governor's chair. His strong civil rights push has been unpopular in some parts of the state. And he has caught much of the blame for higher taxes, including a brand new sales tax passed by the 1963 legislature.

The nature of Indiana is another factor working for Wallace. It was settled mainly by Carolinians and still draws from Kentucky and Tennessee. Copperheads were very active here during the Civil War, and for several years during the 1920s the Ku Klux Klan practically ran the state. Some of this anti-Negro, anti-foreigner, anti-Catholic sentiment is still evident. Indiana is a conservative state, despite the election in the past six years of liberal Democrats Welsh and Senators Vance Hartke and Birch Bayh.

This is the ground Wallace is plowing: Hoosiers who believe Negroes are pushing too hard, conservatives who are leery of big government in Washington and who agree with the States'-rights pitch, and voters dissatisfied with Welsh. Some Republicans are expected to vote in the Democratic primary, but not as many as in Wisconsin. A Republican can ask for a Democratic ballot, but if challenged he must sign an affidavit that he voted for a majority of Democrats in the last general election and intends to do the same in the upcoming one.

Wallace's basic speech, with heavy emphasis on local government, States' rights and individual freedom, plus side attacks on federal aid, foreign aid and the U.S. Supreme Court, goes like this:

The federal civil rights bill is 10 per cent civil rights and 90 per cent a grasp for federal Executive power. It will destroy the free-enterprise system and private ownership of property; it "will destroy the whole cement that holds the U.S. Constitution together."

If the bill passes, your right to sell or rent your home to whom you please will be destroyed; every neighborhood school will be destroyed through mandatory transfers of students; you may lose your job, your seniority, or promotion to make way for a Negro, farmers will lose federal crops supports if they discriminate in hiring workers; the government will control membership in private organizations, and offenders can be jailed without jury trials.

Segregation, says Wallace, is in the best interest of both races in Alabama, but he is not advocating segregation for Indiana or any other state. "This is for each state to decide," he stresses. "If you want integration, have it, but vote it yourselves, decide at the level of Indiana. But if you can't run your schools without the aid of some social engineers up in Washington, you might just as well abolish your Statehouse."

Wallace denies he is a racist. "Not even the left-wing press can show that I have ever made any statement reflecting on anyone because of his race, creed or national origin." Negroes, he says, have excellent schools in Alabama. He himself served two years on the board of trustees of Tuskegee Institute, and his administration appropriates $700,000 a year to that private school for Negroes.

Some eighty students picketed Wallace at Butler. But he got a warm reception inside and beat Welsh, 70 to 55, in a straw vote.

After Indianapolis, Wallace fanned out across the state, to Richmond, Terre Haute, Vincennes, Bloomington—and to more pickets. He is advertising heavily in twenty to twenty-five papers in major cities, and has taken time spots ranging from 5 to 30 minutes, on forty radio and ten television stations.

The Indianapolis *Times* quoted "a reliable source" as saying the tab for all this would come to $50,000, but the Wallace camp says that figure is way too high. Contributions mostly $1 to $5, are coming in steadily, Wallace reports.

The Democratic State Committee, in its counterattack, is relying heavily on the slogan: "Clear the way for L.B.J., vote for Welsh the 5th of May." The committee has reserved a "decent" amount of radio and TV time and newspaper-ad space. All county chairmen and vice chairmen have been given campaign buttons, cards and literature, and have been briefed at a statewide meeting on how to refute what party and church leaders claim are Wallace's blatant misrepresentations of the civil rights bill. All Democratic patronage workers in state, county and local governments have been "urged" to vote May 5 and bring others to the polls.

Welsh returned to the attack at Gary when he compared Alabama to a police state ruled "by the iron fist of would-be dictators." He continued: "On the one hand we're told the Negro schools down there are excellent and in the same breath we are told that thousands upon thousands of Negro graduates of those same schools are illiterate and cannot be allowed to vote." Welsh told a reporter he listened to Wallace's first televised speech and concluded that his appeal is not to Democrats—it was pure John Birch.

The Indiana Council of Churches sent material attacking the Wallace position to 300 church leaders in sixteen denominations in Indiana, asking them to enlist local pastors in the fight. Among other things, the material emphasizes that, Wallace to the contrary, federal-government employment in nonmilitary occupations between 1947 and 1963 remained constant—1.9 per cent of the total population—while state- and local-government employment doubled.

Welsh does not go along with some observers' belief that Wallace will get his heaviest support along the Ohio River, where there is the heaviest concentration of Southerners. He thinks Wallace may do best in such cities as Indianapolis, Gary, South Bend, Fort Wayne, Muncie and Anderson, where Polish and other ethnic minorities live next to Negroes and are in direct competition for jobs. The big question, however, is "the mass of independent voters who normally do not turn out for primaries," he says. "How many will find Wallace's line appealing?"

The nationally known contenders in both Presidential primaries here dispute Wallace's thesis that a big vote for him might kill the civil rights bill. Welsh says only that the election is sure to have some effect on the legislation. Republican Harold Stassen says it would have no effect—that the Democratic vote will simply reflect voters' appraisal of Welsh's performance as Governor.

Republican Barry Goldwater said a big Wallace vote wouldn't kill the bill, "but it might take out two of the most objectionable features—the public-accommodations section and FEPC, and it might delay passage until after the November election."

*January 29, 1968*

# The Black Hessians

*Charles R. Eisendrath*

Along with new assault helicopters, new infantry tactics and new questions about victory and defeat, the "New Kind of War" in Vietnam has bred a new kind of American soldier.

He has been extracted from the urban Negro ghetto by choice, chance and policy, and is being psychologically custom tailored for his war. The result is a semi-mercenary, fighting a campaign characterized by critics and advocates alike as carrying overtones of colonialism, in effect, if not intention. And, like his war, the new kind of American soldier responds to analysis by shattering into paradox.

His family and neighbors of civilian life mount the most militant reform movement in recent American history—one which in annual, incandescent fury flattens whole precincts—but abroad he fights the most conservative of wars. He fights, moreover, as a volunteer—a professional—returning for more than his share of front-line duty in numbers proportionately far greater than his white comrades.

Consequently, he dies in greater numbers. Department of Defense figures indicate that he dies almost twice as fast in the army as he should, statistically. Twelve per cent of the army in Vietnam are Negroes. Twenty-one percent of army deaths by hostile action in Vietnam from January 1, 1961, through July 1, 1967, were Negro deaths.

What brings this poor man—this revolutionary—to fight what *New York Times* columnist James Reston and others have called "a poor man's war"? What makes him re-enlist after fulfilling his military obligation? It becomes clear during interviews that he finds in the Vietnamese War many of the attractions that poor men have always found in fighting rich men's battles.

It is ironic that in this country, where textbooks traditionally malign "The Hessians," hired by George III to fight rebellious colonists, the low-income Negro-turned-soldier increasingly resembles a "Black Hessian." As a hired gun, the Black Hessian, in his own version of army lingo, "re-ups for the benefits." These are considerable. They range from money, security and pensions to some of the goals his civilian neighbors march, demonstrate and destroy to achieve. Nobody seriously argues today that the army—especially the fighting army—throws many obstacles in the path of Negro advancement through the ranks. On the contrary, the nation's largest and only compulsory service is widely cited as its most democratic bureaucracy. Besides equal opportunity and prestige literally wearable on the sleeve, the Black Hessian's hierarchy of benefits includes money— quite a bit of it.

Within two years—when the draftee must "re-up" or get out—an 18-year-old unemployed and possibly "unemployable" Negro from ghetto streets can be making in the normal course of combat more than is earned by the average American male aged 20 to 24 of any race, and almost as much as a newly commissioned second lieutenant. Another three years puts him a full 56 per cent ahead of the average earnings among his Negro age group in civilian life. These relative advances don't take into consideration fringe benefits like free medical attention, clothes and PX prices. And the benefits don't stop with active duty. The Black Hessian can retire in twenty years with a pension—and probably a trade.

Soldiering was made to taste still sweeter last December by the third major Army pay raise since 1965, when the U.S. began its massive build-up for Vietnam. The 5.6 per cent hike lifted basic pay about 25 per cent above 1964 levels—a rate of increase that almost tripled the cost of living climb in the same period. "The raises," remarked an urbane officer attached to the Comptroller of the Army, have been designed "to keep our qualified personnel in the service."

Sgt. Lawyer Jenkins understands all this very well. At 29 and lacking a high school diploma, he looks forward to signing another three-year hitch this year with something of the attitude of a corporation junior vice president facing transfer from New York's glamour to a higher paying job in Peoria. He stands to leave his soft job stateside as a drill sergeant for a fighting job in Vietnam, and he isn't crazy about the idea. As he enjoyed telling his platoon of basic "trainees," he considers himself "a lover, babe, ain't no fighter." Nevertheless, Jenkins, who has repeatedly failed the officer's candidate school test, will "go if they need me."

"They" do. Unable or unwilling to hire enough allied troops with military aid, the United States has come increasingly to press the war with the Lawyer Jenkinses of its manpower pool. His casualties are high, said an army spokesman, because he picks professional line outfits—the Airborne, the Rangers, the Special Forces—to get hazardous duty pay on top of combat pay on top of regular pay, which he considers not bad to begin with. As Jenkins put it: "Where else could I have it this good, man? I'm up tight right here!"

What better attitude could there be in the bosom of a man about to enter a fight with few rules, uncertain backing, and no goals other than to get out of it as soon as possible? Largely without the preconceived notions of world politics that the more fortunate pick up in school or in the press, the Black Hessian is ready to accept the army version—so long as the "benefits is good."

But there are factors beside benefits in the genesis of the Black Hessian. A thicket of prevailing social conditions and deliberate governmental policy brings him from the ghetto to his first confrontation with a drill sergeant—who is often someone very like himself, a Lawyer Jenkins.

Given an initial inclination to stay clear of the army during an unpopular war, any man's route into the service depends to a great degree upon his wherewithal and savvy. The ghetto dweller faces mountainous disadvantages by comparison with the rest of his draft-bait generation in avoiding the military in general, the war in particular. He doesn't go to college, hasn't mastered a critical trade, and hasn't studied the fine points of physical defects and hardship clauses, all of which can lead either to exemption from military duty, or to soft, behind-the-lines jobs once in it.

Moreover, the low-income Negro's inferior education leaves him unarmed against a skillful recruiter's shower of carrots and sticks. Available for dangling before recruits' eyes are, first of all, the purse,

privileges and promotions aforementioned. Then comes the sleeper—
"Choice, Not Chance," indicating that volunteering enables the
recruit to select his assignment.

The selection costs a year and doesn't buy much. The signer often
gains little more choice than appears at the finger tips of his brother
who gets drafted for two years. "This man's army" differs very little
in that respect from "This man's father's army." The infantry is still
full of men who raised their hands to become clerks.

At recruiters' desks and at reception centers, the ghetto man's
education points him toward the rice paddies. Tests given at both
places determine where the army will use a man, and since the Negro
is disadvantaged in general background, verbal skills and vocational
training, he falls flat—which is to say he falls into the infantry—
"Queen of Battle."

These factors do not imply a diabolical racist plot, as some super-
militants of the civil rights movement suggest. They simply result
from the confrontation of a socially isolated group with the demands
of a war nobody wants to fight. Nobody, that is, with anything to lose.

The National Guardsman is the archetypal soldier with something to
lose. If he didn't think his civilian position worth some sacrifice why
wouldn't he submit to the draft and get it over with in two years,
instead of prolonging the agony over six, in periodic parodies of martial rigor? Only by joining reserve programs can young men satisfy
civilian ambitions and military obligations simultaneously.

It was the Guardsman who met the potential Black Hessian in
the streets of Detroit, Milwaukee and Newark last summer. And the
supreme irony of the confrontation was that in many instances the
Negroes failed to realize who he was, or that they "could take his
route" instead of going to "Nam" in his place. The sniper, the brick
thrower, the looter, simply doesn't know who he's up against—
doesn't know that the man with the bayonet or the obsolete M-1 on
Main Street will probably never fight much farther away from
home. If the connection were made, the riots might be worse.

One example of Negro ignorance on this score is a young Negro
enlistee who went AWOL from Ft. Dix last July to be in his home town

of Newark for the riots. Minster Hoops is a man of considerable verve and humor. He took his buddies' orders for color television sets before he left—and he filled them.

But for all Hoops's ghetto savvy, he returned to the barracks full of naive questions. Taking a white Guardsman aside, Hoops had asked him about his unit. Was it really never going to Vietnam? Was the period of active duty really less than six months? Hearing the answers, the Negro's face contorted in a smile bitter as a virgin's first taste of ignorance.

"Whitey wouldn't never tell us nothin' 'bout that thing, would he?" he hissed. Hoops had never heard of the Army National Guard, nor the Army Reserve, nor the Air National Guard, nor the Coast Guard Reserve programs that shield hundreds of thousands of young men from the Vietnamese War—and Hoops's ignorance is typical. Failure of communication probably goes as far as discrimination to explain the Guard's lily-white status.

The riots merely compound the ironies. Uprisings in the ghetto lead to campaigns to preserve the Guard, as Secretary of Defense Robert S. McNamara learned when he first tried to reorganize it. In an age when local political capital can be accumulated by handling a riot with the "home guard" instead of the federal troops, municipal and state leaders argue the riots necessitate leaving the Guard intact. Gov. George Romney of Michigan apparently thought the distinction between federal and home troops vital enough to hesitate precious minutes as Detroit burned before reluctantly sounding the alarm that brought in Maj. Gen. John Throckmorton's 82nd Airborne to bolster the sagging, ill-disciplined Michigan National Guard.

Finally in the making of the Black Hessian there is the Selective Service law itself. Renewed largely unamended last year despite considerable flap, the draft's increased calls reflect the decision not to summon the reserves, and not to do away with deferments for the highly vocal college students.

Unable to skim the cream by eliminating deferments, the draft sank its tap into the silent, dark dregs. In December, 1966, Mr. McNamara announced the "liberalization" of qualifying mental aptitude scores for induction into the army. Thousands of low-income Negroes previously protected by their own ignorance now felt the weight and learned of the opportunities—of the New Kind of War in Vietnam. The raising of the Black Hessians was under way, and continues.

*April 15, 1968*

## Eulogy for Martin Luther King, Jr.

Within the shock of the murder of Dr. Martin Luther King, Jr. rests the additional shock of realizing that he was only 39 when the gunman found him. Dr. King emerged as the leader of his people's strength and dignity in Montgomery in 1956 (he was 27), and since then his has been the senior voice of moral integrity and humane determination in the United States. As Dr. Kenneth Clark said on the night of the slaying, "You have to weep for this country."

And it is by the grace of Dr. King's spirit that this whole country may mourn its loss. His generosity excluded no one, not the most complacent, not the most heedless, not the most bigoted, from the dream he had. He was a man capable of magnificent anger, but hate was not in him; he denounced the act, never the man. Hatred, indeed, was his single foe—both the hatred that steamed out of prejudice and the hatred which, in retaliation and frustration, the black people have been calling down on white society. Violence is now expected, but if Dr. King's spirit can live with us in the next few weeks it need not occur.

'Let Justice roll down like waters in a mighty stream,' said the Prophet Amos. He was seeking not consensus but the cleansing action of revolutionary change. America has made progress toward freedom, but measured against the goal the road ahead is still long and hard.

For many years, it was *The Nation*'s privilege to publish Dr. King's annual report on civil rights, an address on the State of the Nation in the true sense of the phrase. The above quote comes from his article of March 15, 1965; it is typical of how his mind worked: Proud, unhampered by passion, perfectly understanding the size of the job to be done and utterly confident that men endued with his spirit could do it.

The road is still long and hard, and this terrible killing, which could be motivated only by the malice of ignorance, makes it the more difficult to a degree no one can yet estimate.

But one thing is certain: we must march. We must march all together and in his name; violence is always irrelevant, in the context of Dr. King's life it is obscene. As the country knows, he had planned to enter Washington later this month at the head of a "Poor People's Crusade." That appointment must be kept—it is the solemn duty of the government to see that it is kept and that it goes forward in the spirit of magnanimous determination to let justice roll down that animated every action Dr. King took. And we should all be there, for now that Dr. King is slain, the title of his crusade takes on a different meaning: in his shadow, we are all "Poor People." Decency is all he ever asked of the country, and only by the decency of social justice and human respect can the country heal itself of this intolerable deed.

*April 21, 1969*

## Cops & Blacks: Warring Minorities

*Hans Toch*

The United States today is a country in the grip of an internal cold war. Militant ghetto residents are pitted against militant members of metropolitan police forces. Each group watches the other with apprehension, and each plots countermeasures against expected aggression. On both sides are those who proclaim that they will experience Armageddon in their day, in the shape of a premeditated massacre by the opposing force.

There are also those, on both sides, whose pronouncements legit-imize fears. There is much saber rattling, and some of it is literal; blacks collect rifles and steal ingredients for bombs; police fill ware-houses with armor and artillery. And neither side, strangely enough, goes about its business quietly and discreetly. While details are classi-fied, the fact of escalation is loudly and aggressively proclaimed. The suspicion arises that, in addition to psychological warfare, self-stimu-lation is at work—something in the order of a pep rally to doomsday.

Militant spokesmen for the ghetto are prone to characterize the police as an invading army representing the white establishment. This characterization is ironic, because the police, far from being the agents of the majority, are a minority themselves. They have the problems of a minority, they feel like a minority and they think like a minority. In fact, an articulated Blue Power ideology, espoused by militant and self-conscious police spokesmen, in most respects runs fully parallel to the premises and conclusions of Black Power.

The objective situations of blacks and police are in many ways similar. The police inhabit a ghetto of their own, and they are doomed to segregation. They have little hope of man-to-man communication with civilians, who—even if favorably deposed to law enforcement—tend to be nervous and self-conscious in encounters with officers. The average person finds it difficult to feel open and at ease with a man who sports a conspicuous firearm, who is entitled to question, search and arrest him. Even the officer's wife and his children may experi-ence some awe, distance and reserve among peers. This is a standard problem for minorities, and most minorities react to it defensively. They do what they can to convert their liability into an asset. They become self-righteous. ("Our country!" John Crittenden proclaimed when the United States was a minority in the world community, ". . . I will stand by her, right or wrong.") They seek one another's exclu-sive company, and regale one another with their own virtues, some-times enhancing these to superman proportions. Self-regard and pride slide into chauvinism, especially when they are built on a foun-dation of persistent self-doubt.

In the code of minorities, it is important to present a united front. There must be no break in the ranks, no visible division to be exploited by the hostile majority. Among blacks, "soul brothers" are protected, even though they may have courted trouble by losing their cool. Among police, "brother officers" are supported, even when they have proved trigger-happy or brutal. Review boards are anathema to police, because they expose fellow officers to public view; badges must be removed, not so much to avoid blame as to share it.

Obviously, one can carry the analogy between the fate of blacks and the police much too far. There can be no equating of joblessness with insulation, of discrimination with distance, of blind alleys with unpopularity. But often, perceptions are more real than reality, and subjectively the worlds of the police and of blacks are remarkably similar. The police, like the black community, feel themselves discriminated against and unpopular. They feel themselves stigmatized by indices of status. They feel their ambitions thwarted and their objectives misunderstood. They feel impotent and without recourse. They feel hated and persecuted. And they sense that the situation is steadily degenerating into a future of complete hopelessness and utter helplessness. "We are damned on every side" is a favorite police maxim, stated with feeling.

Militant police officers—like militant blacks—react with the premise that they can no longer operate within the system. They feel that, to make themselves heard and respected, they must by-pass the strictures imposed by an insensitive, or even malevolent, power structure. In a sense, this goes beyond the routine gambit of positive minorityism. It represents a super-defensive reaction, which arises when standard group defenses fail. It is found among those members of a minority—mainly the young—who sense behind the self-delusion of their fellows an unresolved, permanent impotence. What they demand is the removal of social institutions that enforce impotence; these, unfortunately, may include competing minorities.

Blue Power advocates among the police are radical dissenters where most officers are moderate critics of the system. For instance, it is a police truism that judges are unfriendly to law enforcement. Every officer will grouse, if he is given the chance, about lenient sentences and Supreme Court rulings. But the Blue Power officer does more than grouse. He may demand the ouster of trial judges (as is happening in New York) or he may circulate Birchite literature calling for the impeachment of Supreme Court Justices.

Police officers usually circumvent the law in minor ways. They arrest people without intending to prosecute them, they dispense justice through negotiation, they garner information not admissible in trials. But such acts are committed without malice, as part of the accommodation process to make our system work. Blue Power advocates would play the game of circumvention grimly and seriously, and carry it to extremes.

If given his way, the Blue Power officer would harass, persecute and punish people, and—if he thinks it "necessary"—would suppress evidence and lie on the witness stand. His object is to "enforce the law" over the dead body of the law. With respect to black militants, such an officer would stand ready to use force (we have seen sad instances of this). He sees the racial issue as a battle between police representatives and black criminals, with society as spectator.

In general, police and blacks are obsessed with the need to instill respect in each other. For both, the demand for respect is for recognition on the basis of group membership rather than for a positive reaction to personal qualities. One reason for this is the feeling that in the past one's kind has been rejected because of blind hatred. The assumption of a "disrespect for law and order," like the premise of "200 years of slavery," leads to the demand for a turned tide.

But there is also a strong component of insecurity here. The men involved feel that their interpersonal skills and their qualities as human beings are insufficient to the problem of coping with the enemy. For each group, the other symbolizes threats that lurk on every corner of the ghetto. The young black does not know how to react to police incursions, and the young officer feels helpless in dealing with difficulties posed by his tense encounters with hostile blacks. Each man comes to feel that he must rely on his group identification—badge or color—as a substitute for answers he cannot find in himself. When the officer stops a black man (for what he considers legitimate reasons) and is rejected and insulted as the invading racist, he is insured against the need for self-examination by knowing that his opponent has no regard "for law and order." When a ghetto resident is humiliated (as he feels, unjustifiably) by a police officer, he can deduce that he has been persecuted by "an agent of white oppression." Neither party need conclude that it has to make the delicate judgments implicit in personal encounters: the matter is prejudged; two men approach each other, not as human beings but as uniformed members of military forces engaged in a doomed truce in a no-man's-land.

Police and blacks act not only as self-appointed representatives of their kind but also as uncompromising representatives, who must "come on strong" as a matter of premeditated policy. Many years ago, Gilbert and Sullivan wrote such an approach into a prescription for individual conduct:

> *His foot should stomp, and his throat should growl*
> *His hair should twirl, and his face should scowl*
> *His eyes should flash, and his breast protrude,*
> *And this should be his customary attitude.*

Such is the militant's stance, and it can be recognized in the baton-swinging swagger of the young officer embarking on his early assignments. The demeanor is a bluff, a transparent effort to convince oneself that one can survive, even conquer, though impotent.

The approach is, of course, partly built into the police subculture and the subculture of the ghetto. Every enforcement training manual stresses the desirability of a firm, loud, no-nonsense command voice. Every ghetto youth learns the need to act tough in his neighborhood jungle. What is new is the consistent, self-conscious policy, in each group, to make the other party the testing ground of valor.

It would be bad enough if militant minorities presented problems for their own kind, but the threats they pose extend to nonmilitants, and to the public at large. No one can speak up to a Blue Power officer without implicating the police as an institution. Anything less than assent to omnipotence becomes an affront to "the law." In turn, anything the officer does, no matter how arbitrary or capricious or stupid or tactless or miscalculated, becomes an act of "law enforcement." Disagreeing with a militant officer lays one open to the accusation of being motivated by perversity, prejudice and incipient anarchism. For his part, the officer feels perpetually persecuted, in that again and again, as he bumbles his way through his awkward personal encounters, the social order appears subjected to unbearable contempt. This leads to cumulative bitterness and increased militancy. When bluff and bluster achieve nothing, it follows that the blame must lie elsewhere. Personal impotence is attributed to national "criminal coddling." The officer feels "handcuffed," not by his own behavior but by bleeding-heart judges and politically motivated civilians.

To date, police excesses and black excesses are approximately equal. We have seen riots initiated by both groups and we have seen confrontations break into open warfare, when pretenses of restraint and self-discipline were dropped. But blue militants are capable of going beyond these limits. Police ideology can reach the point where the officer can question the legitimacy of the obstructions under which he operates. When he comes to see other institutions as unmitigated evils, he can turn law enforcement into anti-law enforcement, and can begin to sabotage the machinery he is sworn to serve. Such a point has not yet been reached with the police, but a few snipings or dramatic court decisions may create incidents (such as the anti-Panther vendettas in New York and Oakland) which fall into the category of officers attacking the fabric of society.

It is then that Blue Power turns into blue racism, and blue pride into blue hate. What emerges is the demand for an autonomous police, or a police state. Unfortunately, the latter (unlike black separatism, which is a weird daydream) can be partially implemented, and that is why Blue Power must be fought. It must be fought, like all ideologies, at its origins. It can be neutralized only by de-alienating police, by depriving them of the stigmas of minority status—stigmas that now separate them from the rest of us, and that force them into tortuous efforts to salvage self-esteem.

The task is difficult, it entails radical restructuring of the police function. It may demand police-civilian collaboration far beyond currently fashionable small-group dialogues and training sessions. Police officers and civilians must labor together intimately and as human beings; they must engage in efforts designed to improve their common lot. They must divest themselves of badges; they must address themselves to social and existential problems of obvious universal import. Through assigned roles, we must restore to each person his primary status as a member of the community, relegating the police role or black role to secondary importance.

Such activity cannot be marketed as "community relations" because it aims at changing people, rather than at improving their images. And it cannot call itself training, because it teaches no skills. It must be, unashamedly, an effort at integration, and—like all integration—it must be total in order to be effective.

Less drastic measures could include the rendering of new kinds of positive police services. What comes to mind here is not social work—at least not as we know it. To be meaningful, positive contacts must be two-sided, and they cannot feature the dispensation of demeaning gratuities. True contacts involve open communication, and permit the other person to participate; they must force helpers to learn as well as to teach or to help; and they must de-emphasize pretense-expertise and empty professionalism. (The "professional" carries a badge of his own, in many respects more dangerous than those worn by the police.)

Another direction of necessary change is personal. It involves redefining the criteria we use to gauge each officer's personal worth. We must give recognition to kindness instead of toughness, to influence rather than force. And we must reward substance in place of bluff and pretense. In some ways, this implies a reversal of the values that currently prevail—making it obvious to the officer that he demonstrates his inadequacy in those situations in which he now feels he proves his manhood and upholds the law. Each officer must be shown that he is weak when "strong," and that he is a pawn where he feels he wages war on his own terms.

None of this is easy, and some of it may be impossible. But where is the alternative? Certainly, no one—least of all the blue minority—can afford accelerated segregation. Apartheid is not a happy state. It produces a climate of fear and hopelessness, and it rests on nagging personal impotence. In its name, human shells in black and blue fearfully eye each other around corners in the dark. We cannot afford this spectacle. And we can afford even less the prospect of militant men—driven by panic—setting out to destroy the social order they serve.

*October 27, 1969*

## Escape from the Dark Cave

*John U. Monro*

*Birmingham*

At Miles College, in Birmingham, I am responsible for trying to develop and conduct a freshman program for some 300 young men and women, all black, who come to us from the local schools in Alabama. It is fifteen years since the great *Brown* decision of the Supreme Court ordered the desegregation of the schools, but hardly one of our 300 freshmen has ever had a white teacher before, or been to school with white classmates. Alabama is now fiftieth on the list of states in per-pupil expenditure for schooling (about $400 per child per year, as compared with about $1,000 in New York State), and in the South—as in the North—black schools seem to get the short end of the budget allocations. So it is no surprise that after twelve years of school, the students coming to Miles seem to be, on average, at about the 9th or 10th grade level in mathematical and language skills.

I recall very well that in my previous incarnation, when I was a dues-paying member of the white community, I had a hard time taking seriously the notion that I and my well-meaning, liberal-minded, church-going friends were bigoted racists. And a couple of years back when I first heard young black people accusing us good white folks of "genocide," I considered the accusation dangerous, and also rather paranoid and absurd. But I see things somewhat differently now. I find it a particularly rich experience to live and work in a black community, mainly because in the black community you develop a clarity of vision about the realities of American life.

I have learned how important it is to listen to the metaphors with which black poets have tried to describe the pain that they feel. For example, one day six years ago a strong, gentle young black man, a Harvard undergraduate, laid on my desk a copy of W.E B. Du Bois' *Souls of Black Folk*. He said "If you really want to know what I'm thinking, and what makes me move, then you must read this book." So, of course, I read it, and admired it in an intellectual way. But now, six years later, I know what my young friend meant and what an honor he conferred on me by inviting me in.

Day by day, in my new incarnation my respect grows for W.E.B. Du Bois. As a Harvard man, I find it incredible that Harvard had Du Bois as an undergraduate and gifted graduate student seventy years ago, and let him go. It sometimes seems to me that our national history might have been different otherwise. But Harvard saw Du Bois as a Negro and let him go. And it seems to me a great national tragedy and loss, and characteristic of us as a people, that we now categorize Du Bois as a Communist, and so turn away from a life and work which would help us to understand our national guilt and our present convulsions. Here is how white America looked to Du Bois:

It is as though one, looking out from a dark cave in a side of an impending mountain, sees the world passing and speaks to it: speaks courteously and persuasively, showing them how these entombed souls are hindered in their natural movement, expression, and development; and how their loosening from prison would be a matter not simply of courtesy, sympathy, and help to them, but aid to all the world.

One talks on evenly and logically in this way but notices that the passing throng does not even turn its head, or if it does, glances curiously and walks on.

It gradually penetrates the minds of the prisoners that the people passing do not hear, that some thick sheet of invisible but horribly tangible plate glass is between them and the world.

They get excited, they talk louder. They gesticulate. Some of the passing world stop in curiosity: these gesticulations seem so pointless; they laugh and pass on. They still either do not hear at all, or hear but dimly, and even when they hear, they do not understand.

Then the people within may become hysterical. They may scream and hurl themselves against the barriers, hardly realizing in their bewilderment that they are screaming in a vacuum, unheard, and that their antics may seem funny to those outside looking in.

They may even, here and there, break through in blood and disfigurement, and find themselves faced by a horrified, implacable, and quite overwhelming mob of people frightened for their own very existence.

What makes Du Bois' metaphor of the black people imprisoned in the cave, behind the plate glass window, so terrible is that it is still true, today, right down to the bloody bit about what happens to the occasional black man who breaks through the barrier and runs into the mob of frightened whites.

Other poets have produced other terrible metaphors for our national curse. Langston Hughes spoke of Harlem, "here on the edge of Hell," "where a nickel costs a dime." Hughes, too, saw racial prejudice as a *wall*; when I was a young man, he said, "the wall rose slowly, slowly, between me and my dream, dimming, hiding the light of my dreams, rose until it touched the sky—the wall." For Richard Wright the terrible thing that thrust in between him and the world was the vision of a horrid lynching, a black man burned, and around the scene "upon the trampled grass . . . buttons, dead matches, butt ends of cigars and cigarettes, peanut shells, a drained gin-flask, and a whore's lipstick." Ralph Ellison's great metaphor was the *Invisible Man*, and I remind you that, though we usually think of Ellison as a moderate and literary man, the first thing his invisible man does, as we meet him, is beat within an inch of his life a blue-eyed white man who bumped and insulted him one dark night. Ellison has his invisible man run from the scene "laughing so hard I feared I might rupture myself."

Or take the metaphor of a sensitive young white man, Jonathan Kozol, who tried to teach in the segregated black schools in Boston, and was fired for having his students read Langston Hughes's poem, "Ballad of the Landlord." Kozol called his book *Death at an Early Age*, and his subtitle was: *The Destruction of the Hearts and Minds of Negro Children in the Boston Public Schools*.

It seems wise to try to communicate what I am trying to say by resorting to metaphor, because the plain statistical facts of our racism are so well known, have been so well known so long, and have so little effect. In this free and rich society, *if* a man is black, just *because* he is black, this is his table of probabilities:

Twice as many black babies as white will die before age 1; because they are black. Four times as many mothers will die in childbirth; because they are black. Between the ages of 30 and 60, twice as many blacks will die as whites. There is three times more chance that a black student will drop out of school before 6th grade, and about one-half the chance that he will finish high or college. In the South, only 15 per cent of young black men and women of college age will get to college, as compared to 50 per cent for young white people; this means that each year some 75,000 black young men and women of college ability, reaching college age, just do not get to college at all; because they are black.

The tabulation goes on, as long as it is familiar. We could go into the matter of jobs, of income levels, of opportunity for real management positions; we could go into housing, what it's like to be confined in a ghetto; we could go into the bloody figures of the military draft for fighting in Vietnam, and the great white sanctuary of college and graduate school; we could document the behavior of white police in black neighborhoods.

In my freshman Social Studies class at Miles I must each day try to explain the American social and political structure to fifteen black young men and women, who, it develops, already know more about the dirty side of that system, and how it *really* operates, than I can ever know. One big, strong, black young man in that class whom I have come to respect particularly is Fred Rogers. Mr. Rogers is a steady man of 24, who has served five years in the Army, three of them in Vietnam. He knows all about the percentage of Negro combat troops in Vietnam, and the high percentage of Negro young men in the daily body counts. He lives in a part of town where there is no sewage system, and no paved streets; where black people live in rickety shacks, Negro schools are third rate, and where the prospect is, if he finished on through college, he can hope maybe some day to be a schoolteacher, if he is careful not to offend anybody. In Alabama he would make better money as a carpenter, or in the steel mills. But he has no real chance of getting a job in business or industry commensurate with his power as a man—his intelligence, his energy, his force.

Fred Rogers is an expert on the brutality of the American social and economic system. He comes to class each day, sits down front, and stares at me unblinking and unsmiling as I try to explain to him and his black classmates how the American social system works.

Mr. Rogers is unfailingly polite and does not say much, but when he does come on, it is like a ton of bricks. And, of course, his presence tends to affect the whole class, my own preparation and presentation of the material, and the response from the other students. I am sure that as a white man trying to present this material, I often annoy and frustrate Mr. Rogers. He seldom shows his annoyance, which is a tribute to his patience and manners. But in that class we are always operating on the edge of annoyance and frustration, and because it is tough and tense, it is the best educational mix in the world.

One day in class we were discussing the phenomenon of "culture," when Mr. Rogers weighed in. "As I listen to this," he said, "it seems to me that I am a man living in two cultures. Or anyway, I was brought up and I live in a black culture; and to get along, I have to learn how to cope with the white culture. And these two cultures are different, in fact one seems very hostile; and it is damned hard."

Given what he has been through in Vietnam, what he lives with every day in Bessemer, and the struggle he faces in the years ahead just to get a decent, self-respecting job in our society, I must say I find Mr. Rogers incredibly moderate. What he has been through, and what he confronts, just because he is black, entitles him to regard me, or any other white man, *categorically*, as the enemy, as part of the evil force oppressing every hour of his life. The miracle—the daily miracle of Miles College and the Birmingham black community—is that Fred Rogers and his classmates, and parents, have not yet come to hate white people categorically. They are still moderate—tough and independent and alert and taking no nonsense—but still willing to talk and listen and work through institutions. The moderation is not for eternity; we are in a terrible race with the erosion of good will in the black community. This fact, already all too visible in the North, is now becoming visible in the South. By a miracle, we still have time, but not much time, and the opportunity to do what must be done is slipping away.

Do I mean by all this that "integration is dead"? That is a central question. In an interview with *Look* Mrs. Betty Shabazz, the widow of Malcolm X, said: "Blacks have been trying to integrate for nearly four centuries, and they have failed. Integration has failed. We have been forced into separate neighborhoods and separate lives, and now we have to go our own way. Now we blacks are going to rule ourselves."

I note certain similarities between Mrs. Shabazz's position and Fred Rogers' position, and what may be a difference. Fred Rogers is planning, somehow, for all the difficulties, to break through and make it in the general national community; and he is planning, at the same time, to turn his energies and talents to the strengthening of the black community. He sees a strong black community as a power base from which he can hope to have some impact on the white community, for himself and his own career, and for others. He would not call what he wants "integration"; what he wants is *equality* of education, of job opportunity; he wants justice, a say in the government, and freedom to move about like any other self-respecting citizen. There's an important difference between "equality" and "integration." For one thing, the idea of integration, as most white people think of it, bores Fred Rogers stiff. He finds most white people cold, hypocritical, inhumane, selfish, impersonal, driven by altogether stupid ambitions involving status and material wealth—in a word depersonalized and "hung up." After two years at Miles College, living in the black community of Birmingham, I think Mr. Rogers sees the white community just about right.

What is more important, Fred Rogers has begun to learn how the United States really works. What white America respects is not weakness but strength; America respects not rational pleas for help but rather any serious threat to vital parts of the system; and most particularly any threat to profits and sacred property. I am old enough to remember the great national labor struggles in the 1930s. We learned then that our great industries—Ford, General Motors, big steel—were not responsive to the needs and concerns of the individual workers, until the workers, with a prolonged, brutal effort, pulled their thing together, and developed the institutional strength to stop the great factories and shut off their profits. Then the working man got attention, and he got respect. He became then a *respectable* threat; an organized, institutional threat.

The American black community will start making real progress in the United States when it discovers the analogy between its own position and the position of unorganized labor a half century ago. It will not work in our society to think of the black community as a separate nation: the metaphor is just wrong. But it will work to think of the black community as a great, national, *black union.* Let me push the analogy one step further. Whereas labor unions were in a position to command respect and attention because they could, and did, close down factories, the black community is in a position to command respect and attention because it can shut down great cities. That threat strikes a nerve in the power structure: it makes its money in the great cities.

So, I believe very strongly in some form of Black Power. I think that the only way any group of people gets along in this country is by strength and not weakness. I observe that our special national genius seems to be the organizing of social institutions, large and small, to accomplish all sorts of purposes. And I observe further that the black people have never gotten seriously into this universal national game, this organizing of effective units of institutional power.

A lot of people I meet, white and black, are scared by the idea of Black Power. I am bound to say that Black Power scares me a whole lot less than industrial power or military power, or the unholy marriage of those two; and scares me a good deal less than what we experience in Alabama as Wallace power, or in Chicago as Daley power. Indeed, it seems to me that the most serious social consequences for us lie not in developing institutional strength and responsibility in the black community—black unity—but in the continuation of a condition of black powerlessness, accompanied by tokenism and oppression. That way surely lie frustration and deepening anger, and terrible social explosions.

One obvious consequence of what I have been saying—obvious

enough to me, anyway—is that as a society we should realize the importance of the predominantly Negro colleges, and find ways to make them strong and effective. There are some 120 junior and senior black colleges, almost all in the South, and they enroll more than 125,000 students, something more than half of all the black students going to college in the United States. This percentage is slowly diminishing as formerly all-white colleges warm up to their responsibilities. But the importance of colleges like Miles increases month by month. In his very constructive and thoughtful study of the black colleges published in 1965, Earl McGrath noted that some 40 per cent of the students come from families with incomes below $4,000; indeed 70 per cent come from families with incomes below $6,000. In the country at large, 80 per cent of all students going to college have family incomes *above* $6,000. The black colleges are reaching a seriously disadvantaged population that no other colleges even know about, much less can reach.

I have already said that the freshman class at Miles College seems, after twelve years of school, to be on the average at the 9th- or 10th-grade level. These figures are not at all atypical, and they do not say a word as to the intelligence or academic potential of the young people; the figures testify only to grossly inadequate schooling. And I noted earlier that each year in the South some 75,000 black boys and girls who have the potential to go to college never get there.

This is the problem that the Negro colleges have been working on, day after day, devotedly, at bare subsistence levels of support, for a hundred years. And it will continue to be the big job for the black colleges in the years ahead. It is not a job the fast-moving, rich white colleges and universities can do, at least not by themselves.

My central point here is that all the colleges in America, black and white, working together, have a most serious task cut out for them in the years ahead. *How* they should be working together is not yet altogether clear. Some notable early examples of cooperative efforts are under way, and we are learning from them. Principally the nation must become aware that the black colleges, for all their weakness and shortcomings, will be essential to thus effort. They are geographically positioned to be in closest contact with some of the most needy areas.

They are accustomed to working with students who are badly prepared for college, and to moving them along to graduate school. Thus they are critical centers of contact and of a growing expertise.

Another critical task for colleges like Miles is to serve as centers for the development of some measure of institutional strength in the black communities of the South. A few recent events will suggest how important such a college can be. When the city and county were slow to develop a local base for poverty programs, Miles College launched the first Head Start program in Birmingham. It developed programs for retraining industrial workers. It is a center for the attack on adult illiteracy; within the year it undertook to manage the VISTA program in the county and in counties to the south. As a consequence of new voting rights, the area is beginning to elect a few black officials into local governments. Miles is trying to provide these new officials with information and research assistance as they attack their new jobs.

So, we must come to see the Negro colleges not just as impoverished and struggling educational institutions but as centers for the development of institutional strength, of coordinated efforts of many kinds, in communities which have dangerously little institutional strength or resources. It is no accident that at Miles College, we now stress more and more the importance, after a student has completed his undergraduate and graduate work, that he come back to the South and put his hard-won skills to work in the community.

So we must quit worrying whether it is the "right thing" to support the black colleges. They are here to stay because, poor though they are, they are performing a critical function, as educational institutions and as centers of community strength. The challenge is to find ways to beef up that effort and make it more effective; through organizations like the United Negro College Fund; through government aid, as through Title III of the Higher Education Act; and through carefully worked out, long-range associations between black colleges and white colleges.

From what I have said about the educational effort in the colleges and the importance of community organization, it follows that I am entirely sympathetic with the insistence of our black communities that they be given control over the schools that serve black children in black neighborhoods. To paraphrase Betty Shabazz on this matter: "White people would consider it insane if black people tried to run white schools. Now it's time for black people to make as much sense, and to take charge of the education of their own children." I say flatly, it is the clearest example I know of white racism, of white people's built-in sense of superiority, to assume that whites should have charge of black children's education. All the facts cry out in the other direction. White people have made schools a weapon of oppression against black children. Read Jonathan Kozol's *Death at an Early Age*.

Consider rural Alabama. The U.S. Civil Rights Commission last year revisited sixteen rural counties in southern Alabama, an impoverished farm area with a population of some 350,000, about three-fifths black. They found, among other things, that for people over 25, the median grade level of school-leaving for white people was eleven grades, and for black people 5.5 grades. The commission found also that, fifteen years after the Supreme Court decision ordering desegregation of schools, only 2 per cent of the black students were attending formerly all-white schools. I would add that the same percentage, about 2 per cent, or less, holds also in metropolitan Jefferson County, around Birmingham.

The commission found further that in Clarke County, for example, virtually all white schools were valued and insured for more than $100,000. No black school was valued above $20,000 and two were insured for $750. The commission asked the State Superintendent of Education, Mr. Ernest Stone, why Clarke County has white schools worth $100,000 and black schools worth $750. Here is Mr. Stone's verbatim reply: "Well, I would assume that the building which is assessed for $110,000 is a more expensive building than the one that is assessed for $750. That would be a reasonable assumption. Now, the state has nothing to do with the building of either one of the buildings. All the plans were promulgated by the local school system. It is a little something that we call democracy and we think it has worked pretty well."

This response will be something to think about if the federal government takes seriously the fervent demands of the South that it send to the states for education "blocks of money with no strings."

I do not find it strange or surprising, but simply inevitable, that black parents should be deeply angry at white racist management of their children's schools and should demand to run the schools themselves.

In the distribution of funds and people for the new effort of schooling, it is critical that we place a great deal of emphasis on strengthening the work in the early grades, in fact strengthen efforts like Head Start, to get the children started before age 6. It is evident, as Ivor Kraft noted in a recent article in *The Nation* ["Second-Class Schools in a First-Class Power," May 26] that improving our elementary schools will be a most difficult job. Most schools and most teachers put an emphasis on rote learning, on conformity, on obedience and order. And most teachers are little prepared to confront racial attitudes, either within themselves, or to the very young. Further, as Kraft observes, elementary schools don't have an internal force pressing hard for changes, as do the colleges. So I sense that another task for our colleges and universities, as responsible members of the nation's educational enterprise, is to try to affect in every way they can what goes on in the grade schools.

We must strive now harder than ever for desegregated education. I do not use the word "integrated," for it has certain connotations of cultural assimilation, and "integration" of that sort is simply over. But "desegregation" is clear. It means requiring the end of separate school systems, and educating young white people and young black people in the same schools, so that they can educate each other. No other item on the national agenda is more important.

The Supreme Court reached the right decision in the *Brown* case of 1954, but for the wrong reason. The Court spoke of the oppression and discouragement that fell upon the minds of young black students by the mere fact of separation, and of the need to relieve this circumstance if black children were to receive the even break guaranteed by the Constitution. What the Court would have done better to stress is the sickness of soul that descends upon white youngsters when *they* are separated and segregated, and brought up willy-nilly with a sub-conscious sense of white superiority.

There may seem to be a contradiction between what I said earlier about Black Power, about black control of black schools, and the need for desegregation that I now stress. The contradiction seems to me more apparent than real. We must arrive at a standoff, a confronta-tion, between black and white America based, not on appeals to gen-erosity and tolerance but on conditions of real strength and self-respect and self-awareness on either side, and an awareness of and respect for the other man. The idea of a black "nation," the use of that word "nation," contains a helpful suggestion. In this crazy world a certain categorical respect attaches to membership in a recognized nation state; a foreign nationality carries more esteem, indeed, than white America renders its black citizens. I do not go all the way with black nationalists, because the metaphor becomes too confused when you think of a nation scattered in pockets large and small across 3,000 miles and surrounded by yet another nation. But the idea of a black community, of a great *black union*, united in righteous anger, and determined to work as one, is just right in the United States. It can become the basis for a position of real social strength and pride. Such a development does not at all rule out desegregation, or other contact with the white community. On the contrary, it assures that desegrega-tion and interracial contact will produce mutual respect.

Another thing we must do if we are to have a rational future is to teach all our people, young and old, in school and out, the long, tor-tured, truthful story of racial confrontation and oppression in our country. The failure of the schools, and especially the colleges, to see the central importance of this dreadful theme to our national life—and to deal with it—is the surest sign we have of the essential insen-sitivity, the habit-ridden conformity, of our educational establishment. We teach every exotic thing you can think of in our great universities: Northern Welsh Literature, Middle Irish, Origins of European Romanticism, Andean Archaeology, *Beowulf,* History of the Byzantine Empire, the Minor Works of Rousseau. And the Lord knows what idi-otic refinements of established professional specialties in the sciences.

In our schools we devote months on end to the *Iliad,* that poeticized story of a two-penny comic-opera war fought 3,000 years ago in the Dardanelles. But our learned faculties cannot see—as history or tragedy—our own terrible racial epic, one of the most agonized struggles in human history, involving millions of men and women over nearly four centuries. That is, they cannot see it until the black students—like the G.M. workers of thirty years ago—stop the works. The students are dead right, and let us get on with it.

Like most Americans, I have been worried that the new student rebellions would produce an uncontrollable backlash; that we would have to grind our way through a long period of repression, and then further response from students, and then still further repression by police and National Guard. We must look forward to a difficult period, no doubt, for there are hundreds of campuses where faculties have yet to discover that the history of black people in America is a topic demanding some priority over ancient Greek dialects. But I am pleased and encouraged that the crucial confrontation is taking place in the colleges and universities, which, for all their conservatism and stuffiness, are still the most responsive large institutions left in this country. We shall go through some bad experiences on the campuses—at least as bad as those of the last two years. But we shall achieve, also, some constructive results. We are having some already.

I was much impressed by President Morris Abrams' thoughtful handling of the Brandeis sit-in; and by President Levy's determination that, come what may, the University of Chicago wants to work through to solutions with its own students, without calling in the law. There are special reasons for not calling in the law of Chicago to help solve student problems, but the underlying principle is nonetheless sound.

I am most of all heartened by the recent action of a faculty committee at Harvard, working its way to a series of suggestions as to how Harvard should proceed to develop a black studies program. To arrive at its recommendation, the faculty committee met regularly with black student groups and their representatives, and the report shows on every page that the faculty was listening and learning.

Two passages from Harvard came through like music in the black community:

The absence of course offerings in many areas of Afro-American culture is emphatically a matter of more than academic or pedagogical concern to black students. Indeed, it seems likely that the absence of such offerings is the single most potent source of the black students' discontent at Harvard. The lack of such courses can strike the black students as a negative judgment by Harvard University on the importance of these areas of knowledge and research, and, by inference, on the importance of the black people themselves.

More pointedly, there is the problem faced by the black student, who, coming to Harvard, may feel more or less consciously, something of a dislocation from the black community. Many students who addressed the committee expressed the need to legitimize, inwardly as well as publicly, their presence at Harvard while other blacks remain in the ghetto, confronting its problems, bearing its burdens. Herein lies one of the major sources of the demand for courses relevant to the black experience. What the black student wants is an opportunity to study the black experience and to employ the intellectual resources of Harvard in seeking solutions to the problems of the black community—so that he will be better prepared to assist the community in solving these problems. Such educational opportunities at Harvard would help the black student to justify his separation from the larger black community—and would attest that the separation was by no means radical or permanent.

And a final statement from the same report:

In our opinion, the *status quo* with respect to Afro-American Studies at Harvard is not satisfactory. Quite a number of courses recognize the existence of black men in the development of America, quite a bit of expertise is already available. However, merely recognizing black men as integral segments of certain overall social processes is not good enough. We are dealing with 25 million of our own people with a special history, culture, and range of problems. It can hardly be doubted that the study of black men in America is a legitimate and urgent academic endeavor. If this be so and if we are determined to launch this field of study successfully, farsighted goals and programs are required. These goals and programs should maintain and even raise academic standards, should avoid considering the black experience in isolation; and finally, should have meaning for all serious students—black and white.

Amen, brothers! Amen!

*September 21, 1970*

## Jim Brown Comes to Mississippi

*Charles Gillespie*

*Memphis*
Holly Springs is the seat of Marshall County, located only thirty (fast) minutes south of Memphis, in the quiet, pleasant hills of northern Mississippi. Yoknapatawpha country, actually. Most of the town proper is submerged in a lake of great trees, and each spring the row of mansions on College and Falconer and neighboring streets, restored years ago to antebellum splendor, are opened to the public for the annual Pilgrimage. The ladies of Holly Springs also restore themselves to antebellum splendor, and visitors from Memphis and from all across the Delta, descendants of carpetbagger and aristocrat alike, gather to relive the fine old minutes of the Old South as Southerners would like them to have been. And perhaps they were.

This year, before the blooming of the gardens and the grounds and the ladies, Holly Springs was the scene of an entirely different sort of tour: sixteen men in a Greyhound bus, black harbingers of a new spring. They eschewed College and Falconer Streets and instead toured a portion of Holly Springs and Marshall County that has yet to gain its place in a Garden Club brochure.

The leader of the sixteen was Jim Brown, most readily identifiable as the best football player of his time, but more recently a movie actor, inspirer of controversy, and the inventor and moving presence of the Black Economic Union, a Cleveland-based Negro organization composed mostly of Brown's former team mates and opponents in the National Football League. His companions on the tour were from among these. They had come, at Brown's summons, first to the Lorraine Motel in Memphis and then on the tour to Holly Springs. Black leaders in Marshall County had asked the BEU for assistance in a campaign against poverty and against an establishment that so far had apparently thrived on assault by boycott, marches, protests and demonstrated misery.

The Lorraine Motel is, of course, the site of Martin Luther King, Jr.'s assassination and as such is inevitably the gathering place for angry blacks in Memphis. The balcony where King stood is now enclosed in glass, the doorway behind it almost obscured by a flower-strewn cross, and souvenirs are available at the front desk. One of Brown's companions stood in the motel driveway, looking across Mulberry Street at the rear of the shabby rooming house, and began to swear.

Brown and a few friends established the BEU not long before Brown retired from football. The plan, as Brown has repeatedly declared, is to provide the capital and the opportunity for blacks to advance themselves "within the system." BEU's notable successes include Magnificent Products of Los Angeles, manufacturers of natural hair products; New Breed Industries of New York, makers of dashikis; and Way Out Records of Cleveland, producers of way-out records.

Any one of Brown's companions in Memphis and Holly Springs, bell-bottomed almost to the last man, might have drawn a crowd. Brown described them to a packed house in the Mississippi Industrial College auditorium as the first group of black football players to "get off their butts" and try to do something for "the people." They included Brig Owens and Jim Snowden of the Washington Redskins; Lonnie Sanders, Jamie Rivers, Ernie McMillan and Cid Edwards of the St. Louis Cardinals; Ray May, Jim Shorter and Roy Jefferson of the Pittsburgh Steelers; Sidney Williams, Erich Barnes and Leroy Kelly of the Cleveland Browns; Mike Taylor of the New Orleans Saints; and Irv Cross of the Philadelphia Eagles. Shorter and Williams had been especially active in bringing together the athletes and setting up the Lorraine beachhead.

In any gathering, however, Jim Brown is almost certain to be the principal presence. He assumes leadership with the ease and grace of his nonchalant strolls back to the gridiron huddles of a few years ago.

Officially, the group came together for the first time on the mezzanine of the Nite Nite Club, a block away from the Lorraine Motel, on Wednesday morning. Brown sat on a table, wearing a short, dark beard and a blue, *avant-garde* outfit with flowing sleeves, and said: "Thanks for coming. It's beautiful." He then proceeded to tell them of BEU's plan to assist Marshall County, which he described as perhaps the most poverty-afflicted area in the United States.

Brown said that the BEU was adopting Marshall County, starting with a Food First program that would include the immediate shipment of food and clothing into Holly Springs for distribution to county residents selected by the local leadership. The second phase of the program would implement government programs already available for food, medicine and the financing of farm and small business development. Finally, the BEU would ask other black organizations—militant, pacific or whatever—to adopt similar counties for similar programs. As he explained, in part for the benefit of outsiders present:

> The BEU is an economic development corporation, organized to enable the black man to help himself. All the other ethnic groups—the Polish, the Irish, the Italians [*laughing*] in another way—have used this to advance themselves within the system. This is the American way and we believe in it.
>
> We're not here as a black group just to help black, starving people. We think we'll find white people there who will accept our help. What makes it appear to be all black is because we

have been put in that position. We're not going to avoid *any* poor family in a place like Holly Springs. We're going to try to work within the system; we're not here to get involved in politics. Unfortunately, the majority of people in Mississippi who are starving are black and they are starving because of the political system.

Athletes aren't a conservative group. There isn't a man here who could turn the other check. That isn't the nature of the profession. The nature of the profession is to come back stronger than the other guy. But that doesn't mean we want to go into guerrilla warfare.

None of you is asked to give a lot of your time. The mistake most make is one great thrust with a program, then they go back home and the project falls on its face. As athletes, you represent one of the highest income groups in the country. There isn't another black group whose income average could approach yours. You paid your way down here and we've used your name, so you've already made a contribution. We're all in certain categories taxwise, so instead of giving to the government you can talk to your lawyer or accountant. It's much better to give to a cause like this than to the federal government.

We're not trying to make people think we're heaven-sent. We're not coming down in dungarees and overalls to tell the people: "Here we are, just like you." I brought my fur coat down here—that's for the people of the press so they won't write, "Here's this man down in a poverty area wearing a fur coat."

Near the conclusion of the meeting Brown accepted an invitation for the group to attend a party "with girls." He said: "When you work with me you go all the way. I don't have any reputation to protect." When his audience had laughed at this, Brown explained his recent difficulties in Los Angeles, where he had been accused of attempting to run down a man and later throwing him bodily from the hood of a car. He was laughing, though bitterly, at the roles played in the affair by the Los Angeles Sheriff's Department and the *Los Angeles Times*: the Sheriff's Department for milking maximum publicity from the arrest, until it was apparent there was no case, and then asking Brown to drop his protests; the *Times* for displaying the opening incidents on page 1 and the verdict "about page 99."

"I got them off my back by attacking the sheriff on national TV," Brown said. "He's running for office this year and now he's calling around and saying to lay off, he's always liked athletes and he's never gotten along with the district attorney's office. But now the public has this image of Big Brown on the rampage again, running over a man. . . . They wouldn't get no satisfaction if I'd been found guilty unless I bowed my head."

Although it would almost be impossible to imagine men like Mike Taylor or Ernie McMillan (both larger than life by any relevant definition) fearing to walk anywhere, there was an abundance of gallows humor, whistling-in-the-graveyard wise cracks, and overemphasized shuffling of feet and, "Yes sah, mistah sheriff" among the players as they prepared for departure.

"They're integrating the schools there [Holly Springs], and they've warned us things might get a little hot," Brown told them. "I'm free myself, but some of you might not want to participate in certain phases in the development of Mississippi. . . . Yesterday was the first time I'd ever been in the state. I've been all over the South, but I used to drive to Alabama, park my car, and fly over Mississippi."

All of the men spoke of the boundary, just south of Memphis, not as the state line but as the border—as though they were about to pass through some shaky Balkan checkpoint. The twenty-odd passengers—Brown and his athletes; Ernest Thomas, community relations director of BEU and discoverer of Marshall County's plight; Maggie Hathaway, a black leader and commissioner on alcoholism in Los Angeles, and a couple of reporters—spread themselves back through the bus. "Just like Sunday morning going to a game," someone said. When the big Greyhound faltered near a Memphis traffic signal, a voice from the rear shouted: "That's the way, bussy. If you're going to break down, break down on this side of the border." A few minutes later, Ray May, the middle linebacker of the Steelers (the first black middle linebacker in the NFL, according to Brown) commented:

"We're spread out now, but watch when we hit the border. There'll be an influx back here with us."

However, there was no incident, or even noticeable interest, as the bus passed the Tennessee-Mississippi line, and drove through Olive Branch and Byhalia; there were no remarks, even, when it braked into Holly Springs. Rust College and Mississippi Industrial College, both black schools, face each other across the highway; the bus turned left onto the Rust campus to pick up new passengers and directions for the Cadet School. Brown and the others met there with Holly Springs black leaders in a cafeteria room bounded on one side by little boys playing basketball and on the other by young voices singing *Where Have All the Flowers Gone?*

At the school, Arverne Moore, George Caldwell, Henry Boyd and other Holly Springs residents who had inspired the presence of the BEU and the black athletes recited the depressing statistics of Marshall County. Its population is 26,000, of which 66 per cent (17,000) is black. (Holly Springs's population is around 8,000, almost evenly divided between black and white.) Approximately 10,000 people in the county are on welfare rolls or the commodity line; the per capita income—based, according to Moore and Caldwell, on government figures—is less than $700 a year. That puts Marshall County on a par with several undeveloped African and Asian countries.

"There are many factors which cause and perpetuate poverty," said Moore. "Number one is the lack of jobs. They just do not exist for black Marshall County. We do have some industry here but past experience has taught us a lesson—when industry does come in, the establishment goes outside the county and recruits white labor."

The athletes were told that only 160 blacks were employed in Marshall County industries (these include firms, like Wurlitzer, owned outside the state), while 1,300 white workers come into Holly Springs every day from neighboring counties. "Our unemployment actually increases every year. If a white man or woman comes in and applies for a job, then a black man or woman is laid off, so there will be room for him."

"In 1971," another speaker vowed, "we'll be able to put black people in office and we'll cull out some who are black on the outside but white on the inside."

Meanwhile, this being 1970, the speakers said they were looking for help—"We've marched, picketed, boycotted. All have failed and the major reason they have failed is that we have nobody to turn to. This is a closed society. There aren't any black-owned stores, no black-owned groceries or industries. You have our support. We don't have anyone else to turn to in Mississippi. We don't have a governor we can go to."

Brown responded by explaining the program he had outlined at the Nite Nite Club in Memphis. He added: "I'm always asked, 'Is this all black? Are you going to help white people too?' No, we're never all black. We're relegated to that position. We're men and we're going to stand and we're not going to apologize because we're black. Mississippi was not set up by us. The politicians have been contacted and informed we're here, and since *they're* not here the white people should be glad there is some black leadership. . . . We didn't come here to get involved in politics but if politics get involved with us . . ."

Following the Cadet School meeting, the BEU members reboarded the bus for a tour of Holly Springs and nearby rural areas. The athletes, most of whom now live in Northern cities and presumably have had some experience with poverty, were shown Negro neighborhoods, the black and gutted remains of a school bombed in October, and "white-owned" churches. At one point a young boy blew kisses at the bus; at another the bus passed a black man and his toddler child carrying firewood into a hovel described over the bus's public address system as a "modern home of the 20th century."

Back on the highway, the bus drove a few miles into the country and stopped at a black home which drew exclamations of disbelief from the passengers. The place had been a storehouse or barn. Windows were covered with strips of tin and the interior walls were insulated against the cold with cardboard and paper. One of the football pros said: "The Monkey's Nest is worse than that and it's in Ohio." Yet there was some reluctance to disturb the residents. Roy Jefferson, later to be introduced by Brown as "one of our fastest receivers and best dancers," said: "I'd just be embarrassed to go in there." But he joined the others when the bus emptied.

Water for the house came from a cistern out back and the privy crouched over a small creek, its mini-pollution emphasized by abandoned stoves and other debris. The woman of the house said she "couldn't get all together" on her age, but was "up there around 63 or somewhere." She was the mother of nine sons and a daughter, only five of the sons still living and one of them in a penitentiary. "We need a new Lincoln," said Maggie Hathaway as she stepped up on the porch.

The above description is dismal, but the woman showed no sense of despair. Erich Barnes noticed this: "These people are to be commended just for staying alive here."

After a second stop at a similar home, the bus took the players back to Holly Springs and an excellent example of living off the lean of the land. Brown and his companions must have become accustomed to excellent food, but in Holly Springs they stopped at Cummings' Goco Service Station, which is also a grocery store, café and laundry. There they plunged into the juke box, jars of pigs' feet, cheeseburgers and French fries. A round of visitors gathered, some of them white and all of them eager for a glimpse at the legends of the television screen.

On the short trip from Cummings' place to the Mississippi Industrial College Auditorium, there were the usual uneasy-but-I'm-laughing remarks. The athletes were obviously growing tired ("too tired to flirt," said Erich Barnes disconsolately as he and Leroy Kelly watched a pretty girl come into the restaurant and depart without eliciting a single gesture of admiration), but they were not too tired to remember self-preservation. "Turn those lights off bussy. I'm serious—didn't you see *Easy Rider*?" When one of the players commented, "There's a woman sitting over there with a flat tire," the response was, "Why don't you help her? They'll lynch your big ass for trying to seduce her."

Holly Springs's black residents filled the auditorium beyond its seating capacity and Brown described it as a turnout "we couldn't have had with just one day's notice in New York or Los Angeles or Cleveland." He told them: "We won't try to carry you on our backs, but we'll help you because you want to do something. . . . You have many battles to fight and I'll tell you out front we can't battle them all with you, but we're going to do what we've promised. Maybe some day, when all our programs are off the ground, we can help you with all your problems."

In May the Governor of Mississippi, John Bell Williams, and the Mayor of Holly Springs, Sam Coopwood, made a publicized visit to Colorado to protest "the unfair image" left by a civic drive in Boulder "to aid the Biafra of America."

The Governor complained that Jim Brown and a group of black militants had spent "a couple of hours" in Holly Springs and made "propaganda photos" in "two or three selected places." The editor of the Marshall County weekly newspaper, former state Sen. George Yarbrough, offered a $100 reward for any person confirming a report of actual starvation in the county.

Jim Brown had participated in the Boulder campaign which resulted in four truckloads of food and clothing and about $10,000 being sent to Holly Springs, and two Mississippi politicians being sent to Colorado.

Brown and a second group of black athletes have since visited Holly Springs and subsequently sponsored Food First dinners in Cleveland and Philadelphia. In New York, the inevitable celebrity party was employed to raise funds, and Brown joined Sen. Jacob Javits, Arthur Ashe and Herb Fitzgibbon in an exhibition tennis match. Basketball games, golf tournaments, fashion shows and jazz concerts have all been used to collect cash and food which the BEU passes on to the United League of Marshall County for distribution.

*July 19, 1971*

## A Fair Trial for Angela Davis?

*Jerome H. Skolnick and Steven A. Brick*

*Berkeley*

Ordinarily, when we speak of a fair trial, we think of the defendant's ability to retain competent counsel and investigators, of being able to exclude illegally seized evidence, or coerced confessions. The Angela Davis-Ruchell Magee case is out of the ordinary. Magee claims he cannot obtain a fair trial in the courts of California. He points to his seven-year-old conviction on a $10 kidnap-robbery charge in Los Angeles and says his guilty plea was fraudulently obtained. He believes that the California courts, district attorneys and appointed counsel want to railroad him to the gas chamber to silence him from protesting his fraudulent conviction. Miss Davis, on the other hand, now says she believes it may be possible for her to receive a fair trial in California courts, although she may not have thought so when she left the state in August 1970. Still, it is questionable that a fair trial is possible for her. The issue must be analyzed in terms of the ability of the criminal justice system to deal impartially with a black, abrasively political defendant accused of serious, violent acts.

On August 7, 1970 James McClain, an inmate at San Quentin prison, was on trial in San Rafael, Calif., for assaulting a prison guard. Ruchell Magee was on the witness stand being examined by the assistant district attorney, Gary Thomas. At about 11 a.m., a young, handsome, light-skinned black man entered the courtroom. After a few minutes he stood up, pointed a gun at the trial's participants and said: "All right, gentlemen, this is it." He took a weapon from a satchel and handed it to McClain. McClain walked to the bench where Judge Harold Haley was sitting and ordered him to call and instruct the sheriff to order his men not to interfere with what was going on. Meanwhile, Magee, who was appearing in handcuffs, ordered a deputy to remove them. McClain then handed a weapon to Magee. Three women jurors, the assistant district attorney and the judge were taken from the courtroom by Magee, McClain and the young man—

later identified as Jonathan Jackson. The armed men also freed William Christmas, another inmate who was to appear as a witness; he joined in moving the hostages out of the building.

A witness testified that as the men were leaving, McClain said: "Free the Soledad brothers by 12:30 or they all die." The four men led their hostages to a yellow Hertz rented van, parked in a lot next to the Civic Center. The van began to move toward an exit. Two cars had arrived at the scene from nearby San Quentin prison and were positioned in the path of the exiting van. The van came to a sudden halt and there was a barrage of gunfire both from without and within the van. When the shooting stopped, McClain, Christmas, Jackson and the judge were dead. Magee, and one of the women jurors and the assistant district attorney suffered gunshot wounds. The assistant district attorney was wounded in the spine, and is permanently confined to a wheelchair. Magee recovered quickly. The woman juror sued Marin County for damages arising from the injuries she suffered.

This invasion of a courtroom is obviously shocking, yet its motives and meaning belie any simplistic interpretation. Certainly, serious crimes were committed, but it is also clear that Jonathan Jackson defined the acts as political. However misguided the means, Jackson's goal was either to "free" political prisoners, or to ameliorate prison conditions by negotiating the return of hostages. The political meaning of the events was further underlined by the indictment of Angela Davis, who was charged with kidnapping, murder and conspiracy. The penalty for these charges is death. The combination of a capital case with international political reverberations promises one of the longest, most complicated and expensive trials in history. This report attempts to summarize the progress of the case and to comment on some of the issues of politics and law in capital cases.

The Marin County grand jury indicted Miss Davis in her absence. That is not an unusual grand jury procedure, but the use of the grand jury is itself unusual in California criminal cases. There are two routes to felony trials in California, the grand jury and the preliminary examination. The prosecutor has complete discretion as to which route will be taken. In an average case, he uses the preliminary examination to convince a municipal court judge that the accused should stand trial. The preliminary examination offers the defendant a major advantage over the grand jury since the evidence necessary to bring him to trial may be tested immediately.

Moreover, the proceedings are public and he has the right to cross-examine witnesses brought by the prosecutor to prove a *prima facie* case. Cross-examination early in the proceedings gives the defendant a chance for early dismissal; if he is "held to answer," cross-examination provides a more thorough record of the witnesses' testimony for possible impeachment at trial. In run-of-the-mill cases, prosecutors don't mind cross-examination of witnesses early in the game—most prefer not to go to trial if the case is weak. Moreover, when the prosecution case proves strong the defendant may be persuaded to plead guilty, thus ending the proceedings with a minimum of time and expense. Finally, a preliminary examination permits a defendant to put forward exculpatory evidence.

Grand jury proceedings in California are usually reserved by prosecutors for cases potentially involving much publicity, or where, for a variety of other reasons, they want to control the initial evidence. From the defendant's point of view there are crucial disadvantages. The grand jury hears only one side of the case, since the prosecutor is unfettered by opposing counsel. He may ask leading questions and put words in the mouths of witnesses.

Further, the grand jury presents special problems for black politically dissident defendants. Such juries are composed of leading citizens—bankers, lawyers and businessmen. Potential discrimination is inherent when the citizens are white, as they usually are, and the defendants are black, or when the defendants are political dissidents who criticize the very sort of people sitting on a grand jury.

Yet in theory, the grand jury exists to protect the defendant. Solid and respectable members of the community presumably make a secret, impartial appraisal of evidence mustered by the prosecutor to bring an indictment. When no indictment is handed down, the potential accused need not be disturbed by knowing that he was so considered; his reputation remains untarnished, his peace of mind unmolested. When the grand jury decides to indict, however, the accused can only suffer from secrecy.

The Davis-Magee case offers one illustration. Miss Davis was confined for six months before the sufficiency of evidence against her was put before a judge. Most of this time was taken up with finding an impartial judge. All the Marin County judges declined to hear the case because they felt they could not be, or certainly could not appear to be, impartial or unprejudiced. Another judge, satisfactory to Miss Davis and her attorneys, disqualified himself after being challenged by Ruchell Magee. The next judge was unsuccessfully challenged for cause by Miss Davis and was disqualified peremptorily by Magee.

The Marin County judges declined to sit on the case for obvious reasons. Yet, how can a judge from an adjoining county or any county in California fail to be moved by the death of a sitting judge kidnapped from his own courtroom? Perhaps the only impartial judge in this case would be one who disqualifies himself. Meanwhile, the case has been widely discussed in the press. The mounting expense of the trial has placed a tremendous financial burden both on the defense and the citizens of Marin County who may ultimately decide Miss Davis' fate.

Once an indictment has been brought, it is not unusual for a number of such legal issues as sufficiency of evidence, discovery and bail, to be raised before trial. On January 5, Miss Davis' attorneys moved to dismiss the indictment on grounds that the evidence was insufficient to support the charges. Primarily because of a variety of legal motions dealing with self-representation, legal jurisdiction, and claims that the judge was prejudiced, the motion to dismiss was not argued until May 27.

The argument for bail was presented on June 2, following which Judge Richard Arnason requested a probation report. The Chief Deputy Probation Officer of Marin County, in his official report to Judge Arnason on Angela Davis' suitability for bail, wrote:

From my investigation of this case, I feel that Miss Davis, if released on bail, will not flee the jurisdiction of the court. Her alleged flight following the August 7, 1970 incident would not in my estimation preclude her from being released on bail. It is not unusual for people who are charged with criminal offenses to hide from the authorities. It is not unusual for people who have avoided the authorities, once arrested and released on bail, to appear for their court hearings. I also feel that since August 7, 1970, some significant things have happened that have a bearing on her case. She has received a great deal of support from numerous people throughout the country for her position. She is looked upon by a great number of people in this country as a leader for social reforms. There is in my estimation a commitment on Miss Davis' part to her family, attorneys and supporters who have given their time, skills and money, to her case. . . . I feel that for Miss Davis to flee the jurisdiction of the court would be a great disappointment to her family, supporters and attorneys. It would also question her role as a leader for social reform. . . .

Yet bail was denied by Judge Arnason on June 15, with the following statement:

Solely and exclusively upon the legal issue . . . I find that she is not eligible for bail under the California statutes and Constitution; not that she is not a fit person, not that she is not the type of person that would be entitled to bail.

That is a remarkable statement. Bail is a civil right guaranteed under the Constitution except in capital cases. The "fitness" of the defendant determines amount of bail, not whether it will be granted. Normally, defendants are jailed before trial because they cannot raise the amount of bail; in fact, they are imprisoned by their poverty. The Marin County probation department recommended that bail be set at $100,000 for Angela Davis, and she probably could raise that amount. Denial of bail reflects the legal erosion of the constitutional right to bail in California.

The California Constitution of 1849 guarantees the right to bail "unless for capital offenses, when the proof is evident or the presumption is great." The special California statute on bail in capital cases alters the constitutional language to: "A defendant charged with an offense punishable with death cannot be admitted to bail, when proof of his guilt is evident or the presumption thereof great. The finding of an indictment does not add to the strength of the proof or the presumptions to be drawn therefrom." By stressing "cannot," the statute seems to alter the expectation concerning right to bail. It becomes something a defendant has to show he is entitled to, rather than a right, except when guilt is evident.

The leading case-law interpretation of the statutory language further waters down the right to bail. The opinion seems to say—in arcane language of 1883—that if the "sufficiency" of the evidence against the defendant is strong enough so that a jury could reasonably bring in a verdict of guilty, even if the judge wouldn't, bail should not be granted. In argument before the court on whether Angela Davis should be admitted to bail, the prosecutor, Albert Harris of the State Attorney General's office, held that "sufficiency" meant something more than the evidence needed to indict, but not much. Howard Moore, representing Miss Davis, argued that the court ought to look to the statute and to the Constitution and that guilt needed to be "evident" to deny bail. The judge, apparently accepting the prosecutor's argument, denied bail.

The law on bail in capital cases is an anachronistic absurdity. It was framed in the 19th century, presumably with the idea that someone facing a death sentence, in a case where the evidence was strong, might flee. After all, it was reasoned, if the defendant faced execution, he would be unlikely to appear for trial. This theory not only erodes the constitutional right to bail—its truth is doubtful. Obviously, the prediction of behavior is sounder when an individual's total situation is taken into account than by a general rule governing all individuals. Moreover, time, society and knowledge are always changing. Executions rarely occur now in capital cases, so the motive for flight is reduced. We have also learned that murderers are often not a threat to the general community. At least such facts can be taken into consideration by a probation officer. But organized probation services did not exist in 1883, when the case relied on by the judge to deny Miss Davis bail was decided.

If the 1883 behavioral assumptions governing bail in capital cases are an anachronism, the law that bail is a constitutional right, *except* in capital cases, is an absurdity. Capital cases are precisely the ones where society should most fear making a mistake, and should therefore offer the defendant the most complete protection of due process of law, including the right to bail. The implications of denying bail are terribly important to the notion of a fair trial, especially in a capital case. Denial materially affects the defendant's position before the court. Despite the presumption of innocence, a jury cannot help noticing whether a defendant walks into court each day as a free man, or in the custody of a sheriff. While the impact of this factor isn't tangible, it is significant. Further, restriction of the defendant to the confines of a jail cell clearly hinders the defense preparation. The defendant is not free to find and talk to witnesses. He cannot consult with his attorneys with the assurance that their conversations are not being monitored, or merely talk with them at their mutual convenience. Ultimately, the most crucial impact is upon the defendant when, as in the Davis case, the defendant is confined to two small rooms, allowed to see only a handful of people, and constantly watched. Inhumanity aside, the defendant's capacity to assist in his or her own defense is jeopardized. Careful studies have shown that, for similar offenses, those who are free on bail fare better than those who are confined before trial.

Political defendants are further hampered by denial of bail. In the Chicago conspiracy case, the defendants were able to raise money by giving speeches around the country during their trial. Angela Davis' presence at rallies and meetings would be an asset to her defense fund, as well as to gaining political support for her cause.

Perhaps most important, the present rule involves the judge in a determination of the strength of the prosecutor's case prior to trial, before evidence has been tested through cross-examination. It is unlikely that a jury, even though admonished to disregard everything but the evidence presented at trial, will be unaware that a defendant has not qualified for bail. If Miss Davis is brought to trial in the custody of the sheriff, the jury may believe she was unfit for bail in the sense that she would flee or present a danger to the community; they might believe bail was denied because evidence of her guilt is "substantial." In either event, can that inference fail to influence their determination of guilt "beyond a reasonable doubt"? It is doubtful that the jury system can work fairly when a prior stigma, over and above the indictment, has been placed on the defendant. With this in mind, we turn now to the evidence against Angela Davis, to see if the additional burden of pretrial confinement can be justified.

Magee undoubtedly picked up a weapon and held it on hostages. It is not yet clear whether he was directly responsible for death or injury, or whether he had prior knowledge that the action would take place. Miss Davis' participation, on the other hand, is entirely inferential. She was not there. The joinder of the cases makes sense for the prosecution because it implicates Angela Davis with Ruchell Magee. Magee was an active participant; the prosecution must prove that Miss Davis was an accessory. Legally, she could move for a separate trial, which the judge has indicated he would grant. But a severance move has personal and political as well as legal implications. Ruchell Magee's history of imprisonment symbolizes the oppression of the poor black man by white society. For Miss Davis, severance might suggest desertion. She cannot abide that personally or politically, even though joinder tends to obscure the absence of evidence directly linking Angela Davis and Ruchell Magee.

The evidence presented to the grand jury indicting Miss Davis shows the following: she purchased the four weapons used in the escape, including a shotgun purchased in San Francisco on August 5, two M-1 carbines, and a Browning automatic pistol; a woman resembling her was seen with Jonathan Jackson by a service station attendant, on August 6, near the Civic Center, in a yellow Hertz van like the one used in the escape; she purchased a ticket at San Francisco International Airport on the afternoon of August 7 for Los Angeles; she and Jonathan Jackson spoke out forcefully at rallies and advocated the release of the Soledad brothers, one of whom is Jonathan's brother George; she was not seen publicly in California after August 7, and was arrested in New York on October 13, 1970. The prosecution contends she was attempting to escape apprehension and subsequent conviction. This pattern of individually lawful acts, alleges the state, is sufficient to bring her to trial on capital charges: murder, kidnapping, conspiracy to murder and kidnap.

Whatever evidence the prosecution may seek to introduce at trial, each act charged by the grand jury to Miss Davis is itself lawful. Purchasing guns is lawful. Moreover, it is not unreasonable for a black militant who had received many threats on her life to purchase guns for self-protection. The state has not introduced evidence showing that she furnished the guns to Jonathan Jackson; even if she had, the state hasn't shown that she did so with the intent that they be used illegally. Indeed, newspaper stories have reported that Jonathan Jackson was her bodyguard. Bodyguards often have access to guns. Even if the woman seen in the van was indeed Angela Davis, accompanying Jonathan Jackson is not a crime. There is no question they were close associates.

Miss Davis says she initially fled because of fear and mistrust in the fairness of California officials. She had recently been fired by the university and, after investigation, the dismissal had been declared unfair by the American Association of University Professors. But Miss Davis says she decided to stay in the United States because her struggle is here and because she is innocent of the charges against her. She also feels that public support has brought her the opportunity for fair judicial treatment.

The Davis-Magee case has yet to go to trial. Miss Davis has been in custody since October 13, 1970, and has not left the confines of the Marin County Civic Center since December 23. The trial, and especially the security measures while Miss Davis is confined, threaten to raise the tax rate of Marin County. The county administrator, in resigning from office, declared that granting bail in this case would be the best possible step to insure a fair trial, and coincidentally save the county a fortune. His judgment was sound.

The legal procedures which have imprisoned Miss Davis and

denied her bail go a long way toward defeating their purported end: a fair trial for the individual defendant and the state. Her grand jury was *de facto* segregated from her in racial, economic, and political terms. Our whole judicial theory demands maximum public disclosure, and adversarial determination of competent evidence, yet the grand jury deliberations were secret and accusatorial. Miss Davis has been denied bail, although the evidence against her is inferential and untested.

Confinement is punishment. The Marin County probation department made a finding that Miss Davis now has many reasons to appear at trial, that her appearance can be insured by high bail, rather than none at all. As for being a threat to the community, her only past crime is a traffic violation. The judge finds her fit for bail but, with less logic than prudence, says that his hands are tied by the grand jury testimony.

If, in light of these circumstances, we ask, "Can Angela Davis get a fair trial?" we must answer on two levels. A model "fair trial" suggests a proceeding that is procedurally correct, with an intelligent judge sensitive to his own prejudices. The ultimate decision of guilt or innocence should be left to a jury which can comprehend the testimony given in behalf of the accused, whether it chooses to believe it or not. Miss Davis is now receiving a "fair" trial only in the sense that she employs a team of able attorneys who will vigorously assert her rights. But they are operating within a social and legal structure that is stacked against her.

In predominantly white middle-class Marin County, communism and black militancy are anathema. The much publicized rise in the tax rate attributed to this trial can hardly fail to influence the county's taxpayers, from whose ranks the jury may be drawn.

Accordingly, an analysis of the fairness of the Angela Davis trial cannot proceed on a purely legal level. It must also examine the community and racial aspects of the trial, and the peculiar but no longer unique combination of race and politics influencing the atmosphere of the trial in and out of the courtroom. Both the state and the accused have an interest in obtaining the fairest trial possible. In reality, fairness can only be approximated; we come closest to it when, while operating in an imperfect system, we strive to remedy imperfections. The worst we can do is deny their existence.

*October 2, 1972*

## Where Did Their Revolution Go?

*J. K. Obatala*

A tall, muscular figure rose slowly and deliberately from the lunch-room table, his semi-clenched fist wavering anxiously in the dimly lighted space above his head; he motioned as if to place a devastating blow in the attentive face of one of the seated students. From the cashier's booth where I was standing, the vague symmetry of the student's body appeared silhouette-like against the pale white background of the Venetian blinds which concealed the card players from the brightness of the world outside.

Although the near-rhythmic rumble of uninhibited voices which came from the darkened corner had now subsided momentarily, elsewhere in the cafeteria the drone of meal-time chatter continued unbroken: even after the wavering black fist, which had probably held an ace of spades, or perhaps a deuce, came slamming down upon the table with a thunderous crash, evoking jubilant cries of "Boston!, Boston!" from the small cluster of black spectators who had huddled around the table.

To the mass of white students this was—so it must have appeared—simply another game of Afro-American-style bid whist being brought once again to its melodramatic conclusion. But to the small group of Afro-American students who gather in the cafeteria at Cal State, Los Angeles, almost every day, a "Boston" is much more than just a flawless card game. It is something in which to immerse oneself, a social ritual, a "trip" whereby participants try to extricate themselves from the humdrum that has once again become life on the college campus.

To be sure, many blacks on college and university campuses manage to find other equally satisfying diversions. Indeed, the chronic card players represent only a small minority of Afro-American students. Yet their reappearance in the cafeterias and lounges on a regular basis is an important indicator of the state of political affairs among black students. For during the heyday of the black student movement, many of the card players could be seen among the rank and file of the protesters and demonstrators; and it is no accident that this and other forms of black student escapism come at a time when political activism among blacks on campus is at the lowest ebb since its emergence in the early 1960s.

Aside from the resurgence of black student escapism, the most important index of the decline of black political activity on campus is the withering away of many of the once ubiquitous Black Student Unions (BSUs) and the stagnant, almost impotent posture of those which manage to survive. This can be seen not only in the case of Cal State University at Los Angeles, where the Black Student Union has been dissolved, but the same phenomenon is also evident on other campuses throughout Southern California (and perhaps the nation). At Cal State, Dominguez Hills, for example, the once militant BSU is gone and in its place is the "Black Caucus," which is nothing more than a negotiating committee, a black students' version of the NAACP. All is calm at the University of Southern California, while at UCLA, the BSU is still intact but has adopted a relatively moderate program of action, one that resembles liberal Republicanism more than revolutionary change. For example:

> Our direction for the *past quarter and the quarter to come* is towards meeting the educational, social, political, and service needs of black students in relation to self-help and co-ordination. Our programs and projects are designed primarily to service the black family *at UCLA* in the most constructive ways we can. The Black Student Union's programs are: Sickle Cell Anemia; Prison Project; Ethnic Film Series; Black Culture Week. [Emphasis added.]

Thus spoke the chairman of UCLA's BSU in a recent issue of the black student newspaper, *Nommo*. It could very well have been Robert Finch.

Whatever happened to the black campus revolution? Whatever happened to the gun-toting nationalist, the uncombed hair, the demonstrations, the handbills, the placards, the protests, the black leather jackets and Malcolm X sweat shirts that came to be symbols of black student militancy in the 1960s? One answer is, of course, that the "true revolutionaries" have either been killed, jailed, driven underground or just plain suppressed by the forces of law and order. In a few instances, this has indeed been the case.

However, a more realistic explanation would be that there simply never was a "black revolution." There was militancy, as well as anger, hate and racial frustration, but—except for radical rhetoric—never much of a genuine revolutionary conviction on the part of most black students. Ironically, if indeed there had been a meaningful degree of revolutionary commitment and understanding among the black student population, much of the chaos and confusion that was generated out of the black campus rebellion in its later stages might never have occurred. For the mature revolutionary understands that real revolutions aren't made in a day and that violence is an important but not an *all-important* part of revolutionary strategy; that there comes a time in any protracted struggle when thought is much more important than action.

Yet the black campus mood today is not one of revolutionary reflection and regroupment; in fact, the black "revolution" has become its opposite: many Afro-Americans on campuses where yesterday blacks declared their willingness to "wipe out the white race" if their demands were not met, seem now prepared to "wipe out" half the black race if the gains from those demands are threatened. Thus it has been reported that a high administration official at UCLA, put there in response to the militant demands of black students, has cautioned the Economic Opportunities Program (EOP) workers on campus against admitting lower-income students with jail records because the latter might "cause trouble"! And strange though it may at first seem, many black students are in sympathy with this conservative approach to student admissions. This is demonstrated, implicitly, by the fact that there has been little opposition from black students—including the BSUs—on the various Southern California campuses to EOP policies which are clearly biased against lower-income students.

Nor should the lingering, if somewhat stale, separatist rhetoric of "blackness" and "nation building" be allowed to obscure the essentially conservative outlook of the Afro-American student population. Even during the peak years of the black campus "revolt"—the middle to late 1960s—such verbiage was nothing more than a fudge coating, beneath which lay the frozen social drives, the frustrated goals and unrealized ideals of an essentially patriotic, pro-American and white-oriented black middle class. Indeed, as the training ground for the Afro-American elite, the colleges and university campuses—not only in Southern California but throughout the nation—have always been the strongholds of black conservatism.

Thus the black world to which the Afro-American student "revolutionary" supposedly declared his allegiance in the 1960s was, in reality, the white world of the 1950s: a world from which the Afro-American middle class was disbarred by the dogs, fire hoses and night sticks of the white-dominated American ruling class. Denied entrance into the white world around whose periphery it had been anxiously pacing since Reconstruction, the black bourgeoisie, led by a radicalized student sector, turned against its white liberal mentors and stormed angrily into the ranks of the growing "separatist" movement. Here they drew crude sketches of an alternative black world—a fantasy world, devoid of hypocritical white liberals, decidedly more humane and, most important, controlled by blacks. This new world of the black bourgeoisie remained without any concrete expression except that it was supposed to be a manifestation of "blackness."

This vagueness, of course, was an attempt to hide the fact that the Afro-American bourgeoisie had little in common with the masses of black people with whom it had formed a temporary and somewhat shaky alliance. The brief alliance between the Afro-American elite and the masses—who, because of their social conditions are frequently susceptible to separatist agitation—expressed itself socially and politically as the Black Power movement.

Though few would dare admit it at the time, Black Power meant totally different things to different people. For the masses, the struggle for power had truly revolutionary implications, in that such a struggle must necessarily concern itself with a redistribution of goods and income and a change in the ownership of productive capacity. This was shown by the fact that looting was a main preoccupation of the ghetto rebellions that erupted among the masses in Watts, Harlem, Detroit and other American cities.

On the other hand, when the Afro-American middle class—including the black student elite—spoke of power, it was, with a few exceptions, speaking mainly in terms of social recognition and social mobility within the present system. Therefore, the vague and abstract nature of the bourgeois ideologies of "blackness" and Black Power was its main strength, it helped to conceal the divergent and contradictory interest of the masses and the Afro-American middle class.

However, in the last half of the 1960s, the Afro-American student community—its ranks swollen by converted integrationists returned from the civil rights struggles in the Southeast—started to organize itself under the umbrella of Black Power. The key issues around which most of the Black Student Unions were organized were the basically elitist notions of black studies, EOP and more black professors on the faculties.

Although these essentially reformist demands were clothed in the rhetorical garb of black nationalism, they were not qualitatively different from the demands Dr. Martin Luther King, Jr. had made upon transit authorities in Montgomery, Ala. more than a decade earlier, when he demanded black bus drivers for the black community. Thus the "separatism" of the black campus elite was, for the most part, back-door integrationism. The programs of the Black Student Unions consisted of nothing more than the deferred dreams of the integrationist movement, transformed by frustrated minds into the surrealistic imagery which flowed so profusely from the pens and lips of petit-bourgeois intellectuals whose influence came to dominate the unions: Blackness! Soul! Negritude! Redneck! House Niggers! White Racist! Indeed, the black student elite cursed the white man with a thousand tongues and, at the same time, implicitly, worshipped his institutions: Miss *Black* America! The *Black* Madonna! Miss *Black* Homecoming! The *Black* Church! *Black* History! *Black* Capitalism! The *Black* University! All of these were the militant harangues of a socially frustrated and alienated people, provocative symbolism which tended to obscure the essentially conservative political and institutional outlook of the Afro-American nationalist movement on campus.

Finally, it should be pointed out that Black Student Unions, as the vehicles of this political and institutional conservatism, contained within themselves the germs of their own destruction. If the unions moved too far to the left, i.e., if they substituted political radicalism for racial militancy—as was the case with the now defunct Black Student Alliance which was based in Southern California—the BSUs would lose their conservative black student following as did the Alliance. On the other hand, if the unions managed to achieve their goals of acceptance for EOP, black studies and other integrationist demands by college and university officials, the BSUs would deprive themselves of further meaningful issues around which to organize and thus remove the need for their own existence. The latter—and, in a few instances, the former—development has already resulted in the decline or disappearance of Black Student Unions on campuses in Southern California.

*December 25, 1972*

## Florence Rice vs. the Utilities

*Steve Murdock*

On one of Madison Avenue's less fashionable blocks—between 125th and 126th Streets in the heart of Harlem—there's a white-painted storefront bearing the sign, "Harlem Consumer Education Council, Inc." You have to knock. They keep the door locked, and there are assorted safeguards against burglary. "Otherwise," explains Mrs. Florence M. Rice, "they steal the typewriters."

Mrs. Rice basically *is* the Harlem Consumer Education Council, although she would be even more hard-pressed than she is if she didn't have the services of Carl Jones, a 37-year-old volunteer researcher who has a penchant for writing briefs to the New York State Public Service Commission that contain his own ironic brand of humor.

Florence M. Rice is a bouncy 53-year-old black woman who accepts the likelihood of burglary as a run-of-the-block risk in Harlem and, after taking the precautions she can, focuses on what she regards as the really important enemies of her people—like the New York Telephone Co. and the Consolidated Edison Co. Mrs. Rice is not going to be deflected by junkies who steal typewriters. "There are not," she says with characteristic candor, "enough Ralph Naders in the world, and there are not enough Florence Rices."

As a self-trained consumer representative, Mrs. Rice concedes that Nader has done some valuable spotlight training on how consumers get cheated, but she isn't exactly one of his fans. She doesn't think he recognizes the special exploitation suffered by the black consumer, and that's where she comes in—to the degree that she can.

If the reaction of the New York Telephone Co. is a yardstick, she can do quite a lot. Edward Goldstein, one of the phone company's vice presidents, came to take her out to lunch after she became a fixture at Public Service Commission hearings on telephone service and rate matters. "Some of the best men," she says, smiling, "take me out to lunch."

*The New York Times* last summer described her as a "telephone militant," and admittedly a lot of her time and energy go into fighting the phone company. At the moment she is involved heavily in Public Service Commission Case No. 26243, a series of hearings known technically as proceedings ". . . on motion of the Commission as to the rules and practices of the New York Telephone Company relating to deposits and suspension of service for non-payment."

As far as Harlem is concerned, she says, the phone company has a double standard. It is much tougher on blacks in demanding deposits and in cutting off service than it is on whites. She is in the process of attempting to prove this through witnesses at the hearings.

Mrs. Rice says she concentrates most of her time and energy on public utilities because Florynce Kennedy, a black activist lawyer, "convinced me that utilities were where the action really was." Before then, "I was chasing pennies."

But, she admits, she will still go in pursuit of an occasional cent. Recently, she ran a consumer education class for a group of neighborhood women. They concentrated on one item—hominy grits. They ran their own survey and found that the price ranged from 31¢ to 39¢ a pound in an area of several blocks surrounding the Council office. The women determined they should pay no more than 34¢. By being concentrated on a single item, she says, the lesson was more dramatic.

A woman of vast energy and enthusiasm, Mrs. Rice seems to have had to do everything the hard way. She grew up in orphanages and in foster homes. She didn't finish high school and started work as a domestic. World War II gave her a chance to get into industry. She found that skills—such as reading blueprints—came quickly to her. After the war she went to work in the garment industry and became a militant rank-and-filer in the International Ladies' Garment Workers' Union. As a result, she says, employment opportunities dried up for her, and she found herself working eventually as a credit clerk in a retail establishment. That was what got her into the consumer movement.

"I saw how black people were exploited at every level. I saw how they were cheated." She realized that blacks couldn't get credit then at the big department stores; now that situation is better, partly as a result of her efforts. "In the beginning of our Council," she says, "I told people to go and shop at the big stores because they could get better buys—even if they couldn't get credit." She started the Council in the early 1960s, and it has led a precarious existence ever since. According to Mrs. Rice, more than 100 foundations have refused the Council any funding. Mostly she keeps it going with lecture fees. She has become an engaging public speaker. Yet the $140 rent for the storefront is a problem every month. "When you have to go out and beg for postage stamps you're in a bad way."

She doesn't like to think in box-score terms—of cases won and lost before the Public Service Commission. "I don't like to think of winning. I like to think of making them change their procedures."

By just being where she is, she feels she has changed the Commission. "We've got them working. I don't think they've ever worked so hard before."

Mrs. Rice is a tempestuous talker. She can range clear across the spectrum of consumer problems and the black human condition in a matter of minutes. She is full of insight into her own problem. "Not enough people know this place is here . . . but you can't talk to a hungry man. . . . When your belly is empty you can't think."

So even she has to put double locks on the door.

*August 14, 1976*

##  Black Power After Ten Years

*Clayborne Carson*

In a single decade, an era of Afro-American politics came and went. A legacy remains, but its full meaning is still to be determined, even by blacks who came of age during the 1960s and were transformed by the events of those years. Now we must search our memories to recall the effect on our lives of the evolution from nonviolent desegregation

sit-ins to massive marches and rallies to convulsive urban rebellions—the evolution from Martin Luther King to Malcolm X to
Stokely Carmichael to Eldridge Cleaver. The 1963 march on Washington is separated from us by thirteen years and three Presidents and
the rise and fall of a succession of movements, leaders and dreams.

Just a decade ago, in the midst of the march through Mississippi
undertaken after James Meredith was wounded by a shotgun blast, a
new form of racial militancy suddenly gained national attention. The
cry for "Black Power" arose as a conscious attempt by the young black
activists in the Student Non-Violent Coordinating Committee (SNCC)
to alter the direction of black politics. Willie Ricks, an Alabama-born
SNCC worker who gained his political education in the streets of
Chattanooga, Albany and Montgomery and in isolated black-belt
regions of Georgia and Alabama, was chosen in June 1966, to test the
readiness of blacks for a new militant vocabulary. Nightly venturing
away from the main body of marchers, Ricks launched a new phase
of Afro-American history in small black Mississippi towns that time
seemed to have ignored. He returned each night with reports of
enthusiastic receptions for the rhetoric of Black Power.

A year earlier, in similar communities of Lowndes County, Ala.,
Ricks and other SNCC workers had organized the Lowndes County
Freedom Organization. In that poor, predominantly black county
between Selma and Montgomery, SNCC organizers took an important and original political departure simply by doing what they
thought necessary. Since their supporters were black and not welcomed by the Democratic Party, they built an independent, all-black
party. Since blacks in the Deep South understood white power and
resented their own powerlessness, they used the slogan, "Black
Power for Black People." And since the panther is black and powerful, they called the new party the Black Panther Party. Stokely
Carmichael's work as an organizer in Lowndes County became the
basis for his successful bid for the chairmanship of SNCC a few weeks
before the Mississippi march, and by June 1966, the SNCC militants
were ready to assert their claim to national black leadership.

Carmichael, who had directed the 1964 voter registration campaign in Mississippi's 2nd Congressional District, when hundreds of

Northern whites came South to help, soon concluded that it was time to break loose from the constraints imposed by SNCC's white liberal supporters. Thus, when the march reached Greenwood, the site of his 1964 headquarters, Carmichael told the nation's press that there was a new black response to the question, "What do you want?" Black Power.

Carmichael—handsome, articulate, always conscious of the effect of his words on his listeners—was quickly identified as the principal spokesman for Black Power. In most reports, he was described as the firebrand who had sparked the new militancy, when in fact he was the mirror of a new mood among blacks. Carmichael, like nearly all important black leaders since the antebellum period, gained a following among blacks not as a prophet of the future but as an interpreter of the past. As was true of Malcolm X, Carmichael was able to surpass other black leaders because he cut through the verbiage of the white oppressors' language to utter the truths that lay dormant in the experiences of oppressed blacks. Most blacks recognized that their leaders could do little to shape the future, but they were willing to give their support to those who understood their lives. Carmichael became an oracle for the Black Power movement, because he was singularly skillful at expressing conclusions, drawn from years of organizing among Southern blacks, in terms that could be understood by urban blacks and whites who were closer than poor black sharecroppers to the mainstream of American politics. He not only expressed the desire of rural Southern blacks to gain control over local institutions but also the desire of urban blacks, like himself, to reject the white-controlled institutions in which they were enmeshed.

Despite their ties to white liberal sympathizers and to the black middle class, Carmichael and other young black proponents of Black Power were heady with a sense of confidence based on what they had accomplished during the early 1960s. They saw more clearly than the established black leadership what the times required, yet saw only vaguely the nature of their historical role. Thus, they did not understand at all the reasons for the rapid demise, later in the decade, of their insurgency.

The initial negative response of white liberals and moderate civil rights leaders helped reinforce the belief of the black militants that they were indeed the harbingers of revolution. They had become accustomed to measuring the radicalness of their goals by the vigor of their opposition, and the initial reaction to the phrase Black Power by most moderate civil rights leaders could hardly have been more vigorous or more negative. Roy Wilkins, executive director of the NAACP, warned that "quick, uncritical and highly emotional" adoption of the demand by "a beleaguered people" could lead only to "black death." Of all the condemnations that appeared in the press during the summer of 1966, perhaps the most menacing, though also honest, was an editorial in *The Saturday Evening Post*:

> We are all, let us face it, Mississippians. We all fervently wish that the Negro problem did not exist, or that, if it must exist, it could be ignored. Confronted with the howling need for decent schools, jobs, housing, and all the other minimum rights of the American system, we will do our best, in a half-hearted way, to correct old wrongs. The hand may be extended grudgingly and patronizingly, but anyone who rejects the hand rejects his own best interests. For minimum rights are the only rights that we are willing to guarantee, and above those minimum rights there is and will continue to be a vast area of discrimination and inequity and unfairness, the area in which we claim the most basic right of all—the right to be stupid and prejudiced, the right to make mistakes, the right to be less and worse than we pretend, the right to be ourselves. When this majority right is threatened, the majority will react accordingly—with results that could be disastrous to all of us.

As they endured such verbal attacks, the Black Power advocates became even more convinced that the unfulfilled aspirations of blacks could be achieved by courageous leaders willing to sacrifice for the sake of racial ideals. Their confidence was buoyed by the fact that the masses of blacks reacted positively to the new militant thrust. Only as the opposition began to shift its ground did the movement lose momentum. Moderate black and white leaders soon recognized that, on the one hand, they could not stem the tide of black discontent and that, on the other, there was nothing inherently radical about a phrase that simply made explicit the importance of group identity in American political life.

As early as the summer of 1966, the Commission on Religion and Race of the National Council of Churches sponsored an advertisement in *The New York Times*, signed by forty-eight black clergymen, which defended the demand for racial power and advised the press to listen to black voices other than those of the radicals. In the summer of 1967, the Congress of Racial Equality (CORE) joined the Black Power bandwagon. That same year representatives of the black middle class assumed leading roles at the Newark Black Power Conference. Carmichael had once been certain that Black Power would not be used by white political leaders in the way President Johnson had appropriated the cry, "Freedom Now," to rally black support, but in the spring of 1968, while hundreds of young blacks were "picking up the gun" for the Oakland-based Black Panther Party, Richard Nixon was already offering his own interpretation of Black Power as the ability of blacks to "affect their own communities." Nixon and others realized that, although black militant rhetoric attacked liberal political orthodoxy, it did not actually offer radical alternatives to conventional liberalism. Moreover, it provided an excuse for cutting back federal social programs.

Of course, the federal government's vicious domestic counterinsurgency programs partially account for the decline of black militancy during the late 1960s and early 1970s. However, it would be too much to say that repression, and particularly the FBI's Cointelpro program, was responsible for the demise of racial militancy. It is debatable whether the iron fist was more effective in the velvet glove. Despite the fact that J. Edgar Hoover professed to believe that black leftist radicalism and black nationalism posed serious threats to the American political system, few black activists of the late 1960s offered ideas that departed significantly from the dominant ideological assumptions underlying American politics. Looking back today, it is astonishing that objectives like full employment, decent housing and education, an end to police brutality, and trial by a jury of peers could inspire such vehement opposition. The only radical goals put forward by the Oakland-based Black Panther Party—freedom for imprisoned blacks and a U.N.-supervised plebiscite to determine "the will of black people as to their national destiny"—were not rooted in revolutionary ideology and had little effect on the appeal of the party among blacks.

There were, of course, many contenders for the position of black "Messiah"—one who, in the words of an August 1967 memorandum sent from Washington to the FBI branch office, "could unify and electrify the militant black nationalist movement." But the fact that Hoover branded most black political leaders, from Martin Luther King to Bobby Seale, as threats to the American way of life does not in itself demonstrate their revolutionary importance.

The celebrated black militants of the past decade gained almost overnight a fame they did not deserve, and gradually they fell into an obscurity they could not have expected. There is little to suggest that they learned enough from their experiences to build a movement capable of achieving fundamental changes in American society; at present, few militant black leaders possess even the illusion of revolutionary potential. Ricks and Carmichael were among those blacks who came to identify with Africa during the late 1960s, but their political views are now separated both from the Marxist programs of most African revolutionary movements and from the pragmatism and opportunism that dominate contemporary Afro-American politics. They have been unable to transform the black discontent expressed by the Black Power slogan into mass support for their present goal of building a power base in a unified Africa.

Other militant spokesmen have similarly found themselves exiled, imprisoned, or simply ignored. Bobby Seale of the Black Panther Party has long since left that moribund organization. Huey Newton, the other co-founder of the party, is now in Cuban exile. Eldridge Cleaver, whose obscenities once helped shape the image of the party, has become a repentant fugitive who expresses support for the American political system and wishes to be allowed to make his singular contribution to men's fashion design. Imamu Amiri Baraka (formerly LeRoi Jones), the poetic ideologue of black separatism, has more recently concluded that Marx was right as well as white and found that his audience has decreased as dialectics replaced theatrical diatribes. James Foreman, whose "Black Manifesto," as delivered to white religious organizations, revealed a prevalent confusion of militant tactics and rhetoric with revolutionary strategy, seems now a burned-out firebrand.

Formerly controversial ideas have become accepted, but the ideas no longer rouse blacks to collective action. Leaders were once discovered; now they are memorialized. A movement that probed to the bone of American political realities has become mired, as insights are transformed into cant and militancy into posturing.

The significant changes that did occur during the past decade merely illustrate the paradoxes of the period. The limited nature of those gains has made many blacks more skeptical about the possibility of fundamentally improving their positions in U.S. life through collective action. Racial pride has risen, but it has neither created an effective national black political movement nor measurably increased racial unity. The attempt by blacks to prove themselves "blacker than thou" has proved quite as divisive as earlier efforts to gain acceptance from whites. Blacks who rejected the term Negro did not abandon the term "niggah."

An increase in the number of black politicians holding public office has been accompanied by a decrease in the proportion of blacks who bother to vote and by an increase in factionalism as blacks compete for leadership. Indeed, black political power has grown largely as a result of the inability of blacks to escape from deteriorating conditions in segregated communities. Mass activism among poor and working-class blacks provided the push for the gains of the 1960s, but the poorest segment of the black population has profited least from those gains. Black leaders who claim to speak for "the people" have diverted the black struggle from the effort to wrest economic concessions directly from the white establishment to the problematic strategy of interposing between the black masses and the white elite a buffer of black businessmen and bureaucrats who equate their own success with that of the race. Although the overall failure of blacks to advance economically in recent years can be attributed to the economic downturn affecting the larger society, it is significant that the black middle class has expanded during this period—from 1965 to 1974—the percentage of blacks making more than $15,000 a year increased by more than 100 percent (to 19 percent of the total black population). Growth of black college enrollment, white-collar employment and entrepreneurship has gone hand in hand with continued high unemployment. The rising black bourgeoisie urges self-reliance on the black poor and working classes, while it as a class has gradually abandoned the relative independence of self-employment for jobs as hired hands of government and big business. Black students have learned to market their blackness as well as to find it. If affirmative-action programs suddenly were to alter their criteria in order to provide greater opportunities for those who are poor rather than simply for those who are black, the loudest cries of protest would doubtless come from middle-class blacks, many of whom claim that class analysis does not apply to them.

The demand for Black Power was basically a response to the recognition that blacks were effectively powerless, but the demand was often tied to the naive notion that power could be achieved by unifying a black populace whose common concerns and objective bases for unity were being rapidly eroded by the advances in the struggle for civil rights. To go on repeating some variant of the assertion that, no matter how rich or educated, a black man is still a "nigger," is to obscure the fact that the battle against racism has widened rather than narrowed the class divisions among blacks. Those who ignore this trend not only condemn Afro-American politics to a future of stagnation but also contribute to the erosion of the racial trust and empathy that made past gains possible.

Despite the remarkable upsurge in political mobilization and militancy that occurred among blacks during the 1960s, real power has remained outside their communities. Civil rights laws were achieved because protests took place when the national political climate was sympathetic to their goals. This climate enabled the champions of civil rights to prod powerful forces into action and, to some extent, restrained the Southern repression that could have destroyed the movement in the South. The most perceptive of the black leaders of the 1960s were able to view their own activism in its proper perspective: as a catalyst in the process of social change, but not as a determinant.

A source of the 1960s militancy was Afro-American awareness of the rise of independent Third World leaders who seemed to have broken free of the constraints imposed by the Western political and economic order. There is irony, however, in the fact that, while young black radicals in this country were making their initial contacts with Third World leaders, they were losing the leverage that had been provided by the attempt of the United States to win support in the non-white world. During the early 1960s the State Department was directly involved in attempts to end domestic segregation policies that generated negative publicity abroad and to prevent embarrassing incidents involving African diplomats on visits here. By the mid-1960s, however, as the war in Vietnam escalated, it became evident that the future of Africa and Asia would not be decided primarily through propaganda battles but through the use of military and economic power, and American leaders became less concerned about the effect of domestic racial conflicts on the hearts and minds of Africans and Asians. Thus, the indirect relationship between the domestic and foreign policies of the United States during the early 1940s had greater impact on the fortunes of Afro-Americans than did the haphazard efforts of black radicals later in the 1960s to establish direct ties with distant revolutionary movements.

The belief that Afro-Americans were a colonized group analogous to subject peoples elsewhere in the world was widely accepted by the black radical intelligentsia of the late 1960s, but the colonial analogy obscured as much as it clarified. While many blacks identified with the African demand for nationhood, some Third World revolutionary writers were noting that the direction of change in the newly independent African and Asian nations was toward military domination, economic exploitation by native elites, and the continued disruption of internal affairs by the covert and overt agents of Western capitalism. Robert Allen, author of *Black Awakening in Capitalist America*, was among the few blacks in this country who understood by the late

1960s that the crucial lesson to be learned from the recent experiences of Third World nations was that colonization was no longer the principal issue. Allen argued that black nationalism in the United States was being manipulated and co-opted by the white establishment in order to achieve the kind of neo-colonial domination it had already gained in many Third World nations. However, he was no more able than most African and Asian leaders to offer a viable program to end economic exploitation, and the absence of such a program led to cynicism and disillusionment.

Within the United States, blacks gained their equivalent of political independence—that is, nominal control of a few areas where blacks were in the majority—but, as had been the case for African nations, it was a hollow prize. Large corporations were able to retain the benefits of a black market and labor force, while avoiding the problems that arose from the fact that many blacks were not needed by the economic system. Whites were somewhat upset by the growth of black electoral power, but they were also relieved of a burden of guilt and responsibility. As "blackness" became a much desired commodity (there were many rewards for those who could mimic the distinctive forms of black lower-class behavior) there were some expressions of dismay among whites. But the communications media quickly appropriated the exotic behavior of the black masses as another faddish diversion to attract mass audiences to their clients. As in Africa during the early 1960s, apparent agreement regarding the desirability of black control masked internal divisions that were deep and exploitable.

The failure of the Black Power movement to make significant improvements in the material conditions of most blacks has recently caused some black nationalists to undertake a re-examination of their own earlier positions. Ron Karenga, a major theorist of Afro-American cultural nationalism, is one who has had second thoughts. He now distinguishes between separatism and "national liberation" as strategic models for struggle. Separatists, he concludes, were "unable to make a concrete analysis of the subjective and objective conditions that mold our people's minds, limit and encourage their imagination and aspirations, and determine and direct their behavior." As a result, they became muddled in mysticism. Advocates of national liberation, he says in contrast, recognize objective conditions and call for "revolutionary engagement of blacks in constant confrontation and negation of the oppressive conditions which every day in a merciless multitude of ways cripple and kill them."

Such words reflect commendable self-criticism but they are also vague and imprecise. In any case, Karenga and other erstwhile black separatists, who have discovered that the search for black unity is a futile pursuit that reduces the chances for effective unity among some blacks, are themselves far from centers of power, even within the black political community. At present, after an exceptional period of militancy, black leadership is most effectively exercised by those who have traditionally exercised it: black professionals, businessmen, clergymen and elected officials. The Congressional Black Caucus has emerged as the most significant national black political institution, but it has offered neither consistent nor farsighted leadership. The black legislators recognize, perhaps more clearly than most of their constituents, that the period when the issue of racial status took precedence over all others is coming to an end and that the crucial concerns of the future will be economic. Yet they have developed no plans that avoid the drawbacks of previous liberal social welfare programs. Such programs have succeeded only in supplying temporary jobs outside the manufacturing sector and some more permanent jobs for those who study, evaluate, advise and speak for the poor and needy.

For better or worse, the future of Afro-American society will involve a gradual and inexorable movement from the periphery closer to the center of the world economic system. It is this movement that made possible the emergence of viable black social movements during the 1960s, and the same trend will define the character and potential of future black movements. Doubtless, some blacks will remain outside the mainstream of change, but they will also be at the margins of the main currents of Afro-American life. The common experiences that once permeated black racial consciousness are rapidly being displaced as blacks assume new and varied roles in the modern industrial world. Racial unity has become increasingly difficult to achieve as Afro-American society becomes less distinguishable from the pervading mass culture surrounding it. New opportunities exist, however, to develop collective movements among blacks who recognize that important aspirations have remained submerged in order to maintain the illusion that all blacks share the same interests. The persistence of the outworn rhetoric of the past has obscured the continued widening of class divisions among blacks. The present course of Afro-American politics must be reassessed, not only to confront future realities but also to allow all segments of the black populace a share in the valuable legacy from earlier struggles: an awareness of the potential power of people who come to realize their common destiny.

*December 25, 1976*

## Was Fred Hampton Executed?

*Jeff Gottlieb and Jeff Cohen*

In the predawn hours of December 4, 1969, Chicago police, under the direction of the Cook County State's Attorney's Office, raided the ramshackle headquarters of the local chapter of the Black Panther Party. When the smoke cleared, Chairman Fred Hampton and party member Mark Clark were dead; four others lay seriously wounded.

Today in Chicago, seven years after the raid, the facts are slowly emerging, as a civil trial crawls through its tenth month. The families of Hampton and Clark, along with the seven who survived the foray, have filed a $47.7 million damage suit. Edward Hanrahan, three former and present FBI agents, an ex-FBI informant, and twenty-six other police personnel stand accused of having conspired to violate the civil rights of the Panthers, and then of covering it up. In essence, the plaintiffs and their lawyers are out to prove that the FBI/police conspired to execute Fred Hampton.

At 17, Hampton was a black youth on the road to "making it" in white America. He was graduated from high school in Maywood, Ill. with academic honors, three varsity letters, and a Junior Achievement Award. Four years later he was dead.

As youth director of the Maywood NAACP, he had built an unusually strong 500-member youth group in a community of 27,000. After his nonviolent, integrationist activities aroused the hostility of Maywood authorities, Hampton moved to Chicago where he organized a local chapter of the Black Panther Party.

As Panther chief in Chicago, Hampton built a reputation as a uniter, bringing together the "Rainbow Coalition" of Puerto Rican, white and black poor people, and engineering a tenuous peace among several warring ghetto gangs. His death was a blow to this multiracial united front.

Within hours of the raid, the authorities offered their explanation of what had occurred. Chicago Police Sgt. Daniel Groth, who led the fourteen police raiders, said:

> There must have been six or seven of them firing. The firing must have gone on ten or twelve minutes. If 200 shots were exchanged, that was nothing. . . . It's a miracle that not one policeman was killed.

At a press conference that day, State's Attorney Edward Hanrahan issued a statement, saying in part:

> The immediate, violent and criminal faction of the occupants in shooting at announced police officers emphasizes the extreme viciousness of the Black Panther Party. So does their refusal to cease firing at police officers when urged to do so several times.

On December 11, the *Chicago Tribune* ran an account drawn from the policemen involved in the assault, and accompanied by a photograph of the apartment on which circles were drawn around what purported to be holes caused by bullets fired at the police.

Hanrahan later had a full-scale model of the apartment constructed so that the participating policemen could re-enact the raid on WBBM-TV, the local CBS affiliate. Each officer acted out his part step by step for the TV cameras as if rehearsing a scene for a SWAT episode in slow motion. One cop said that as soon as he announced he was a police officer, occupants of the apartment responded with shotgun fire. Two raiders demonstrated how as they approached the front room, they were greeted by a woman who fired a shotgun blast at them as they stood in the doorway. Another cop explained how he had fired through a door and then received return fire, presumably from Mark Clark.

Despite the elaborate re-enactment for TV and the explanations given by the fourteen policemen, it soon became apparent that the official version was at variance with the facts. The "bullet holes" in the *Tribune* photograph turned out to be nail heads. Although officers Groth and Davis both alleged that Brenda Harris fired a shotgun blast at the doorway as they approached, there was absolutely no evidence of such a blast.

Ultimately, a federal grand jury determined that the police had fired between eighty-three and ninety shots—the Panthers a *maximum* of one. The grand jury indicated that, if the Panthers fired at all, it was one shot that Mark Clark fired—apparently *after* he had been shot in the heart. If the cops had, in fact, demanded a cease-fire on three occasions, they were talking only to themselves. The official explanation amounted to a cover-up, and a massive one.

In attempting to resolve this issue, the raid on Chicago Panther headquarters must be put into context. That the FBI supervised a nationwide effort to destroy the Black Panther Party is no longer seen as the paranoid rantings of leftists, but as a fact documented by the *Staff Report* of the Church committee. The report stated that the FBI's COINTELPRO (Counter-Intelligence program) used "dangerous, degrading or blatantly unconstitutional technique" to disrupt Left and black organizations. It went on to liken the FBI's harassment of Martin Luther King to the treatment usually afforded a Soviet agent.

On March 4, 1968 (exactly one month before King was assassinated), Hoover issued this directive:

• • •

Prevent the *Coalition* of militant black nationalist groups. In unity there is strength, a truism that is no less valid for all its triteness. An effective coalition . . . might be the first step toward a real "Mau Mau" in America, the beginning of a true black revolution.

Prevent the *rise of a "messiah"* who could unify, and electrify, the militant black nationalist movement. Malcolm X might have been such a "messiah"; he is the martyr of the movement today . . . Elijah Muhammad is less of a threat because of his age. King could be a very real contender for this position should he abandon his supposed "obedience" to "white liberal doctrines" (nonviolence) and embrace black nationalism. Stokely Carmichael has the necessary charisma to be a real threat in this way.

This memo was drafted three weeks after the Panthers had accomplished a short-lived alliance with Stokely Carmichael and SNCC. (Until the Hampton suit released this document in full, the names had been deleted.)

After King's death, Hoover called the Panthers "the single most dangerous threat to the internal security of the United States." Of the 295 actions taken to disrupt black groups, 233 were aimed at the Panthers. The bureau's main tactic was to provoke warfare between the Panthers and other black organizations. These actions, according to the *Staff Report*, "involved risk of serious bodily injury or death to the targets."

Over the years of COINTELPRO, the FBI paid out more than $7.4 million in wages to informants and provocateurs, more than twice the amount allocated to organized crime informants. Operating out of forty-one field offices, COINTELPRO agents supervised agents-provocateurs, placed "snitch jackets" on bona-fide Panthers by having them mislabeled as informants, and drafted poison-pen letters and cartoons in attempts to incite violence against the Panthers, and divide the party leadership.

All the weapons in COINTELPRO's arsenal were used against the rising "black messiah," Chairman Hampton of the Illinois Black Panther Party. Documents released by the suit have exposed the local "get-Hampton" campaign. Roy Mitchell, a defendant in the case and an ace handler of FBI informants, testified that he had between seven to nine informants in the Chicago Panthers at the time of the raid. Adding that number to those working for the state and the Gang Intelligence Unit of the Chicago Police, one comes up with approximately thirty informants reporting on about sixty-five active members. The names of these informants have been deleted from the documents. This estimate does not include any informants working for the CIA or military intelligence, a subject which the plaintiffs have not been allowed to probe.

One informant whose name we do know, William O'Neal, figures very prominently in the case. He was planted in the chapter almost from its inception and soon became head of security. Among his many schemes as security chief was the construction of an electric chair to be used on informers. It was disassembled on Hampton's orders. After the raid, O'Neal suggested to remaining party members that the steps leading to the apartment on W. Monroe be electrified so that any future raiders would be fried.

Not simply an informant, O'Neal tried to provoke others into "kamikaze"-type activities. Former Panther member Louis Truelock has submitted an affidavit stating that during a visit to O'Neal's father's home, the informer showed him putty, blasting caps and "plastic bottles of liquid," enough material to produce several bombs. He proposed that they blow up an armory and later suggested robbing a McDonald's restaurant. Truelock and others who heard O'Neal's provocative proposals rejected them as useless to the cause.

Although he was infatuated with weapons and tried to involve other Panthers in criminal activities, O'Neal was tolerated because he was an exceptionally hard worker around the office. Ronald "Doc" Satchel, a Panther leader who was wounded in the raid, recalls, "The only person who didn't want O'Neal in the Panthers was Fred Hampton."

O'Neal was also instructed to carry out the FBI's "divide-and-conquer" plan. The bureau most feared a pact between the Panthers and the Blackstone Rangers, Chicago's most powerful black gang. Defendant Marlin Johnson, former Chicago FBI chief, now head of the Chicago Police Board, and a defendant in the present trials, testified before the Church committee that he approved the sending of an anonymous letter to Ranger leader Jeff Fort which read, "The brothers that run the Panthers blame you for blocking their thing and there's supposed to be a hit out for you. . . . I know what to do if I was you." When pressed for an explanation, Johnson claimed that he thought a hit "is something nonviolent in nature," and maintained that the letter-writing scheme was aimed at preventing violence. He added, "We didn't think he [Fort] would pay too much attention to the letter."

William O'Neal's crowning achievement was his advance work on the December 4th raid. Two weeks before the attack, he provided the FBI with a detailed floor plan of Panther headquarters, complete with an "X" over Fred Hampton's bed. Most of the shots were fired at that spot.

Following the lethal raid, O'Neal was rewarded with a $300 bonus after Agent Robert Piper, also a defendant in the suit, explained in a memo to Washington, "Our source [O'Neal] was the man who made the raid possible." In another memo, listing the amounts and dates that O'Neal was paid, the bureau acknowledged his information on national Panther leaders, anti-war activists from the New Mobilization Committee and the Chicago 8, and the furnishing of the floor plan: "It is noted that most information provided by this source is not available from any other source." O'Neal was so valuable that Roy Mitchell once dished out $1,600 to buy him a car and $1,000 to bail him out of jail.

When FBI agents began to shop around for a police agency to raid Panther headquarters, they approached the Chicago Police Department twice, in October and November 1969, but were turned down both times. The FBI then approached Cook County State's Attorney Edward Hanrahan, who agreed to carry out the operation. Hanrahan, in a TV interview, said that he agreed to the raid after the FBI told him that the Panthers were stockpiling illegal weapons at their headquarters. However, on November 19, O'Neal had reported to the FBI that the guns had been legally obtained. This was corroborated by Maria Fisher, an infiltrator who worked for both the FBI and the state.

The raid was originally scheduled for December 3 at 8 p.m., but the State's Attorney's office, without notifying the FBI, postponed it by several hours, on the stated ground that it would be too dangerous to move in while the occupants were awake. But the floor plan submitted by O'Neal specifically marked Hampton's bed, and some people wonder what the real reason was for the delay.

It was not the first time Black Panther headquarters had been raided. In June 1969, a force led by FBI Agent Marlin Johnson, but also involving other police agencies, met no resistance when the raiders informed those inside of their intent to search the office, allegedly for a fugitive. O'Neal admitted in a deposition that he had set up that raid. No fugitive was found, but several Panthers were arrested on a variety of charges, all of which were later dropped. The point is that, once the authorities announced themselves, the Panthers made no attempt to resist.

At 4:30 on the morning of December 4, police raiders burst into the apartment with their guns ablaze. Harold Bell, one of the wounded survivors, testified that everyone immediately surrendered. Bell and two others, including Hampton's girl friend, Deborah Johnson, were ordered out of Hampton's bedroom, where he lay motionless. Then, says Bell, police fired from point-blank range into Hampton's body. Bell's testimony about Hampton's execution-style death has been supported by Deborah Johnson and other survivors. Johnson testified that, after emptying his gun into Hampton's bed, the cop walked away muttering, "He's good and dead now."

Why didn't Hampton get out of bed and try to resist? Photographs of his blood-soaked mattress make it obvious that he did not. According to the independent Commission of Inquiry, headed by NAACP chief Roy Wilkins and former Atty. Gen. Ramsey Clark, there are strong indications that he had been drugged. About three hours before the shooting, at 1:30 a.m. Hampton was in bed talking to his mother on the telephone, when he fell asleep in mid-conversation. Deborah Johnson tried to rouse him but failed. During the raid others tried to wake him, but his only movement was to raise his head briefly. And, of course, the sound of gunfire is not usually conducive to sleep.

The day after the raid, the Cook County coroner performed the first of four official autopsy examinations. It "failed to show the presence of barbiturates." Later postmortems by the coroner's office, the FBI and a federal grand jury also failed to turn up any trace of barbiturates. However, an independent autopsy and blood analysis which were performed at the request of the Hampton family by Dr. Victor Levine, former chief pathologist for the Cook County coroner's office, and Dr. Eleanor Berman, a toxicologist and acting director of the Department of Biochemistry at Cook County Hospital, found a potentially lethal quantity of drugs in Fred Hampton's bloodstream—a dosage which, at the least, would have induced a coma.

The Commission of Inquiry attempted to resolve these differences. It consulted experts who concluded that technical errors had been made during the official autopsies. The scientists found no reason to reject the Berman-Levine verdict.

With up to nine informants inside the Panthers, including the resourceful William O'Neal, the FBI had ample opportunity to have the chairman drugged. Informant Maria Fisher has asserted in a signed statement to the *Chicago Daily News* that one week before the killings, local FBI chief Marlin Johnson asked her to slip Hampton a colorless and tasteless drug which would put him to sleep so that the FBI could raid the apartment. She says that when she refused, Johnson told her she was "being very foolish."

O'Neal has admitted in a deposition that he was in Hampton's apartment on December 3, but his memory is hazy as to the precise time. A criminal associate of his testified under oath, in another case, that, one time when he and O'Neal were high on marijuana, O'Neal said that the raid on the Panthers was unnecessary because he had drugged Hampton the night of the assault.

Robert Piper, a defendant and the FBI agent in charge of the "Racial Matters" squad in Chicago throughout 1968-9, admitted on the stand that the Black Panthers had broken no laws and had never been prosecuted locally. He testified that the FBI's sole purpose was to harass the group and contribute to its breakup.

Within months of the raid, a federal grand jury roundly criticized the police, but offered no indictments. Panther attorney G. Flint Taylor provided an explanation when he stated in court: "I have a document from the government showing that there was a deal that there would be no indictments [of Hanrahan and the police] in return for Hanrahan's dropping of indictments [against the survivors of the raid].

Because of rising anger in Chicago's black community at the failure to indict any law-enforcement officials, Joseph Power, Chief Judge of the Cook County Criminal Court, established a special county grand jury on June 27, 1970. Barnabas Sears, a prominent Chicago lawyer, was appointed special prosecutor and promised a free hand in investigating the affair.

Rumors began making the rounds in late April 1971 that indictments against Hanrahan and other police officials were imminent. But when the grand jury handed Power an envelope containing the indictments, the judge sought to prevent their return by refusing to open the envelope. The matter was resolved on August 24 by a unanimous opinion from the seven-man Illinois State Supreme Court that "the interests of justice would best be served by opening the indictment and proceeding pursuant to the law." The indictments against Hanrahan and thirteen others for conspiracy to obstruct justice in the investigation that followed the raid were finally made public. Still, no one was held accountable for the deaths of Hampton and Clark.

The obstruction of justice case went to trial on July 10, 1972, with Cook County Criminal Court Judge Philip Romiti presiding without a jury. At the close of the prosecution's case, defense attorneys for Hanrahan and the police moved for an acquittal on the ground that not enough evidence had been presented to convict. The judge granted the motion.

Against this backdrop, the civil suit began on January 5, 1976. Now the familiar courtroom roles have been reversed—never before have the Black Panthers been the plaintiffs, with law-enforcement officials the defendants. Judge Joseph Sam Perry is on the bench. In November 1975, lawyers for the plaintiffs asked for his removal on the ground that at the age of 79, Perry is too old and too deaf to function competently. He has given credence to these objections by several times falling asleep in court. Attorneys for the victims also contend that he is unable to understand the complexities of the case.

One of Perry's first rulings was to eliminate many defendants from the suit, including Mayor Daley; former Police Chief James Conlisk, Cook County; the estate of J. Edgar Hoover, and several officials of the FBI or Justice Department. The judge also dismissed complaints against Hanrahan and his assistants, but was overruled on appeal.

Although the Northern District of Illinois has a 31 per cent black population, only 6 per cent of the 400 prospective jurors were black. Panther attorneys watched helplessly as one of their best prospects disqualified herself with an honest answer. When asked if she could judge the word of an FBI agent without prejudice, the prospective juror replied, "Judge, to tell you the truth, with all I've been reading recently about them, I think I would find it difficult." Ultimately, one elderly black woman ended up on the six-person jury.

At the start, Perry told prospective jurors that both sides have agreed "there was a gun battle." If that had been true, there would be no civil suit. The basis of the plaintiffs' case is that only one bullet, and perhaps none at all, was fired at police, and that conclusion is endorsed by the federal grand jury and the Commission of Inquiry's report, *Search and Destroy*. Calling this a gun battle is like calling the assassination of Martin Luther King a duel.

Lawyers for both sides feel that Perry committed a reversible error by delaying the enforcement of Panther subpoenas for FBI ties until two days before the trial opened. Up to then Perry had declared FBI files inadmissible unless they mentioned the name of Hampton or Clark, his explanation being that "the Black Panther Party is not on trial here." The judge has since conceded that his mistake on the Panther subpoenas, and a second blunder, have been responsible for greatly prolonging the proceedings. Perry's second error was to give the defense a free hand in deleting "irrelevant" information from the files.

In January, Richard Held, then head of the FBI's Chicago field office and now an associate director of the bureau, was served with a subpoena, signed by Perry, calling for all FBI documents relevant to the case. Held appointed FBI Agent Robert Piper, *a defendant in the case,* and some fifteen agents working under him, to make deletions from these files. Justice Department lawyers repeatedly assured the court that the order to deliver all relevant material had been complied with. However, in mid-March, during testimony from defendant Roy Mitchell, it come out that 90 per cent of the file had been withheld. This included 130 volumes of information, a stack of papers 30 feet high. Mitchell let that cat out of the bag when he referred to a document that Panther attorneys had never seen.

Immediately, lawyers for the plaintiffs called for contempt citations against seven Justice Department and FBI officials, including defense attorneys Kanter and Kwoka, and FBI agents Piper and Held. Complaints by Roy Wilkins and an open letter from two Illinois state legislators prompted Attorney General Levi to appoint Assistant U.S. Attorney Charles Kocoras to head an inquiry into the matter of the hidden documents. This choice was criticized because Kocoras had prosecuted a case in which FBI informant O'Neal and Agent Mitchell were the main government witnesses. Lawyer Taylor called the selection of Kocoras "like naming John Mitchell to investigate Watergate."

Kocoras was soon replaced by another Assistant U.S. Attorney, Stephen Kadison. An aide to Kadison told the authors that, although plaintiffs' lawyers and FBI agents have been among those interviewed, the probe is an *internal* Justice Department matter, and that the findings may not be revealed publicly. After seven months, no conclusions have been announced.

The dispute over the documents placed the Hampton case on the front pages of the local papers for one of the few times during the trial. Because of this, Perry agreed to a plea from defense attorney Camilio Volini that the jury be polled to determine if any member was aware of the controversy. During the polling, one juror pulled a clipping of a *Chicago Daily News* story from her purse. The judge immediately stopped the canvassing process because it could, in his words, "lay the grounds for a mistrial."

At the next court session Volini reiterated his motion to poll. In a surprise move, the Panther lawyers joined in the request, probably the only time both sides have agreed on anything. As all ten lawyers converged on the bench arguing in favor of the motion, the overwhelmed judge shouted, "Just leave me alone!" Perry regained his composure in time to deny the motion, saying, "I have confidence that this jury is not going to be influenced by a few headlines. The court disagrees with all parties, and I happen to be the final word."

Perry then announced to the jury that it was his fault, not the defendants', that the case was being delayed because of the withheld documents. Defense attorneys were stunned when the judge took the blame for what appeared to be suppression of vital information by the defendants.

In mid-April Panther lawyers renewed their call for a mistrial, this time asking for a default judgment because of "wholesale deceit, bad faith, and manipulation of evidence by the FBI defendants and the U.S. Attorney's Office." Perry stated that he would delay a ruling on the motion until the end of the trial.

The 130 volumes of FBI documents were finally turned over to the plaintiffs, but not before the bureau tried to charge them $17,353 for labor and materials in making the copies. According to Taylor, Judge Perry said he wanted to assess those charges to the panthers but could find no law to back him up.

The plaintiffs are faced with the problem of how to digest and utilize the mass of new material. The judge would not postpone the trial. Once, when attorney Haas asked permission to delay an interrogation until he could study the relevant FBI documents, a flushed Perry rose from the beach and yelled, "You're stalling, you're stalling, you're stalling." When fellow counsel Taylor answered, "No, we are not," Perry ordered him to sit down or be found in contempt. When Dennis Cunningham, a third Panther lawyer, attempted to say something, Perry screamed at him, "Sit down or you'll be held in contempt of court!" Needless to say, permission for a postponement was not granted.

As the trial inches along, the taxpayers continue to foot the bill for those who planned and carried out the raid. Cook County and the city of Chicago are paying for the defense of Hanrahan, his assistants, the fourteen raiders, and other police personnel to the tune of $20,000 per week. The federal government is covering the defense of the three agents and O'Neal. The cost is already well beyond $1 million and the trial isn't expected to end until March 1977 at the earliest.

While the defense is well funded, financial woes have beset the plaintiffs. The Panther legal staff cannot afford to buy daily transcripts, an indispensable resource, but one that would cost $50,000 for the trial. The lawyers' request to make copies from the judge's or defense's transcripts was denied, but Perry agreed that they could inspect his when necessary.

Fred Hampton had been fond of proclaiming, "You can kill a revolutionary, but you cannot kill a revolution. You can jail a liberation fighter, but you cannot jail liberation." Between 1968 and 1971, more than a score of Panthers were killed by police agencies, and more than 1,000 were jailed. That the party has survived at all is a minor miracle. While the death of Fred Hampton dealt a crippling blow to the Illinois chapter, the charter chapter in Oakland has never been stronger. The party currently runs fifteen *free* "survival programs" in its Oakland stronghold, including free clothing, legal aid, ambulance, pest control, plumbing and maintenance, a breakfast for children program, a food co-op, medical clinics and the Oakland Community School.

Although many talk about the FBI's destruction of the Black Panther Party as if it were a *fait accompli*, perhaps it is too early to discard the favorite slogan of exiled Panther leader, Huey Newton: "The spirit of the people will defeat the technology of the Man."

*September 20, 1980*

## Blacks Only Need Apply

*Richard Severo*

What you are about to read is really two stories. One is the E. I. du Pont de Nemours & Company's curious expedition into genetic screening in the workplace, a relatively new science that essentially takes the position that no workplace can be totally cleaned up and made safe enough for all workers. The result, not unpredictable, is that industry has an obligation to remove from the workplace those people whose genes may make them more susceptible to chemical hazards. The other story concerns itself with *The Washington Post's* unlikely role as apologist for that part of Du Pont's genetic screening effort focused on black workers.

The genesis of the genetic-screening controversy goes back to May 16, 1972, when President Richard Nixon signed $115 million worth of legislation that promised intensified efforts to find a "cure" for sickle-cell anemia and to persuade a wary black community that the Government really was interested in its problems.

The Administration's effort was apparently successful in heightening Dr. Alston Meade's awareness of sickle-cell anemia. Meade, a senior research biologist at Du Pont, was president of the Black Du Pont Employees Association, and he sent a letter to Du Pont's public relations and employee relations departments requesting that the company consider giving tests for sickle-cell anemia routinely to all black employees.

Meade says that the letter was written without a clear understanding of the difference between sickle-cell anemia and sickle-cell trait. The actual anemia occurs mainly in black people (although white Mediterraneans get it too), but only if the individual receives a sickle-cell gene from both of his parents and is thus homozygous for the disease. People with the sickle trait are heterozygous, i.e., they inherited only one gene with the anemia trait and may exhibit absolutely no anemic symptoms at all. The 0.2 percent of American blacks who have the anemia don't need a company to tell them they have it. They know about their problem early in life, long before they reach employment age. They know about the jaundice and recurrent attacks of fever and pains in the arms, legs and abdomen. They may also have experienced paralysis, convulsions and renal damage. In contrast, the carriers of the sickle trait are no more aware that they carry such a gene than is a brown-eyed person aware that he may carry a gene for blue eyes.

Du Pont says that as a result of Meade's letter a testing program was begun, not for the actual anemia, which was what Meade requested in his letter, but for sickle trait, which is carried by 8 to 10 percent of American blacks. The test was offered to blacks only prior to employment. At first it was offered locally, then in all Du Pont plants in the United States. The company says it was and is voluntary, although company medical officials say that no black has ever declined to take it.

This is not to suggest that blacks should not know if they carry a single gene for sickle-cell anemia. But the only reason for knowing is personal. For example, if both parties to a marriage knew that they had the sickle trait, they might elect to adopt children, rather than run the risk of having a child who might be burdened with the actual anemia. It is much the same concern Jews have about Tay-Sachs disease, a genetically transmitted neurological disorder that kills most of its victims by the age of three years.

And so Du Pont began its sickle-trait test. It all went quickly enough, but after five years of testing, it was clear that the company had transformed a personal physical problem affecting blacks into a screening to determine the suitability of blacks with sickle trait to work for Du Pont. This purpose was clearly stated in a 1978 article by Du Pont's Dr. Charles Reinhardt entitled "Chemical Hypersusceptibility" as "a condition of inordinate or abnormally increased susceptibility to chemicals, infective agents, or other agents which in the normal individual are entirely innocuous."

In a section dealing with sickle-cell anemia, Reinhardt, who is the director of the company's Haskell Laboratory for Toxicology and Industrial Medicine, wrote:

Several screening tests for sickle-cell trait have now been devel-

oped and a number of mass screening programs have been conducted. In Du Pont, as a service, we routinely offer all black
employees a test for sickle-cell trait. If the test is positive, we will
ask the applicant to check with his or her personal physician or
a community health service. At our Chambers Works plant, het-
erozygotes with a hemoglobin of less than 14 grams per 100 milliliters [of blood] are restricted from work involving the
handling of nitro and amino compounds; if their hemoglobin is
greater than 14 grams per 100 milliliters, no restrictions are
made. We generally employ individuals with sickle-cell trait
who appear otherwise to fill job requirements.

So there it was in *The Journal of Occupational Medicine*. A request
that had been made out of a feeling that blacks should know if they
carried sickle-cell genes had become the focus of a scientific paper on
"hypersusceptibility" in the chemical workplace. Something that
might have been a factor in family planning had become an employment issue. Blacks at Du Pont had thus become the only ethnic or
racial group to be singled out because of alleged special risk on the
job, even though many whites with roots in the Mediterranean, as
well as East Indians and Orientals, have genetically caused anemia
problems too.

In the process of researching a series of articles on genetic
screening in the workplace for *The New York Times*, I interviewed
Reinhardt and confirmed that he still meant what he said in that
article. I also interviewed Dr. Bruce Karrh, Du Pont's medical
director, who offered a different version from Reinhardt's. He
insisted that no job-placement decisions were based on the tests
and that they were "purely for the education and edification of the
individual involved."

My findings on the Du Pont sickle-trait tests were published in
*The New York Times* on February 4. Du Pont's response was immediate. The next day Irving Shapiro, the Du Pont chairman, sent a letter
to *The Times* in which he wrote that the sickle-trait test was never used
in job placement and that my report was "offensive" to a management
that "has worked diligently to foster an end to racism in this country."

He made no mention of the Reinhardt article, but no matter: *The Times* printed his letter on February 7.

A few days later, Meade, along with John Fisher, the current president of the Black Du Pont Employees Association, also wrote a letter to the editor of *The Times* and to newspapers in Wilmington and Philadelphia that had run portions of the *Times* series. They said they were not aware of any "abuse" of Du Pont's sickle-cell testing program and that they welcomed "any information to the contrary." Like the Shapiro letter, the Fisher-Meade letter made no mention of Reinhardt's article. In subsequent conversations, Meade admitted that he had only read the edited version of my story in *The Philadelphia Bulletin*, and said there was no mention of Reinhardt's article. As it turned out, *The Bulletin*'s version did mention the Reinhardt article.

Then, on March 10, *The Washington Post* ran an editorial that was quite supportive of my series. Du Pont's public-relations department reacted quickly and sent to the newspaper a letter written by company president Edward Jefferson that said much the same thing Shapiro's letter had said. In the same envelope Du Pont enclosed a copy of the original 1972 letter by Meade along with his more recent missive written with Fisher. On March 26, *The Post* ran a second editorial apologizing to Du Pont for its first editorial. "As it turns out, our sources were wrong," the newspaper explained.

In what way were *The Post*'s sources "wrong"? The retraction ran, I learned, because Jessica Mathews, the writer of the first editorial, had become convinced that it was necessary after reading the Fisher-Meade letter and the supporting material from 1972. Mathews told me she hadn't spoken to Meade, nor to Fisher, nor to any members of the Black Du Pont Employees Association, nor to any scientist or policy maker at Du Pont. "I am not a reporter," she said, adding that she had telephoned three of her own sources, people who had nothing to do with Du Pont or the workers there. Mathews felt that even if Reinhardt wrote what I reported he wrote (and she was going to check that out right away in a medical library), he probably didn't know anything about company testing policy because, after all, he ran a research facility and research scientists tend not to know very much about medical practices in individual plants. She had no response when I informed her that Reinhardt was formerly employed at Du Pont's Chambers Works plant in Deepwater, New Jersey, where he was instrumental in starting a genetic-screening program.

And so her editorial stands, and Du Pont sends it out, along with the Fisher-Meade letter, when people inquire as to what Du Pont's genetic-screening program is all about. When Lewis Milford of the National Veterans Law Center at American University made such an inquiry, he was told by Matthew Cooney Jr., a Du Pont public-relations man, that "a major paper like *The Post* doesn't apologize lightly." As for Reinhardt's description of Du Pont's screening program in *The Journal of Occupational Medicine*, Cooney says, "This language clearly says that it is a standard hemoglobin test, not a sickle test, that is used to restrict a person with a low hemoglobin count from certain areas as a health safeguard." But Dr. Samuel Epstein, professor of occupational and environmental health at the University of Illinois School of Public Health, and Dr. Nicholas Ashford, associate professor of technology and policy at the Massachusetts Institute of Technology, to whom I showed the article, were unable to find any reference to a "standard hemoglobin test." Ashford said it showed "insensitivity to America's racial problems to produce an article that applied the level of hemoglobin only to blacks with sickle trait and to no one else."

And so the questions remain: Why are blacks alone singled out in the Reinhardt article? If the tests are only for the personal benefit of blacks, why are they mentioned in an article that purports to deal with people who are said to be abnormally susceptible to chemicals? If no blacks have ever been transferred to other jobs because of their sickle trait, how can one explain the statement of William Golt, president of the Chemical Workers Association, a company union, who told me he knew of at least one black who was transferred because of the test? Just where are the hard data that would justify stigmatizing chemical workers who carry the sickle trait as special risks? Furthermore, Karrh's contention that no job-placement decisions were made on the basis of the test, that it was "purely for the education and edification of the individual involved," seems suspect too. I have recently learned that the company does not even have a uniform national policy for explaining the sickle-trait test to its black employees. Cooney said the only time the company explained the test to black workers was in 1972, when it was started.

The genetic-screening issue has aroused the interest of legislators like New York State Assemblyman Frank Barbaro of Brooklyn, who is proposing legislation to prohibit the use of genetic testing in his state. Nationally, it certainly isn't against the law. In fact, there is a redundant, ambiguous regulation on the books of the Occupational Safety and Health Administration that some have taken as a Federal mandate to screen. The rule is contained in Part 1910, Title 29 of the Code of Federal Regulations promulgated for general industry by the agency. A section entitled "Medical Surveillance" says that workers are to take a "preassignment physical examination" which is to include "the personal history of the employee, family and occupational background, including genetic and environmental factors." I learned of this obscure rule only because a laboratory employee happened to tell me his company was considering starting a genetic-screening program, even though they didn't want to, in order to be in compliance with the law.

Dr. Eula Bingham, OSHA's assistant secretary, was unaware of the rule until I informed her of it but has made it clear she doesn't want it used as an exclusionary tool against any group of people by industry. Bingham also says she doesn't think the language of the rule creates the mandate. But how can "genetic factors" be obtained without a test? If the Government simply wanted to obtain genetic information gleaned from family history, they could have done so without making "genetic factors" a separate entity in the rules. At any rate, the rule remains on the books.

As for Du Pont, the current situation remains unclear, in view of the company's propaganda smokescreen. If the screening program continues as before, then black employees have grounds for questioning the Du Pont slogan, "There's a lot of good chemistry between us."

*September 4, 1982*

## On Cussing Out White Liberals

*Randall Kennedy*

One of the most debilitating tendencies among black activists today is the indiscriminate "cussing out" of white allies. This tendency was evident in the controversy that recently erupted at Harvard Law School when two campus groups—the Harvard Black Law Students Association and the Third World Coalition—urged students to boycott a course in antidiscrimination law. The course is to be taught this winter by Jack Greenberg, a white attorney who has been director of the NAACP Legal Defense Fund for the past twenty-two years, and Julius Chambers, a black attorney who is president of the fund.

The opposition to Greenberg's appointment stems mainly from the law school's failure to hire more minority professors. At present, there is only one black tenured professor and one black assistant professor. To the student groups, the fact that a white attorney was hired to teach anti-discrimination law—an area in which, not surprisingly, many of the finest practitioners are black—blatantly demonstrated the law school's unwillingness to create a racially diverse faculty.

The organizations, however, went beyond attacking Harvard's hiring policies. They also challenged the ability of a white professor to teach effectively a course in antidiscrimination law, and they challenged the qualifications of Jack Greenberg in particular. In its statement opposing Greenberg's appointment, the Third World Coalition declared: "It is extremely important that [the course] be taught by an instructor who can identify and empathize with the social, cultural, economic and political experiences of the Third World community." The Harvard Black Law Students Association stated that the choice of Greenberg was "especially inappropriate" given what it termed his "adamant refusal to relinquish directorship of the NAACP Legal Defense Fund to a black attorney."

These charges have a familiar ring to them. They are variations on a recurring theme—the festering conflict between black activists and white reformers over the role of whites in the struggle for civil rights.

Some minimize this conflict or even deny that it exists. That was essentially the position Greenberg took in responding to the charge that he has refused to turn over his post to a black attorney: "It never has been seriously suggested," he wrote to the students, that he step aside in favor of a black.

However, the choice of Greenberg in 1961 to succeed Thurgood Marshall as head of the fund has long been the focus of criticism. As Louis Lomax recounts in *The Negro Revolt*, Greenberg's appointment struck a sour note with many blacks. "The argument invariably comes in these words: 'The Jews would die before they would let a Negro rise to the leadership of one of their organizations; so why should we let a Jew, or any white man for that matter, head our organization?' " Within the ranks of black attorneys, it has often been argued that the appointment of a white to direct the fund is a mistake that should be rectified. This resentment toward Greenberg is largely what fuels the suit recently initiated by the N.A.A.C.P. against the Legal Defense Fund to divest it of its right to use the initials "NAACP" as part of its official title. The views of the minority organizations at Harvard Law School, then, are not aberrational; they are widespread and deep-rooted.

But does all this justify the students' wholesale rejection of Greenberg? There are, to be sure, criticisms that can rightly be leveled against certain whites who proclaim themselves friends of the black cause. Some are able to work with blacks only in a leadership role. Others are only fair-weather friends. Still others invite skepticism by making excessive references to the aid they have rendered to black struggles. But criticism should take into account sensible distinctions. And, as I have said, the trouble with much of the cussing out is that it is indiscriminate.

I have often heard blacks say that white liberal hypocrites pose as great a threat to black advancement as overt racists do. With the latter one knows, as the saying goes, exactly where they're coming from. This is nonsense. The liberal hypocrite who cannot reject all forms of racism is clearly less of a threat than the reactionary who enthusiastically embraces white supremacy. There is, in other words, an important difference between Daniel Patrick Moynihan and Jesse Helms.

The white liberal hypocrite is likely to be restrained by his rhetoric and inhibited by his conscience, after all, hypocrisy by definition implies allegiance to an ideal of behavior coupled with a failure to practice it fully. The hypocrites who figure so prominently on the enemies lists of those who despise white liberals *do* often fail to live up to the ideals they profess. But at least they are aspiring to a worthy standard.

In criticizing white liberals, it is also necessary to distinguish between liberal hypocrites and liberal heroes—those whites who have dedicated themselves to the struggle against racial oppression. From Wendell Phillips and Thaddeus Stevens to Andrew Goodman and Michael Schwerner to Thomas I. Emerson and Arthur Kinoy, there have been whites who have seized every opportunity to enlarge the scope of freedom for blacks. Jack Greenberg belongs in this category. He has devoted his entire legal career to the fight against racism and has been a central figure in many of the epic legal battles of the civil rights movement, beginning with *Brown v. Board of Education* in 1954.

It is precisely Greenberg's prominence as a civil rights champion, however, that aggravates some blacks. After all, they say, Greenberg has by no means martyred himself. Rather, he has profited from his association with the civil rights movement. Some even contend that he gained his prominence at the expense of black attorneys who never received credit for their contributions to the black rights struggle. These, too, are familiar complaints. They stem from the fact that disproportionate attention is paid to white advocates of black rights. One of the things that helped sour relations between black and white civil rights workers in the South in the 1960s was the media's penchant for highlighting the efforts of whites while relegating to the background the sacrifices of blacks. The death of a black activist in the cause of civil rights might occasion a brief mention in the establishment press. The death of a white would make headlines.

The difference in coverage can be explained, in part, by the public's understandable fascination with privileged people who take great risks on behalf of the oppressed. But it is mainly attributable to racism. In this country, white lives mean more than black ones. This ugly aspect of racism must be confronted and overcome. The best way to overcome it, however, is not by purveying a further distortion of reality—such as the notion that people like Jack Greenberg haven't helped and can't identify with our struggle.

White allies are not above criticism, but they should be criticized for their real flaws, not for specious ones such as having the "wrong" skin color. Furthermore, blacks themselves have reinforced some of the white attitudes they criticize. Blacks complain, for example, that white intellectuals exclude them from the mainstream of academic and political discourse. Yet, in all too many cases, black intellectuals and activists have ghetto-ized themselves by confining their interests to race-oriented issues and by disparaging the involvement of others with issues not directly linked to black rights. Feminism and the gay rights movement, for example, have frequently been denigrated by blacks on the grounds that these struggles—invariably described con-descendingly as "fashionable"—siphon resources away from the fight against racism.

Such hostility is ill-considered. It increases our isolation, rein-forces the belief that we are intellectually narrow and gives credence to the charge that we are nothing more than a typical interest group, selfishly grasping for all it can get and heedless of the obstacles others face.

It is also important to keep in mind that some of the attitudes of our white allies that have frequently been ridiculed are actually com-mendable responses to a racist society. Take white liberal guilt, for example, the butt of innumerable bitter jokes by blacks and whites. But what is wrong with feeling guilty about the role one's group has played in the subjugation of others, or with feeling uneasy about having benefited from wrongs done to others, or with feeling respon-sible for righting those wrongs? Of course, a commitment to social justice should not be based solely on guilt. But that does not justify the wholesale debunking of a quality of mind and spirit that inspires a sense of social responsibility within the white community.

The attempts of whites to gain acceptance among blacks are also often ridiculed. Whites are derided for seeking to learn about the cer-emonies of black culture, for seeking to establish friendships across the color line, for seeking to show that they care about black people and want to help them in their struggles. Again, what is wrong with such conduct? Even when it is awkward and self-conscious, it represents a gesture of solidarity and respect. Certainly it is preferable to the neglect and unconcealed repugnance that are thriving under the aegis of Reaganism.

It is ironic that blacks' belittlement of their white liberal allies in many ways parallels the attacks on liberals launched by the right. Reaganites also disparage white liberal guilt, scoff at white liberal hypocrisy and claim that liberals insidiously mislead blacks about what their true interests are. This is an effective strategy. It makes reformist impulses suspect. It generates the cynicism and ill-will that nurture the politics of greed. And it stultifies the idealism that is necessary for a renewed campaign against the hatred and insensitivity that blight our society. Attacked from all sides, white supporters of racial justice begin to accept as true the charges flung at them. Having been repeatedly told that there is no difference between them and their racist or indifferent white brethren, many liberals lose the nerve and perseverance needed to sustain their commitment to the fight against racism.

These attacks, of course, are not the only reason for the falling away of white liberals from the struggle for black advancement. Opportunism is also an important factor. Indeed, some liberals are undoubtedly relieved by black rejection, for it covers their retreat from a battle they are tired of waging. Still, by criticizing white liberals unfairly, blacks are playing an important role in encouraging their retreat.

There are those who will argue that the black community's greater vulnerability in these reactionary times makes criticism (especially in publications read mainly by whites) ill-advised. This kind of claim, grounded as it is on the notion that criticism weakens rather than strengthens a community, is always suspect. But it is particularly mistaken now, precisely because of the ascendance of the right. We can no longer afford to gratuitously alienate allies or potential allies. Hence, when friends of racial justice are needlessly insulted, it is the duty of progressives—especially black progressives—to speak up.

Furthermore, as the Harvard controversy shows, abuse of white liberals diverts attention from the conditions that give rise to black protest. What prompted the black students' anger was the law school's failure to name more blacks to the faculty. Yet, in an editorial condemning the students, *The New York Times* never mentioned Harvard's hiring record. According to *The Times*, "black law students at Harvard are calling for a boycott of a course in race and legal issues because one of its teachers, Jack Greenberg, is white." This is merely half of the truth. The students' protest did involve an ill-considered attack on Greenberg. But the object of the protest was the stifling homogeneity of a law school faculty of more than seventy professors, of whom only two are black.

That protest was marred by a self-defeating and narrow-minded urge to cuss out whites. But any response to the students' demands that does not consider the larger context in which they arose is similarly narrow-minded. Racial oppression spawns problems of great complexity, and attempts to address them must be discriminating. One-dimensional responses cannot hope to alleviate injustices whose ramifications, unfortunately, seem endless.

*April 9, 1988*

## Flo Don't Know

*Andrew Kopkind*

*Detroit*

In 1950, when she was 19, Bertha Gillespie left the hot, rich, farm land of Columbus, Mississippi, and rode the train a thousand miles north to Detroit to find good work and raise her family. She had high hopes. Right away she got a job as a housekeeper in the new Howard Johnson's motel, the perfect orange-and-aqua symbol for the triumph of the auto-industrial age and the mass car culture it spawned. She already had two children, and they moved into the sprawling

Brewster housing project. Her new neighbors were black migrants from all over the rural South who had come to work in the factories— and make the beds—of the corporate families that had fashioned Detroit into a great war machine and the foundation of the consumer civilization.

"Oh, things were nice then," Bertha Gillespie told me as we walked around Brewster-Douglas, as the project is now known, just behind Jesse Jackson and a platoon of Secret Service men on the afternoon of the Michigan Democratic caucuses. Gillespie, her daughter and several friends had joined hundreds of residents in an impromptu march to get out the vote and drum up enthusiasm for a campaign that was already at fever pitch in the projects.

"It was a real nice place to live in, most times," Gillespie recalled. "The buildings were so new, they wouldn't let us barbecue outside, 'cause they said we'd smoke up the bricks." The place was full of possibilities. Joe Louis, the Brown Bomber of Detroit, was a Brewster boy. "See over there, that's where Diana Ross grew up. I used to see her all the time," Gillespie said proudly. "And on the second floor of that high-rise there, that's where Mary Wilson lived. And behind, the other Supreme, the one who died, she lived there." They don't remember Flo so well.

"Things started to go down after that," Gillespie recounted. "We lacked police protection. There was a lot of drugs and guns, and the police would come and circle the block, they'd pull over somebodies and take their money and drugs and keep on going. They still do it, but they don't come around that much anymore."

Detroit went up in flames in the riots of 1967, and there are still broad fields of dirt and rubble where nothing has been rebuilt. The bricks of Brewster grew grimy and the paint peeled, but it wasn't from the smoke of barbecues. The entry to Diana Ross's apartment and hundreds of others are boarded up with plywood, and windows in Mary Wilson's high-rise are broken and the stairwells are littered and foul. They closed Bertha Gillespie's apartment block and moved her out of the project, but she still works as a housekeeper in one of the buildings, where old people live. Her seven kids are grown; the "baby," she says, is "coming out" of school this year. She's thinking of going back to Mississippi. "Things down there ain't so bad anymore," she thought. In Detroit, hopes are no longer high.

It is impossible to understand Jesse Jackson's extraordinary political achievement in Michigan without some sense of the social transformations that have produced the conditions his campaign addresses. When Jackson talks about the "dispossessed and the disenfranchised," he does not refer only to the poor or the voteless but to people who are radically removed from the nourishing institutions and the enlivening spirit of American society. In Michigan, especially, that includes whites as well as blacks, and people who are just getting by in the economy as well as those who are suffering on welfare. Hundreds of thousands of white workers have lost their jobs, and the ones who are still working live with a permanent sense of insecurity. A pall of pessimism has settled over the scene.

The precipitous decline of "the industry" has ravaged souls as well as cities. It has exacerbated racial and class differences and has called into question all the old strategies for economic development and social improvement. Detroit Mayor Coleman Young, an undoubted hero of black political power in the early 1970s, has failed utterly to redistribute resources from the declining corporate coffers in the suburban ring to his miserable base in the core. His de facto endorsement of Michael Dukakis, who represents the old strategies and the traditional poetics, was a last act of loyalty that was rejected by both the base and the ring.

Jim Settles, an official of United Automobile Workers Local 600 in Dearborn, explained that Jackson's "message" was getting through to workers of all stripes in his union, but it was not merely the promise of paychecks or food stamps. "Jackson does something no one else has done," Settles said. "He gives people hope." Richard Gephardt, who was favored for a time by the union's top brass, scored some emotional points with his Hyundai-bashing, but Jackson won by locating villainy in the system rather than in Asia. Dukakis halfheartedly appealed to white blue-collar workers on the basis of their ethnicity and certain cultural icons. He endlessly repeated sentimental stories of his parents' arrival at Ellis Island; in Detroit's Polish enclave of Hamtramck he actually told a small and dispirited audience that his wife, Kitty, "the love of my life," is supposed to "look just like Jackie Kennedy." At which point his sponsors presented him with a signboard with his name spelled out in kielbasa. Not too many of those folks came out to vote for him the next day.

Jackson has known all along that a populist campaign runs on hope and the prospect of power. His jingly chant, "I am somebody" (heard more frequently four years ago than today), turns out to be the essential statement of the populist ideology. He is more sophisticated now, but no less consistent. In Michigan he could be recognized as a great communicator of hope to the victims of transformations that he himself has lived through and triumphed over. The Brewster kids have a new model for success. What Flo don't know (in the Supremes' phrase) is that a new level of political possibility has come out of the projects, out of the shuttered factories along the Rouge, out of the dead city and the besieged suburbs. It's a powerful tide that Jackson is riding now, and it energizes constituencies in ever-widening rings.

Although anything *could* happen in this highly volatile primary season, not everything *will*. Jackson's appeal is still limited—as evidenced by his second-place showing in the Connecticut primary last week—by the class character of his campaign, his race base and by the historical conditions he engages. Michigan displays virtually every difficulty of postindustrial America. Connecticut is about as good as the new entreprenunal, service society can get. If Jackson can get from the one to the other, he will make his own history.

*February 27, 1989*

## Racial Hatred on Campus

*Jon Wiener*

The Boston Red Sox had just lost the World Series to the New York Mets. At the University of Massachusetts, Amherst, hundreds of students, many of them drunk, poured out of the dorms. White Red Sox fans began shoving Mets fans who were black; soon a white mob of 3,000 was chasing and beating anyone who was black. Ten students were injured. Joseph Andrade recalls thinking, "My God, my life is being threatened here—and it's because I'm black."

The U-Mass explosion—on October 27, 1986—may be the most emblematic outbreak of student hatred of the 1980s. But it is by no means the only one. The upsurge in campus racism is the most disturbing development in university life across the nation during the past decade. More than anything, it reveals how white attitudes toward minorities have changed on campus during the Reagan years, even at institutions that historically have been bastions of liberalism.

At the University of Michigan, Ann Arbor, for example, the campus radio station broadcast a call from a student who "joked": "Why do blacks always have sex on their minds? Because all their pubic hair is on their head. . . . Who are the two most famous black women in history? Aunt Jemima and Mother Fucker." At Dartmouth College, the *Dartmouth Review* attacked a black music professor, William Cole, describing him as "a cross between a welfare queen and a bathroom attendant." Then four *Review* staff members confronted Cole after a class last February and, in front of his students, apparently attempted to provoke him into a fight. Esi Eggleston, a black student who witnessed the confrontation, told PBS's *Frontline*: "That moment let me know that there are people in this world who hate you just because of your color. Not dislike you, or choose not to be friends with you, but hate you."

At the University of Wisconsin, Madison, a fraternity held a "slave auction" as part of a pledge party last October. At U.C.L.A. white and Chicano students fought on campus last spring during a student election. At Purdue, a black academic counselor found "Death Nigger" scratched on her office door. A headline in a recent issue of *The Montclarion*, the student newspaper at Montclair State College in New Jersey, read, "Attention focused on racial tension at M.S.C."

Why is all this happening now? Shelby Steele, a black associate professor of English at San Jose State University, tends to blame the victim. In the February *Harper's*, he argues that the problem on campus is not white racism but rather black "feelings of inferiority," which give rise to "an unconscious need to exaggerate the level of racism on campus to make it a matter of the system, not just a handful of students." Instead of "demonstrating for a black 'theme house,' " Steele writes, black students "might be better off spending their time reading and studying."

Duchesne Paul Drew, a Columbia University junior who is black, offers a different explanation: "Reagan was President during the formative years of today's students." When Reagan was elected in 1980, this year's freshman class was 10 years old. Their political consciousness was formed while the White House used potent code words and attacked social programs to legitimize a subtle racism. Columbia students report that racist remarks are seldom made to blacks but frequently are heard in conversations among whites. The litany is that black people tend to be criminals, drug addicts and welfare cheats; that they don't work; and that black students aren't as smart as whites.

This, of course, is the image of blacks George Bush sought to project in his campaign to succeed Reagan. The Republicans' Willie Horton television spots suggesting that blacks are rapists and murderers played not just in living rooms but in dormitories and student centers for most of the fall semester. Undergraduate viewers may have been even more vulnerable to the Horton propaganda than was the rest of the TV audience, because most of them lacked the experience and knowledge required to challenge racist imagery—especially after eight years of Ronald Reagan.

The Reagan Administration gave its blessing to the *Dartmouth Review*, the best-known purveyor of campus racism and intolerance. The *Review* (which is not an official Dartmouth publication) boasts that several of its former staff members have gone on to prestigious jobs in Reagan's Washington: One became a speechwriter for President Reagan, another for Vice President Bush. *Review* columnist and president Keeney Jones penned a notorious racist parody, "Dis Sho Ain't No Jive Bro," that purported to quote a black student at Dartmouth: "Dese boys be sayin' that we be comin' here to Dartmut an' not takin' the classics. You know, Homa. . . ." Jones was subsequently hired as a speechwriter for Secretary of Education William Bennett. The editor who published that column, Dinesh D'Souza, went on to a career as a policy analyst in the Reagan White House.

This legitimization of racism has been accompanied by other developments. Admission to top colleges, including some public universities like the University of California, Berkeley, and U.C.L.A., has become fiercely competitive: Berkeley had 21,200 applications to its 1987 freshman class, and enrolled 3,700—14 percent. Many students with straight A averages in high school were denied admission. At the same time, some college campuses are beginning to reflect the diversity of the American population: Berkeley's incoming class in 1987 was 12 percent black, 17 percent Latino, 26 percent Asian and only 40 percent white.

This new alignment comes as a shock to many white students, especially those who grew up in all-white, middle-class suburbs. Some of them respond to campus racial diversity by proclaiming that all blacks and Latinos have been admitted under affirmative action programs and thus are taking places away from "more qualified" whites. That argument is often turned around, however, as a justification for hostility toward Asians, who are criticized for being super-competitive.

University administrators at many campuses prefer to ignore racial incidents or keep them out of the news, but antiracist student organizations have successfully focused attention on the problem. After the U-Mass incident following the World Series, campus officials at first denied that race had played any part in what the campus police termed a brawl among sports fans. That made it hard for black students to follow Shelby Steele's advice and spend their time "reading and studying." Not until students demonstrated did U-Mass Chancellor Joseph Duffey admit that his campus had a racial problem. At Penn State, eighty-nine students were arrested at a campus sit-in last April. At U-Mass a year ago, 200 students held a five-day sit-in; at Wisconsin in November 1987, 100 protesters marched outside the Phi Gamma Delta ("Fiji") fraternity house, where a racist incident had occurred, chanting, "Hey, Fijis, you can't hide, drop the sheets and come outside!" As a result of dozens of scenes like these, the student campaign against racism has provided the focus for campus politics at many colleges and universities.

Campus antiracist activists have put forward a variety of strategies. One of these identifies the problem as ignorance among white kids, many of whom grew up in isolated lily-white suburbs and need to learn about the diversity of American culture. Advocates of this approach insist that all students should take a course in ethnic studies or cultural diversity, often taught by newly hired minority faculty members. The Universities of Indiana and Minnesota each require two courses in U.S. cultural pluralism; the University of Wisconsin, Madison, has just established a one-course ethnic studies requirement and the University of California, Berkeley, is currently debating a similar measure.

Minority student organizations across the country enthusiastically support an ethnic studies requirement for graduation. Charles Holley, co-president of the Black Student Union of the Madison campus, argues that the courses teach "what minorities are all about, where we came from, what we feel." The student government officers at Berkeley, in a joint statement, declared that "students commonly graduate without reading the work of a minority author, studying under a minority professor, or having learned the vital histories of people of color. In a state that will soon have a non-white majority, such an undergraduate experience dangerously perpetuates false stereotypes."

Another strategy focuses on the empowerment of targets of violence. Much racial harassment typically goes unreported, even though it makes life miserable for minority students. When these students have their own campus centers and organizations, they don't have to suffer in isolation; they can—and increasingly do—rally their forces against their antagonists. In the aftermath of racial flare-ups minority students have frequently demanded university support for such centers. At U-Mass, participants in last winter's sit-in called on school administrators to renovate New Africa House as a cultural center for minority students.

A third strategy strives to reduce campus violence in general as a way of thwarting racial violence. Jan Sherrill, director of the Center for Study and Prevention of Campus Violence at Towson State University, in Maryland, argues that American culture condones violent means of resolving disputes as a legitimate form of male self-expression. Reagan's oft-proclaimed "values" glorified the macho response to international problems. Terrorism at a disco in Berlin? Send the Air Force to Tripoli to bomb Qaddafi. Men longed to join the President in saying, "Go ahead, make my day." A media culture of exploding cars, free-swinging cops and bone-crunching sports is reinforced by campus norms that say it's O.K. for young men to get drunk, wreck their dorm rooms and slug it out with one another. A program at Towson State's Richmond Hall has focused on reducing property damage in the dorm and violence of all kinds between students by setting strict rules and giving residents responsibility for enforcing them. As a result, there have been no racist incidents or attacks on gays or women this academic year in the dorm, which has become "a violence-free zone," according to Sherrill. It's not yet clear whether incidents elsewhere on campus will decline.

On many campuses, racism is endemic to the fraternity subculture. The house that held the slave auction at Madison last October, Zeta Beta Tau (Z.B.T.), is predominantly Jewish and had itself been a target of an attack: Members of Fiji crashed a Z.B.T. party, beat three persons and taunted them with anti-Semitic slurs. In another racist incident involving fraternities on that campus, a Kappa Sigma party in 1986 had a "Harlem Room," with white students in blackface, watermelon punch, graffiti on the walls and garbage on the floor.

Racism among fraternities is fostered by the fact that most are completely segregated, and it is exacerbated by rituals of heavy drinking on party weekends. Last November the Chancellor at Madison, Donna Shalala, established a Commission on the Future of Fraternities and Sororities, which is to recommend ways to reduce their racist and sexist behavior. The possibilities, Shalala said, range from attacking "substance abuse" as a cause of "misconduct" to elimination of the Greek system altogether.

A more problematic strategy for reducing campus racism focuses on criminalizing racist speech, which constitutes the most prevalent form of harassment. At the University of Michigan, Ann Arbor, interim president Robben Fleming implemented a new code last year that allows university administrators to place on probation, suspend or expel students engaged in "discriminatory" behavior, including racist speech. Under the code, the student who told the racist "jokes" over the radio would be put on probation; if he made "other blatantly racist remarks" while on probation he could be suspended or expelled. Most of the university Regents support the code, *The Michigan Daily* reports, as do several deans and professors. But the student representatives of the University Council have denounced the proposal as a "terrible misuse of power," and the United Coalition Against Racism, a student group that has demanded university action against racial abuse, has voiced a similar sentiment.

At Madison, Z.B.T. was cleared by the student government disciplinary committee of all charges of violating university rules against racial discrimination. Committee chair Rana Mookherjee said of the fraternity's slave auction, "There is no rule you can write to eradicate bad taste and insensitivity." Many minority students expressed outrage at the decision; one was in tears. A spokesman for the Madison campus's Minority Coalition, Peter Chen, said, "By hiding behind the issue of free speech, the administration is making this campus safe for racism."

The protection of offensive speech will always cause frustration, but it nonetheless provides an important lesson in the meaning of the First Amendment. Campus leaders need not limit themselves to defending the First Amendment just because of constitutional barriers to criminalizing offensive speech, however. On the contrary, they have an obligation to speak out, forcefully and frequently, explaining why racist speech is objectionable. Chancellor Shalala did that: Although fraternity members have a First Amendment right to objectionable speech, she said, "using slavery as a basis for humor should be offensive to every American."

Donna Shalala began her term as chancellor last February by announcing the "Madison plan." It calls for the University of Wisconsin to double the number of minority undergraduates over the next five years; create 150 financial aid packages for low-income students; raise $4 million in private money to increase the scholarship endowment and another $4 million to endow twenty-five new minority graduate and professional fellowships; hire seventy new minority faculty members over the next three years, more than doubling the current number; and require ethnic studies courses in each college. In addition, the university will hire or promote 125 minority academic staff members over the next three years. Shalala has budgeted $4.7 million to implement this program over the next three years, part of which must come from new appropriations, which the Wisconsin legislature is currently considering.

The Minority Coalition at Madison criticized the plan for failing to establish a strong racial harassment policy, an adequate multicultural center or antiracism workshops during student orientation. But the goals, the budget and the timetable make the Madison plan one of the most far-reaching attempts to overcome institutional racism undertaken by any major university. The University of Wisconsin's effort is important, among other reasons, because of the school's size: It has the fourth largest student body in the nation, numbering almost 44,000. It's especially heartening that Wisconsin is making such an extensive commitment at a time when people feel beaten down and defeated by eight years of losing battles against the Reagan White House.

Unfortunately, the promises made at Madison and at other progressive institutions to hire more black faculty run up against a major obstacle: the small pool of available black college teachers. These men and women are being intensely wooed, and Madison's recruitment successes will inevitably hurt the campaigns on other campuses. The shortage of black faculty is part of a larger problem—the declining number of blacks in higher education, from the undergraduate through the professorial ranks. Most talented black undergraduates opt for law or medicine or business over academia—and why not? The prospect of spending years as an isolated, underpaid, overworked assistant professor is not an inviting one.

The Madison plan addresses this problem in several ways: by pledging that the university will work with local high schools to improve their graduation rates; will in the future recruit twice as many minority students to its freshman class and provide them with financial support to help them stay through graduation; and will double the number of fellowships for graduate and professional schools, to encourage minority students to finish dissertations.

Defensive administrators at colleges and universities across the country argue that the recent spread of racism on campus shows only that the university is a part of American society, which itself seems to be increasingly racist and violent. That's true, but it shouldn't provide an excuse for educators who prefer to wait for the larger society to change. More universities need to make the kind of commitment demonstrated by Chancellor Shalala at the University of Wisconsin if they are going to overcome the racism that has stained the campus during the Age of Reagan.

*January 21, 1991*

## The Rise of Louis Farrakhan (Part 1)

*Adolph Reed Jr.*

Louis Farrakhan is all over America. In the past year he has been the subject of widely publicized feature-length interviews in *The Washington Post* and *The Washington Times*, and in other non-black publications as well. He tore up the campaign trail on behalf of local and Congressional candidates in the Nation of Islam's first direct foray into electoral politics. He was prominent at rallies and demonstrations in support of embattled former Washington Mayor Marion Barry, despite having denounced him only a few months earlier as a drug fiend and philanderer. Farrakhan has even been a featured solo guest on *Donahue*. He has kept up a torrid pace of speaking engagements and, of late, has begun to stake out a position critical of U.S. intervention in the Persian Gulf [see box on page 400].

Recognition of Farrakhan as a public figure has been growing since his involvement in Jesse Jackson's first campaign for the Democratic presidential nomination in 1984. But understanding what his rise means in American life requires going back much further than that.

Louis Farrakhan, now 57, has been around a long time. Like Otis Redding, Aretha Franklin and hip-hop, he had considerable visibility among blacks before whites discovered him. For well over thirty years he has propagated a vision of political separatism and a program of moral rearmament, "self-help" business development and an idiosyncratic brand of Islamic religion. That vision and program, as well as his personal stature, grew from the soil of black nationalist politics in the civil rights/black power era. To make sense of Farrakhan requires situating him within the organizational and ideological contexts from which he emerged. Doing so, moreover, indicates that his anti-Semitism and whatever he might think of whites in general are ephemeral in comparison with the truly dangerous tendencies he represents.

In the early 1960s, as Louis X, Farrakhan was minister of the Nation of Islam's important Boston mosque and a kind of understudy to Malcolm X. He sided conspicuously with Elijah Muhammad, founder and "Messenger" of the Nation, against Malcolm in the bitter 1963-65 conflict that ended with the latter's murder. Farrakhan replaced Malcolm as minister of the Harlem mosque and later became Muhammad's national representative.

The Messenger's core teachings include claims that blacks were the world's "original" race, from which all others derived; that black Americans are descended from an ancient, "lost" Asian tribe; that the white race originated from a demonic laboratory experiment and that Elijah Muhammad was divinely inspired. Following nationalist convention, the Muslims advocate the subordination of women, drawing on a rhetoric of domesticity, moral purity and male responsibility; predictably, they denounce feminism and gay rights as white decadence and as strategies to undermine black unity and moral fiber.

The Nation's secular program has always focused on "nation building," which in practice has meant business development and the creation of separate schools and other institutions. Those activities have been harnessed to the ultimate goal of political separation and the formation of an independent state. Under Muhammad that goal remained inchoate, appearing mainly as a millenarian dream, but for Farrakhan it figures more directly into programmatic rhetoric. Discussion of the proposed state's citizenry characteristically elides the distinction between the membership of the Nation of Islam and black Americans in general, but Farrakhan recently has indicated that one possible model entails putting the former in charge of the latter. The nation-building agenda also reinforces the organization's natalist ideology and longstanding opposition to abortion, which both Muhammad and Farrakhan have denounced as genocidal as well as immoral.

Farrakhan rose to prominence during the late 1960s and early 1970s, when Muhammad's Nation was trying to become more visible in public life and to establish a greater presence in the black activist arena. As Muhammad's representative, he participated in national black political forums, addressed the 1970 Pan-African Congress of nationalist activists (as did first-time black Mayors Richard Hatcher of Gary, Indiana, and Kenneth Gibson of Newark; Ralph Abernathy; National Urban League director Whitney Young Jr.; Jesse Jackson and others) and frequently spoke on black college campuses. During that period the Nation also expanded its business development agenda, which until then had centered mainly on mom-and-pop restaurants, takeout sandwich and baked goods shops, cut-and-sew operations catering to the organization's members (to satisfy the Muslim dress code) and the newspaper *Muhammad Speaks*. The Nation unveiled a set of ambitious goals, including establishment of agribusiness in the South, a medical complex in Chicago and large-scale international commerce anchored by fish imports from Peru. There was even talk that Muhammad would take advantage of Richard Nixon's definition of "black power" as "black capitalism" and apply for funds from minority economic development programs in the Office of Economic Opportunity or the Small Business Administration.

Two personal encounters I had with Farrakhan in late 1970 and early 1971 neatly reflect the discordant aspects of the Nation of Islam's thrust then and his place in it. One was a speech he gave at the predominantly black Fayetteville State University in North Carolina, where he scored mainstream civil rights spokespersons for their spinelessness and lack of vision. Of Ralph Abernathy's pledge to pursue King's "dream" as his successor at the Southern Christian Leadership Conference, Farrakhan quipped, "Talking about dreaming somebody else's dream! Don't you know that when you're dreaming, you're *asleep*? *Wake up*, black man!" And he chastised his mainly student audience for putative moral weakness. "Just as a boot-maker molds a boot, so the teacher molds the hearts and minds of the youth of our nation," he said, playing on the institution's history as a teachers' college. "And what are you going to teach them, *drunkard*? What are you going to teach them, *dope fiend*? What are you going to teach them, *foul, frivolous woman* who will lie down with a teacher to get a passing grade?" (Note that the woman, not the teacher, is his target.) With striking theatricality and stage presence, he punctuated each charge by pointing to a different section of the auditorium, as if exposing particular culprits.

The second encounter came soon thereafter. Along with other field-staff members of the North Carolina–based Foundation for Community Development, I was called in to Durham to attend a meeting with Farrakhan. He had come to the area as Muhammad's delegate, mainly to pursue contacts with officials of a well-established black bank and the North Carolina Mutual Life Insurance Company, then one of the largest black-owned businesses in the United States. He also wanted to examine the operations of the community development corporation that our agency had helped the local poor-people's organization create. At the meeting his demeanor was reserved, almost stilted, and he seemed (or tried to seem) in thrall to an image of black Durham as a center for business enterprise. (He had attended college in Winston-Salem during the early 1950s and quite likely imbibed that image then.) Although he made perfunctory gestures of appreciation for our reputation for grass-roots activism and black-power radicalism, he expressed only polite interest in the participatory and cooperative aspects of our community development approach. He was not much moved by the idea of organizing poor people to act on their own behalf.

While the Nation seemed to be growing and consolidating itself as a corporate enterprise, many of us in movement circles who watched from the outside wondered then how it would resolve the evident tension between its flamboyant rhetorical posture, so clear that night at Fayetteville State, and its very conventional business aspirations. Central in our minds was anticipation of the succession crisis likely to occur when Muhammad, who in 1970 was already a feeble septuagenarian, died or stepped down. For not only could Muslim operatives be seen hanging out with denizens of the underworld, but sectarian zealotry often condoned a strong-arm style.

The Uhuru Kitabu bookstore in Philadelphia, for example, was firebombed in 1970 when its proprietors—former Student Non-Violent Coordinating Committee workers—refused to remove a Malcolm X poster from the store's window after threats from local Muslims. In Atlanta in 1971 a dispute between Muslims and Black Panthers over turf rights for street-corner newspaper hawking erupted into a hundred-person brawl. In 1972 strife within New York's Temple Number 7 culminated in a three-hour fight and shootout that began in the mosque and spilled outside. A purge of remaining Malcolm X loyalists followed in New York and elsewhere, and factions within the Nation were implicated in assassinations of outspoken followers of Malcolm in Boston and in Newark, where the presiding minister of the mosque was gunned down.

Most chilling, in January 1973 a simmering theological dispute with members of the Hanafi Islamic sect in Washington ignited into an attack of which only zealots or hardened killers are capable. Seven Hanafis were murdered in their 16th Street residence, owned by Kareem Abdul-Jabbar; five of the victims were children, including babies who were drowned in the bathtub. (The Hanafis held the Nation responsible and four years later occupied a government building and B'nai B'rith center and took hostages to press their demands for retribution.)

In that climate it was reasonable to worry, upon Elijah Muhammad's death in 1975, that the friction might lead to open warfare among the organization's contending factions, particularly between those identified with Farrakhan, who stood for the primacy of ideology, and the Messenger's son Wallace (Warith) Deen Muhammad, who had been linked much more with the Nation's business operations than with its ideological mission. Consequences of that sort did not materialize, and W.D. succeeded his father without apparent conflict, or at least with no immediate, publicly noticeable disruption.

The tension between the two agendas inevitably came to a head, however. Since the early 1970s the Nation had sought explicitly to recruit a middle-class membership as part of its drive for economic development. College students and professionals who joined were likely to be rewarded with responsible positions in the administrative hierarchy, but the Nation had only limited success in gaining petit-bourgeois adherents. It was, after all, a bit much to expect a college-educated constituency to accept as religious principle that the pig is a hybrid of the dog, the cat and the rat or that whites derive from an evil wizard's botched experiment on subhuman creatures.

At the same time, instability grew in the Muslim business operations. For whatever reasons—probably among them was a reluctance to open records to outside scrutiny—the organization retreated from its ambivalent interest in pursuing federal economic-development support. Yet the projects on the board required both considerable specialized expertise and capitalization surpassing the Nation's liquidity. A $3 million "loan" from the Libyan government in 1972 was a stopgap. Despite its ideological boost as a statement of Islamic solidarity, however, the Libyan deal was also a signal that the Messenger Muhammad could not finance his bold schemes internally and was unwilling to do so through regular outside sources.

The desire to broaden the Nation's class base rested on more than a need for expertise. The early newspaper and the bean pie, restaurant and fish ventures relied on the super-exploitation of members' labor. The religio-racial ideology—much like family ideology in a mom-and-pop store—could impose on members, at least in the short run, jobs offering low wages, no benefits and sometimes even no wages. But while it might help keep a newspaper solvent or finance a new restaurant, that ideologically driven accumulation strategy could not begin to support hospital construction or complex international commerce. Tithes or direct investment by a more affluent membership might better help meet capital needs.

Thus, when W. D. Muhammad inherited the Nation of Islam, it was stymied by a fundamental contradiction: The motors of its success—the religio-racial ideology, hermetic separatism and primitive strategy of capital accumulation—had become impediments to realizing the objectives that success had spawned. Negotiating the contradiction was constrained, moreover, by Farrakhan, who constituted himself on the right flank as guardian of the Messenger's orthodoxy, ready to challenge deviations.

Those contrary tendencies coexisted no more than three years. Before the split became public knowledge Muhammad had introduced sweeping changes. He repudiated his father's idiosyncratic religious doctrines—no more Yacub, the evil wizard—in favor of conventional Islamic beliefs. He changed the sect's name to the World Community of Islam in the West to reflect a move toward traditional Islam. He rejected the Messenger's insistence on abstaining from secular politics; instead, he actively urged political participation. In 1976 Muhammad gave up on the goal of economic independence, dismantled the group's holdings and considered seeking Small Business Administration assistance for member-entrepreneurs. (Rumor has it that titles to all the Nation's assets were held not by the organization but by the Messenger himself, who died intestate. Supposedly, W.D. hastened to sell off everything and divided the proceeds equally among all his father's legitimate and illegitimate offspring.)

W.D. had been a very close ally of Malcolm X, reputedly even through the break with his own father, and within his first year as leader of the organization he renamed the Harlem mosque in Malcolm's honor. To Farrakhan's partisans, who often pointed to W.D.'s support for Malcolm as evidence of filial impiety, that gesture must have affirmed suspicions of his blasphemous inclinations. More strain must have developed from W.D.'s proclamation in 1975 that whites thenceforth would be welcome as members of the sect. In 1978 Farrakhan announced his departure and the formation of a new Nation of Islam on the basis of the Messenger's original teachings. In 1985 the World Community of Islam in the West officially disbanded, leaving Farrakhan's group as Elijah Muhammad's sole organizational legacy.

Through the early 1980s Farrakhan maintained a relatively low profile as he built his organization by replicating the old Nation's forms and cultivating a membership drawn from its main social base on the margins of black working-class life. He re-established the Fruit of Islam, the paramilitary security force, and he restored the old ideology, Yacub and all. He even concocted a version of the old bean pie-and-fish economic development formula via Power Products, a line of household and personal items. (To date, the line has not done well, and Farrakhan seems not to have given it much attention.) As if to underscore his loyalty to the elder Muhammad's vision, Farrakhan resumed his old title, national representative of the Honorable Eli ah Muhammad and the Nation of Islam. The chief public signal of the Nation of Islam's return was the appearance of young men on inner-city streets wearing the group's distinctive suit and bow tie and aggressively selling the *Final Call* newspaper, which, but for the different title, follows the format of the old *Muhammad Speaks*.

The original Nation of Islam had grown in prominence in the years after the Supreme Court's 1954 *Brown v. Board of Education* decision because the organization, primarily through Malcolm, chose to operate within the discursive realm created by the developing activist movement. Debate about politics and racial strategy—at widely varying levels of sophistication—was extensive, and the rising tide of activism lifted all ideological and organizational boats.

In the early 1980s, though, there was no hint of a popular movement, and black political discourse had withered to fit entirely within the frame of elite-centered agendas for race-relations engineering. The cutting edge of racial advocacy, for example, was what political scientist Earl Picard described astutely at the time as the "corporate intervention strategy," pioneered by Jesse Jackson at Operation PUSH and adopted with less rhetorical flair by the National Urban League and the N.A.A.C.P. This strategy consisted in using the threat of consumer boycott to induce corporations to enter into "covenants" binding them to hire black managers, contract with black vendors, deposit in black banks and recruit black franchisees. (For a while, the

N.A.A.C.P. concentrated on Hollywood, identifying the fate of the race with its representation in the film industry.) At the same time Ronald Reagan was pressing ahead with a rhetoric and battle plan steeped in racial revanchism, and official black opposition ranged from feeble to incoherent. In that context, the Fruit of Islam selling newspapers outside the supermarket looked for all the world like living anachronisms.

In the race for the 1984 Democratic presidential nomination, however, Farrakhan demonstrated the new Nation of Islam's political departure from the old. Unlike Elijah Muhammad, Farrakhan did not remain publicly aloof from electoral politics. He openly supported Jackson's candidacy and even provided him with a Fruit of Islam security force. Because of Farrakhan's and the Nation's long association with anti-Semitic rhetoric, his closeness to Jackson was thrown into relief in the wake of the "Hymietown" controversy.

Milton Coleman, the *Washington Post* reporter who disclosed Jackson's remarks, was condemned widely as a race traitor, but Farrakhan raised the ante: "We're going to make an example of Milton Coleman. One day soon, we will punish you by death, because you are interfering with the future of our babies—for white people and against the good of yourself and your own people. This is a fitting punishment for such dogs." (Farrakhan has always denied he made these remarks.)

That inflamed rhetoric, along with Farrakhan's reference to Judaism as a "gutter religion," prodded a temporizing Jackson to distance himself publicly from Farrakhan, and the incident made sensationalistic copy throughout the information industry. For those with longer memories Farrakhan's attack on Coleman was a chilling reminder of the thuggish currents of the past. Indeed, his theretofore most notoriously threatening pronouncement—against Malcolm X— had set a frightening precedent. In December 1964 he wrote in *Muhammad Speaks*:

Only those who wish to be led to hell, or to their doom, will follow Malcolm. The die is set and Malcolm shall not escape, especially after such foolish talk about his benefactor in trying to rob him of the divine glory which Allah has bestowed upon him. Such a man as Malcolm is worthy of death—and would have met with death if it had not been for Muhammad's confidence in Allah for victory over the enemies.

Two months later Malcolm was assassinated.

In retrospect, the significance of the Milton Coleman incident lay in how it propelled Farrakhan into the new, mass-mediated space in Afro-American politics first carved out by Jesse Jackson. Jackson's 1984 campaign oscillated between simplistic racial appeals ("It's our turn now!") and claims to represent some larger "moral force." As I have argued in *The Jesse Jackson Phenomenon*, that oscillation was rooted in a contradiction between the campaign's public posture as the crest of a broadly based social movement and the reality that it could rely on black votes only. The pressure to increase the black vote justified a mobilization strategy that often approached pure demagogy. In an August 1984 interview with *Ebony*, Jackson described himself as the carrier of "the emotions and self-respect and inner security of the whole race." The messianism implicit in that perception of his racial role appeared more clearly in his insinuation in that same interview that a Virginia supporter's terminal cancer was cured by going to a Jackson rally. In the midst of the Reagan counterrevolution and black elites' typically uninspired and ineffectual responses, that sort of demagogic appeal found a popular audience. With no more promising agenda available, racial cheerleading at least offered a soothing catharsis. The promise of deliverance by proxy, of racial absorption into Jackson's persona, consoled some with simple explanations and apparently easy remedies ("If all black people could just get together behind Jesse . . .").

But between 1984 and 1988 Jackson moved to consolidate his position as a racial broker in mainstream national politics and to expand his domain to include putative representation of all the "locked out." That shift required soft-pedaling the race line, and instead of making sharp denunciations of the nasty grass-roots racism expressed in Howard Beach and Forsyth County, Georgia, he attempted to invoke the common interests of poor whites and poor blacks. Jackson's transition from the posture of militant insurgent to a more subdued insider's style left vacant the specific racist space that he had created and that had proved to be marketable. Louis Farrakhan's emergence as a national political figure is largely the story of his efforts to replace Jackson as central embodiment and broker of the black race-nationalist political persona. Those efforts began, at least symbolically, with Jackson's grudging acquiescence to white pressure to criticize Farrakhan after the "Hymietown" incident.

The notoriety acquired in that incident fueled Farrakhan's rise in two ways. First, it simply increased his name recognition, especially among a younger generation with no recollection of the old Nation of Islam and his role therein. Second, the heavy barrage of sensationalistic coverage and the sanctimonious white response to the affair afforded an image of Farrakhan and Jackson joined in racial martyrdom. Repudiation of Farrakhan has become a litmus test imposed by white opinion makers for black participation in mainstream politics, and many blacks perceive the test as a humiliating power play. Farrakhan's messianic pretensions, moreover, give him a style something like a counterpunching boxer, and he deftly turned the assault on him into evidence of his authenticity as a race leader. Whites and their agents, the argument goes, expend so much energy on discrediting him because he is a genuine advocate of black interests and thus a threat to white racial domination. In that view, the more he is attacked, the greater his authenticity and the more emphatically he must be defended.

Farrakhan hardly invented this style. Jackson and his black supporters have routinely dismissed criticism by accusing critics of either racism or race treason. Marion Barry, Gus Savage and legions of less prominent malefactors have wrapped themselves in red, black and green rhetoric to conceal abuses of public trust or other failings. Nor is the practice an "African survival." Jimmy Swaggart, Billy James Hargis, Richard Nixon and Oliver North all claim to have been beleaguered by a comparable conspiracy of liberal-communists. Farrakhan stands out because he has been cast in our public theater—like Qaddafi and Noriega, both of whom he has defended—as a figure of almost cartoonishly demonic proportions. He has become uniquely notorious because his inflammatory nationalist persona has helped to center public discussion of Afro-American politics on the only issue (except affirmative action, of course) about which most whites ever show much concern: What do blacks think of whites?

## Louis Farrakhan on the Persian Gulf: 'Mr. Bush, Send Your Son'

Farrakhan has denounced in strident terms the Bush Administration's troop deployment and saber rattling in the Persian Gulf. In the December 10 issue of *The Final Call*, he attacked Bush for cynically sending "Blacks, Native Americans, Chicanos, Hispanics and even poor white boys and girls" to fight a possible war motivated only by "greed, material gain and to keep people in power [in the region] who bow down to the will of America." But he stopped short of calling for an immediate withdrawal of troops and had nothing to say about Saddam Hussein's actions. So far, he has appealed to King Fahd of Saudi Arabia—as a fellow Muslim and not an enemy—to ask the United States to withdraw its troops, and he pledges to mount an antiwar campaign if the United States refuses to comply with such a request. By invoking Islamic solidarity and carefully avoiding any expression of support for Saddam or any hint of criticism of the deposed Kuwaiti regime or the Saudis, Farrakhan shows a concern not to alienate any possible Arab or Muslim source of good will. His linking of his threat to mobilize against the war to such an unlikely condition reflects a reluctance to put to a public test his claim to be a major force in black American political life. Farrakhan has been successful in filling auditoriums and titillating rallies, but he has neither won mass adherence to the Nation of Islam nor ever demonstrated a capacity to galvanize popular action toward any end. Thus on the gulf he has opted for a characteristic Nation of Islam stance: a militant rhetorical posture that preserves an aversion to real political mobilization.     A.R.

*January 28, 1991*

# All for One and None for All (part 2)

*Adolph Reed Jr.*

The hypocrisy in the white reaction to Louis Farrakhan's "hate mongering" is transparent. And beneath the platitudes and fatuities about Martin Luther King Jr.'s dream, black Americans are aware of the dual standard governing public outcry. David Duke's racism and anti-Semitism have been more direct and vitriolic than Farrakhan's, but Duke has not provoked comparable public anxiety and denunciation—despite the fact that the ex-Nazi/Klansman has won a seat as a Louisiana State Representative, has run as a "legitimate" candidate for the U.S. Senate and harbors gubernatorial intentions. The heavy metal group Guns n' Roses maintains a repertoire that is unremittingly and unapologetically misogynistic, homophobic, racist and xenophobic, yet the group has escaped the outrage and public censure heaped upon the no more (nor less, certainly) racist and misogynistic Public Enemy. The scurrilous Andrew Dice Clay is granted television specials and a film contract; the no more repugnant 2 Live Crew is censored for obscenity. Recognition of this hypocritical Jim Crow standard for targeting public scorn naturally breeds resentment and racial defensiveness. The retrograde racial climate fostered by Reaganism particularly stimulates that defensive tendency. It is also reinforced and cultivated by black elites of all sorts—from the national civil rights advocacy organizations, the Congressional Black Caucus and Jesse Jackson to small-town politicians, journalists and academics, who opportunistically reproduce a political discourse among black citizens that takes race as its only significant category of critical analysis.

The Marion Barry case exemplifies the dangerous limitations of that discourse. With very few honest exceptions, black spokespersons failed to take a principled stand denouncing both the Bush Administration's disingenuous, irresponsible (and yes, racist) use of public power in pursuit of Barry and the Mayor's culpability—not simply for his tawdry personal life but, much more seriously, for the contempt and neglect that his entire pattern of governance has directed toward his poor black constituents. One source of the reticence is the mutual protectiveness that operates within all elite networks; it is intensified no doubt by being in a beleaguered community. But it also reflects the absence of explicit norms of civic life and ideals of poetical economy other than those connected immediately to principles of equity among racial groups. Without such norms and ideals, race stands out as the sole unequivocal criterion of good and bad, right and wrong, truth and falsity. That context nurtures a variety of demagogues, hustlers and charlatans; in addition, it underlies an important characteristic of Farrakhan's black support.

Farrakhan has been attacked so vigorously and singularly *in part* because he is black. He is seen by whites as a symbol embodying, and therefore justifying, their fears of a black peril. Blacks have come to his defense *mainly* because he is black and perceived to be a victim of racially inspired defamation; he gets points in principle for saying things that antagonize whites. Few who rally to vindicate him know or have anything substantive to say about his program; most defend him as a strong black voice that whites want to silence. Farrakhan's wager is that he can build a personal following by asserting his apparent victimization as de facto evidence of political legitimacy.

Can he succeed? To what extent has he already succeeded? What difference does it make whether or not he ensconces himself as a major force in national Afro-American politics? The first two questions, commonly asked, express clear, immediate concerns but can be answered only contingently. The third is almost never asked, but it goes to the heart of the most disturbing qualities of the Farrakhan controversy and what it says about the state of black politics.

If mass conversion to the Nation of Islam is the measure of success, then Farrakhan does not seem to have got very far. Nor is it likely that he will. The organization's strict dietary code and other behavioral disciplines—not to mention its bizarre and non-Christian theology—greatly limit his membership pool, as they did Elijah Muhammad's. There is, however, an intermediate zone between adhering to the Nation's doctrines and *pro forma* support, and I suspect that is the terrain on which Farrakhan has staked his aspirations.

He seems to have made some headway, at least within the college-age population, in propagating an image of himself as the quintessential representative of black assertiveness. Black student groups now almost routinely make headlines and raise hackles by paying top-shelf lecture fees (reportedly $17,000 for speaker and entourage at the University of Massachusetts, Amherst) to hear Farrakhan's message. And those in both college and noncollege networks drop his name as a signifier of being conversant with the state of chic in race militancy, just as semireverent, faux intimate invocations of Michael Jordan or Teddy Riley convey being *au courant* in other contexts.

Embracing Farrakhan's image—like wearing an Africa medallion—is an act of vicarious empowerment. More clearly on the campuses but probably outside student life as well, it is a totemic act of the sort distinctive to mass-consumption culture: highly salient but without clear meaning, effortlessly accessible but somehow bestowing in-group status. For college students, inviting Farrakhan forges identity with a power that counterattacks racism and isolation and soothes the anxieties around upward mobility or class maintenance. For nonstudents, invoking his name forges identity with a power that consoles fleetingly in the face of a marginalized life showing little hope for improvement.

Not surprisingly, the youthful Farrakhan constituency in each domain seems preponderantly male. On the one hand, Farrakhan's stridency and martial style have a distinctly macho appeal. On the other, women of any stratum are not likely to respond enthusiastically to his philosophy, which assigns them subordinate status in a patriarchal family, stresses childbearing and child raising as their main functions and ties them to the domestic realm in a state of modified purdah.

How far that kind of ephemeral constituency can go is an open question. Some slender cohort will enter the Nation of Islam from the student and nonstudent populations, and Farrakhan's decision to have the Nation operate in electoral politics will probably help campus recruitment by providing a visible public career path, though that tactic has yet to produce any substantive victories. The vast majority will either retain a mainly symbolic identification by recycling signature catch phrases, lose interest entirely or move back and forth between those two positions according to the vagaries of biography.

The impetus to invite Farrakhan to speak on campuses is driven by a combination of localized *cri de coeur* and protest, competition and solidarity with black students at other institutions, faddishness and racially mediated adolescent rebelliousness and anxiety. But what happens when he comes? What message does he deliver? What do students hear and how do they receive it? What can that tell us about the depth and meaning of his support?

For many the act of consuming the event is the principal gratification. In that sense going to a Farrakhan speech is identical to going to an M. C. Hammer concert; it is the happening place to be at the moment. Farrakhan is a masterful performer and spellbinding orator. He offers his audience a safely contained catharsis: visceral rebellion without dangerous consequences, an instant, painless inversion of power and status relations. As a talented demagogue, Farrakhan mingles banalities, half-truths, distortions and falsehoods to buttress simplistic and wacky theories. The result is a narrative in which he takes on the role of racial conscience and, in Malcolm's old phrase, "tells it like it is." He cajoles, berates, exhorts, instructs and consoles— all reassuringly, without upsetting the framework of conservative petit-bourgeois convention.

Indeed, Farrakhan has reproduced the contradiction within the old Nation of Islam, the tension between militant posture and conservative program. But that contradiction fits the ambivalent position of the student audience. Their racial militancy often rests atop basically conventional, if not conservative, aspirations: for example, the desire to penetrate—or create black-controlled alternatives to—the "glass ceiling" barring access to the upper reaches of corporate wealth and power. Radical rhetoric is attractive when it speaks to their frustrations as members of a minority, as long as it does not conflict with their hopes for corporate success and belief in their own superiority to a benighted black "underclass."

The combination of cathartic, feel-good militancy and conservative substance is the source as well of whatever comparable following Farrakhan may have generated among the older population. It is also what makes him a dangerous force in American life—quite apart from what he thinks of whites in general or Jews in particular. He weds a radical, oppositional style to a program that proposes private and individual responses to social problems; he endorses moral repressiveness; he asserts racial essentialism; he affirms male authority; and he lauds bootstrap capitalism. In defining his and the Nation's role as bringing the holy word to a homogeneous but defective population, moreover, he has little truck for cultivation of democratic debate among Afro-Americans, and he is quick to castigate black critics with the threatening language of race treason.

Reports of Farrakhan's grooving presence typically note that the crowds drawn to his speaking tours include many older, apparently well-off people who indicate that they appreciate his message of race pride and self-help community development. Observers from Benjamin Hooks to Phil Donahue have anointed his antidrug and bootstrap rhetoric as level-headed and unobjectionable, the stuff of an appropriate and reasonable approach to the problems of black inner cities. But his focus on self-help and moral revitalization is profoundly reactionary and meshes perfectly with the victim-blaming orthodoxy of the Reagan/Bush era.

To Farrakhan the most pressing problems confronting the poor and working-class Afro-American population are not poverty and dispossession themselves but their putative behavioral and attitudinal byproducts: drugs, crime, social "pathology." In an August interview in *Emerge* he declared that to improve black Americans' condition it is necessary first to "recognize that we as a people are sick." In his March 13, 1990, *Donahue* appearance he maintained that blacks suffer from a dependent, welfare mentality inculcated in slavery; there and elsewhere (in a March 1, 1990, *Washington Post* interview, for example) he has implicitly trivialized and challenged the propriety of the Thirteenth Amendment, alleging that at Emancipation the infantilized blacks "didn't have the mentality of a free people to go and do for ourselves." (In this view Farrakhan echoes not only Daniel Patrick Moynihan's notorious 1965 report on the black family but also much older racist representations: the common belief in the early twentieth century that emancipated blacks would die out because of their incompetence at independent life in civilized society and the antebellum view that justified slavery as a humanitarian service for childlike savages who could not exist independently.)

Farrakhan romanticizes the segregation era as a time of black business success and laments that "throughout the South the economic advancement that we gained under Jim Crow is literally dead." He suggested in *Emerge* that civil rights legislation has done black citizens general harm because "women, gays, lesbians and Jews have taken advantage of civil rights laws, antidiscrimination laws, housing laws, and they have marched on to a better life while the people who made it happen are going farther and farther behind economically." He proposed the "real solution" in a very sympathetic July 23, 1990, interview in *The Spotlight*, organ of the ultra-reactionary Liberty Lobby:

> If I am sick and I'm a member of your household and I have a communicable disease, what you do (so that the disease does not affect the whole family) you remove me from the house and you put me in a place which is separate to allow me to come back to health. Then I can return to my family. Here, when people have been under oppression for 400 years, it produces an ill effect. . . . You have . . . millions of [Black] people who are out of it in terms of our ability to take advantage of even the laws that are on the books right now. We are not creating jobs for ourselves. We are sitting in a dependent posture waiting for white people to create a job for us. And if you don't create a job for us we threaten to picket or wait on welfare to come.

Farrakhan's views of politics and government also share significant features with the Reaganite right. The flip side of his self-help notion is rejection of government responsibility for the welfare of the citizenry. The highly touted Muslim "Dopebusters" drug program in Washington's Mayfair Mansions (where I lived as a child, incidentally) is, after all, advertised as a case of successful privatization. Predictably, Farrakhan shows little regard for the state's integrity as a secular institution. In announcing the Nation's foray into running candidates for public office (for the Washington school board and two Congressional seats, one of them contested by Dr. Abdul Alim Muhammad of Dopebusters fame), he maintained in the Nation's organ, *The Final Call*, that politics needs "somebody trained in divine law, then trained in the law of the land" and announced that the Nation of Islam has been "given by Allah the right guidance for our people and the right guidance for our nation." Like Reagan, he assumes the classic demagogic tack of an antipolitical politics, presenting himself and his subalterns as redeemers coming from outside the political realm and untainted by its corruptions. Their mission is to bring moral order.

Clearly, this is a very disturbing, regressive social vision, and it is instructive that Farrakhan has received the Liberty Lobby's enthusiastic stamp of approval. The good news is that his vision is most unlikely to win mass Afro-American adherence; the bad news is that doing so is not a necessary condition for Farrakhan's becoming a central race spokesperson. Instead, he seems to be following the route that Jesse Jackson pioneered.

With his 1983 speaking tour Jackson gained acclamation as a paramount figure in Afro-American politics by parlaying media images of enthusiastic audiences into a claim to represent a mass constituency. He succeeded without having articulated a program or coherent vision for those supposed constituents to accept or reject. In claiming to embody their aspirations simply in his being, he also sought to merge collective racial fortunes into his own, a strategy that entailed defining support of Jackson as an act of race loyalty.

Jackson's strategy exploited longstanding and hegemonic presumptions in American society that black people naturally speak with a single voice as a racial group, that the "leaders" who express the collective racial interest emerge organically from the population and that the objectives and interests of those organic leaders are identical with those of the general racial constituency. Those presumptions eliminate the need to attend to potentially troublesome issues of accountability, legitimacy and democratic process among Afro-Americans, and they give whites easy, uncomplicated access to a version of black thinking by condensing the entire race into a few designated spokespersons. They also simplify the management of racial subordination by allowing white elites to pick and choose among pretenders to race leadership and, at their own discretion, to confer "authenticity." Thus Jackson generated the dynamic of personalistic legitimation that created his national status almost as self-fulfilling prophecy, without regard to the specific character of his popular support. Jackson has shown that it is possible to penetrate the innermost circles of the national race-relations management elite without coming from a clearly denominated organizational, electoral or institutional base. Farrakhan could follow that same path, though he might be constrained as well as aided by the fact that he does have an organizational base, and by that base's particular nature.

Operation PUSH under Jackson was purely an extension of his person, and it cohered around opportunism as a raison d'être. The National Rainbow Coalition Inc. today is an organizational fiction. Both have therefore been well suited to the protean style that Jackson employed to establish himself first as embodiment of insurgent mass racial aspirations and then as generic "moral force" in elite national political circles. While the Nation of Islam is an extension of Farrakhan's objectives, it also has a governing ideology and world view. He may be limited—in the same way that he hampered Wallace Muhammad—in his ability to bend that orthodoxy to suit his immediate political purposes.

Farrakhan may differ from Jackson in yet another consequential way. Where Jackson's history has been marked by self-promotion more than propagation of a durable set of beliefs, Farrakhan—though obviously opportunistic—has built his career and organization around a clear, aggressive ideology. His ambitions appear to be in a way narrower, in a way broader than Jackson's. Farrakhan is more likely to be content with a status defined in purely racial terms and has been less inclined to moderate his race line in exchange for access to privileged insider status. On his own and through the Nation he has been sharply censorious and disparaging of what he construes as Jackson's knuckling under to white criticism. In part, I suspect, that difference reflects the fact that Farrakhan has an organizational apparatus that permits him to maximize the returns of a purely racial focus by engineering symbols of legitimacy and continual mobilization (rallies, conferences, community visibility). The difference also underscores the fact that Farrakhan's ideology decrees an explicit racial mission—purification (by the Nation's standards) of Afro-American life. Unlike Jackson, who has capitalized on the image of control of the black American population, Farrakhan wants real control.

His suggestion that some 600,000 incarcerated blacks be released to his authority in Africa is more than a publicity stunt. It expresses a belief that in the best-case scenario he should be put in charge of black Americans. His request in the *Washington Post* interview to be "allowed the freedom to teach black people unhindered" sounds mild enough, but only because it leaves ambiguous what he considers improper hindrances. Opposition of any sort falls into that category, and his 1984 threat to Milton Coleman for race treason in the "Hymietown" affair reveals the place of dissent in the society he would make. Of the model of racial authority he would assert, he makes a revealing comparison in the *Emerge* interview: "I am to black people as the Pope is to white people." That enlarged self-image can approach a lunatic megalomania. He alleges in *Emerge* that the revival of interest in Malcolm X is the work of a conspiracy aimed at undermining his mission; to *The Washington Post* he traced the spread of crack in inner cities to a similar conspiracy against him, and he claimed to have been transported in 1985 into a spaceship where Elijah Muhammad gave him general instructions and prophesied Reagan's attack on Libya.

How can it be that Farrakhan's actual vision of and for black America has been so noncontroversial? Why have the civil rights establishment and other liberal black opinion leaders not publicly expressed more vocal concern about its protofascist nature and substance? Some of the reticence may derive from fear of being attacked for race disloyalty, but the black petit-bourgeois chorus of praise for the Nation's rhetoric of self-help and moral rearmament reveals a deeper reason for the absence of criticism. The same repugnant, essentially Victorian view of the inner-city black poor as incompetent and morally defective that undergirds Farrakhan's agenda suffuses the political discourse of the black petite bourgeoisie. That view informs the common sense, moreover, even of many of those identified with the left. Of course, not many would admit to the level of contempt that Farrakhan has expressed publicly:

> Not one of you [*Spotlight* editorial staff] would mind, maybe, my living next door to you, because I'm a man of a degree of intelligence, of moral character. I'm not a wild, partying fellow. I'm not a noisemaker. I keep my home very clean and my lawn very nice. . . . With some of us who have learned how to act at home and abroad, you might not have problems. . . . Drive through the ghettoes, and see our people. See how we live. Tell me that you want your son or daughter to marry one of these. No, you won't.

Some, like Harvard sociologist Orlando Patterson, share Farrakhan's contention that the black poor's pathology is a product of the slavery experience. Others, like the Carter Administration's Equal Employment Opportunity Commission director and newly elected Washington Congressional delegate Eleanor Holmes Norton or Chicago sociologist William Julius Wilson, maintain that this pathology is a phenomenon of the post–World War II or even post-segregation era. Still others, like Roger Wilkins, have embraced both narratives of origin. There is, however, nearly unanimous agreement with Farrakhan's belief that defective behavior and attitudes are rampant among the poor. In a recent article in *Dissent*, Patterson points to an underclass bent on "violence and destruction." Norton, calling for "Restoring the Traditional Black Family" in *The New York Times Magazine* (June 2, 1985), sees a "self-perpetuating culture of the ghetto," a "destructive ethos" that forms a "complicated, predatory ghetto subculture." Wilson frets over the "sharp increase in social pathologies in ghetto communities" in his opus on urban poverty, *The Truly Disadvantaged* (1987). Wilkins cites in *The New York Times* the authority of Samuel Proctor—retired Rutgers professor, civil rights veteran and minister emeritus of Harlem's Abyssinian Baptist Church—who fears that the "uneducated, illiterate, impoverished, violent underclass" will "grow like a cancer," producing "losers who are destroying our schools . . . who are unparented and whose communities are morally bankrupt." Being associated with the more radical left does not imply immunity from the rhetoric of spreading pathology among the black poor. In *The Progressive* Manning Marable reproduces uncritically the mirage of "growing numbers of juvenile pregnancies" among his litany of "intractable social problems proliferating" in black inner cities despite his observation that such problems have structural causes and his call for good social-democratic solutions. Cornel West in *Prophetic Fragments* sounds the alarm about the cities' "cultural decay and moral disintegration."

This often lurid imagery of pathology naturally points toward a need for behavioral modification, moral regeneration and special tutelage by black betters, and black middle-class paternalism is as shameless and self-serving now as at the turn of the century. Patterson, Norton, Wilson and Wilkins announce the middle class's special role in making certain that the poor are fit into properly two-parent, male-headed families. Proctor, presumably giving up on adults, wants to use military discipline to insure that children have "breakfasts with others at a table." West would send them into churches for moral rehabilitation. And the Committee on Policy for Racial Justice of the Joint Center for Political Studies (whose members include Norton, Wilkins and Wilson) lauds self-help in its manifesto, *Black Initiative and Governmental Responsibility*, and calls on black "religious institutions, civic and social organizations, media, entertainers, educators, athletes, public officials, and other community leaders" to "emphasize . . . values." It was a master stroke of Reagan's second-term spin doctors to sugarcoat the offensive on the black poor with claptrap about special black middle-class responsibility for "their" poor and the challenge of self-help. The black leadership elite fell right into line and quickly institutionalized a cooing patter of noblesse oblige.

From that hegemonic class standpoint there is little room and less desire to criticize Farrakhan's contemptuous, authoritarian diagnosis and remedy. As he instructed *The Spotlight*:

We must be allowed the freedom first to teach our people and put them in a state of readiness to receive justice.... Blacks in America have to be concentrated upon, to lift us up in a way that we will become self-respecting so that the communities of the world will not mind accepting us as an equal member among the community of family of nations. . . . But when we [the Nation of Islam] get finished with these people, we produce dignified intelligent people. The American system can't produce that. We can.

In sum, Louis Farrakhan has become prominent in the public eye because he appeals symbolically both to black frustration and alienation in this retrograde era and to white racism, disingenuousness and naiveté. He also responds to the status anxiety, paternalistic class prejudice and ideological conservatism embedded within black petit-bourgeois race militancy. His antiwhite or anti-Semitic views are neither the most important issue surrounding Farrakhan nor the greatest reason for concern about his prospects for growing influence.

After all, he will never be able to impose his beliefs—no matter how obnoxious or heinous—on any group of white Americans. More significant, and more insidious, is the fact that racial units are his essential categories for defining and comprehending political life. That fact obviously establishes him on common conceptual ground with all manner of racists. (*The Spotlight* was happily curious about whether he and David Duke actually would disagree on anything in a debate rumored to be in the works.)

His racial essentialism has an appeal for many blacks in a purely demagogic way. It also gives him an outlook that seems disarmingly sensible to whites—at least those who can overlook his fiery pro-black sentiments and devil theories—because it fits into the hoary "What do your people want?" framework for discussing black Americans. That essentialist outlook also underlies his self-help rhetoric, which appeals to both whites and middle-class blacks. Whites like it because it implies that blacks should pull themselves up by their bootstraps and not make demands on government. Middle-class blacks like it because it legitimizes a "special role" for the black petite bourgeoisie over the benighted remainder of the race. In both views, "self-help" with respect to ordinary black Americans replaces a standard expectation of democratic citizenship—a direct, unmediated relation to the institutions and processes of public authority. Self-help ideology is a form of privatization and therefore implies cession of the principle that government is responsible for improving the lives of the citizenry and advancing egalitarian interests; it also rests on a promise that black Americans cannot effectively make demands on the state directly as citizens but must go through intermediaries constituted as guardians of collective racial self-interest. Ironically, "self-help" requires dissolution of the autonomous civic self of Afro-Americans.

The link between self-help rhetoric and racial custodianship is as old as Booker T. Washington, the model of organic racial leadership Farrakhan articulates. The idea that black racial interests can be embodied in a single individual has always been attractively economical for white elites. Giving Washington a railroad car for his own use to avoid Jim Crow was a lot cheaper for white elites and less disruptive than socioeconomic democratization and preservation of citizenship rights. Jesse Jackson updated the claim to organic racial leadership and brokerage by enlisting mass media technology to legitimize it, and Farrakhan is following in Jackson's steps. Because of his organization and ideology, however, Farrakhan more than his predecessors throws into relief the dangerous, fascistic presumptions inscribed at the foundation of that model. That—underscored by the brownshirt character of the Fruit of Islam and the history of the old Nation during Farrakhan's ascent—is what makes him uniquely troubling. But demonizing him misses the point; it is the idea of organic representation of the racial collectivity that makes him possible.

It is that idea, whether expressed flamboyantly by Farrakhan or in the more conventional petit-bourgeois synecdoche that folds all black interests into a narrow class agenda, that most needs to be repudiated. Its polluting and demobilizing effects on Afro-American political life have never been more visible, thanks to promotion by the mass media's special combination of racist cynicism and gullibility. Cheap hustlers and charlatans, corrupt and irresponsible public officials and perpetrators of any sort of fraud can manipulate the generic defensiveness decreed by a politics of organic racial representation to support their scams or sidestep their guilt—all too often for offenses against black constituents. A straight line connects Washington's Tuskegee Machine, which sought to control access to philanthropic support for racial agendas, to Jackson's insinuation that "respect" for him is respect for all black Americans to Farrakhan's death threat against Milton Coleman to the pathetic specter of the rogues' gallery of Farrakhan, Illinois Representative Gus Savage, the Rev. Al Sharpton, the Rev. George Stallings and Tawana Brawley sharing the stage with Marion Barry at a rally to defend the corrupt Mayor's honor. That image captures the depth of crisis of political vision that racial organicism has wrought.

*July 5, 1993*

## Where's the Revolution?

*Barbara Smith*

July 5, 1993—Revolution seems like a largely irrelevant concept to the gay movement of the nineties. The liberation politics of the earlier era, which relied upon radical grass-roots strategies to eradicate oppression, have been largely replaced by an assimilationist "civil rights" agenda. The most visible elements of the movement have put their faith almost exclusively in electoral and legislative initiatives, bolstered by mainstream media coverage, to alleviate *discrimination*. When the word "radical" is used at all, it means confrontational, "in your face" tactics, not strategic organizing aimed at the roots of oppression.

Unlike the early lesbian and gay movement, which had both ideological and practical links to the left, black activism and feminism, today's "queer" politicos seem to operate in a historical and ideological vacuum. "Queer" activists focus on "queer" issues, and racism, sexual oppression and economic exploitation do not qualify, despite the fact that the majority of "queers" are people of color, female or working class. When other oppressions or movements are cited, it's to build a parallel case for the validity of lesbian and gay rights or to expedite alliances with mainstream political organizations. Building unified, ongoing coalitions that challenge the system and ultimately prepare a way for revolutionary change simply isn't what "queer" activists have in mind.

When lesbians and gay men of color urge the gay leadership to make connections between heterosexism and issues like police brutality, racial violence, homelessness, reproductive freedom and violence against women and children, the standard dismissive response is, "Those are not our issues." At a time when the gay movement is under unprecedented public scrutiny, lesbians and gay men of color and others committed to antiracist organizing are asking: Does the gay and lesbian movement want to create a just society for everyone? Or does it only want to eradicate the last little glitch that makes life difficult for privileged (white male) queers?

The April 25 March on Washington, despite its historical importance, offers some unsettling answers. Two comments that I've heard repeatedly since the march is that it seemed more like a parade than a political demonstration and that the overall image of the hundreds of thousands of participants was overwhelmingly Middle American, that is, white and conventional. The identifiably queer—the drag queens, leather people, radical faeries, dykes on bikes, etc.—were definitely in the minority, as were people of color, who will never be Middle American no matter what kind of drag we put on or take off.

A friend from Boston commented that the weekend in Washington felt like being in a "blizzard." I knew what she meant. Despite the fact that large numbers of lesbians and gay men of color were present (perhaps even more than at the 1987 march), our impact upon the proceedings did not feel nearly as strong as it did six years ago. The bureaucratic nineties concept of "diversity," with its superficial goal of assuring that all the colors in the crayon box are visible, was very much the strategy of the day. Filling slots with people of color or women does not necessarily affect the politics of a movement if our participation does not change the agenda, that is, if we are not actually permitted to lead.

I had had my own doubts about attending the April march. Although I went to the first march in 1979 and was one of the eight major speakers at the 1987 march, I didn't make up my mind to go to this one until a few weeks before it happened. It felt painful to be so alienated from the gay movement that I wasn't even sure I wanted to be there; my feelings of being an outsider had been growing for some time.

I remember receiving a piece of fundraising direct mail from the magazine *Outlook* in 1988 with the phrase "tacky but we'll take it" written next to the lowest potential contribution of $25. Since $25 is a lot more than I can give at any one time to the groups I support, I decided I might as well send my $5 somewhere else. In 1990 I read Queer Nation's manifesto, "I Hate Straights," in *Outweek* and wrote a letter to the editor suggesting that if queers of color followed its political lead, we would soon be issuing a statement titled, "I Hate Whiteys," including white queers of European origin. Since that time I've heard very little public criticism of the narrowness of lesbian and gay nationalism. No one would guess from recent stories about wealthy and "powerful" white lesbians on TV and in slick magazines that women earn 69 cents on the dollar compared with men and that black women earn even less.

These examples are directly connected to assumptions about race and class privilege. In fact, it's gay white men's racial, gender and class privileges, as well as the vast numbers of them who identify with the system rather than distrust it, that have made the politics of the current gay movement so different from those of other identity-based movements for social and political change. In the seventies, progressive movements—especially feminism—positively influenced and inspired lesbians' and gays' vision of struggle. Since the eighties, as AIDS has helped to raise consciousness about gay issues in some quarters of the establishment, and as some battles against homophobia have been won, the movement has positioned itself more and more within the mainstream political arena. Clinton's courting of the gay vote (at the same time as he did everything possible to distance himself from the African-American community) has also been a cru-cial factor in convincing the national gay and lesbian leadership that a place at the ruling class's table is just what they've been waiting for. Of course, the people left out of this new gay political equation of mainstream acceptance, power and wealth are lesbians and gay men of color.

It was talking to radical lesbians and gay men that finally made me decide to go to the April 25 march. Earlier in the month, I attended an extraordinary conference on the lesbian and gay left in Delray Beach, Florida. The planners had made a genuine commitment to racial and gender parity; 70 percent of the participants were people of color and 70 percent were women. They were also committed to sup-porting the leadership of people of color and lesbians—especially les-bians of color—which is almost never done outside of our own autonomous groupings. The conference felt like a homecoming. I got to spend time with people I'd worked with twenty years before in Boston as well as with younger activists from across the country.

What made the weekend so successful, aside from the humor, gossip, caring and hot discussions about sex and politics, was the huge relief I felt at not being expected to cut off parts of myself that are as integral to who I am as my sexual orientation as the price for participating in lesbian and gay organizing. Whatever concerns were raised, discussions were never silenced by the remark, "But that's not our issue." Women and men, people of color and whites, all agreed that there desperately needs to be a visible alternative to the cut-and-dried, business-as-usual agenda of the gay political mainstream. Their energy and vision, as well as the astuteness and tenacity of rad-ical lesbians and gays I encounter all over the country, convince me that a different way is possible.

If the gay movement ultimately wants to make a real difference, as opposed to settling for handouts, it must consider creating a multi-issue revolutionary agenda. This is not about political correctness, it's about winning. As black lesbian poet and warrior Audre Lorde insisted, "The master's tools will never dismantle the master's house." Gay rights are not enough for me, and I doubt that they're enough for most of us. Frankly, I want the same thing now that I did thirty years ago when I joined the civil rights movement, and twenty years ago when I joined the women's movement, came out and felt more alive that I ever dreamed possible: freedom.

*May 23, 1994*

## The Freedom of Employment Act

*Derrick Bell*

*Civil rights proponents fought valiantly but in vain to forestall the enactment of the Freedom of Employment Act of 1997. The President, whose election the previous year was partly based on his pledge to push for the legislation, quickly signed the measure. The law, according to its preamble, would allay growing racial hostility by eliminating policies that undermined fundamental principles of fair play in a misguided and socially disruptive effort to remedy instances of past racial discrimination, problems that had mostly disappeared with the enactment of civil rights laws three decades earlier.*

*In summary, the act bans all affirmative action programs, including preferential recruitment, hiring promotions or other employment policies practices, rules and regulations based in whole or in part on race or ethnicity. The act assumes that all persons who, because of their race or ethnicity, were actual or potential beneficiaries of affirmative action policies obtained the positions they now hold unfairly. Under the act, such positions are rendered "vulnerable to challenge" by individuals (job challengers) not eligible for affirmative action preferences and presumed harmed by them.*

*If any such challenger can show that he or she had superior training or experience at the time the job was filled, the presumed affirmative action beneficiary holding the position must, upon formal demand, vacate the position within thirty days. Judicial review, after the exhaustion of extensive administrative remedies, is available, but the cost must be borne by the suspect jobholder. Jobholders who contest bona fide challenges and are subsequently held not entitled to the jobs they hold are liable for damages to the job challenger in the amount of job salary from the date thirty days after the challenge was filed.*

"Stop right there, Geneva Crenshaw. Given my difficulties in the past with your unorthodox racial beliefs, I don't know why I asked you to help me prepare an essay commemorating the fortieth anniversary of the Supreme Court's 1954 decision in *Brown v. Board of Education.*"

"Why indeed," Geneva responded, ready as ever to challenge what she considered my out-of-touch civil rights views. "What is there to commemorate about a four-decades-old decision that, like Lincoln's Emancipation Proclamation, promised more than it could deliver, and enabled the progress that occurred only because so many blacks and liberal whites treated its symbols as real and gave them substance in countless nonviolent protests and endless lawsuits? Now, what we hailed as *Brown*'s new nondiscriminatory legal standard has been twisted into a more subtle barrier to racial equality, one that is hardly less pernicious than was the separate but equal standard that *Brown* replaced."

"Geneva. I share your disappointments with *Brown*, but surely you are not predicting that its shortcomings are going to lead to this Freedom of Employment Act, possibly the most repressive legislation I've ever heard of. With the possible exception of a few superstars in sports, entertainment and science, it will place at risk every job held by a nonwhite. Whites can challenge our jobs under a law that unrelentingly stacks the deck in their favor. Within a few months, this law would drop middle-class blacks who don't run their own businesses right into poverty, alongside the one-third of blacks who are already struggling in the economic basement."

"Precisely," Geneva said, calmly.

Geneva is a wonderful person, but she is also a trial. As some of you know, Geneva holds strange, unnerving views about racial issues, gained during the long period she spent in a coma following a car crash while she was a civil rights lawyer in the South. She gained, as well, other extraordinary abilities—including the ability to appear and disappear at will—that she accepts as normal and that I never question because, to tell the truth, I am not sure I really want to know the source of her mysterious, otherworldly gifts.

For the past several years I have been sharing her prophecies in allegorical-story form with the public in books and other writings. Even so, I usually resist her allegorical insights. "Why would Congress pass such a bill, Geneva, and why on earth would the President sign it?"

"Considering the current economic and political problems the nation is facing and refusing even to acknowledge—much less address—why not? If Jesse Helms, a conservative on many issues other than race, could overcome the substantial lead of former Charlotte Mayor Harvey Gantt, a black man, and get re-elected to the Senate by using an infamous television ad attributing affirmative action as the reason whites did not get jobs, why couldn't a President be elected on a similar campaign?"

"I see your point, Geneva, but you surely don't expect me to publish a piece predicting that when your new law takes effect in 1997, most blacks will find their jobs in jeopardy."

"Their jobs are already in jeopardy, as they should know from the contraction in the labor market that continues even as the economy improves. And you are right, many will lose their jobs when this act takes effect. But most of them will work again," Geneva assured me.

"Well, that's a relief. In other words, the bill is less drastic than you described it."

"*Au contraire, mon ami.* The act is much more drastic—as you would have learned had you not interrupted me. Another provision states that all those who held or were eligible to hold affirmative action positions are, upon surrender of those positions, required to find work within thirty days, or be subject to induction into a national work force."

"Sort of like the Civilian Conservation Corps of the 1930s?" I ventured.

"More like the military services," Geneva replied. "All those found physically and mentally able must go. The terms of service are for three years, except that failing to locate a job within thirty days of mustering out results in automatic extensions of service for another three years. Oh yes, the government, at its discretion, can assign inducted workers to civilian employers with labor-intensive work deemed in the public interest."

"Like environmental clean-up operations," I suggested.

"Yes, but also farming—particularly harvests of fruits and vegetables—mining, reforestation projects and the maintenance of parks and other public facilities."

"Even as a hypothetical, Geneva, your Freedom of Employment Act is scary. Dick Gregory, commenting on the thousands of blacks without jobs, joked that slavery, with all its evils, was at least a full employment act for black people. It sounds like someone was taking Gregory seriously."

"Slaves work without pay," Geneva reminded me. "Inducted workers will receive the minimum wage, and, while deemed on duty at all times, they will normally work eight-hour days and will receive room, board and recreational facilities at no cost. Charges that the law violates the Thirteenth Amendment's indentured servitude prohibition will not slow the bill's enactment by Congress, and they likely will not work in the courts."

"Why do you look so concerned?" Geneva asked. "Aren't you the author who has been writing—with some persistent prompting from me—about the permanence of racism, which makes a Freedom of Employment Act not only possible but quite probable—and quite soon?"

I ignored her question and tried another tack. "Assuming that you are reading the future accurately, won't my revelation of this monstrous measure provide our enemies with a plan that they might not come up with on their own?"

"Just the opposite. By spelling it out, you delegitimize this particular plan for adoption by affirmative action opponents. They will devise other schemes, though, some likely even more devastating. My Freedom of Employment Act is a hypothetical warning of what can become all too real."

"Listen," she continued. "I have to leave for a while. Think about the act and how it might be countered."

I could tell Geneva was annoyed. She didn't bother to use the door. She just vanished—a habit she knows irritates me.

As many of you know, for the past two years I have been suggesting that racism is a permanent condition in America. I have argued that American racism is not, as Gunnar Myrdal concluded in his massive study *An American Dilemma*, an anomaly on our democratic landscape, a holdover from slavery that the nation both wants to cure and is capable of curing. Rather, I agree with Jennifer Hochschild's *The New American Dilemma* that racism is a critically important stabilizing factor that enables whites to bond across a wide socioeconomic chasm. Without the deflecting power of racism, masses of whites would likely wake up and revolt against the severe disadvantage they suffer in income and opportunity when compared with those whites at the top of our system.

Making the "racism is permanent" case has proved relatively easy for black people who have heard it. Whites are more resistant, running the gamut from those who are deeply troubled by my thesis but unable to refute it, to those who angrily reject the idea, charging that I am racist for even suggesting it. Even so, there is a long leap from concluding that racism is permanent to predictions that it will generate policies subjecting millions of people of color to what amounts to forced labor.

This society has always been willing to advance black interests when those interests coincide with the perceived needs of whites. Indeed, it is not too much to suggest that all positive racial policies come about in this way. For example, Lincoln, while personally finding slavery abhorrent, issued the Emancipation Proclamation only when he recognized that ending slavery would help preserve the Union; the post–Civil War amendments clearly served the political power-preserving interest of Republicans who had been victorious on the military front but wanted to insure that battles won in the field were not lost on the political scene by too quickly allowing the defeated Southern Democrats back into the halls of Congress. Even the Supreme Court's decision in *Brown v. Board of Education* illustrates the point. While depriving whites of the status and resource priorities of segregation, *Brown* provided whites in policy-making positions the benefits of economic and political advantages both at home and abroad that followed abandonment of apartheid in our national law. The *Brown* decision, as University of Iowa law professor Mary Dudziak made clear, gave America credibility in the struggle with Communist nations for the hearts and minds of emerging Third World peoples. It offered reassurance to blacks that the precepts of equality and freedom so heralded during World War II might yet be given meaning at home. And, without state-enforced segregation, it opened the way for the South to make the transition from a rural, plantation society to the modern Sunbelt, with all its potential and profit.

On the other hand, serious differences between whites are often resolved through compromises that sacrifice the rights of blacks. The pattern was set in the seventeenth century, when, as Edmund Morgan explains in *American Slavery—American Freedom*, an alliance between poor whites and plantation owners utilized the enslavement of blacks as the bridge across the broad expanse of wealth disparity.

The classic example is the Hayes-Tilden Compromise following the disputed presidential election of 1876. To avoid a threatened new civil war, the nation's political leaders effected a deal that conceded the election to the Republican, Hayes, in return for a commitment to withdraw Northern troops from the South, an action that left the fate of the newly freed blacks to their former masters.

A few decades later, when working-class whites insisted on formal segregation as the price for their continued allegiance to elite policy-makers, they were granted state-supported superior status at the expense of blacks—a support the Supreme Court ratified in 1896 with its "separate but equal" decision in *Plessy v. Ferguson*. Of course, the definitive sacrifice of black rights was made by the Constitution's Framers in 1787 when, to secure the backing of Southern representatives, they approved the Constitution with no fewer than ten provisions directly or indirectly recognizing and protecting property in slaves.

For the reasons stated earlier, after World War II segregation became a luxury the nation could no longer afford. Blatant discrimination fell out of fashion, a fact that some whites in the South learned slowly, much to the embarrassment of the rest of the country. Through the courts, Congress and the media, these Southern whites became the enemy and those peaceful blacks with their white allies became the heroes. It was a sometimes dangerous but no less glorious time for those of us involved in what we thought would be the final struggle for civil rights.

But while the Jim Crow signs came down after prolonged battles in the courts and on the streets, society quickly devised means to limit the substantive value of the pro–civil rights decisions and the new civil rights laws enacted during the 1960s. The frustrations engendered by these barriers led to the Black Power movement in the middle and late 1960s, a phenomenon that alienated some whites, and the riots in Watts and other places that turned off still more. The real disenchantment came when whites began to recognize that civil rights for blacks meant more than condemning the use of fire hoses and police dogs on peacefully protesting children in a Deep South town. It meant, as well, giving up privileges and priorities long available to whites simply because they were white.

Applying this history to the current social scene can be deeply disturbing. Black workers are a disproportionately large percentage of those "downsized" out of jobs, but whites too are victims of the current disemployment trend. From 1989 to 1993, the United States lost 1.6 million manufacturing jobs. As the business sections of the papers report almost daily, those losses continue to mount.

With good reason, millions of white Americans are fearful about their jobs, and yet there has been remarkably little criticism of corporate America for its downsizing policies. During the same period, opposition to affirmative action programs has increased. Callers and audience participants on a Phil Donahue show strongly indicated their view that antiblack feelings were a predictable reaction to affirmative action policies. Donahue, trying to ease the tension, said, tongue-in-cheek, "Yes, I know. Every white person in America has a relative who lost out on a job or promotion to a less-qualified black." To his chagrin, the audience broke into wild applause. Caught up in the myth they find comforting, they missed Donahue's effort to use humor to illustrate a truth they are determined not to see.

The fact is that we are at the end of an era when work was the society's sustaining force. We can expect serious dislocations that government—influenced as it is by those who are either profiting from or willing to maintain the economic status quo—will find it difficult to address in any effective fashion. The likely result will be a move to the political right and a growing antipathy toward this society's traditional scapegoats: black people.

Of course, those of us who are lawyers may hope that our skills will convince the courts to strike down freedom-of-employment-type laws. But historians will point out the slim reed such reliance is likely to provide.

"Well, I would hope so." Geneva was back, having entered my study as mysteriously as she had departed. "It might help," she continued, "if all law students, particularly those with civil rights inclinations, gained a thorough grounding in black history."

"Not a bad idea, Geneva," I agreed, "but the long shadow of concern cast by your Freedom of Employment Act demands a more specific response. The question is whether a legal challenge is an appropriate response given the Court's hostility to affirmative action policies over the past ten to twelve years."

"Your question answers itself, friend," Geneva replied. "Even when approving them, the Supreme Court has always been uneasy about affirmative action plans. And in the past several years that unease has turned to outright opposition for a majority of the Court, who ignore the decades of discrimination these programs were intended to remedy. The more pressing need for the Court's majority is, *We must protect the innocent.*"

"The innocent, of course," I interjected, "are those whites who might conceivably be disadvantaged by an affirmative action plan and who are not themselves guilty of overt, invidious discrimination. Given the Court's current antipathy, Geneva, how should civil rights lawyers challenge the Freedom of Employment Act?"

"The arguments should not dwell on the law's harm to blacks— that is all too obvious. Rather, they should focus on the harm it will do to the country, which is to say, to whites or many of them."

"And what harm might that be?" I asked. "It seems to take blacks out of competition for any jobs whites want, while reducing us to a permanent status of minimum wage servitude."

Geneva smiled, sadly. "The fact is, all too many blacks—and whites as well—are trying to support themselves at minimum wage levels right now, and without the room-and-board benefits the new law would provide for inducted workers. But a possibly effective argument is quite like the one used by many whites who opposed slavery. The law, by providing subsidized work for blacks and Latinos, will take the jobs of thousands of whites. This fear was crucial to the ending of slavery in the Northern states after the Revolutionary War. It also led many Midwestern and Western states to bar not only slavery but all black people as well. They were protecting white men's jobs."

"So," Geneva continued, "the argument may still work. My only concern is that if black people rely so heavily on the courts, other approaches will be drained of energies and resources. For example, if thousands of blacks declare that they will not allow themselves to be inducted or, if inducted, they will refuse to work, the plan may fail."

"There is also the chance that many blacks will die," I said. "You didn't mention it, but I am sure the new law has adequate provisions for court-martial-type proceedings for those who disobey orders, or leave their post."

"It does," Geneva said, "but the harshness of the act, its obvious hostility not only to affirmative action but to blacks and Latinos as a group, could serve as a much-needed wake-up call reminding all of us that the racial policies of the past three centuries have not really changed as we approach a new millennium."

"So, Geneva, you view your Freedom of Employment Act as something of a blessing for the victims of racial discrimination."

"Blessing? Hardly. It is a disaster, but opportunity can be found even in disaster and, if availed, could lead to events, impossible to predict, that many would hail as blessings. Slavery was certainly no blessing, but perhaps a law that forces us to face up to the fact that we are imprisoned by the history of racial subordination in America will enable us to recognize—as our enslaved forebears had no choice but to recognize—our true condition. Acknowledging where we are is the prerequisite to understanding that the history of black people in this country is less a story of success than of survival through an unending struggle that guarantees a triumph of the spirit even as we suffer defeat after defeat."

*March 27, 1995*

## Racism Has Its Privileges

*Roger Wilkins*

The storm that has been gathering over affirmative action for the past few years has burst. Two conservative California professors are leading a drive to place an initiative on the state ballot to 1996 that will ask Californians to vote affirmative action up or down. Since the state is beloved in political circles for its electoral votes, advance talk of the initiative has put the issue high on the national agenda. Three Republican presidential contenders—Bob Dole, Phil Gramm and Lamar Alexander—have already begun taking shots at various equal opportunity programs. Congressional review of the Clinton Administration's enforcement of these programs has begun. The President has started his own review, promising adherence to principles of nondiscrimination and full opportunity while asserting the need to prune those programs that are unfair or malfunctioning.

It is almost an article of political faith that one of the major influences in last November's election was the backlash against affirmative action among "angry white men," who are convinced it has stacked the deck against them. Their attitudes are shaped and their anger heightened by unquestioned and virtually uncheckable anecdotes about victimized whites flooding the culture. For example, *Washington Post* columnist Richard Cohen recently began what purported to be a serious analysis and attack on affirmative action by recounting that he had once missed out on a job someplace because they "needed a woman."

Well, I have an anecdote too, and it, together with Cohen's, offers some important insights about the debate that has flared recently around the issues of race, gender and justice. Some years ago, after watching me teach as a visiting professor for two semesters, members of the history department at George Mason University invited me to compete for a full professorship and endowed chair. Mason, like other institutions in Virginia's higher education system, was under a court order to desegregate. I went through the appropriate application and review process and, in due course, was appointed. A few years later, not long after I had been honored as one of the university's distinguished professors, I was shown an article by a white historian asserting that he had been a candidate for that chair but that at the last moment the job had been whisked away and handed to an unqualified black. I checked the story and discovered that this fellow had, in fact, applied but had not even passed the first threshold. But his "reverse discrimination" story is out there polluting the atmosphere in which this debate is taking place.

Affirmative action, as I understand it, was not designed to punish anyone; it was, rather—as a result of a clear-eyed look at how America actually works—an attempt to enlarge opportunity for *everybody*. As amply documented in the 1968 Kerner Commission report on racial disorders, when left to their own devices, American institutions in such areas as college admissions, hiring decisions and loan approvals had been making choices that discriminated against blacks. That discrimination, which flowed from doing what came naturally, hurt more than blacks: It hurt the entire nation, as the riots of the late 1960s demonstrated. Though the Kerner report focused on blacks, similar findings could have been made about other minorities and women.

Affirmative action required institutions to develop plans enabling them to go beyond business as usual and search for qualified people in places where they did not ordinarily conduct their searches or their business. Affirmative action programs generally require some proof that there has been a good-faith effort to follow the plan and numerical guidelines against which to judge the sincerity and the success of the effort. The idea of affirmative action is *not* to force people into positions for which they are unqualified but to encourage institutions to develop realistic criteria for the enterprise at hand and then to find a reasonably diverse mix of people qualified to be engaged in it. Without the requirements calling for plans, good-faith efforts and the setting of broad numerical goals, many institutions would do what they had always done: assert that they had looked but "couldn't find anyone qualified," and then go out and hire the white man they wanted to hire in the first place.

Affirmative action has done wonderful things for the United States by enlarging opportunity and developing and utilizing a far broader array of the skills available in the American population than in the past. It has not outlived its usefulness. It was never designed to be a program to eliminate poverty. It has not always been used wisely, and some of its permutations do have to be reconsidered, refined or, in some cases, abandoned. It is not a quota program, and those cases where rigid numbers are used (except under a court or administrative order after a specific finding of discrimination) are a bastardization of an otherwise highly beneficial set of public policies.

President Clinton is right to review what is being done under present laws and to express a willingness to eliminate activities that either don't work or are unfair. Any program that has been in place for thirty years should be reviewed. Getting rid of what doesn't work is both good government and good politics. Gross abuses of affirmative action provide ammunition for its opponents and undercut the moral authority of the entire effort. But the President should retain— and strengthen where required—those programs necessary to enlarge social justice.

What makes the affirmative action issue so difficult is that it engages blacks and whites exactly at those points where they differ the most. There are some areas, such as rooting for the local football team, where their experiences and views are virtually identical. There are others—sometimes including work and school—where their experiences and views both overlap and diverge. And finally, there are areas such as affirmative action and inextricably related notions about the presence of racism in society where the divergences draw out almost all the points of difference between the races.

## This Land Is My Land

Blacks and whites experience America very differently. Though we often inhabit the same space, we operate in very disparate psychic spheres.

Whites have an easy sense of ownership of the country; they feel they are entitled to receive all that is best in it. Many of them believe that their country—though it may have some faults—is superior to all others and that, as Americans, they are superior as well. Many of them think of this as a white country and some of them even experience it that way. They think of it as a land of opportunity—a good place with a lot of good people in it. Some suspect (others *know*) that the presence of blacks messes everything up.

To blacks there's nothing very easy about life in America, and any sense of ownership comes hard because we encounter so much resistance in making our way through the ordinary occurrences of life. And I'm not even talking here about overt acts of discrimination but simply about the way whites intrude on and disturb our psychic space without even thinking about it.

A telling example of this was given to me by a black college student in Oklahoma. He said whites give him looks that say: "What are *you* doing here?"

"When do they give you that look?" I asked.

"Every time I walk in a door," he replied.

When he said that, every black person in the room nodded and smiled in a way that indicated recognition based on thousands of such moments in their own lives.

For most blacks, America is either a land of denied opportunity or one in which the opportunities are still grudgingly extended and extremely limited. For some—that one-third who are mired in poverty, many of them isolated in dangerous ghettos—America is a land of desperadoes and desperation. In places where whites see a lot of idealism, blacks see, at best, idealism mixed heavily with hypocrisy. Blacks accept America's greatness, but are unable to ignore ugly warts that many whites seem to need not to see. I am reminded here of James Baldwin's searing observation from *The Fire Next Time*:

> The American Negro has the great advantage of having never believed that collection of myths to which white Americans cling: that their ancestors were all freedom-loving heroes, that they were born in the greatest country the world has ever seen, or that Americans are invincible in battle and wise in peace, that Americans have always dealt honorably with Mexicans and Indians and all other neighbors or inferiors, that American men are the world's most direct and virile, that American women are pure.

It goes without saying, then, that blacks and whites remember America differently. The past is hugely important since we argue a lot about who we are on the basis of who we think we have been, and we derive much of our sense of the future from how we think we've done in the past. In a nation in which few people know much history these are perilous arguments, because in such a vacuum, people tend to weave historical fables tailored to their political or psychic needs.

Blacks are still recovering the story of their role in America, which so many white historians simply ignored or told in ways that made black people ashamed. But in a culture that batters us, learning the real history is vital in helping blacks feel fully human. It also helps us understand just how deeply American we are, how richly we have given, how much has been taken from us and how much has yet to be restored. Supporters of affirmative action believe that broad and deep damage has been done to American culture by racism and sexism over the whole course of American history and that they are still powerful forces today. We believe that minorities and women are still disadvantaged in our highly competitive society and that affirmative action is absolutely necessary to level the playing field.

Not all white Americans oppose this view and not all black Americans support it. There are a substantial number of whites in this country who have been able to escape our racist and sexist past and to enter fully into the quest for equal justice. There are other white

Americans who are not racists but who more or less passively accept the powerful suggestions coming at them from all points in the culture that whites are entitled to privilege and to freedom from competition with blacks. And then there are racists who just don't like blacks or who actively despise us. There are still others who may or may not feel deep antipathy, but who know how to manipulate racism and white anxiety for their own ends. Virtually all the people in the last category oppose affirmative action and some of them make a practice of preying upon those in the second category who are not paying attention or who, like the *Post*'s Richard Cohen, are simply confused.

**The Politics of Denial**

One of these political predators is Senate majority leader Bob Dole. In his offhandedly lethal way Dole delivered a benediction of "let me now forgive us" on *Meet the Press* recently. After crediting affirmative action for the 62 percent of the white male vote garnered by the Republicans, he remarked that slavery was "before we were born" and wondered whether future generations ought to have to continue "paying a price" for those ancient wrongs.

Such a view holds that whatever racial problems we once may have had have been solved over the course of the past thirty years and that most of our current racial friction is caused by racial and gender preferences that almost invariably work to displace some "qualified" white male. Words and phrases like "punish" or "preference" or "reverse discrimination" or "quota" are dropped into the discourse to buttress this view, as are those anecdotes about injustice to whites. Proponents of affirmative action see these arguments as disingenuous but ingenious because they reduce serious and complex social, political, economic, historical and psychological issues to bumper-sticker slogans designed to elicit Pavlovian responses.

The fact is that the successful public relations assault on affirmative action flows on a river of racism that is as broad, powerful and American as the Mississippi. And, like the Mississippi, racism can be violent and deadly and is a permanent feature of American life. But while nobody who is sane denies the reality of the Mississippi, millions of Americans who are deemed sane—some of whom are powerful and some even thought wise—deny, wholly or in part, that racism exists.

It is critical to understand the workings of denial in this debate because it is used to obliterate the facts that created the need for the remedy in the first place. One of the best examples of denial was provided recently by the nation's most famous former history professor, House Speaker Newt Gingrich. According to *The Washington Post*, "Gingrich dismissed the argument that the beneficiaries of affirmative action, commonly African Americans, have been subjected to discrimination over a period of centuries. 'That is true of virtually every American,' Gingrich said, noting that the Irish were discriminated against by the English, for example."

That is breathtaking stuff coming from somebody who should know that blacks have been on this North American continent for 375 years and that for 245 the country permitted slavery. Gingrich should also know that for the next hundred years we had legalized subordination of blacks, under a suffocating blanket of condescension and frequently enforced by nightriding terrorists. We've had only thirty years of something else.

That something else is a nation trying to lift its ideals out of a thick, often impenetrable slough of racism. Racism is a hard word for what over the centuries became second nature in America—preferences across the board for white men and, following in their wake, white women. Many of these men seem to feel that it is un-American to ask them to share anything with blacks—particularly their work, their neighborhoods or "their" women. To protect these things—apparently essential to their identity—they engage in all forms of denial. For a historian to assert that "virtually every American" shares the history I have just outlined comes very close to lying.

Denial of racism is much like the denials that accompany addictions to alcohol, drugs or gambling. It is probably not stretching the analogy too much to suggest that many racist whites are so addicted to their unwarranted privileges and so threatened by the prospect of losing them that all kinds of defenses become acceptable, including insistent distortions of reality in the form of hypocrisy, lying or the most outrageous political demagogy.

### 'Those People' Don't Deserve Help

The demagogues have reverted to a new version of quite an old trick. Before the 1950s, whites who were busy denying that the nation was unfair to blacks would simply assert that we didn't deserve equal treatment because we were *inferior*. These days it is not permissible in most public circles to say that blacks are inferior, but it is perfectly acceptable to target the *behavior* of blacks, specifically poor blacks. The argument then follows a fairly predictable line: The behavior of poor blacks requires a severe rethinking of national social policy, it is said. Advantaged blacks really don't need affirmative action anymore, and when they are the objects of such programs, some qualified white person (unqualified white people don't show up in these arguments) is (as Dole might put it) "punished." While it is possible that color-blind affirmative action programs benefiting all disadvantaged Americans are needed, those (i.e., blacks) whose behavior is so distressing must be punished by restricting welfare, shriveling the safety net and expanding the prison opportunity. All of that would presumably give us, in William Bennett's words, "what we want—a color-blind society," for which the white American psyche is presumably fully prepared.

There are at least three layers of unreality in these precepts. The first is that the United States is not now and probably never will be a color-blind society. It is the most color-conscious society on earth. Over the course of 375 years, whites have given blacks absolutely no reason to believe that they can behave in a color-blind manner. In many areas of our lives—particularly in employment, housing and education—affirmative action is required to counter deeply ingrained racist patterns of behavior.

Second, while I don't hold the view that all blacks who behave badly are blameless victims of a brutal system, I do believe that many poor blacks have, indeed, been brutalized by our culture, and I know of no blacks, rich or poor, who haven't been hurt in some measure by the racism in this country. The current mood (and, in some cases like the Speaker's, the cultivated ignorance) completely ignores the fact that some blacks never escaped the straight line of oppression that ran from slavery through the semislavery of sharecropping to the late mid-century migration from Southern farms into isolated pockets of urban poverty. Their families have always been excluded, poor and without skills, and so they were utterly defenseless when the enormous American economic dislocations that began in the mid-1970s slammed into their communities, followed closely by deadly waves of crack cocaine. One would think that the double-digit unemployment suffered consistently over the past two decades by blacks who were *looking for work* would be a permanent feature of the discussions about race, responsibility, welfare and rights.

But a discussion of the huge numbers of black workers who are becoming economically redundant would raise difficult questions about the efficiency of the economy at a time when millions of white men feel insecure. Any honest appraisal of unemployment would reveal that millions of low-skilled white men were being severely damaged by corporate and Federal Reserve decisions; it might also refocus the anger of those whites in the middle ranks whose careers have been shattered by the corporate downsizing fad.

But people's attention is kept trained on the behavior of some poor blacks by politicians and television news shows, reinforcing the stereotypes of blacks as dangerous, as threats, as unqualified. Frightened whites direct their rage at pushy blacks rather than at the corporations that export manufacturing operations to low-wage countries, or at the Federal Reserve, which imposes interest rate hikes that slow down the economy.

**Who Benefits? We All Do**
There is one final denial that blankets all the rest. It is that only society's "victims"—blacks, other minorities and women (who should, for God's sake, renounce their victimological outlooks)—have been injured by white male supremacy. Viewed in this light, affirmative action remedies are a kind of zero-sum game in which only the "victims" benefit. But racist and sexist whites who are not able to accept the full humanity of other people are themselves badly damaged—

morally stunted—people. The principal product of a racist and sexist society is damaged people and institutions—victims and victimizers alike. Journalism and education, two enterprises with which I am familiar, provide two good examples.

Journalistic institutions often view the nation through a lens that bends reality to support white privilege. A recent issue of *U.S. News & World Report* introduced a package of articles on these issues with a question on its cover: "Does affirmative action mean NO WHITE MEN NEED APPLY?" The words "No white men need apply" were printed in red against a white background and were at least four times larger than the other words in the question. Inside, the lead story was illustrated by a painting that carries out the cover theme, with a wan white man separated from the opportunity ladders eagerly being scaled by women and dark men. And the story yielded up the following sentence: "Affirmative action poses a conflict between two cherished American principles: the belief that all Americans deserve equal opportunities and the idea that hard work and merit, not race or religion or gender or birthright, should determine who prospers and who does not."

Whoever wrote that sentence was in the thrall of one of the myths that Baldwin was talking about. The sentence suggests—as many people do when talking about affirmative action—that America is a meritocratic society. But what kind of meritocracy excludes women and blacks and other minorities from all meaningful competition? And even in the competition among white men, money, family and connections often count for much more than merit, test results (for whatever they're worth) and hard work.

The *U.S. News* story perpetuates and strengthens the view that many of my white students absorb from their parents: that white men now have few chances in this society. The fact is that white men still control virtually everything in America except the wealth held by widows. According to the Urban Institute, 53 percent of black men aged 25–34 are either unemployed or earn too little to lift a family of four from poverty.

Educational institutions that don't teach accurately about why America looks the way it does and why the distribution of winners and losers is as it is also injure our society. Here is another anecdote.

A warm, brilliant young white male student of mine came in just before he was to graduate and said that my course in race, law and culture, which he had just finished, had been the most valuable and the most disturbing he had ever taken. I asked how it had been disturbing.

"I learned that my two heroes are racists," he said.

"Who are your heroes and how are they racists?" I asked. "My mom and dad," he said. "After thinking about what I was learning, I understood that they had spent all my life making me into the same kind of racists they were."

Affirmative action had brought me together with him when he was 22. Affirmative action puts people together in ways that make that kind of revelation possible. Nobody is a loser when that happens. The country gains.

And that, in the end, is the case for affirmative action. The arguments supporting it should be made on the basis of its broad contributions to the entire American community. It is insufficient to vilify white males and to skewer them as the whiners that journalism of the kind practiced by *U.S. News* invites us to do. These are people who, from the beginning of the Republic, have been taught that skin color is destiny and that whiteness is to be revered. Listen to Jefferson, writing in the year the Constitution was drafted:

The first difference that strikes us is that of colour. . . . And is the difference of no importance? Is it not the foundation of a greater or less share of beauty in the two races? Are not the fine mixtures of red and white . . . in the one, preferable to that eternal monotony, which reigns in the countenances, that immoveable veil of black which covers all the emotions of the other race? Add to these, flowing hair, a more elegant symmetry of form, their own judgment in favor of the whites, declared by their preference for them, as uniformly as is the preference of the Oranootan for the black women over those of his own species. The circumstance of superior beauty, is thought worthy attention in the propagation of our horses, dogs, and other domestic animals; why not in that of man?

• • •

In a society so conceived and so dedicated, it is understandable that white males would take their preferences as a matter of natural right and consider any alteration of that a primal offense. But a nation that operates in that way abandons its soul and its economic strength, and will remain mired in ugliness and moral squalor because so many people are excluded from the possibility of decent lives and from forming any sense of community with the rest of society.

Seen only as a corrective for ancient wrongs, affirmative action may be dismissed by the likes of Gingrich, Gramm and Dole, just as attempts to federalize decent treatment of the freed slaves were dismissed after Reconstruction more than a century ago. Then, striking down the Civil Rights Act of 1875, Justice Joseph Bradley wrote of blacks that "there must be some stage in the progress of his elevation when he takes the rank of a mere citizen, and ceases to be the special favorite of the laws, and when his rights, as a citizen or a man, are to be protected in the ordinary modes by which other men's rights are protected."

But white skin has made some citizens—particularly white males—*the special favorites of the culture.* It may be that we will need affirmative action until most white males are really ready for a color-blind society—that is, when they are ready to assume "the rank of a mere citizen." As a nation we took a hard look at that special favoritism thirty years ago. Though the centuries of cultural preference enjoyed by white males still overwhelmingly skew power and wealth their way, we have in fact achieved a more meritocratic society as a result of affirmative action than we have ever previously enjoyed in this country.

If we want to continue making things better in this society, we'd better figure out ways to protect and defend affirmative action against the confused, the frightened, the manipulators and, yes, the liars in politics, journalism, education and wherever else they may be found. In the name of longstanding American prejudice and myths and in the service of their own narrow interests, power-lusts or blindness, they are truly victimizing the rest of us, perverting the ideals they claim to stand for and destroying the nation they pretend to serve.

*August 10/17, 1998*

## Performance and Reality
### Race, Sports and the Modern World

*Gerald Early*

Last year's celebration of the fiftieth anniversary of Jackie Robinson's breaking the color line in major league baseball was one of the most pronounced and prolonged ever held in the history of our Republic in memory of a black man or of an athlete. It seems nearly obvious that, on one level, our preoccupation was not so much with Robinson him- self—previous milestone anniversaries of his starting at first base for the Brooklyn Dodgers in April 1947 produced little fanfare—as it was with ourselves and our own dilemma about race, a problem that strikes us simultaneously as being intractable and "progressing" toward resolution; as a chronic, inevitably fatal disease and as a test of national character that we will, finally, pass.

Robinson was the man white society could not defeat in the short term, though his untimely death at age 53 convinced many that the stress of the battle defeated him in the long run. In this respect, Robinson did become something of an uneasy elegiac symbol of race relations, satisfying everyone's psychic needs: blacks, with a redemp- tive black hero who did not sell out and in whose personal tragedy was a corporate triumph over racism; whites, with a black hero who showed assimilation to be a triumphant act. For each group, it was important that he was a hero for the other. All this was easier to accomplish because Robinson played baseball, a "pastoral" sport of innocence and triumphalism in the American mind, a sport of epic romanticism, a sport whose golden age is always associated with childhood. In the end, Robinson as tragic hero represented, paradox- ically, depending on the faction, how far we have come and how much more needs to be done.

As a nation, I think we needed the evocation of Jackie Robinson to save us from the nihilistic fires of race: from the trials of O. J. Simpson (the failed black athletic hero who seems nothing more than a symbol of self-centered consumption), from the Rodney King trial and subsequent riot in Los Angeles and, most significant, from the turmoil over affirmative action, an issue not only about *how* blacks are to achieve a place in American society but about the perennial existential question: *Can* black people have a rightful place of dignity in our realm, or is the stigma of race to taint everything they do and desire? We know that some of the most admired celebrities in the United States today—in many instances, excessively so by some whites—are black athletes. Michael Jordan, the most admired athlete in modern history, is a $10 billion industry, we are told, beloved all over the world. But what does Michael Jordan want except what most insecure, upwardly bound Americans want? More of what he already has to assure himself that he does, indeed, have what he wants. Michael Jordan is not simply a brilliant athlete, the personification of an unstoppable will, but, like all figures in popular culture, a complex, charismatic representation of desire, his own and ours.

Perhaps we reached back for Jackie Robinson last year (just as we reached back for an ailing Muhammad Ali, the boastful athlete as expiatory dissident, the year before at the Olympics) because of our need for an athlete who transcends his self-absorbed prowess and quest for championships, or whose self-absorption and quest for titles meant something deeper politically and socially, told us something a bit more important about ourselves as a racially divided, racially stricken nation. A baseball strike in 1994–95 that canceled the World Series, gambling scandals in college basketball, ceaseless recruiting violations with student athletes, rape and drug cases involving athletes, the increasing commercialization of sports resulting in more tax concessions to team owners and ever-more-expensive stadiums, the wild inflation of salaries, prize money and endorsement fees for the most elite athletes—all this has led to a general dissatisfaction with sports or at least to some legitimate uneasiness about them, as many people see sports, amateur and professional, more and more as a depraved enterprise, as a Babylon of greed, dishonesty and hypocrisy, or as an industry out to rob the public blind. At what better moment to resurrect Jackie Robinson, a man who played for the competition and the glory, for the love of the game and the honor of his profession, and as a tribute to the dignity and pride of his race in what many of us perceive, wrongly, to have been a simpler, less commercial time?

What, indeed, is the place of black people in our realm? Perhaps, at this point in history, we are all, black and white, as mystified by that question as we were at the end of the Civil War when faced with the prospect that slave and free must live together as equal citizens, or must try to. For the question has always signified that affirmative action—a public policy for the unconditional inclusion of the African-American that has existed, with all its good and failed intentions, in the air of American racial reform since black people were officially freed, even, indeed, in the age of abolition with voices such as Lydia Maria Child and Frederick Douglass—is about the making of an African into an American and the meaning of that act for our democracy's ability to absorb all. We were struck by Jackie Robinson's story last year because it was as profound, as mythic, as any European immigrant's story about how Americans are made. We Americans seem to have blundered about in our history with two clumsy contrivances strapped to our backs, unreconciled and weighty: our democratic traditions and race. What makes Robinson so significant is that he seemed to have found a way to balance this baggage in the place that is so much the stuff of our dreams: the level playing field of top-flight competitive athletics. "Athletics," stated Robinson in his first autobiography, *Jackie Robinson: My Own Story* (ghostwritten by black sportswriter Wendell Smith), "both school and professional, come nearer to offering an American Negro equality of opportunity than does any other field of social and economic activity." It is not so much that this is true as that Robinson believed it, and that most Americans today, black and white, still do or still want to. This is one of the important aspects of modern sports in a democratic society that saves us from being totally cynical about them. Sports are the ultimate meritocracy. Might it be said that sports are what all other professional activities and business endeavors, all leisure pursuits and hobbies in our society aspire to be?

If nothing else, Robinson, an unambiguous athletic hero for both races and symbol of sacrifice on the altar of racism, is our most magnificent case of affirmative action. He entered a lily-white industry amid cries that he was unqualified (not entirely unjustified, as Robinson had had only one year of professional experience in the Negro Leagues, although, on the other hand, he was one of the most gifted athletes of his generation), and he succeeded, *on merit*, beyond anyone's wildest hope. And here the sports metaphor is a perfectly literal expression of the traditional democratic belief of that day: If given the chance, anyone can make it on his ability, with no remedial aid or special compensation, on a level playing field. Here was the fulfillment of our American Creed, to use Gunnar Myrdal's term (*An American Dilemma* had appeared only a year before Robinson was signed by the Dodgers), of fair play and equal opportunity. Here was our democratic orthodoxy of color-blind competition realized. Here was an instance where neither the principle nor its application could be impugned. Robinson was proof, just as heavyweight champion Joe Louis and Olympic track star Jesse Owens had been during the Depression, that sports helped vanquish the stigma of race.

In this instance, sports are extraordinarily useful because their values can endorse any political ideology. It must be remembered that the British had used sports—and modern sports are virtually their invention—as a colonial and missionary tool, not always with evil intentions but almost always with hegemonic ones. Sports had also been used by their subjects as a tool of liberation, as anti-hegemonic, as they learned to beat the British at their own games. "To win was to be human," said African scholar Manthia Diawara recently, and for the colonized and the oppressed, sports meant just that, in the same way as for the British, to win was to be British. Sports were meant to preserve and symbolize the hegemony of the colonizer even as they inspired the revolutionary spirit of the oppressed. Sports have been revered by fascists and communists, by free-marketers and filibusters. They have also been, paradoxically, reviled by all those political factions. Sports may be among the most powerful human expressions in all history. So why could sports not serve the United States ideologically in whatever way people decided to define democratic values during this, the American Century, when we became the most powerful purveyors of sports in all history?

Both the left and the right have used Jackie Robinson for their own ends. The left, suspicious of popular culture as a set of cheap commercial distractions constructed by the ruling class of post-industrial society to delude the masses, sees Robinson as a racial martyr, a working-class member of an oppressed minority who challenged the white hegemony as symbolized by sports as a political reification of superior, privileged expertise; the right, suspicious of popular culture as an expression of the rule of the infantile taste of the masses, sees him as a challenge to the idea of restricting talent pools and restricting markets to serve a dubious privilege. For the conservative today, Robinson is the *classic, fixed* example of affirmative action properly applied as the extension of opportunity to all, regardless of race, class, gender or outcome. For the liberal, Robinson is an example of the *process* of affirmative action as the erosion of white male hegemony, where outcome is the very point of the exercise. For the liberal, affirmative action is about the redistribution of power. For the conservative, it is about releasing deserving talent. This seems little more than the standard difference in views between the conservative and the liberal about the meaning of democratic values and social reform. For the conservative, the story of Robinson and affirmative action is about conformity: Robinson, as symbolic Negro, *joined* the mainstream. For the liberal, the story of Robinson and affirmative action is about resistance: Robinson, as symbolic Negro, *changed* the mainstream. The conservative does not want affirmative action to disturb what Lothrop Stoddard called "the iron law of inequality." The liberal wants affirmative action to create complete equality, as all inequality is structural and environmental. (Proof of how much Robinson figured in the affirmative action debate can be found in Steve Sailer's "How Jackie Robinson Desegregated America," a cover story in the April 8, 1996, *National Review*, and in Anthony Pratkanis and Marlene Turner's liberal article, "Nine Principles of Successful Affirmative Action: Mr. Branch Rickey, Mr. Jackie Robinson, and the Integration of Baseball," in the Fall 1994 issue of *Nine: A Journal of Baseball History and Social Policy Perspectives*.) Whoever may be right in this regard, it can be said that inasmuch as either side endorsed the idea, both were wrong about sports eliminating the stigma of race. Over the years since Robinson's arrival, sports have, in many respects, intensified race and racialist thinking or, more precisely, anxiety about race and racialist thinking.

Race is not merely a system of categorizations of privileged or discredited abilities but rather a system of conflicting abstractions about what it means to be human. Sports are not a material realization of the ideal that those who succeed deserve to succeed; they are a paradox of play as work, of highly competitive, highly pressurized work as a form of romanticized play, a system of rules and regulations that govern both a real and a symbolic activity that suggests, in the stunning complexity of its performance, both conformity and revolt. Our mistake about race is assuming that it is largely an expression of irrationality when it is, in fact, to borrow G. K. Chesterton's phrase, "nearly reasonable, but not quite." Our mistake about sports is assuming that they are largely minor consequences of our two great American gifts: marketing and technology. Their pervasiveness and their image, their evocation of desire and transcendence, are the result of marketing. Their elaborate modalities of engineering—from the conditioning of the athletes to the construction of the arenas to the fabrication of the tools and machines athletes use and the apparel they wear—are the result of our technology. But modern sports, although extraordinary expressions of marketing and technology, are far deeper, far more atavistic, than either. Perhaps sports, in some ways, are as atavistic as race.

**The Whiteness of the White Athlete**
In a December 8, 1997, *Sports Illustrated* article, "Whatever Happened to the White Athlete?" S. L. Price writes about the dominant presence of black athletes in professional basketball (80 percent black), professional football (67 percent black) and track and field (93 percent of gold medalists are black). He also argues that while African-Americans make up only 17 percent of major league baseball players, "[during] the past 25 years, blacks have been a disproportionate

offensive force, winning 41 percent of the Most Valuable Player awards." (And the number of blacks in baseball does not include the black Latinos, for whom baseball is more popular than it is with American blacks.) Blacks also dominate boxing, a sport not dealt with in the article. "Whites have in some respects become sports' second-class citizens," writes Price. "In a surreal inversion of Robinson's era, white athletes are frequently the ones now tagged by the stereotypes of skin color." He concludes by suggesting that white sprinter Kevin Little, in competition, can feel "the slightest hint—and it is not more than a hint—of what Jackie Robinson felt 50 years ago." It is more than a little ludicrous to suggest that white athletes today even remotely, even as a hint, are experiencing something like what Robinson experienced. White athletes, even when they play sports dominated by blacks, are still entering an industry not only controlled by whites in every phase of authority and operation but also largely sustained by white audiences. When Jackie Robinson departed the Negro Leagues at the end of 1945, he left a sports structure that was largely regulated, managed and patronized by blacks, inasmuch as blacks could ever, with the resources available to them in the 1920s, '30s and '40s, profitably and proficiently run a sports league. Robinson's complaints about the Negro Leagues—the incessant barnstorming, the bad accommodations, the poor umpiring, the inadequate spring training—were not only similar to white criticism of the Negro Leagues but they mirrored the criticism that blacks tended to levy against their own organizations and organizational skills. As Sol White makes clear in his seminal 1907 *History of Colored Base Ball*, black people continued to play baseball after they were banned by white professional leagues to show to themselves and to the world that they were capable of *organizing* themselves into teams and leagues. When Robinson left the Kansas City Monarchs, he entered a completely white world, much akin to the world he operated in as a star athlete at UCLA. It was, in part, because Robinson was used to the white world of sports from his college days that Branch Rickey selected him to become the first black man to play major league baseball. Today, when white athletes enter sports dominated by blacks, they do not enter a black *organization* but something akin to a mink-lined black ghetto. (My use of the word "ghetto" here is not meant to suggest anything about oppression, political or otherwise.) Although blacks dominate the most popular team sports, they still make up only 9 percent of all people in the United States who make a living or try to make a living as athletes, less than their percentage in the general population.

What I find most curious about Price's article is that he gives no plausible reason for why blacks dominate these particular sports. He quotes various informants to the effect that blacks must work harder than whites at sports. "Inner-city kids," William Ellerbee, basketball coach at Simon Gratz High in Philadelphia, says, "look at basketball as a matter of life or death." In a similar article on the black makeup of the NBA in the *Washington Post* last year, Jon Barry, a white player for the Atlanta Hawks, offers: "Maybe the suburban types or the white people have more things to do." Much of this is doubtless true. Traditionally, from the early days of professional baseball in the mid-nineteenth century and of professional boxing in Regency England, sports were seen by the men and boys of the poor and working classes as a way out of poverty or at least out of the normally backbreaking, low-paying work the poor male was offered. And certainly (though some black intellectuals may argue the point, feeling it suggests that black cultural life is impoverished) there probably is more to do or more available to amuse and enlighten in a middle-class suburb than in an inner-city neighborhood, even if it is also true that many whites who live in the suburbs are insufferably provincial and philistine.

Nonetheless, these explanations do not quite satisfy. Ultimately, the discussion in both articles comes down to genetics. There is nothing wrong with thinking about genetic variations. After all, what does the difference in human beings mean and what is its source? Still, if, for instance, Jews dominated football and basketball (as they once did boxing), would there be such a fixation to explain it genetically? The fact of the matter is that, historically, blacks have been a genetic wonder, monstrosity or aberration to whites, and they are still burdened by this implicit sense that they are not quite "normal." From the mid-nineteenth century—with its racist intellectuals like Samuel

Cartwright (a Southern medical doctor whose use of minstrel-style jargon, "Dysesthaesia Ethiopica," to describe black people as having thick minds and insensitive bodies is similar to the talk of today's racist geneticists about "fast-twitch" muscles) and Samuel Morton (whose *Crania Americana* tried to classify races by skull size), Louis Agassiz, Arthur de Gobineau and Josiah Nott (who with George Gliddon produced the extremely popular *Types of Mankind* in 1854, which argued that races had been created as separate species)—to Charles Murray and Richard Hermstein's most recent defense of intelligence quotients to explain economic and status differences among racial and ethnic groups in *The Bell Curve*, blacks have been subjected to a great deal of scientific or so-called scientific scrutiny, much of it misguided if not outright malicious, and all of it to justify the political and economic hegemony of whites. For instance, Lothrop Stoddard, in *The Revolt Against Civilization* (1922), a book nearly identical in some of its themes and polemics to *The Bell Curve*, creates a being called the Under-Man, a barbarian unfit for civilization. (Perhaps this is why some black intellectuals loathe the term "underclass.") "The rarity of mental as compared with physical superiority in the human species is seen on every hand," Stoddard writes. "Existing savage and barbaric races of a demonstrably low average level of intelligence, like the negroes [*sic*], are physically vigorous, in fact, possess an animal vitality apparently greater than that of the intellectually higher races." There is no escaping the doctrine that for blacks to be physically superior biologically, they must be inferior intellectually and, thus, inferior as a group, Under-People.

But even if it were true that blacks were athletically superior to whites, why then would they not dominate all sports instead of just a handful? There might be a more plainly structural explanation for black dominance in certain sports. This is not to say that genes may have nothing to do with it but only to say that, at this point, genetic arguments have been far from persuasive and, in their implications, more than a little pernicious.

It is easy enough to explain black dominance in boxing. It is the Western sport that has the longest history of black participation, so there is tradition. Moreover, it is a sport that has always attracted poor and marginalized men. Black men have persistently made up a disproportionate share of the poor and the marginalized. Finally, instruction is within easy reach; most boxing gyms are located in poor neighborhoods, where a premium is placed on being able to fight well. Male fighting is a useful skill in a cruel, frontierlike world that values physical toughness, where insult is not casually tolerated and honor is a highly sensitive point.

Black dominance in football and basketball is not simply related to getting out of the ghetto through hard work or to lack of other amusements but to the institution most readily available to blacks in the inner city that enables them to use athletics to get out. Ironically, that institution is the same one that fails more often than it should in fitting them for other professions: namely, school. As William Washington, the father of a black tennis family, perceptively pointed out in an article last year in the *New York Times* discussing the rise of tennis star Venus Williams: "Tennis, unlike baseball, basketball or football, is not a team sport. It is a family sport. Your immediate family is your primary supporting cast, not your teammates or the players in the locker room. . . . The experiences [of alienation and racism] start soon after you realize that if you play this game, you must leave your neighborhood and join the country club bunch. You don't belong to that group, and they let you know it in a variety of ways, so you go in, compete and leave." In short, because their families generally lack the resources and connections, indeed, because, as scholars such as V. P. Franklin have pointed out, black families cannot provide their members the cultural capital that white and Asian families can, blacks are at a disadvantage to compete in sports where school is not crucial in providing instruction and serving as an organizational setting for competition. When it comes to football and basketball, however, where school is essential to have a career, not only are these sports played at even the poorest black high schools, they are also the dominant college sports. If baseball were a more dominant college sport and if there were no minor leagues where a player had to toil for several years before, maybe, getting a crack at the major leagues, then I think baseball would attract more young black men. Because baseball, historically, was not a game that was invented by a school or became deeply associated with schools or education, blacks could learn it, during the days when they were banned from competition with white professionals, only by forming their own leagues. Sports, whatever one might think of their worth as activities, are extremely important in understanding black people's relationship to secular institutions and secular, non-protest organizing: the school, both black and white; the independent, nonprofessional or semiprofessional league; and the barnstorming, independent team, set up by both whites and blacks.

Given that blacks are overrepresented in the most popular sports and that young black men are more likely than young white men to consider athletics as a career, there has been much commentary about whether sports are bad for blacks. The March 24, 1997, issue of *U.S. News & World Report* ran a cover story titled "Are Pro Sports Bad for Black Youth?" In February of that year Germanic languages scholar John Hoberman published *Darwin's Athletes: How Sport Has Damaged Black America and Preserved the Myth of Race*, to much bitter controversy. *The Journal of African American Men*, a new academic journal, not only published a special double issue on black men and sports (Fall 1996/Winter 1997) but featured an article in its Winter 1995/96 number titled "The Black Student Athlete: The Colonized Black Body," by Billy Hawkins. While there are great distinctions to be made among these works, there is an argument about sports as damaging for blacks that can be abstracted that tends either toward a radical left position on sports or, in Hawkins's case, toward a militant cultural nationalism with Marxist implications.

First, Hoberman and Hawkins make the analogy that sports are a form of slavery or blatant political and economic oppression. Superficially, this argument is made by discussing the rhetoric of team sports (a player is the "property" of his team, or, in boxing, of his manager; he can be traded or "sold" to another team). Since most relationships in popular culture industries are described in this way—Hollywood studios have "properties," have sold and swapped actors, especially in the old days of studio ascendancy, and the like—usually what critics who make this point are aiming at is a thorough denunciation of popular culture as a form of "exploitation" and "degradation." The leftist critic condemns sports as a fraudulent expression of the heroic and the skilled in capitalist culture. The cultural nationalist critic condemns sports as an explicit expression of the grasping greed of white capitalist culture to subjugate people as raw resources.

On a more sophisticated level, the slavery analogy is used to describe sports structurally: the way audiences are lured to sports as a false spectacle, and the way players are controlled mentally and physically by white male authority, their lack of access to the free-market worth of their labor. (This latter point is made particularly about college players, since the breaking of the reserve clause in baseball, not by court decision but by union action, has so radically changed the status and so wildly inflated the salaries of many professional team players, regardless of sport.) Probably the most influential commentator to make this analogy of sport to slavery was Harry Edwards in his 1969 book, *The Revolt of the Black Athlete.* Richard Lapchick in his 1984 book, *Broken Promises: Racism in American Sports*, extends Edwards's premises. Edwards is the only black writer on sports that Hoberman admires. And Edwards is also cited by Hawkins. How convincing any of this is has much to do with how willing one is to be convinced, as is the case with many highly polemical arguments. For instance, to take up Hawkins's piece, are black athletes more colonized, more exploited as laborers at the university than, say, graduate students and adjunct faculty, who teach the bulk of the lower-level courses at a fraction of the pay and benefits of the full-time faculty? Are black athletes at white colleges more exploited than black students generally at white schools? If the major evidence that black athletes are exploited by white schools is the high number who fail to graduate, why, for those who adopt Hawkins's ideological position, are black students who generally suffer high attrition rates at such schools not considered equally as exploited?

What is striking is the one analogy between slavery and team sports that is consistently overlooked. Professional sports teams operate as a cartel—a group of independent entrepreneurs who come together to control an industry without giving up their independence as competitive entities. So does the NCAA, which controls college sports; and so did the Southern planters who ran the Confederacy. They controlled the agricultural industry of the South as well as both free and slave labor. The cartelization of American team sports, which so closely resembles the cartelization of the antebellum Southern planters (the behavior of both is remarkably similar), is the strongest argument to make about slavery and sports or about sports and colonization. This is what is most unnerving about American team sports as an industry, and how the power of that industry, combined with the media, threatens the very democratic values that sports supposedly endorse.

The other aspects of the sports-damage-black-America argument, principally made by Hoberman, are that blacks are more likely to be seen as merely "physical," and thus inferior, beings; that society's promotion of black sports figures comes at the expense of promoting any other type of noteworthy black person; that black overinvestment in sports is both the cause and result of black anti-intellectualism, itself the result of virulent white racism, meant to confine blacks to certain occupations. Implicit in Hoberman's work is his hatred of the fetishization of athletic achievement, the rigid rationalization of sports as a theory and practice. He also hates the suppression of the political nature of the athlete, and hates, too, both the apolitical nature of sports, mystified as transcendent legend and supported by the simplistic language of sportswriters and sports-apologist intellectuals, and the political exploitation of sports by ideologues and the powerful. As a critical theorist, Hoberman was never interested in proving this with thorough empiricism, and, as a result, was attacked in a devastatingly effective manner by black scholars, who blew away a good number of his assertions with an unrelenting empiricism. But he has got into deep trouble with black intellectuals, in the end, not for these assertions or for the mere lack of good empiricism. Hoberman, rather, has been passionately condemned for suggesting that blacks have a "sports fixation" that is tantamount to a pathology, a word that rightly distresses African-Americans, reminiscent as it is of the arrogance of white social scientists past and present who describe blacks as some misbegotten perversion of a white middle-class norm.

There is, however, one point to be made in Hoberman's defense. Since he clearly believes high-level sports to be a debased, largely unhealthy enterprise and believes that the white majority suffers a sports obsession, he would naturally think that blacks, as a relatively powerless minority and as the principal minority connected to sports, would be especially damaged by it. The black intellectual who most influenced Hoberman was Ralph Ellison; and, as Darryl Scott pointed out in a brilliant analysis delivered at a sports conference at New York University this past April that dealt almost exclusively with Hoberman's book, Ellison might rightly be characterized as "a pathologist" and "an individualist." But he was, as Scott argued, "a pathologist who opposed pathology as part of the racial debate." Yet one of the most compelling scenes in *Invisible Man* is the Battle Royal, a surreal perversion of a sports competition in which blacks fight one another for the amusement of powerful whites. Although racism has compelled blacks to participate in this contest, the characters come willingly, the winner even taking an individualistic pride in it. Such participation in one's own degradation can be described as a pathology. How can an Ellison disciple avoid pathology as part of the debate when Ellison made it so intricately serve the artistic and political needs of his novel? Ellison may have loved jazz, and growing up black and poor in Oklahoma may have been as richly stimulating as any life, just as going to Tuskegee may have been the same as going to Harvard—at least according to Ellison's mythologizing of his own life—but he found black literature generally inadequate as art and thought that blacks used race as a cover to avoid engaging the issues of life fully. For Ellison, black people, like most oppressed minorities, intensely provincialized themselves.

This is not to say Hoberman is justified in adding his own pathologizing to the mix, but his reasoning seems to be something like this: If racism is a major pathology and if we live in a racist society, one might reasonably suspect the victims of racism to be at least as pathologized by it as the perpetrators. If the victims are not pathologized at all by it, why single out racism as a particularly heinous crime? It would, in that instance, be nothing more than another banal example of man's inhumanity to man.

In response to an article like *SI*'s "Whatever Happened to the White Athlete?" blacks are likely to ask, Why is it whenever we dominate by virtue of merit a legitimate field of endeavor, it's always seen as a problem? On the one hand, some blacks are probably willing to take the view expressed in Steve Sailer's August 12, 1996, essay in *National Review*, "Great Black Hopes," in which he argues that black achievement in sports serves very practical ends, giving African-Americans a cultural and market niche, and that far from indicating a lack of intelligence, blacks' dominance in some sports reveals a highly specialized intelligence: what he calls "creative improvisation and on-the-fly interpersonal decision-making," which also explains "black dominance in jazz, running with the football, rap, dance, trash talking, preaching, and oratory." I suppose it might be said from this that blacks have fast-twitch brain cells. In any case, blacks had already been conceded these gifts by whites in earlier displays of condescension. But black sports dominance is no small thing to blacks because, as they deeply know, to win is to be human.

On the other hand, what the *SI* article said most tellingly was that while young whites admire black athletic figures, they are afraid to play sports that blacks dominate, another example of whites leaving the neighborhood when blacks move in. This white "double-consciousness"—to admire blacks for their skills while fearing their presence in a situation where blacks might predominate—is a modern-day reflection of the contradiction, historically, that has produced our racially stratified society. To be white can be partly defined as not only the fear of not being white but the fear of being *at the mercy* of those who are not white. Whiteness and blackness in this respect cease to be identities and become the personifications not of stereotypes alone but of taboos, of prohibitions. Sports, like all of popular culture, become the theater where the taboos are simultaneously smashed and reinforced, where one is liberated from them while conforming to them. Sports are not an idealization of ourselves but a reflection.

### The Prince and His Kingdom

Arguably the most popular and, doubtless, one of the most skilled boxers in the world today is the undefeated featherweight champion, Prince Naseem Hamed of England. (The "Prince" title is a bit of platonic self-romanticism; Naseem, of lower-middle-class origins—his father a corner-store grocer—has no blood tie to any aristocracy.) When he was boy, Hamed and his brothers fought all the time in the street, usually against white kids who called them "Paki." "I'd always turn around and say, 'Listen, I'm Arab me, not Pakistani,'" said Hamed in an interview some years later. "They'd turn round and say you're all the same." Indeed, Hamed was discovered by Brendan Ingle, his Irish manager, fighting three bigger white boys in a Sheffield schoolyard and holding his own very well. The fight was probably instigated by racial insult. Although his parents are from Yemen and Naseem is worshiped nearly as a god among the Yemeni these days, he was born in Sheffield, is a British citizen, never lived in Yemen and, despite his Islamic religious practices, seems thoroughly British in speech, taste and cultural inclination. Yet when Naseem was fighting as an amateur, he was sometimes taunted racially by the crowd: "Get the black bastard." Even as a professional he has sometimes been called "Paki bastard" and "nigger." He was once showered with spit by a hostile white audience. But Naseem was far more inspired than frightened by these eruptions, and was especially impressive in winning fights when he was held in racial contempt by the audience, as he would wickedly punish his opponents. For Hamed, these fights particularly became opportunities to rub white Anglo faces in the dirt, to beat them smugly while they hysterically asserted their own vanquished superiority. But his defiance, through his athleticism, becomes an ironic form of assimilation. He is probably the most loved Arab in England, and far and away the most popular boxer there. As he said, "When you're doing well, everyone wants to be your friend."

On the whole, these displays of racism at a sporting event need to be placed in perspective. For what seems a straightforward exhibition of racialist prejudice and Anglo arrogance is a bit more complex. And deeper understanding of the Naseem Hamed phenomenon might give us another way to approach the entangled subject of race and sports.

It must be remembered that professional boxing has been and remains a sport that blatantly, sometimes crudely, exploits racial and ethnic differences. Most people know the phrase "Great White Hope," created during the reign (1908–15) of the first black heavyweight boxing champion, Jack Johnson, when a white sporting public that had, at first, supported him turned against him in part because he flaunted his sexual affairs with white women; in part because he seemed to be so far superior to the white opponent, Tommy Burns, from whom he won the title. The advent of Johnson did not, by any means, invent the intersection of race and sports but surely heightened it as a form of national obsession, a dark convulsion in an incipient American popular culture. The expression "Great White Hope" is still used today, in boxing, track and field, and professional basketball, whenever a white emerges as a potential star.

But ethnicity and racialism in boxing has a more intricate history than white against black. Boxers have often come from racially and ethnically mixed working-class urban environments where they fought racial insults as street toughs. This was particularly true of white ethnic fighters—Jews, Italians and Irish—in the United States from the turn of the century to about the fifties, when public-policy changes widened economic and educational opportunities, and suburbanization altered white ethnic urban neighborhoods, changing the character of boxing and big-city life. John L. Sullivan, the last great bare-knuckle champion, may have been "white" when he drew the color line and refused to fight the great black heavyweight Peter Jackson (at nearly the same time that Cap Anson refused to play against blacks in baseball, precipitating a near-sixty-year ban on blacks in professional baseball), but to his audience he was not merely white but Irish. Benny Leonard was not just a white fighter but a Jewish fighter. Rocky Graziano was not merely a white fighter but an Italian fighter. Muhammad Ali, reinventing himself ethnically when the fight game became almost exclusively black and Latino, was not just a black fighter but a militant black Muslim fighter. Fighters, generally, as part of the show, tend to take on explicit ethnic and racial identities in the ring. One needn't be a deconstructionist to understand that race aspires to be a kind of performance, just as athletic performance aspires to be something racial. This is clear to anyone who has seriously watched more than, say, a half-dozen boxing matches. Today, basketball is a "black" game not only because blacks dominate it but because they have developed a style of play that is very different from the style when whites dominated the pro game back in the fifties. It is said by scholars, writers and former players that Negro League baseball was different from white baseball and that when Jackie Robinson broke the color line, he introduced a different way of playing the game, with more emphasis on speed and aggressive base-running. In the realm of sports, this type of innovation becomes more than just performance. The political significance of race in a sporting performance is inextricably related to the fact that sports are also contests of domination and survival. It should come as no surprise that the intersection of race and sports reached its full expression at the turn of the century when social Darwinism was the rage (Charles Murray is our Herbert Spencer); when sports, imitating the rampant industrialism of the day, became a highly, if arbitrarily, rationalized system; when business culture first began to assimilate the values of sports; when it was believed that blacks would die out in direct competition with whites because they were so inferior; when Euro-American imperialism—race as the dramaturgy of dominance—was in full sway.

In most respects, the racialism displayed at some of Naseem Hamed's fights is rather old-fashioned. This racialism has three sources. First, there is the old Anglo racism directed against anyone nonwhite but particularly against anyone from, or perceived to be from, the Indian subcontinent. (Hamed is insulted by being called a "Paki," not an Arab, a confusion that speaks to something specific in white British consciousness, as does the statement "they are all the same.") In short, in British boxing audiences, we see Anglo racism as a performance of competitive dominance as well as a belief in the superiority of "whiteness."

Second, there is the way that Hamed fights. "Dirty, flash, black bastard," his audience shouts, meaning that Named has stylish moves, is very fast, but really lacks the heart and stamina to be a true boxer, does not have the bottom of a more "prosaic" white fighter. Hamed is derided, in part, because his showy, flamboyant style seems "black," although there have been several noted white fighters in boxing history who were crafty and quick, like Willie Pep. Hamed is immodest, something the white sporting crowd dislikes in any athlete but particularly in nonwhite athletes. He fights more in the style of Sugar Ray Leonard and Muhammad Ali than in the mode of the traditional stand-up British boxer. To further complicate the ethnicity issue, it must be remembered that famous black British boxers such as Randy Turpin, John Conteh and Frank Bruno have been very much accepted by the British sporting public because they fought in a more orthodox manner.

Third, traditional working-class ethnocentrism is part of most boxing matches, as it is a seamless part of working-class life. Hamed calls his manager "Old Irish," while Ingle calls him "the little Arab." A good deal of this ethnocentrism is expressed as a kind of complex regional chauvinism. Below the glamorous championship level, boxing matches are highly local affairs. Hamed has received his most racist receptions when fighting a local boy on that boy's turf. This almost always happens, regardless of ethnicity, to a "foreign" or "alien" boxer. In international amateur competitions, Hamed himself was constantly reminded that he was "fighting for England." It is all right if Hamed is a "Paki" as long as he is "our Paki."

What we learn from the example of Hamed is that race is a form of performance or exhibition in sports that is meant, in some way, for those at the bottom, to be an act of assertion, even revolt, against "how things are normally done." But also, in boxing, ethnic identities are performances of ethnic hatreds. As Jacques Barzun wrote, "In hatred there [is] the sensation of strength," and it is this sensation that spurs the fighter psychologically in the ring, gives him a reason to fight a man he otherwise has no reason to harm. So it is that within the working-class ethnic's revolt there is also his capitulation to playing out a role of pointless, apolitical resentment in the social order. This is why boxing is such an ugly sport: It was invented by men of the leisure class simply to bet, to make their own sort of sport of their privilege; and it reduces the poor man's rightful resentment, his anger and hatred, to a form of absurd, debased, dangerous entertainment. The Hameds of the boxing world make brutality a form of athletic beauty.

Postscript: O Defeat, Where Is Thy Sting?

*She: Is there a way to win?*
*He: Well, there is a way to lose more slowly.*
—*Jane Greer and Robert Mitchum in* Out of the Past

*I'm a loser*
*And I'm not what I appear to be.*
—*Lennon and McCartney*

It is a certainty that sports teach us about defeat and losing, for it is a far more common experience than winning. It might be suggested that in any competition there must be a winner and a loser and so winning is just as common. But this is not true. When a baseball team wins the World Series or a college basketball team wins a national title or a tennis player wins the French Open, everyone else in the competition has lost: twenty-nine other baseball teams, sixty-three other basketball teams, dozens of other seeded and unseeded tennis players. Surely, all or nearly all have won at some point, but most sports are structured as elaborate eliminations. The aura of any sporting event or season is defeat. I am not sure sports teach either the participants or the audience how to lose well, but they certainly teach that losing is the major part of life. "A game tests, somehow, one's entire life," writes Michael Novak, and it is in this aspect that the ideological content of sports seems much like the message of the blues, and the athlete seems, despite his or her obsessive training and remarkable skill, a sort of Everyperson or Job at war, not with the gods but with the very idea of God. Sports do not mask the absurdity of life but rather ritualize it as a contest against the arbitrariness of adversity, where the pointless challenge of an equally pointless limitation, beautifully and thrillingly executed, sometimes so gorgeously as to seem a victory even in defeat, becomes the most transcendent point of all. Black people have taught all of us in the blues that to lose is to be human. Sports, on any given day, teaches the same.

My barber is a professional boxer. He fights usually as a light-heavyweight or as a cruiser-weight. He is 34 and would like to fight for a championship again one day, but time is working against him. He has fought for championships in the past, though never a world title. It is difficult to succeed as a boxer if you must work another job. A day of full-time work and training simply leaves a fighter exhausted and distracted. I have seen him fight on television several times, losing to such world-class fighters as Michael Nunn and James Toney. In fact, every time I have seen him fight he has lost. He is considered "an opponent," someone used by an up-and-coming fighter to fatten his record or by an established fighter who needs a tune-up. An opponent does not make much money; some are paid as little as a few hundred dollars a fight. My barber, I guess, is paid more than that. This is the world that most boxers occupy—this small-time world of dingy arenas and gambling boats, cramped dressing rooms and little notice. It is the world that most professional athletes occupy. He last fought on June 2 against Darryl Spinks for something called the MBA light-heavyweight title at the Ambassador Center in Jennings, Missouri. Darryl Spinks is the son of notorious St. Louis fighter and former heavyweight champion Leon Spinks. Spinks won a twelve-round decision, and my barber felt he was given "a hometown decision" in his own hometown, as he felt he decisively beat young Spinks. But Spinks is an up-and-coming fighter, and up-and-coming fighters win close fights. When I talked to my barber after the fight, he seemed to accept defeat with some equanimity. What upset him was that the local paper, or the local white paper, as it is seen by most blacks, the *St. Louis Post-Dispatch*, did not cover the fight. It was prominently covered by the *St. Louis American*, the city's black paper. I told him I would write a letter to the editor about that; he appreciated my concern. As things turned out, the fight was mentioned in the *Post-Dispatch* ten days later as part of a roundup of the local boxing scene. My barber's fight earned three paragraphs. It probably wasn't quite what he wanted, but I am sure it made him feel better. After all, a local fighter has only his reputation in his hometown to help him make a living. Nonetheless, I admired the fact that he took so well being unfairly denied something that was so important to him. Most people can't do that.

I might quarrel a little with my good friend Stanley Crouch, who once said that the most exquisite blues statement was Jesus, crucified, asking God why he had been forsaken. It's a good line Jesus said on the old rugged cross. But for us Americans, I rather think the most deeply affecting blues statement about losing as the way it is in this life is the last line of a song we learned as children and we sing every time we go to the park to see our favorite team: " 'Cause it's one, two, three strikes you're out at the old ball game."

*July 26, 1999*

## Rhyme and Resist
### Organizing the Hip-Hop Generation

*Angela Ards*

*Each generation must out of relative obscurity discover its mission, fulfill it, or betray it.*

> —*Frantz Fanon,* The Wretched of the Earth

*I have stood in a meeting with hundreds of youngsters and joined in while they sang, "Ain't Gonna Let Nobody Turn Me Around." It's not just a song; it is resolve. A few minutes later, I have seen those same youngsters refuse to turn around before a pugnacious Bull Connor in command of men armed with power hoses. These songs bind us together, give us courage together, help us march together.*

> —*Martin Luther King Jr.,* Why We Can't Wait

• • •

"You'll turn around if they put you in jail," a young black man quips to a peer as counselor LaTosha Brown belts out the classic freedom song.

It's the kickoff of the 21st Century Youth Leadership Movement's annual winter summit, held last December at Tuskegee University in Alabama. In 1985 former SNCC activists and their children founded 21st Century on the anniversary of the Selma marches, which ushered in the 1965 Voting Rights Act. Three times a year the group convenes camps to teach movement history to a generation with little appreciation of its accomplishments. They've heard of sit-ins but little of SNCC. Media soundbites provide piecemeal knowledge of Malcolm X and Martin Luther King, but who was Ella Baker? 21st Century seeks to fill in the gaps before this generation slips through. Yet the paradoxical pull of preparing for the future by building a bridge to the past reveals just how wide the chasm has grown.

"When spirits got low, the people would sing," Brown explains: "The one thing we did right/Was the day we started to fight/Keep your eyes on the prize/Oh, Lord." Her rich contralto, all by itself, sounds like the blended harmonies of Sweet Honey in the Rock, but it's not stirring this crowd of 150 Southern youth. Two fresh-faced assistants bound on stage to join in like cheerleaders at a pep rally. Most of the others, however, take their cues from the older teens, slouched in their seats in an exaggerated posture of cool repose. Brown hits closer to their sensibilities when she resorts to funk. "Say it loud," she calls. "I'm black and I'm proud," they respond. But a brash cry from the back of the room speaks more to their hearts. "Can we sing some Tupac?" Another cracks, "Y'all wanna hear some Busta Rhymes?"

By the weekend's close, 21st Century co-founder Rose Sanders is voicing a sentiment activists who work with young people increasingly share. "Without hip-hop," says Sanders, 53, "I don't see how we can connect with today's youth."

In *Hiphop America*, cultural critic Nelson George writes that this post–civil rights generation may be the first black Americans to experience nostalgia. Although it's proverbial that you can't miss what you never had, or what never truly was, romantic notions of past black unity and struggle—despite the state violence that created the sense of community—magnify the despair of present realities. Public schools are almost as segregated today as at the time of the 1954 *Brown v. Board of Education* ruling. "Jail, no bail"—the civil-disobedience tactic used by sixties activists to dismantle Southern apartheid—could just as easily refer to the contemporary incarceration epidemic, ushered in by mandatory minimum sentencing, three-strikes-you're-out laws and the "war on drugs." The voter registration campaigns for which many Southern blacks lost jobs, land and lives are now mocked by the fact that 13 percent of African-American men—1.4 million citizens—cannot vote because of criminal records meted out by a justice system proven to be neither blind nor just.

Hip-hop was created in the mid-seventies as black social movements quieted down, replaced by electoral politics. It has deep sixties cultural and political roots; Gil Scott-Heron and The Last Poets are considered the forebears of rap. But once the institutions that supported radical movements collapsed or turned their attention elsewhere, the seeds of hip-hop were left to germinate in American society at large—fed by its materialism, misogyny and a new, more insidious kind of state violence.

Under the watch of a new establishment of black and Latino elected officials, funding for youth services, arts programs and community centers was cut while juvenile detention centers and prisons grew. Public schools became way stations warehousing youth until they were of prison age. Drugs and the violence they attract seeped into the vacuum that joblessness left. Nowhere was this decay more evident than in the South Bronx, which came to symbolize urban blight the way Bull Connor's Birmingham epitomized American racism—and black and Latino youth in the Boogie Down made it difficult for society to pretend that it didn't see them.

In the tradition of defiance, of creating "somethin' outta nothin'," they developed artistic expressions that came to be known as hip-hop. Rapping, or MCing, is now the most well-known, but there are three other defining elements: DJing, break dancing and graffiti writing. For most of the seventies hip-hop was an underground phenomenon of basement parties, high school gyms and clubs, where DJs and MCs "took two turntables and a microphone," as the story has come to be told, creating music from the borrowed beats of soul, funk, disco, reggae and salsa, overlaid with lyrics reflecting their alienated reality. On city streets and in parks, hip-hop crews—the peaceful alternative to gangs—sought to settle disputes through lyrical battles and break-dancing competitions rather than violence. On crumbling city walls and subways, graffiti writers left their tags as proof that they'd passed that way, or that some friend had passed on. Eventually, all of these mediums shaped in New York morphed into regional styles defined by the cities in which they arose—Los Angeles, Oakland, Chicago, Philadelphia, Atlanta.

Underground tapes showcasing a DJ's skills or an MC's rhymes were all the outside world knew of rap music until 1979, when the Sugar Hill Gang released "Rapper's Delight" on a small independent black label. It wasn't the first rap album; many of the lyrics were recycled from artists with more street credibility. But it was a novelty to the mainstream. The record reached No. 36 on US charts and was a huge international hit, purchased largely by young white males, whose tastes have dictated the way rap music has been marketed and promoted ever since. From those classic "a hip hippin to the hip hip hop" lyrics and risqué "hotel-motel" rhymes, rap music has gone through various phases—early eighties message raps, late-eighties Afrocentricity, early nineties gangsta rap, today's rank materialism—and shows no signs of stopping.

This past February, *Time* trumpeted hip-hop on its cover: "After 20 years—how it's changed America." In the past year it has been the subject of at least five academic conferences—from Howard to Harvard to Princeton to UCLA to NYU. In January 2000, the Postal Service plans to issue a hip-hop stamp. *Nation* colleague Mark Schapiro reports that in Macedonian refugee camps, Kosovar Albanian youth shared tapes of home-grown hip-hop, raging against life in prewar Kosovo. This creation of black and Latino youth whom America discounted is now the richest—both culturally and economically—pop cultural form on the planet.

Given hip-hop's social origins and infectious appeal, there's long been a hope that it could help effect social change. The point of the music was always to "move the crowd," for DJs to find the funkiest part of the record—the "break beat"—and keep it spinning until people flooded the dance floor and the energy raised the roof. In the late eighties, Chuck D of Public Enemy declared rap "the black CNN" and argued that the visceral, sonic force that got people grooving on the dance floor could, along with rap's social commentary, get them storming the streets.

If nothing else, rapping about revolution did raise consciousness. Public Enemy inspired a generation to exchange huge gold rope chains, which the group likened to slave shackles, for Malcolm X medallions. From PE and others like KRS-ONE, X-Clan and the Poor Righteous Teachers, urban youth were introduced to sixties figures like Assata Shakur and the Black Panther Party, then began to contemplate issues like the death penalty, police brutality, nationalism and the meaning of American citizenship.

These "old school hip-hop headz," in the parlance of the culture, have come of age along with the music. Many of them are activists, artists, educators, academics, administrators, entrepreneurs, hoping to use hip-hop to awaken a younger generation in the way it began to politicize them. Much of this "hip-hop activism" is in New York, emanating from the culture's Bronx birthplace, but flashes of organizing are being seen in San Francisco, Los Angeles, Washington, Atlanta and cyberspace.

Last September former Nation of Islam minister Conrad Muhammad launched A Movement for CHHANGE (Conscious Hip Hop Activism Necessary for Global Empowerment) and its Million Youth Voter Registration Drive. El Puente Academy for Peace and Justice in Williamsburg, Brooklyn, has a Hip Hop 101 course that borrows from Paulo Freire's teaching model: Educate to liberate. In 1993 the Central Brooklyn Partnership, which has trained people since 1989 to organize for economic justice, opened the first "hip-hop credit union" in Bedford-Stuyvesant to offer low-interest loans. The Prison Moratorium Project, a coalition of student and community activists dedicated to ending prison growth and rebuilding schools, is producing *No More Prisons*, a hip-hop CD featuring Hurricane G, The Coup and Cornel West. In Atlanta, the Youth Task Force works with rap artists Goodie Mobb to teach youth about environmental justice and political prisoners. In the Bay Area, the Third Eye Movement, a youth-led political and arts organization, has initiated a grassroots campaign against police brutality that combines direct action, policy reform and hip-hop concerts that serve as fundraisers, voter education forums and mass demonstrations. The New York chapter of the Uhuru Movement, a black nationalist organization that promotes communal living and self-determination, has as its president Mutulu Olugbala, M1 of the rap group Dead Prez. In cyberspace, Davey D's Hip-Hop Corner, produced by an Oakland radio personality, keeps aficionados up-to-date on the latest industry trends and issues affecting urban youth. On his own Web site, Chuck D is waging a campaign to get rap artists to plunge into the new MP3 technology, which offers musicians creative control and immediate access to a global audience, bypassing corporate overhead and earning more profits for themselves and, potentially, their communities.

For many activists, the creation of hip-hop amid social devastation is in itself a political act. "To—in front of the world—get up on a turntable, a microphone, a wall, out on a dance floor, to proclaim your self-worth when the world says you are nobody, that's a huge, courageous, powerful, exhilarating step," says Jakada Imani, a civil servant in Oakland by day and a co-founder of the Oakland-based production company Underground Railroad. Concerted political action will not necessarily follow from such a restoration of confidence and self-expression, but it is impossible without it. Radical movements never develop out of despair.

It's too early to say whether the culture can truly be a path into politics and not just a posture, and, if it can, what those politics might be. But what is emerging throughout the country—when the influence of the black church has diminished, national organizations seem remote from everyday life and, in some sense, minority youth have to start from scratch—is an effort to create a space where youth of color can go beyond pain to resistance, where alternative institutions, and alternative politics, can develop.

As Tricia Rose, professor of Africana studies and history at New York University and author of *Black Noise: Rap Music and Black Culture in Contemporary America*, puts it, "The creation, and then tenacious holding on, of cultural forms that go against certain kinds of grains in society is an important process of subversion." It is "about a carving out of more social space, more identity space. This is critical to political organizing. It's critical to political consciousness." Because of its osmotic infusion into the mainstream, Rose argues, hip-hop culture could be used to create a conversation about social justice among young people, much as black religious culture influenced the civil rights discourse of the sixties.

> *Come on, baby, light my fire/Everything you drop is so tired/Music is supposed to inspire/How come we ain't getting no higher?*
> —Lauryn Hill, "Superstar"

The parallel may stop with broad social appeal. There are critical distinctions between black religious culture and hip-hop that make using hip-hop for social change a complicated gesture, suggests Richard Yarborough, English professor and director of the Center for African-American Studies at UCLA. "Black religious culture didn't threaten mainstream white liberals the way hip-hop does," notes Yarborough. "It grew directly out of black social institutions, while hip-hop has few sustained institutional bases. Black religious culture never became fodder for the mainstream commodity economy the way hip-hop has. It provided a central role for black women, while the role of women in hip-hop is still problematic. Black religious culture was associated with the moral high ground, while hip-hop is too often linked to criminality."

Indeed, Davey D dubbed 1998 "The Year of the Hip-Hop Criminal." Scores of artists, from Busta Rhymes and DMX to Ol' Dirty Bastard and Sean "Puffy" Combs, were arrested that year on charges ranging from assault to drug and weapons possession to domestic and sexual violence. Given the hip-hop mandate to "keep it real," to walk the talk of rap music, the inescapable question becomes, What kind of perspectives are youth tapping into and drawing on in hip-hop music?

At the 21st Century youth camp, students are attending the workshop "Hip-Hop 2 Educate." Discussion facilitator Alatunga asks the students to list the music's major themes, prompting a lugubrious litany, in this order: death, pain, drugs, sex, alcohol, gangbanging, guns, struggling in life, reality, murder and childbirth (an odd inclusion, perhaps provoked by Lauryn Hill's joyful ode to her firstborn). The young woman who offers "childbirth" then suggests "love." A fan of Kirk Franklin's hip-hop-inflected gospel says "God." It is Alatunga who suggests "politics." The students duly note it on their list.

For the next exercise, he has each person name a "positive" rapper. The first to respond cite the obvious: Lauryn Hill, Goodie Mobb, Outkast. The rest struggle, coming up with current, though not necessarily politically conscious, chart toppers: Jay-Z, DMX, the whole No Limit family. Gospel singer Fred Hammond is allowed because Kirk Franklin was before. Tupac gets in because everyone feels bad he died before fulfilling his potential. Master P, chief exec of the No Limit label, raises some eyebrows because of his hustler image but slides in because it's argued that the distribution contract he negotiated with Priority Records, which secures him 80 percent of the sales revenue, upsets the classic master-slave relationship between the industry and artists. Alatunga finally draws the line at master marketer Puff Daddy, reminding the group that by "positive" he means political, not just "getting paid."

It's a tricky business fitting culture into politics. Adrienne Shropshire, 31, is a community organizer in Los Angeles with AGENDA (Action for Grassroots Empowerment and Neighborhood Development Alternatives), which came together after the 1992 "Rodney King riots." "Oftentimes the music reinforces the very things that we are struggling against," she says. "How do we work around issues of economic justice if the music is about 'getting mine'? How do we promote collective struggle when the music is about individualism?"

In 1995, AGENDA tried using hip-hop culture in its organizing efforts against Prop 209, the anti-affirmative action ballot measure that eventually passed. Organizers hoped to get youth involved in canvassing around voter education and peer education workshops in schools through open-mike poetry nights. The organizers succeeded in creating a space to talk about social justice issues. They also were able to introduce themselves to artists whom they often failed to reach doing campus-based work. And the events were fun, balancing the unglamorous work of organizing.

Overall, though, Shropshire said, "people didn't make the leap" between raising issues and taking action. They would attend the Friday night poetry reading but pass on the Saturday morning rally. "The attitude was 'If I'm rapping about social justice, isn't that enough?' They wanted to make speeches on the mike, but there was not a critical mass who could take the next step in the process."

This failed experiment forced AGENDA organizers to return to more tried and true techniques: door-to-door canvassing; editorials for local, college and high school newspapers; educational workshops on campuses; collaboration with on-campus student organizations. At their meetings they passed out "action cards" for people to note the areas in which they had expertise: media, outreach, fundraising, event security, etc. And they came to understand that the solid core of people who remained were not the dregs of the hip-hop open-mikes but the die-hard troops who could be counted on over the long haul of a campaign.

As AGENDA learned firsthand, the pitfall organizers have to avoid is becoming like advertisers, manipulating youth culture for their own ends. About a decade ago, Tricia Rose recalls, Reynolds Wrap had a campaign with a cartoon figure reciting rhymes over corny beats about using the plastic wrap. Since teenagers rarely purchase Reynolds Wrap, the commercial was rather odd and largely unsuccessful. "But once the advertisers moved into the realm of youth products," says Rose, "then the fusion was complete. There was no leap. You could do sneakers, soda, shoes, sunglasses, whatever, because that's what they're already consuming."

*We don't pull no rabbits from a hat/we pull rainbows/from a trash can/we pull hope from the dictionary/n teach it how to ride the*

*subway/we don't guess the card in yo hand/we know it/aim to change*
*it/yeah/we know magic/and don't be so sure that card in yo hand/is*
*the Ace*

—*Ruth Forman, "We Are the Young Magicians"*

"I believe in magic," poet/actor Saul Williams chants into the
mike at CBGB in New York's East Village, backed up by a live band
with violin, viola, drum, bass and electric guitars, and accompanied
by a "live performance painting" by Marcia Jones, his partner. In 1996
Williams won the Grand Slam Championship, a competition among
spoken-word artists who bring a hip-hop aesthetic to poetry. "Magic,"
Williams riffs, "not bloodshed," will bring on "the revolution." The
transformative power of art is the theme of his hit movie *Slam*, in
which Williams plays a street poet cum drug dealer incarcerated for
selling marijuana. Through his poetry, and beautiful writing teacher,
the protagonist transforms himself and fellow inmates. At the movie's
end, he raps, "Where my niggas at?" both demanding to know where
all the troops are who should be fighting against injustice, and
lamenting that they are increasingly in jail. At CBGB, when Williams
asks, "Where my wizards at?" the challenge to the hip-hop community to transform society through art is clear.

Later, Williams predicted a "changing of the guard" in hip-hop,
from a commodity culture to an arts renaissance that reconnects with
hip-hop's sixties Black Arts Movement roots. There are plenty of
skeptics. Last September, at a festival of readings, panels and performances in Baltimore and College Park, Maryland, sixties poet Mari
Evans argued that while the Black Arts Movement was the cultural
arm of a political movement, the work of contemporary artists is "an
expression of self rather than the community."

Considering that these are not the sixties and there is not yet a
movement to be the arm of, a better analogy would be to the Beat
poets of the fifties, whose subversive art prefigured the political
tumult that would arise only a few years later, even if they didn't
anticipate it. Today, what look like mere social events may represent a
prepolitical phase of consciousness building that's integral to organizing. Often, these open-mike nights and poetry slams have politically

conscious themes that the poets address in their rhymes. They are also increasingly used for education and fundraising. For instance, Ras Baraka, son of Black Arts father Amiri Baraka, used the proceeds from his weekly Verse to Verse poetry nights in Newark to raise money for his political campaigns for mayor in 1994 and city council in 1998. (He lost both races narrowly, in runoffs.)

Others are developing companies, curriculums and performance spaces to institutionalize hip-hop and reclaim it as a tool for liberation. Mannafest, a performance company, seeks to develop the voice of black London by creating a space where people can express their ideas on political and social issues. This fall the Brecht Forum in New York will sponsor a nine-week "course of study for hip-hop revolutionaries." Akila Worksongs, an artist-representation company, evolved out of president April Silver's work in organizing the first national hip-hop conference at Howard University in 1991. One of its missions is to "deglamorize" hip-hop for school-age kids. About the responsibility of artists, Silver says, "You can't just wake up and be an artist. We come from a greater legacy of excellency than that. Artists don't have the luxury to not be political."

At the Freestyle Union (FSU) in Washington, DC, artist development isn't complete without community involvement. That philosophy grew out of weekly "cipher workshops," in which circles of artists improvise raps under a set of rules: no hogging the floor, no misogyny, no battling. The last of those, which defies a key tenet of hip-hop, has outraged traditionalists, who see it feminizing the culture. What this transformation has created is a cadre of trained poet-activists, the Performance Corps, who run workshops and panels with DC-based universities, national educational conferences, the Smithsonian Institution and the AIDS Project, on issues ranging from domestic violence to substance abuse and AIDS prevention. This summer FSU and the Empower Program are holding a twelve-week Girls Hip-Hop Project, which tackles violence against women.

Obviously, as Tricia Rose points out, this stretching of the culture, even if it does raise political consciousness, "is not the equivalent of protesting police brutality, voting, grassroots activism against toxic waste dumping, fighting for more educational resources, protecting young women from sexual violence." Toni Blackman, the founder of FSU, admits as much. "As artists," she says, "we're not necessarily interested in being politicians. We are interested in making political statements on issues that we care about. But how do you give young people the tools to decide how to spend their energy to make their lives and the world better?"

It's a good question, but activist/artist Boots of the Oakland-based rap group The Coup laid the challenge far more pointedly in an interview with Davey D in 1996: "Rappers have to be in touch with their communities no matter what type of raps you do, otherwise people won't relate. Political rap groups offered solutions only through listening. They weren't part of a movement, so they died out when people saw that their lives were not changing. On the other hand, gangsta groups and rappers who talk about selling drugs are a part of a movement. The drug game has been around for years and has directly impacted lives, and for many it's been positive in the sense that it earned people some money. Hence gangsta rap has a home. In order for political rap to be around, there has to be a move-ment that will be around that will make people's lives better in a material sense. That's what any movement is about, making people's lives better."

*In order to have a political movement, you have to have education and consciousness. It's very difficult to mix education and consciousness with capitalism. And most people, when confronted with an option, will pick money over everything else.*

*—Lisa Williamson, a k a Sister Souljah*

*It's all about the Benjamins, baby.*

*—Sean "Puffy" Combs, a k a Puff Daddy, "No Way Out"*

Organizing the hip-hop generation is "an idea whose time has come," says Lisa Sullivan, president of LISTEN (Local Initiative Sup-port Training Education Network), a youth development social change organization in Washington. "But there's no reason to believe that it will happen naturally."

No organizing ever does. The grassroots work that is going on around the country is mostly small, diffuse and underfunded. For it ever to reach a mass scale, Sullivan argues, there will have to be an independent infrastructure to support close-to-the-ground organizing. That means training, coordination and leadership building. It also means money. There is plenty of that among the most successful rappers—for the uninitiated, "the Benjamins" refers to $100 bills—but for the most part they, and the projects they get behind, are in thrall to the corporate ideology that made them stars.

Consider Rock the Vote's Hip-Hop Coalition, designed to register black and Latino youth for the 1996 presidential election using the same model by which rock artists have tried to convince white youth that voting is relevant to their lives. The brainchild of rapper LL Cool J, the Hip-Hop Coalition was led by former Rock the Vote executive director Donna Frisby and involved artists Chuck D, Queen Latifah and Common Sense, among others, registering almost 70,000 youth of color, versus hundreds of thousands of white youth.

This media strategy didn't succeed as Frisby had hoped, so the coalition took its show on the road, staging political forums where rap artists and local politicians talked to teenagers about the political process. What was clear from these open forums was that, besides the political apathy characteristic of most young people, there is a deeper sense of alienation. "African-American and low-income youth feel that the Constitution and the Declaration of Independence were not created with us in mind," says Frisby. "So people felt, the system isn't doing anything to help me, why should I participate in it?"

From these experiences Frisby learned that not only will programs for minority youth always be given short shrift by mainstream underwriters—the Hip-Hop Coalition never got the media support of its white counterpart—but they won't even reach their audience unless they are specifically designed for youth of color. Now she and Chuck D have a new venture, Rappers Educating All Curricula through Hip-Hop (REACH). Building on the Hip-Hop Coalition, REACH is recruiting a cadre of artists as "conduits of learning," making public appearances at schools, juvenile detention centers, community centers. In nurturing more conscious artists, Chuck D and Frisby hope more conscious art will result. The group also plans to develop educational tools incorporating hip-hop songs. "Hip-hop is first and foremost a communication tool," says Chuck D. "For the last twenty years, hip-hop has communicated to young people all across the world, people in different time zones, who speak different languages, teaching them more about English, or black hip-hop lingo, quicker than any textbook can." REACH aims to narrow the cultural and generational gap between teachers and students in the public schools, and to promote the idea that "being smart is being cool."

As described by Chuck D, however, REACH seems in many ways to be an if-you-can't-beat-'em-join-'em approach. To compete for the short attention spans of youth, he says, social change organizations have to be like corporations. "A lot of organizations that have been out there for a long time are not really on young people's minds. In the information age, there are so many distractions. Organizations have to market themselves in a way so that they are first and foremost on young people's minds and supply the answers and options that they might need."

But political organizing isn't about supplying "answers." As Sister Souljah puts it, "Just because you have the microphone doesn't mean you know what you're talking about. Just because you can construct a rhyme doesn't mean that you know how to organize a movement or run an organization." Souljah came to broad public attention during the 1992 presidential campaign when Bill Clinton, gunning for Jesse Jackson to woo the conservative vote, distorted a statement she had made about the LA riots. But before there was Sister Souljah, rap icon, there was Lisa Williamson, activist. At Rutgers University, she was involved in campaigns against apartheid and police brutality. With the United Church of Christ's Commission for Racial Justice, she mobilized young people for various events in the black community and organized a star-studded concert at Harlem's Apollo Theater to fund a summer camp she'd developed. Impressed with her organizing skills, Chuck D christened her "Sister Souljah" and designated her minister of information for Public Enemy.

Today, Souljah is executive director of Daddy's House—the nonprofit arm of Puffy's rap empire, Bad Boy Entertainment—which runs a summer camp for urban youth and provides meals for the homeless during the holidays. "The stars we choose to celebrate are reflections of who we are as a people," she says. "Right now we celebrate those with money, but that has nothing to do with understanding history, culture or understanding your future. And I think that's missing in hip-hop right now."

Last November in an *Essence* profile, Combs said that he wanted to use his popularity and influence to galvanize his generation to exercise their political power in the 2000 presidential election. Last September Master P's nonprofit foundation helped finance the Million Youth March. Rap artists are clearly not political leaders—they might be better described as representatives of their record labels than of their communities—but they do have one obvious role to play if they want to foster activism. While Sullivan embodies the idea of organizing as a fundamentally grassroots undertaking, she knows that it can't survive on sweat alone. "Hip-hop is a billion-dollar industry," she says, "and there are people who can play a venture philanthropist role. But that would require educating them about different ways to be philanthropists." No doubt, Master P and Puffy get capitalism. In 1998, the two were the top-selling rap artists, with Master P earning $57 million and Combs $54 million. But "the $64,000 Question," says Sullivan, "is could [they] become what Sidney Poitier and Harry Belafonte were for the civil rights movement? Those two guys actively financed how people got from Mississippi to Atlantic City," she recalls, referring to the historic all-black Mississippi State delegation, led by Fannie Lou Hamer, that demanded to be seated at the 1964 Democratic convention in place of the state's white segregationists.

Sullivan was the field coordinator of the Children's Defense Fund and, until 1996, manager of its Black Student Leadership Network, a service and child advocacy program. Her subsequent stint as a consultant at the Rockefeller Foundation convinced her that a movement of the hip-hop generation will have to fund itself. "Traditional foundations are not going to support this work. You have a couple of program officers in the arts and humanities who get how important youth culture is to reaching alienated young people. While they tend to be radical and politicized, the institutions that they money-out from are not anywhere comfortable supporting what a mature hip-hop political agenda could be."

For Sullivan, such an agenda would address three issue areas. Top on the list is the criminal justice system, including police brutality and the incarceration epidemic. "It's the whole criminalization of poor, urban youth," she says. "That's a policy area that folks have got to get a handle on quickly. And it's also a place where our constituency numbers—our power—if organized well, could move the policy agenda away from its current punitive, negative stance." Public education is agenda item number two: "People are being set up. This is the system that is the most dysfunctional in the country, and something drastic has to occur so that people acquire the skills and have a fighting chance in terms of the economic future. A bad public education system feeds a whole generation of young people into the criminal justice system." Finally, activists need to address people losing the vote because of incarceration: "This is about the health of American democracy. What is happening to the hip-hop community around the loss of citizenship is permanently preventing many of us from ever being able to participate in the democratic process."

> *If you ain't talkin' about endin' exploitation/then you just another sambo in syndication/always sayin' words that's gon' bring about elation/never doin' shit that's gon' bring us vindication/and while we getting strangled by the slave-wage grippers/you wanna do the same,/and say we should put you in business?/so you'll be next to the ruling class, lyin' in a ditch/cuz when we start this revolution all you prolly do is snitch.*
>
> —*The Coup, "Busterismology"*

Once all this activism matures, it's hard to say whether it will resemble hip-hop, or the left, as we know it. But a few operations on the ground suggest some necessary features. First off, it has to be youth led and defined. At the weekly rally for A Movement for CHHANGE, everyone is frisked as they enter the National Black Theater in Harlem, women on the left, men on the right. "Hip-hop minister" Conrad Muhammad, the motive force behind the group, is waging a mass voter registration drive in preparation for 2001, when he hopes to sponsor a convention to announce a bloc of young urban voters with the political clout to influence the mayoral agenda. The minister's roots lie in the Nation of Islam, but at the rally he sounds more like a Southern Baptist preacher.

"Would you, please, brother, register today?" Muhammad pleads with a dreadlocked black man sitting with his wife. Their new baby just had a harrowing hospital stay. They're relieved that the baby is healthy and that insurance will pay for the visit, but initially neither was a certainty. After the minister's hourlong pitch, the man is still unconvinced that casting a ballot and then hounding politicians, of any color, will assure strong black communities of healthcare, good schools and intact families.

Voter registration is an odd, and hard, sell coming from a man who, until three years ago, never cast a ballot and, while minister of the Nation of Islam's Mosque #7 in Harlem, preached against it. But Muhammad, 34, tries. It's mid-November 1998, the same week Kwame Ture, *a k a* Stokeley Carmichael, died and the Madd Rapper, *a k a* Deric "D-Dot" Angeletti, ambushed and battered the then-editor in chief of the hip-hop magazine *Blaze*. Someone, Muhammad figures, ought to be the bridge between the civil rights tradition and the hip-hop generation, and it might as well be him.

He appeals to that sense of competition supposedly at the core of hip-hop: "If Kwame at 21 could go down to Lowndes County and register his people to vote, so can we." He appeals to a sense of shame: "This is the talented tenth that Du Bois said was supposed to come up with solutions to the problems of our people, and here they are fighting and killing each other up in corporate offices. Brothers and sisters, you know we got to make a change from that kind of craziness." He goads: "Talkin' 'bout you a nationalist, you don't believe in the system. You're a part of the system!" He suggests outright poverty: "Somebody had to say, 'I'll forgo the riches of this world to make sure that my people are in power.' If Stokeley died with $10 in his pocket I'd be surprised." He pushes the willingness-to-suffer motif that characterized the early civil rights movement: "James Meredith decided to have a march against fear. We need one of those today in the 'hood, where dope is being sold, people are destroying themselves, frivolity and ignorance are robbing this generation of its substance. Meredith marched by himself—of course, he was shot down. You make that kind of stand, you're going to be shot down." At long last, he gets to his point: "If A Movement for CHHANGE can organize the youth, get them off these street corners, get them registered, make them conscious, active players in the political landscape, maybe we can vote Sharpton into office as mayor or Jesse as President."

The grandmothers of the amen gallery in the audience punctuate each exhortation with cheers, and a few raised fists. The young folks quietly mull over the prospects: poverty, suffering, Sharpton, Jesse. At one point, a 17-year-old decked in the "ghetto fabulous" hip-hop style—baggy jeans, boots, black satin do-rag, huge rhinestone studs weighing down each lobe—challenges the voter registration model of political empowerment. "They [politicians] always say things, do things, but soon as they get in office, they don't say and do what they're supposed to. The community that I live in is mostly, like, a drug environment. And they're always talking about, we're going to get the drug dealers, we're going to bust them, we're going to stop all the gangs, we're going to stop all the black-on-black crime, we're going to have our own businessmen. And they never follow their word, so what's the sense in voting?"

"Let's put you in office," says Muhammad. "In 2001, when forty-two City Council seats come up [in New York City], let's run you."

"Run me?" the young brother asks incredulously, biting a delighted grin. He is clearly interested in the idea of being involved, even a leader, in his community. But if these are the terms, he and his peers don't seem so sure.

Secondly, a mature hip-hop political movement will have more than a race-based political analysis of the issues affecting urban youth. Increasingly, the face of injustice is the color of the rainbow, so a black-white racial analysis that pins blame on some lily-white power structure is outdated. At the 21st Century meeting in Tuskegee the theme of the weekend was miseducation and tracking. In the Selma public schools, however, more than 90 percent of the students are black, so whatever the remedial tracking, it is happening along class lines, instituted by black teachers, principals and superintendents. "All teachers except for the whites told me that I wasn't going to be anybody," says a heavyset, dark, studious young man, who transferred from the public school system to a Catholic school. When he asked many of the black teachers for help, the response was often flip and cutting: "Your mama's smart, figure it out."

Ras Baraka tells of how Black NIA F.O.R.C.E., the protest group he founded while at Howard University in the late eighties, descended on a Newark City Council meeting to oppose an ordinance banning citizens from speaking at its sessions. They were arrested for disrupting city business on the orders of Donald Tucker, a black councilman. "Stuff like 'the white man is a devil' is anachronistic," Baraka says. "The white man didn't make Donald Tucker call the police on us. He did that on his own."

In explaining his actions, Tucker invoked his own history in civil rights sit-ins. "That's their disclaimer to justify doing anything," Baraka says. "If it were white people [jailing peaceful demonstrators], the people would be outraged. The irony is that we went down there singing civil rights songs. We thought we would call the ghosts of Martin Luther King and Medgar Evers and Kwame Ture on their asses, but it didn't even faze them. They have more in common now with the people who oppress us than with us. In that sense the times are changing, so our level of organizing has to change."

Like many activists working on a range of issues across the left in this country, these organizers are beginning to shift focus from civil rights to human rights. As Malaika Sanders, the current executive director of 21st Century, puts it, "Civil rights is based on the state and what the state has defined as the rights of the people." Human rights, on the other hand, is based on the rationale that "no matter who or where I am, I have some basic rights, so it's not about voting rights or what the law is." She argues that human rights presents a more motivating rationale for activism. Whereas a civil rights philosophy—focused on a finite set of principles that define citizenship—can lead to despair as those rights are never fully attained or are subject to the mood of the times, "a human rights approach allows a vision that's bigger than your world or what you think on a day-to-day basis."

On the West Coast, the Third Eye Movement has developed a theory of organizing that goes from civil rights to human rights, from nationalism to internationalism. It couples grassroots organizing with programs and policy analysis, using hip-hop culture not just to educate and politicize but to help young people express their concerns in their own language, on their own terms. Third Eye activists used rap and song to testify before the San Francisco Police Commission in 1997 after Officer Marc Andaya stomped and pepper-sprayed to death Aaron Williams, an unarmed black man. By the sixth week of these appearances, three of the five commissioners had resigned. Their replacements fired Andaya for his brutal police record shortly after being seated. Third Eye also worked recently on the case of Sheila DeToy, a 17-year-old white girl shot in the back of the head by police.

"They've taken hip-hop where it's never been before. They've taken hip-hop ciphers to the evening news," boasts Van Jones, executive director of the Ella Baker Center for Human Rights in San Francisco, one of the principals of Third Eye. Mixed with hip-hop's aggressive attitude, the political message can get "scary," he says. "You won't find it in a traditional civics-class curriculum: We're willing to take issues into our hands if the system won't work. As scary as people thought gangsta rap was, it's nothing compared to young people using hip-hop to express what they're going through and targeting the people who are really responsible."

Jones says he founded the Ella Baker Center—named to honor the soul mother of SNCC—in response to the failures of the civil rights establishment, which had become "too tame and too tired." "I don't believe the true power of the people can be confined to a ballot box," he says, but must express itself in strikes, boycotts, pickets, civil disobedience. "We need to be about the whup-ass. Somebody's fucking up somewhere. They have names and job descriptions. You have to be creative about how you engage the enemy, because if you do it on his terms, the outcome is already known."

Most important, a mature hip-hop movement will have to deal with the irony of using hip-hop. Organizing for social change requires that people tap into their mutual human vulnerability and acknowledge their common oppression before they can bond, and band, together in solidarity. Though born in and of alienation and extreme social vulnerability, hip-hop culture is not eager to boast of it. Whereas the blues embraced pain to transcend it, hip-hop builds walls to shield against further injury. So getting to that place where the music might once again speak of individual frailty and collective strength is a difficult task.

At a December 12 rally for Mumia Abu-Jamal—co-sponsored by Third Eye and STORM (Standing Together to Organize a Revolutionary Movement), among others—students from the Bay Area crowd the steps of Oakland's City Hall. It's the kind of rally a traditional leftist would recognize. White radicals pass out socialist papers, petitions to end the death penalty and "Free Mumia" decals. Placards and banners quote Malcolm X, Assata Shakur, Che Guevara. The difference is that hip-hop headz take center stage, leaving older white lefties on the periphery with their pamphlets.

It is not exactly a changing of the guard. The rally begins on a shaky note. The Ella Baker Center's youth coordinator, Jasmin Barker, steps to the mike and calls for a moment of silence. Minutes before, the sound system was blaring what might be called less than conscious rap. It's difficult for some to make the switch from the gangsta lyrics to a spirit of solidarity with Mumia. Barker persists like a schoolmarm and finally gets the reverence she demands. She then calls for a "moment of noise" to put the city government on notice. But it's Saturday. City Hall is closed. Downtown Oakland is empty. If mass demonstrations are for the onlookers, at first glance it seems as if these young activists have made the most basic of organizing errors: staging an action for a targeted constituency that's not even around. But soon enough it's evident that the objective here, this day, is to assert a generational identity, a collective sense of political possibility.

"Chill with the sellin' papers while the rally's goin' on," a young brother named Ryan scolds a man passing out *Workers Vanguard* during a step routine by seven Castlemont High School students. They are wearing blue jeans, sneakers, white T-shirts and fluorescent orange decals that say "Free Mumia," distributed by Refuse and Resist. They stand at attention, in single file, each girl holding two empty aluminum cans end to end. The lead girl sets the beat with a syncopated chant: "Mu-miiiiii-aa! Free Mumia, yeah! Mu-miiiiii-aa!"

The other six chime in, and the line begins to move like a locomotive, with hands and legs clapping and stomping to recreate the diasporan rhythms that are at the heart of hip-hop.

Speakers pass the mike. Castlemont junior Muhammad, 15, explains the uses of the criminal justice system, from police brutality to the death penalty, to uphold the interests of the ruling class in his own hip-hop lingo. Latifah Simon, founder of the Center for Young Women's Development in San Francisco, relates Mumia's predicament to their lives: "If they should kill Mumia what will they do to you? If they should kill a revolutionary, people got to be in the streets screaming. It was young people like the ones here," she reminds the 300 on the steps of City Hall, "who made the civil rights movement happen." A white kid named Michael Lamb, with UC Berkeley's Poetry for the People collective, pays tribute to Saul Williams and *Slam* in reciting a rap with the refrain "Where my crackers at?" suggesting that the struggle for true democracy in America needs to be an equal opportunity affair.

It is Dontario Givens, 15, who best illustrates the impact a burgeoning hip-hop movement could have on a generation so long alienated. His favorite record at the moment is Outkast's tribute to Rosa Parks, the mother of the civil rights movement. But when his social studies teacher asked him to speak at the rally on behalf of Mumia, his first response was pure hip-hop: "Why should I care?" It took him three weeks to sort through his initial resistance before hitting on that space of empathy and recognition that is the cornerstone of organizing. "What would I want the world to do if I was Mumia?" he asked himself. "Come together and make the revolution."

*January 21, 2002*

## Unforgiven

*Amy Bach*

On August 21 in Lake Charles, Louisiana, a struggling oil-refinery town on the Texas border, Wilbert Rideau walked to the center of the modern courtroom, hobbled by shackles. The man *Life* magazine called "the most rehabilitated man in America" lifted up his furrowed brow and looked at the judge. And stillness came over the crowd of mostly elderly blacks, as Rideau pleaded not guilty to a murder committed forty years ago.

Interest in the case lies not in Rideau's innocence or guilt. On numerous occasions he has accepted responsibility for murdering a woman after robbing a bank in 1961. Rideau, 59, received the death penalty, but by an accident of history, lived to become a famous journalist. As editor of a prison magazine called *The Angolite*, he has won almost every journalistic award and become a national expert on prison life; he's been "Person of the Week" on *World News Tonight* with Peter Jennings and a pundit on *Nightline*—all from behind prison bars in Angola, Louisiana. In 1994 Rideau's lawyers, in a last-ditch effort to free him, filed a habeas corpus petition in federal court. In December 2000 the Fifth Circuit Court of Appeals in New Orleans found that the original prosecutor of the case had excluded blacks from the grand jury in blatant violation of the Constitution, and ruled that the state must retry Rideau or release him.

This year Rideau is set to stand trial in the same Louisiana town where he was first convicted forty years ago. Many thought that Lake Charles and Calcasieu Parish would look the other way rather than reprosecute an age-old case with lost evidence and a manifestly rehabilitated defendant. Rideau's lawyers have said he would settle by pleading guilty to manslaughter and walk away with more time served than all but four convicted murderers in Louisiana history. But the state won't offer any deal.

The reason can be found in Lake Charles, a town where redemption may not be possible when a black man kills a white woman. Powerful people in the parish have blocked Rideau's release, whereas other inmates sentenced for similar crimes have received parole. During Rideau's time in Louisiana State Penitentiary in Angola, nearly 700 convicted murderers have been freed. Four pardon boards have recommended Rideau for release—but two governors have denied clemency. "Why Not Wilbert Rideau?" was the title of a *20/20* segment exploring why he has not been able to get parole. "I think he is a con artist," said District Attorney Rick Bryant. "He's a master manipulator of the media and people who have supported him."

The vehemence stems in part from the fact that Rideau is a prosecutor's nightmare. This is the fourth time the parish has tried him. Each time Rideau is convicted, he appeals and exposes shameful structural flaws in how the justice system here really works. And he's doing it again. This past November 29 the Louisiana Supreme Court struck down the parish's process for selecting judges in capital cases, which the court faulted for allowing judge-picking, a practice used by prosecutors to obtain judges favorable to the state. The prosecution had filed its new case against Rideau when the only ball left in the bingolike hopper was the one for Michael Canaday, a white judge who had never before tried a felony. After watching Judge Canaday in court, Marjorie Ross, 68, a retired department store salesperson, said, "I look back forty years ago and things haven't changed. It's because of this." She pointed to her dark-skinned face.

But the new judge, selected "at random" with all seven balls in the hopper, happens to be one Wilford Carter, who is black and was elected from a black district with many voters fixated on this case. It's a boon that has become Rideau's signature—the grace of luck appears just when it seems to have run out. "The fact that I excelled beyond anybody's wildest expectations not only vindicated official decisions but increased the hostility of my enemies," Rideau said in a series of telephone interviews. "Everything I became, everything I have achieved, has been in spite of this unholy force from Lake Charles dedicated to destroying me and denying me the ability to be anything more than the criminal they wanted me to be."

His crime has been hard for the town to forget. According to the original prosecutor, Frank Salter, on February 16, 1961, Wilbert Rideau, then 19, knocked on the door of the Gulf National Bank at closing time. Bank manager Jay Hickman unlocked the door. He knew Rideau as the errand runner at Halperin's, the sewing shop next door, who would fetch sodas for bank employees, until the relationship became too friendly for the whites. "We stopped [asking him for sodas] because he started talking," said victim Dora McCain in her trial testimony, "calling us by our first names. So we just—we just got a refrigerator for the bank." That day, Rideau produced a gun and demanded that Hickman empty the money drawer. Rideau put $14,000 in a gray suitcase (leaving $30,000 on the floor and in coffers) and forced Hickman and two women bank tellers into a car. They drove to a country road in a wooded area, where Rideau lined up his three hostages and began firing. One bullet landed in Jay Hickman's arm. Hickman rolled off into a bayou out of sight. The two women fell to the ground with gunshot wounds. Julia Ferguson, 49, cried out, "Think of my poor old daddy," who lived with her. "Don't worry, it will be quick and cool," Rideau allegedly said before slitting her throat and stabbing her in the heart. Ferguson died at the scene. Rideau approached the other teller, Dora McCain, a pretty twentysomething with a well-known family, who lay facedown. He kicked her in the side three times to see if she was dead. When she didn't cry out, Rideau took the car and left. Two state troopers stopped Rideau in his car as he was leaving town. They found the suitcase with the money in the back seat. (Rideau's counsel declined to comment on the facts before trial.)

That year, the first of three all-white, all-male juries convicted Rideau and sentenced him to death. Rideau appealed on grounds that a TV station, KPLC-TV, had secretly filmed the sheriff posing questions to Rideau, who had no access to a lawyer, and aired his mumbled answers as a confession. The US Supreme Court slammed the parish's "kangaroo court proceedings" and found that the broadcast had unfairly prejudiced the jury pool. The Court reversed the conviction and said Rideau could not be tried anywhere within the reach of KPLC. In 1964 at a second trial, in Baton Rouge, the jury deliberated for fifteen minutes before deciding to give him the electric chair.

Rideau appealed again, and a federal court overturned his conviction on grounds that the state court had rejected jurors with doubts about the death penalty, in effect stacking the jury with death penalty proponents—a violation of due process. In 1970 at a third trial, in Baton Rouge, the jury took eight minutes to give Rideau the death penalty. His appeals were unsuccessful, and he returned to death row—just in time to benefit from *Furman v. Georgia*, the 1972 Supreme Court decision that temporarily found the death penalty unconstitutional. As a result, every death-row inmate in America, including Rideau, had his death sentence commuted to life imprisonment.

Rideau won't comment on the crime because he is facing a new trial. But he agreed to talk about the person he was at the time and how he has changed. Though he usually speaks quickly, in perfect sentences, his cadence is deliberate in describing the man he was when he entered prison. "I wouldn't recognize him today," he said. "I was typical in a lot of ways. I was another dumb black, immature, angry. Not even aware that there is a world bigger than me." He says he had a fairly normal childhood, moving to Lake Charles when he was 6. "My home life wasn't the best," Rideau says. "But that doesn't say much because a lot of people's family lives weren't." His problems, he says, began during adolescence. "People used to pass by and they would throw Coke bottles and spit and holler at you," he says. "You could be walking by with your girl and they would call at you talking about you—'Hey nigger, blah blah blah, whatever.' " Rideau knew it wasn't directed at him alone. But he took it as "the end of the world." "I saw whites as enemies responsible for everything wrong with my world. Whites created this bizarre segregated world where racism ruled," he says. In his segregated school, he dismissed the hand-me-down books from white schools, which held forth ideas of "rights" and "how life was so wonderful." Though he had a straight-A average, he quit school in the eighth grade because he saw no use for an education. "I wanted to be a spaceman like Flash Gordon," he says. At 13, he began a series of low-paying jobs and spent most of his time in pool halls and gin joints. "I didn't even know the name of the governor of the state," he said. "I was totally out of it."

Eventually, he became an errand runner in the fabric shop, his last job before being sent to Angola. In prison, he noticed the strange ethics of prison life, starting with white guards who smuggled him novels and science texts. "I read a library on death row," he says. And in a Baton Rouge jail, where he stayed for part of his appeals, Rideau lived in the segregated white section as punishment for leading a "strike" in protest against prison conditions—flooding the commodes and burning mattresses. When Rideau led white prisoners in a strike as well, the prison put him in solitary confinement. And to Rideau's shock, whites began secretly sending him food and kind words. "Whites started taking care of me," he said.

Within the first year of his life sentence, Rideau asked to join the then-all-white newspaper, the *Angolite*, only to have administrative officials turn him down. "I read in the paper that they couldn't find a black who could write," he says. The rejection stung. Over the past decade, he had penned a book-length analysis of criminality and corresponded with a young editor at a New York publishing house, who tutored him in the art of writing. Rideau rounded up an all-black staff and started *The Lifer*, which chronicled stories like that of a group of elderly women who brought a truckload of toilet paper to the prison and were turned away. Eventually, the administration put him out of business. "They threw me in the dungeon saying I was advocating insurrection," he says. White prisoners petitioned a black senator to demand Rideau's release from solitary confinement. "Along the way, the whites that I initially saw as enemies befriended me and fought for me, not blacks," he says. "That experience caused hell with the way I saw things."

In 1975, the warden made Rideau editor of the *Angolite* as part of compliance with a federal court order mandating integration of the segregated Angola prison. A year later a new warden, C. Paul Phelps, arrived and offered to strike a deal. Phelps promised that the *Angolite* would operate under the same standards that applied to journalists in the free world—he could print whatever he could prove—so long as Rideau would teach him about life at Angola. Over the years, the two men had many philosophical and political discussions. And they ate together in the dining hall. "He told me that like begets like," Rideau says. Phelps permitted Rideau to become a public speaker, a reward for well-behaved prisoners to travel and explain the dangers of prison life to youth at risk. And with his new freedom, Rideau jettisoned a longtime plan to escape. "The thing that is most respected in prison is character, loyalty, keeping your word," says Rideau. "These are things that are highly valued in the real world, but they are really, really valued in ours." This and the passage of time have changed him. "Part of it is just growing up," he says. And growing up has meant a realization that he may die in prison. Since 1997 Rideau has been president of the Angola Human Relations Club, which cares for elderly inmates by providing such essentials as toiletries, warm caps and gloves, and which buries the dead.

After Rideau became editor of the *Angolite*, the paper changed from a mimeographed newsletter into a glossy magazine exposing systemic problems and an emotional inner life. One story revealed that the Department of Corrections had doled out money for AIDS programs that were never implemented. Another issue featured pictures of inmates after electrocution—a portrait so horrifying that Louisiana changed its method to lethal injection. The magazine has won seven nominations for a National Magazine Award, and Rideau has won the Robert F. Kennedy Journalism Award, the George Polk Award and an Academy Award nomination for *The Farm*, a documentary film about Angola that he co-directed. He co-edited a book, *Life Sentences* (Random House). He addressed the convention of the American Society of Newspaper Editors in 1989 and 1990. And he's a correspondent for National Public Radio's *Fresh Air* program. While Lake Charles watched, the man many faulted with ushering in an era of crime became a nationally respected writer and commentator. "There's no way you're going to give life back where it's been taken," Rideau opined on *Nightline* in 1990. "But you—you just try to make up. . . . When it's all over and done with, Wilbert Rideau will have tried."

One blistering August afternoon in Lake Charles, I locked my keys in my rental car and called "Pop-A-Lock" for help. As owner Jim Rawley jimmied the lock, he recalled the night Rideau committed the crime.

Rawley was in high school then. His friends wanted to kill Rideau and mobbed the courthouse. "There was a group of vigilantes among us," he says. "I can't remember the specifics. But I remember the atmosphere. Macho kind of stuff, except that we were scared too." Years later, Rawley became a Calcasieu Parish deputy and knew Rideau, who was awaiting trial in the Lake Charles jail, as "a trouble-maker." Once, he says, a friend and fellow officer "beat the hell out of [Rideau]" for being "belligerent and uncooperative." When asked if he thought Rideau had changed, he said, "By all appearances he has rehabilitated himself, for lack of a better word. He seems to be a different man than he used to be. But that doesn't negate what he did. . . . It doesn't change the fact that he was convicted three times. He has never claimed that he didn't commit the crimes. He is fortunate he didn't receive the death penalty." He also said Rideau is a burden to the courts and should stop appealing his case. "If he's a different person he needs to go through the pardon board," he argued. But everyone knows that governors have blocked his release. Rawley shrugs, "It's already been decided, then."

Rawley's reaction was typical of whites I met. Rideau's good actions matter little next to the fact that he escaped the death penalty, as if death had somehow been cheated. And one has to wonder if there isn't some jealousy of his fame in the world outside Lake Charles. Elliott Currie, a professor of criminology at the University of California, Berkeley, calls the unceasing and vindictive punishment of those who have committed bad acts, without regard for the genuineness of their remorse or rehabilitation, "punitive individualism." Law-abiding people don't want prisoners to have anything they can't have—thus the 1994 elimination of Pell Grants (federal educational scholarships) for prisoners and the conflicts over whether taxpayers should pay for weightlifting equipment for prisoners. Rideau represents the extreme of this line of thinking: *Most of us are never going to get to be on* Nightline. *Why does this murderer get to do it?* Many white observers view the legal mistakes in his case as technicalities, and his appeals a waste of taxpayer money. After the arraignment, a blue-blazered security guard grabbed my hand very tightly and muttered, "If I killed your grandmother could you rehabilitate her?"

And the more well-known a defendant, the more the public focuses on preventing release. In this sense, Rideau is not unlike famous white prisoners who can't get a break despite impeccable prison records—like Kathy Boudin, the former Weather Underground radical, denied parole last August for a 1981 murder conviction; or Karla Faye Tucker, a convicted murderer executed in 1998, even after the victim's brother begged Texas Governor George W. Bush to pardon her. Their violent offenses do not elicit leniency. "It's not that people are afraid he is going to do it to her again," says Currie. "They are saying, 'Anybody who does this can't be free again; in our moral universe that can't happen.'" This attitude pervades public policy. Federal laws passed in 1994 provide matching funds to states to keep violent criminals in prison longer by denying parole.

But perhaps the biggest strike against Rideau is his race: No black man convicted of murdering a white person in Lake Charles has ever been released from prison, according to The Rideau Project, a research effort at Loyola University in New Orleans (see www.wilbert-rideau.com). Whether or not people were alive at the time of the crime, feelings seem to be as strong as they were forty years ago. A 33-year-old white saleswoman at an electronics store, who asked not to be identified, said, "He should die the same death like everyone else," adding that she had to put her kids in private schools because of the "kids who cause trouble." She then mouthed the word "blacks." Her co-worker, a 30-year-old white man, used lynching imagery to say he agreed: "They should have swung him a long time ago." But then he asked, "What did he do?"

This is what gives District Attorney Rick Bryant his mandate. He's up for re-election in November, which means trying Rideau during campaign fundraising season. In two conversations, one at his desk and a second in a downtown bar, he said that even if Rideau were rehabilitated (and he wouldn't admit this), he would reprosecute. "He did the crime, didn't he?" Bryant refuses to recognize his own prosecutorial discretion, implying that he actually doesn't have the power to decide not to prosecute. This may be true, but only in the sense that his political survival in this majority-white town depends on a conviction. "They are trying to make me into a glorified pardon board. I am not a pardon board. I am a DA. Like I should be God of this case! Like I don't care! Or that I should decide he's a good guy in prison! That is not my job. The only reason I would not retry him is if there is no evidence, he's innocent or the victims want his release," he says. I suggest that his job is to seek justice, not just to convict, and that a retrial can only divide the town. "They line up and tell me to keep him in prison," Bryant says.

Of course, there are those—mostly black and some influential whites—lining up on the other side, too. Cliff Newman, an attorney and Democratic state senator from 1980 to 1988, once lobbied the governor to keep Rideau in prison at the behest of Dora McCain, the only victim who is still alive today. In the following years, Newman met Rideau in Angola at the prison rodeo and followed his story in the media. Today Newman has changed his mind: "From a political point of view it is not popular to ever say a murderer should be released. But I am not in politics anymore. And I am not going to be. Everyone is capable of rehabilitation."

Even conservative whites are hard pressed to argue that Rideau is not a different man today. Bill Shearman, owner of the town's conservative weekly newspaper, said, "Well, yeah, I think Rideau is rehabilitated," explaining that his view isn't representative. "Only a scant minority realized he has changed." Jim Beam, 68, a columnist of the *American Press*, the conservative daily that has opposed Rideau's freedom, admitted, "If you asked me if he's rehabilitated I would say yes." And Peggi Gresham, retired assistant warden and *Angolite* supervisor for twelve years, said, "I am not a bleeding-heart liberal. I don't think that everybody should get out. But when a person is as successful as some individuals are they can get out and have a good life. Wilbert is one of those people."

Young black professionals I met generally thought Rideau should be released because he has changed but see his plight as a remnant of past prejudice that doesn't really concern them. Rideau's real support in Lake Charles has come from the local NAACP and black press who believe that Rideau didn't commit the crime alone and is part of a larger conspiracy. "Blacks don't rob banks and they don't commit suicide," says Lawrence Morrow, publisher and editor of the black magazine *Gumbeaux*. Rideau had a good job, they argue, at a time when it was difficult for blacks to find jobs, and he took only $14,000, leaving $30,000 in the bank. Joshua Castille, 73, a retired black law enforcement officer, had drinks with Rideau the night before the crime and saw no peculiar behavior. He believes Rideau acted in concert with bank manager Hickman. Even back then, he said, a bank would never open its doors after closing hours. For a black person? "For anyone," he says. "They just wouldn't do it." The contrasting perceptions of the Rideau case among blacks and whites is emblematic of the different ways the two groups view crime, as well as issues like the death penalty. "Blacks are more likely to understand that people like Rideau are less likely to have committed the crime because they are monsters than because of circumstances that put them in that situation—'there but for their fortune go I,' " says Currie. "And they know that the criminal justice system has been pushed toward punishing blacks more than whites for as long as the justice system has existed."

Rideau's trial could go either way. On the one hand, Lake Charles elects its judges and Judge Carter is accountable to a black constituency that cares about this case enormously, which could mean openness to arguments about prosecutorial vindictiveness. On the other hand, when Carter's son, then 16, was charged with second-degree murder, he received a plea deal from Bryant reducing the charge to manslaughter—which, critics say, could predispose the judge to be friendly to the prosecution. And while, after so many years of appeals, the evidence is mostly lost, Dora McCain's lawyer, Frank Salter, the original prosecutor, said she would testify, which could mean a conviction based on her testimony alone (McCain did not respond to interview requests). Rideau's lawyer is the formidable George Kendall of the NAACP Legal Defense & Educational Fund, but it isn't yet clear how Judge Carter feels about counsel who swoops in from New York.

Rideau says if he does get out, he wants to leave Louisiana and write two books. "And neither one of them is about me," he says, explaining that he hopes to redefine criminality. "But I am telling you they are going to give me the Pulitzer Prize for this." It's hardly what

Lake Charles wants to hear. When does he believe punishment should stop? "Whatever it should be, it should be," he says. "But it should be equal."

# Contributors

**Paula J. Giddings** is the author of *When and Where I Enter: The Impact of Black Women on Race and Sex in America* and *In Search of Sisterhood: Delta Sigma Theta and the Challenge of the Black Sorority Movement.* Her articles have appeared in the *New York Times,* the *Washington Post,* and *Jeune Afrique* (Paris) among other publications. She is currently Professor of Afro-American Studies at Smith College.

(Most of these biographies are contemporaneous to the period)

**Faith Adams** was a pseudonym for Martha Gruening, the sister of *Nation* editor (and later senator) Ernest Gruening. A prominent suffragist at Smith College, she ran the International School of Revolution in Marlboro, New York, and was active in the NAACP.

**Sherwood Anderson** was born in Camden, Ohio. His novels and poetry won praise from Theodore Dreiser, Carl Sandburg, and Ben Hecht, especially on the publication of the collection of his short stories *Winesburg, Ohio* (1919). His autobiographies are *Tar, A Midwest Childhood* (1926), and *Sherwood Anderson's Memoirs* (1942).

**Angela Ards** was the Nation Institute's Haywood Burns Fellow in 1999. Her writing has appeared in *Ms., Village Voice, The New Crisis* and *The Women's Review of Books.*

**Amy Bach** was The Nation Institute's Haywood Burns Fellow in 2001. Her work has appeared in *The American Lawyer, Content, New York* and *Salon.*

**James Baldwin** was a member of *The Nation*'s Editorial Board from 1978 to 1987, and the author of many novels, including *Giovanni's Room, The Fire Next Time, Nobody Knows My Name,* and *Another Country.*

**Carleton Beals** established a reputation as a leading radical journalist specializing in international affairs, especially Latin American affairs, in the twenties and thirties, covering Mussolini's march on Rome and interviewing Augusto Sandino in 1928 for *The Nation.* He authored a highly regarded book on Cuba, *The Crime of Cuba,* for which Walker Evans took the photographs. He served on the Dewey Commission, which exonerated Leon Trotsky from Stalin's charges during the Moscow trials of 1938.

**Derrick Bell** is a Scholar in Residence at New York University Law School. His books include *Faces at the Bottom of the Well* and *And We Are Not Saved.*

**Dora Byron** was a writer and professor who taught at Emory University, West Georgia College and State University in Carrollton. She died in 2001.

**Clayborne Carson** is a professor of History at Stanford University and director of the King Papers Project.

**Horace R. Cayton**, an ex-slave, came to Seattle in the late 1880s and in a few years was publishing the *Seattle Republican*, a newspaper directed at both white and Black readers and which at one point had the second largest circulation in the city. He was a frequent delegate to the Republican Party county and state nominating conventions, secretary of the party's King County convention in 1902, and for several years a member of the Republican State Central Committee.

**Jeff Cohen** is the founder of FAIR, the New York-based media watch organization.

**Paul Delaney** is the director of the Center for the Study of Race and Media at Howard University, writes regularly for the *Baltimore Sun*, and was a reporter for twenty-three years for the *New York Times*.

**Peter de Lissovoy** is the author of the memoir *Feelgood*.

**Barbara Deming** was a writer, civil rights and peace activist, and feminist. She died in 1984. Her books include *Remembering Who We Are* and *To Fear Jane Alpert is to Fear*.

**W.E.B. (William Edward Burghardt) Du Bois** was one of the most influential Black leaders of the first half of the twentieth century. Du Bois shared in the founding of the National Association for the Advancement of Colored People (NAACP) in 1909. He served as director of research and editor of the magazine *Crisis* until 1934. Du Bois was the first African American to receive a Ph.D. from Harvard University in 1896. He is author of *The Souls of Black Folk* and *Biography of a Race*.

**Wilma Dykeman** (the pen name of Mrs. James Stokely) is the author of *The French Broad*, one of the Rivers of America Series. Her husband **James Stokely**, the poet and farmer, died in 1977.

**Gerald Early** is Merle Kling Professor of Modern Letters at Washington University in St. Louis and author of *The Culture of Bruising* and *The Muhammad Ali Reader*.

**Gordon Englehart** is a veteran reporter from Indiana.

**Charles R. Eisendrath** is the director of the University of Michigan Journalism Fellows program.

**F. Franklin Frazier** was a protégé of W.E.B. Du Bois and taught at Fisk, Howard, and Atlanta universities. His most important work was *The Negro Family in the United States* (1939), his most controversial *The Black Bourgeosie* (1957). He died in 1962.

**Hoyt W. Fuller** was a writer, editor, college professor, activist, and promoter of the black arts movement. He was editor of the *Negro Digest*. He died in 1981.

**Charles Gillespie** is a free-lance writer living in Memphis, Tennessee.

**Jeff Gottlieb** is a reporter for the *Los Angeles Times*.

**Robert Herrick**, described by Alfred Kazin as a "pioneer realist" novelist, was appointed secretary to the governor of the Virgin Islands in 1935 and died three years later from overwork.

**Langston Hughes** is particularly known for his insightful, colorful portrayals of Black life in America from the twenties through the sixties. He wrote novels, short stories, and plays as well as poetry, and is also known for his engagement with the world of jazz and the influence it had on his writing, as in "Montage of a

Dream Deferred." His life and work were enormously important in shaping the artistic contributions of the Harlem Renaissance of the 1920s.

**LeRoi Jones** (Amiri Baraka), poet and playwright, is the author of *Dutchman* and *The Slave*.

**Randall Kennedy** is the author of *Nigger: The Strange Career of a Troublesome Word* and a professor at Harvard Law School.

**Martin Luther King, Jr.,** was the leader of the civil rights movement in the 1950s and 1960s, and led the successful boycott by Montgomery blacks that propelled him to national recognition. He won the Nobel Peace Prize in 1964, and was assassinated in Memphis, Tennessee, in 1968.

**Andrew Kopkind** joined *The Nation* in 1982, where he was an associate editor and senior political writer until his death in 1994. His essays are collected in *The Thirty Years' War: Dispatches and Diversions of a Radical Journalist 1965-1994*.

**John Leonard** is a *Nation* contributing editor and media critic for *CBS Sunday Morning*.

**William Ellery Leonard** was an English professor for many years at the University of Wisconsin. He was also a renowned poet and translator of *Beowulf* and Lucretius.

**Claude McKay,** Jamaican-born novelist and poet, was one of the most prominent figures in the Harlem Renaissance. During his lifetime he often spoke out against and wrote about the institutionalized racism of governments in the world's most powerful countries, like America and England. In 1937 McKay published his autobiography, *A Long Way from Home*, the culmination of his life as a political activist, novelist, essayist, and poet. McKay died a few years later at the age of 58.

**Carey McWilliams** was the editor of *The Nation* from 1955 to 1975. Before that he wrote on social, economic, and political issues in California for the national press and served as California Commissioner of Immigration and Housing. He was the author of many books, including the classic *Factories in the Fields* and *Southern California: An Island on the Land*, which was a partial inspiration for Robert Towne when he wrote the *Chinatown* screenplay.

**John U. Monro** was the Dean of Students at Harvard University from 1957 to 1968, and then ran the freshman education program at Miles College, Birmingham, until his resignation in 1978, after which he joined Tougaloo College, another black institution.

**Mary Mostert,** a former civil rights activist, runs a conservative website called Banner of Liberty ( www.bannerofliberty.com).

**Steve Murdock** was an editor for ILWU Dispatcher, a sports writer in Montana and an editor of Local 1199 publications in New York City.

**John O'Kearney** was a veteran newspaperman in New York.

**J.K. Obatala** was Associate Professor and Chairman of Black Studies at Long Beach State University.

**Roi Ottley** was the author of *New World a' Coming* and *Black Odyssey*.

**Nell Irvin Painter** was the author of *Sojourner Truth, a Life, a Symbol*.

**William Pickens** was a writer, scholar, and activist who was involved in the Niagara movement, a precursor to the NAACP, and the author of, among other works, *The Heir of Slaves*.

**Adolph Reed, Jr.,** is a professor of political science at the New School for Social Research.

**Richard Severo** is an award-winning reporter for the *New York Times*.

**Jerome H. Skolnick** is the co-director of the Center for Research in Crime and Justice, NYU Law School.

**Barbara Smith** is the author of *Home Girls: A Feminist Anthology*, and the publisher of Kitchen Table: Women of Color Press.

**Gustavus Adolphus Steward** was educated at the University of Montana and Oberlin College, taught at the Tuskagee Institute and other southern schools, and was a contributor to many magazines.

**Hans Toch** is a Distinguished Professor at the School of Criminal Justice at SUNY-Albany.

**Patricia Vigderman** teaches film and creative writing at Kenyon College.

**Oswald Garrison Villard** (1872-1949) joined the staff of his father's newspaper, the *New York Evening Post* and eventually became the owner of that newspaper and *The Nation*. Villard held radical political opinions and gave his support to women's suffrage, trade union law reform, and equal rights for African Americans. Villard and his mother were both founder members of the National Association for the Advancement of Colored People (NAACP).

**Aaron O. Wells**, a physician practicing in New York, was national chairman of the Medical Committee for Human Rights.

**John Edgar Wideman** is an author and professor of English at the University of Massachusetts.

**Jon Wiener**, a contributing editor to *The Nation*, teaches history at the University of California, Irvine.

**Patricia J. Williams** is a professor at Columbia University and a columnist for *The Nation*.

**Roger Wilkins** is a professor of history at George Mason University.

**Howard Zinn** is the author of *A People's History of the United States: 1492 to Present* and *The Zinn Reader: Writings on Disobedience and Democracy*, among other titles.

## Permissions

"Brotherly Love" © by Langston Hughes originally appeared in *The Nation* in 1956. Collected in *Collected Poems by Langston Hughes*. Copyright © 1994 by the estate of Langston Hughes. Reprinted by permission of Alfred A. Knopf. Reprinted by permission of Harold Ober Associates.

"Report on Civil Rights. Fumbling on the New Frontier" © 1963 by Dr. Martin Luther King, Jr. Copyright renewed 1991 by Coretta Scott King. Reprinted by arrangement with the Estate of Martin Luther King Jr., c/o Writers House as agent for the proprietor, New York, NY.

"In the Ring" © by Amiri Baraka (LeRoi Jones) originally appeared in *The Nation* in 1964. Reprinted by permission of Sterling Lord Literistic, as agents for the author.

"Tell It Like It is, baby" © by Ralph Ellison, originally appeared in *The Nation* in 1965. Collected in *The Collected Essays of Ralph Ellison*, published by Modern Library. Reprinted by permission of Random House, Inc.

"An Open Letter to the Born Again" © by James Baldwin originally appeared in *The Nation* in 1979. Collected in *The Price of the Ticket*, published by St. Martin's Press. Used by arrangement with the James Baldwin Estate.

"Notes on the House of Bondage" © by James Baldwin originally appeared in *The Nation* in 1980. Collected in *The Price of the Ticket*, published by St. Martin's Press. Used by arrangement with the James Baldwin Estate.